HAPPINESS
#6

SHUZO OSHIMI

Chapter 26: Sakurane   Page   3
Chapter 27: A Wounded Heart   Page 39
Chapter 28: Reunion   Page 75
Chapter 29: Looking Back   Page 111
Chapter 30: Discovery   Page 147

Chapter 26: Sakurane

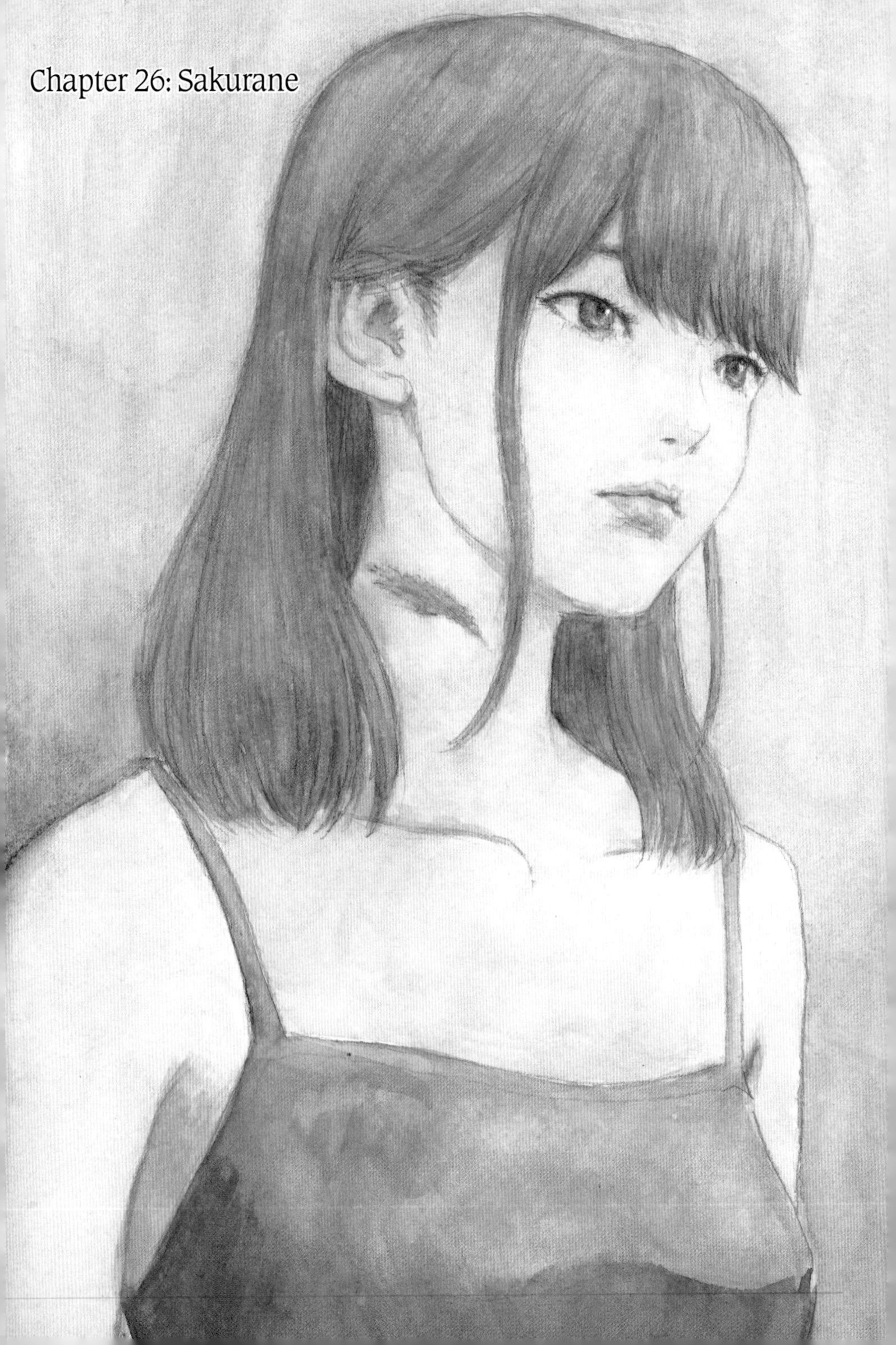

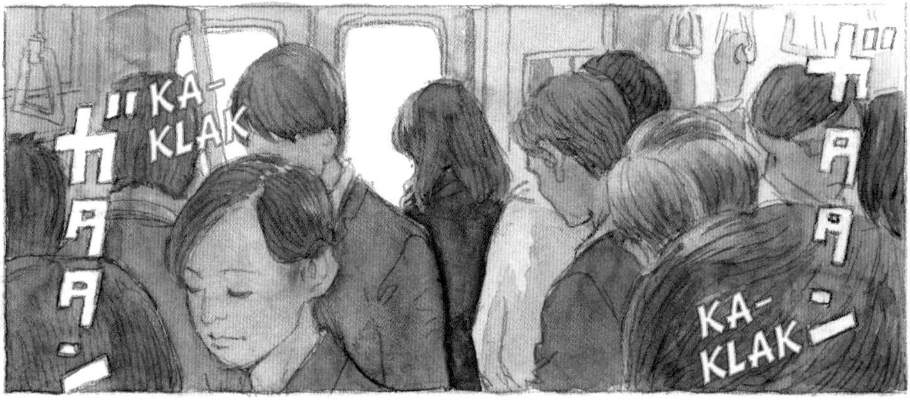
ガタタン
KA-
KLAK
ガタタン
KA-
KLAK

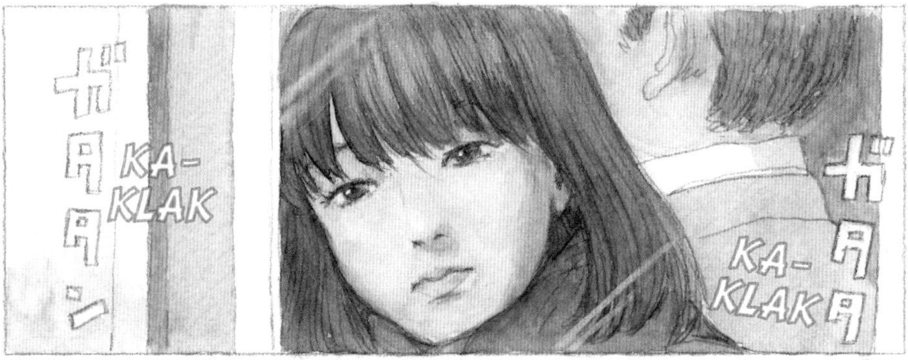
ガタタ
KA-
KLAK
ガタタン
KA-
KLAK

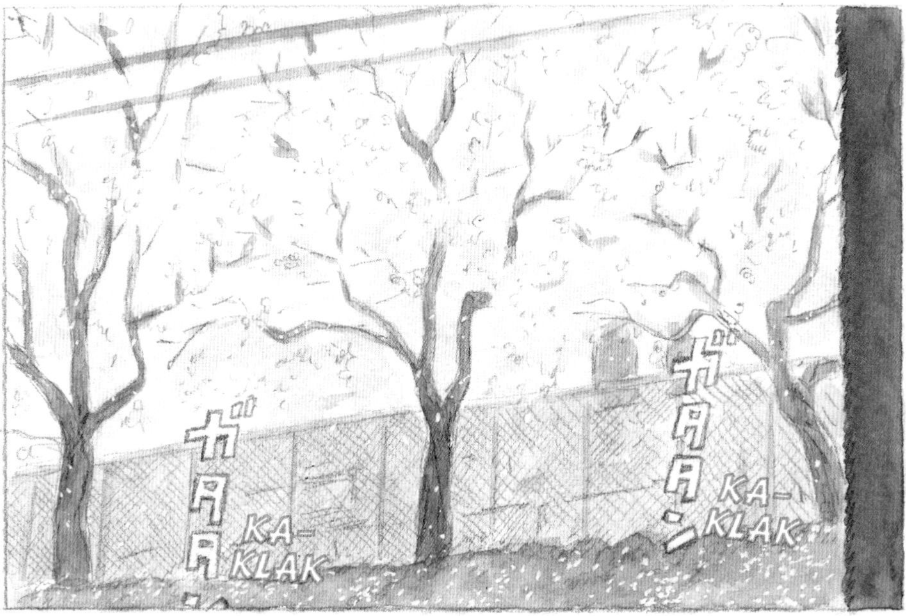
ガタタン
KA-
KLAK
ガタタ
KA-
KLAK

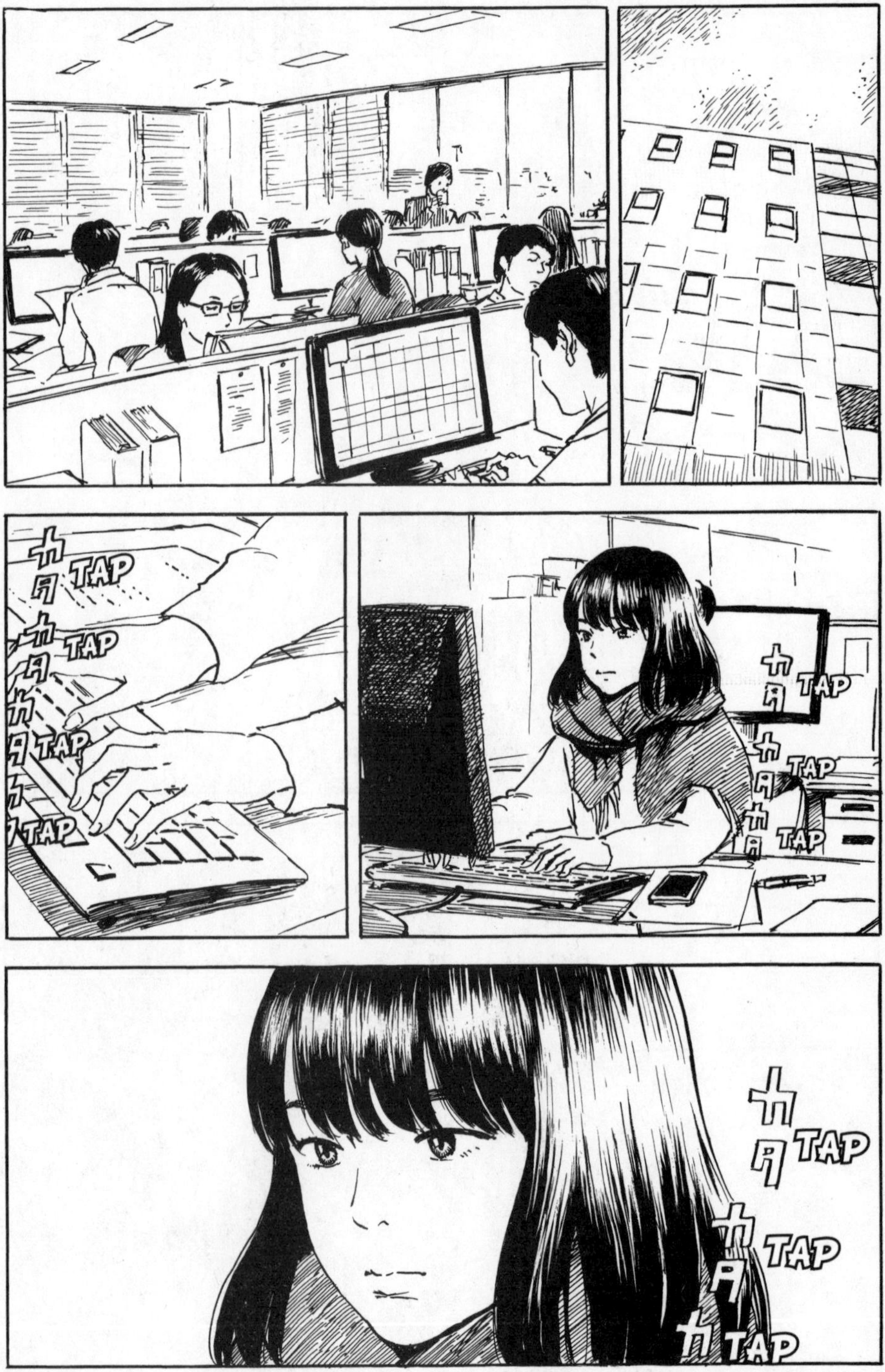
カタ TAP
カタ TAP
カタ TAP
カタ TAP
カタ TAP
カタ TAP
カタ TAP
カタ TAP
カタ TAP
カ TAP

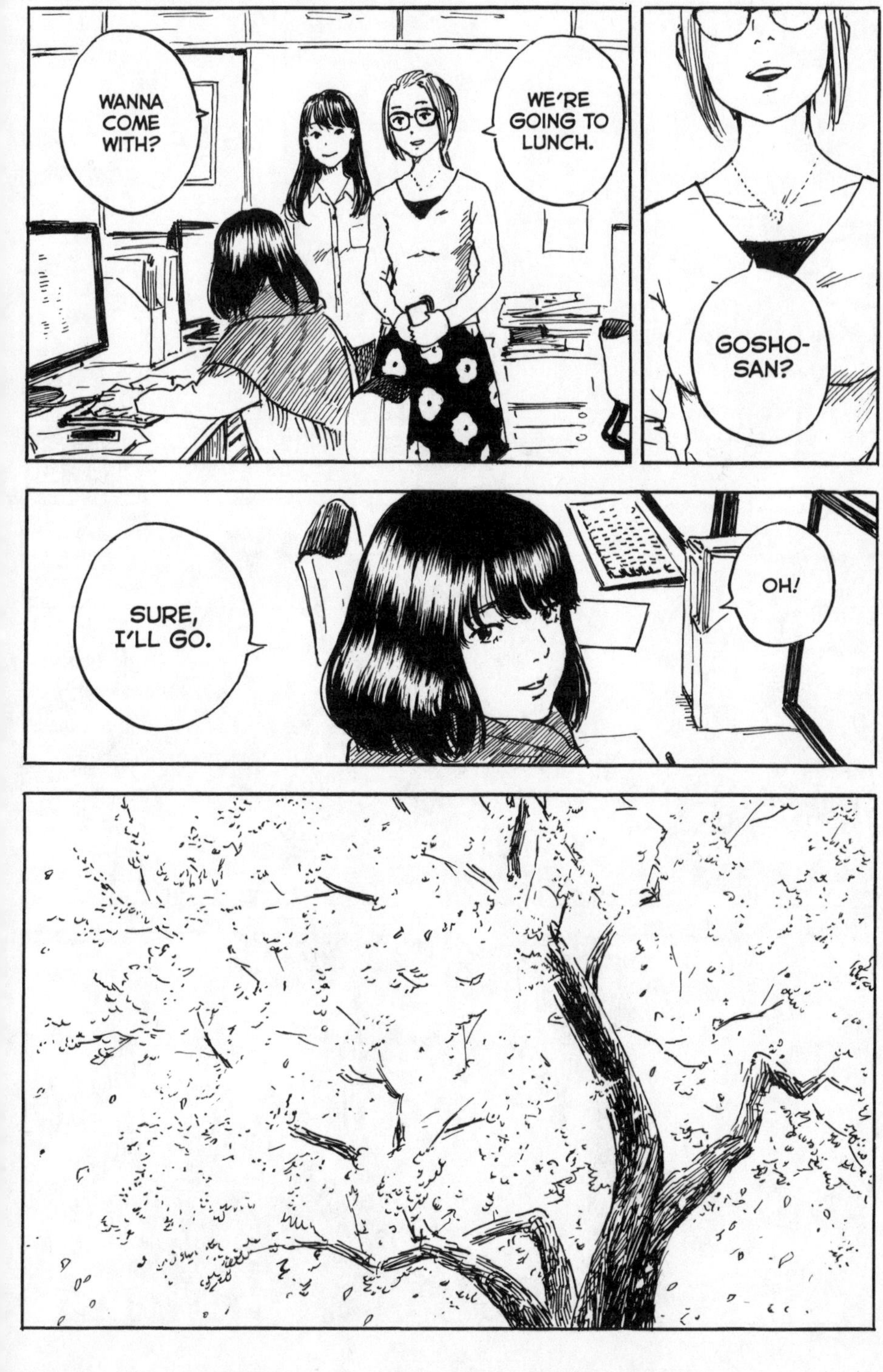
GOSHO-SAN?
WE'RE GOING TO LUNCH.
WANNA COME WITH?
OH!
SURE, I'LL GO.

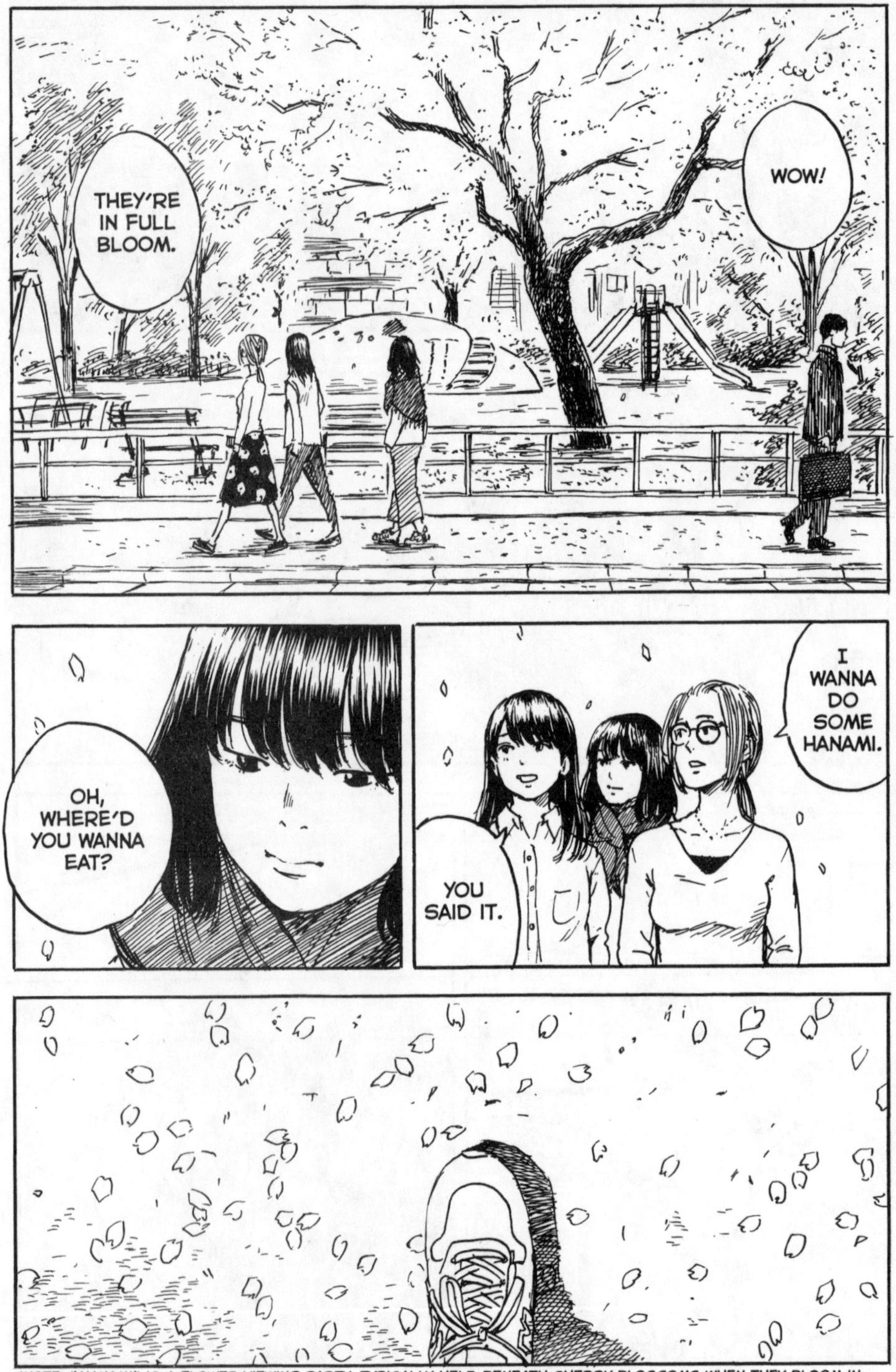
WOW!
THEY'RE IN FULL BLOOM.
I WANNA DO SOME HANAMI.
YOU SAID IT.
OH, WHERE'D YOU WANNA EAT?

NOTE: "HANAMI" IS A FLOWER-VIEWING PARTY, TYPICALLY HELD BENEATH CHERRY BLOSSOMS WHEN THEY BLOOM IN MID-SPRING.

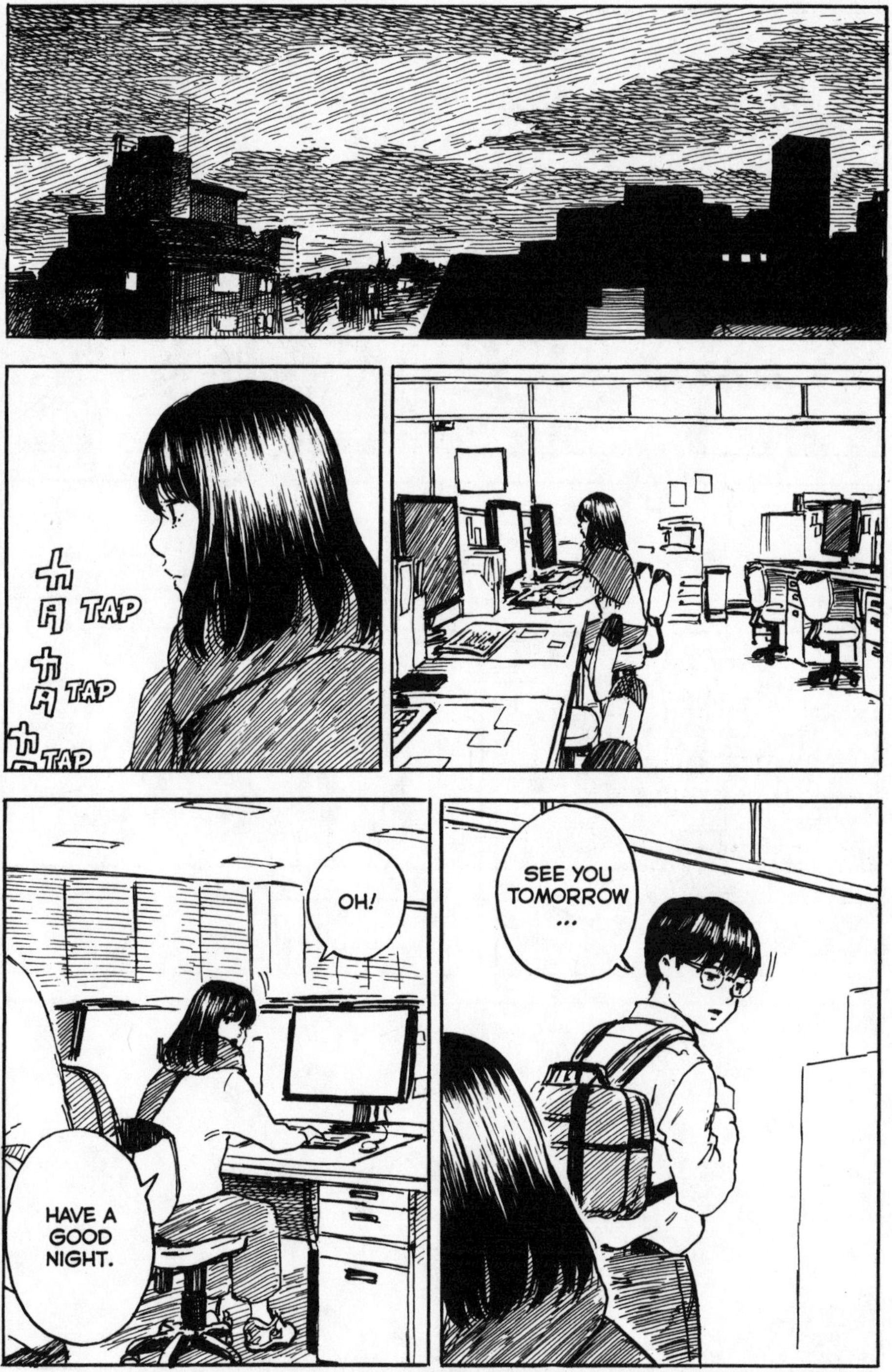
カタ TAP
カタ TAP
TAP
SEE YOU TOMORROW ...
OH!
HAVE A GOOD NIGHT.

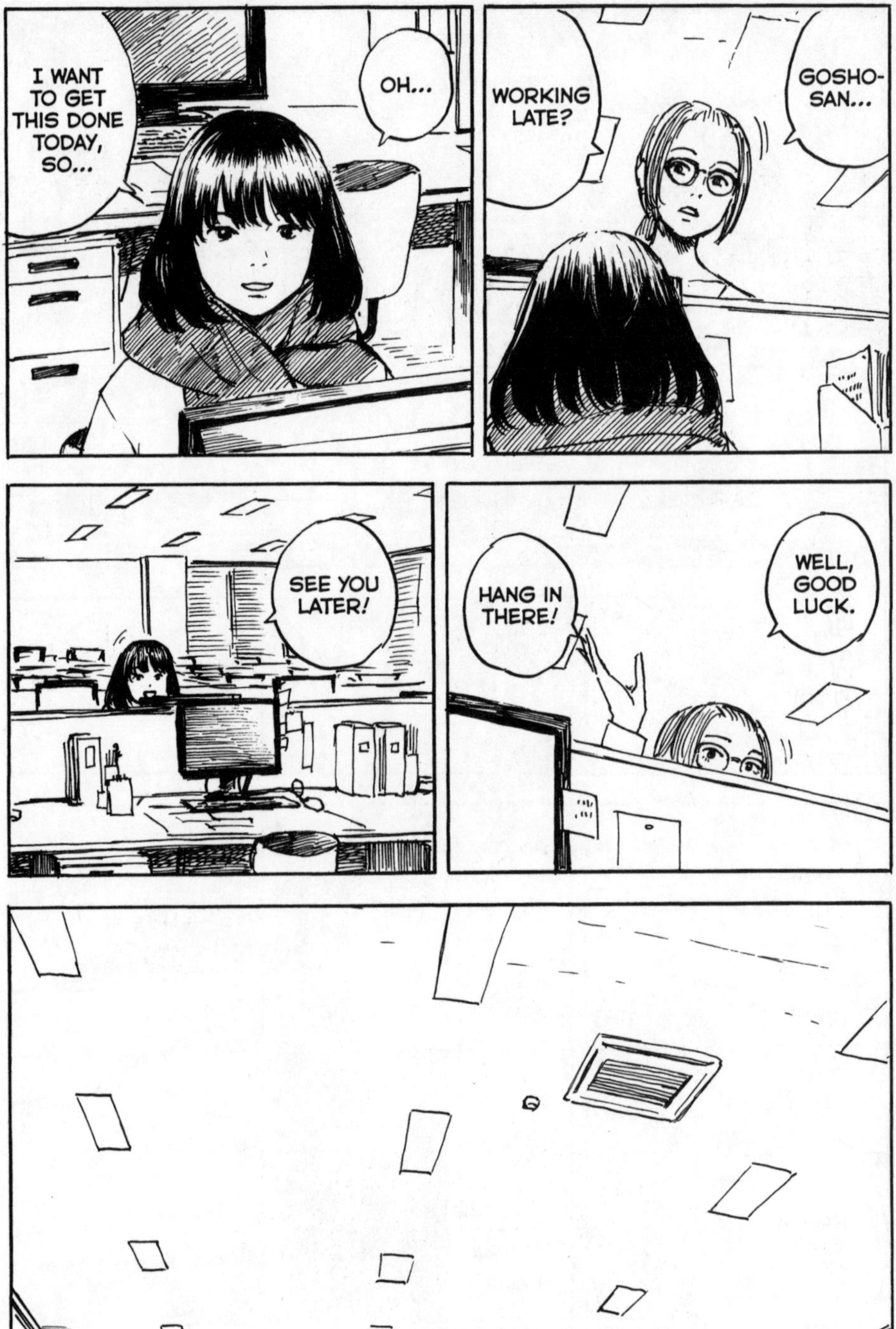
GOSHO-SAN...
WORKING LATE?
OH...
I WANT TO GET THIS DONE TODAY, SO...
WELL, GOOD LUCK.
HANG IN THERE!
SEE YOU LATER!

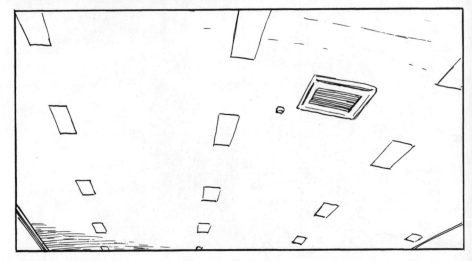

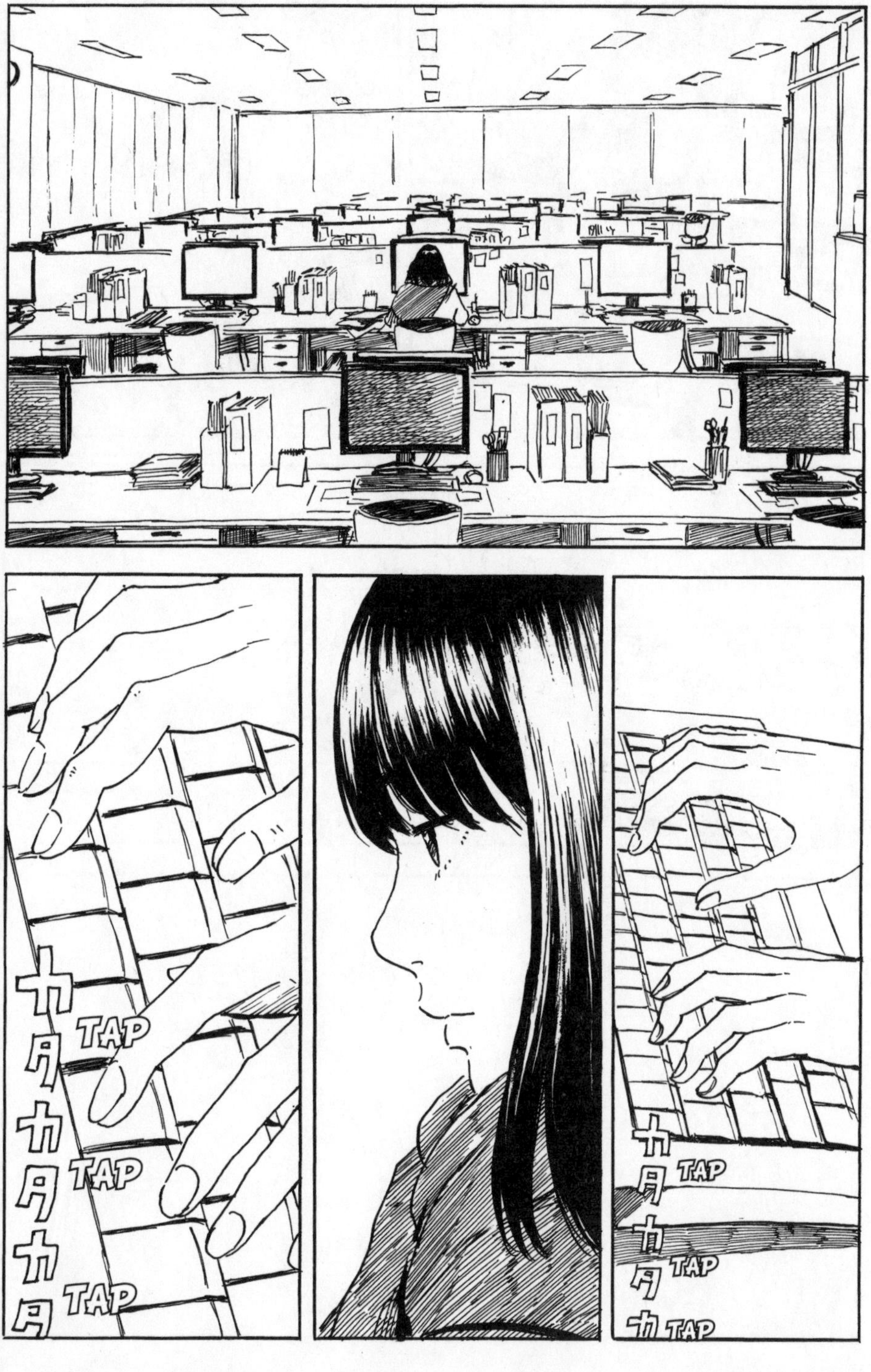
カ TAP タ カ TAP タ カ TAP
カ TAP タ カ TAP タ カ タ TAP

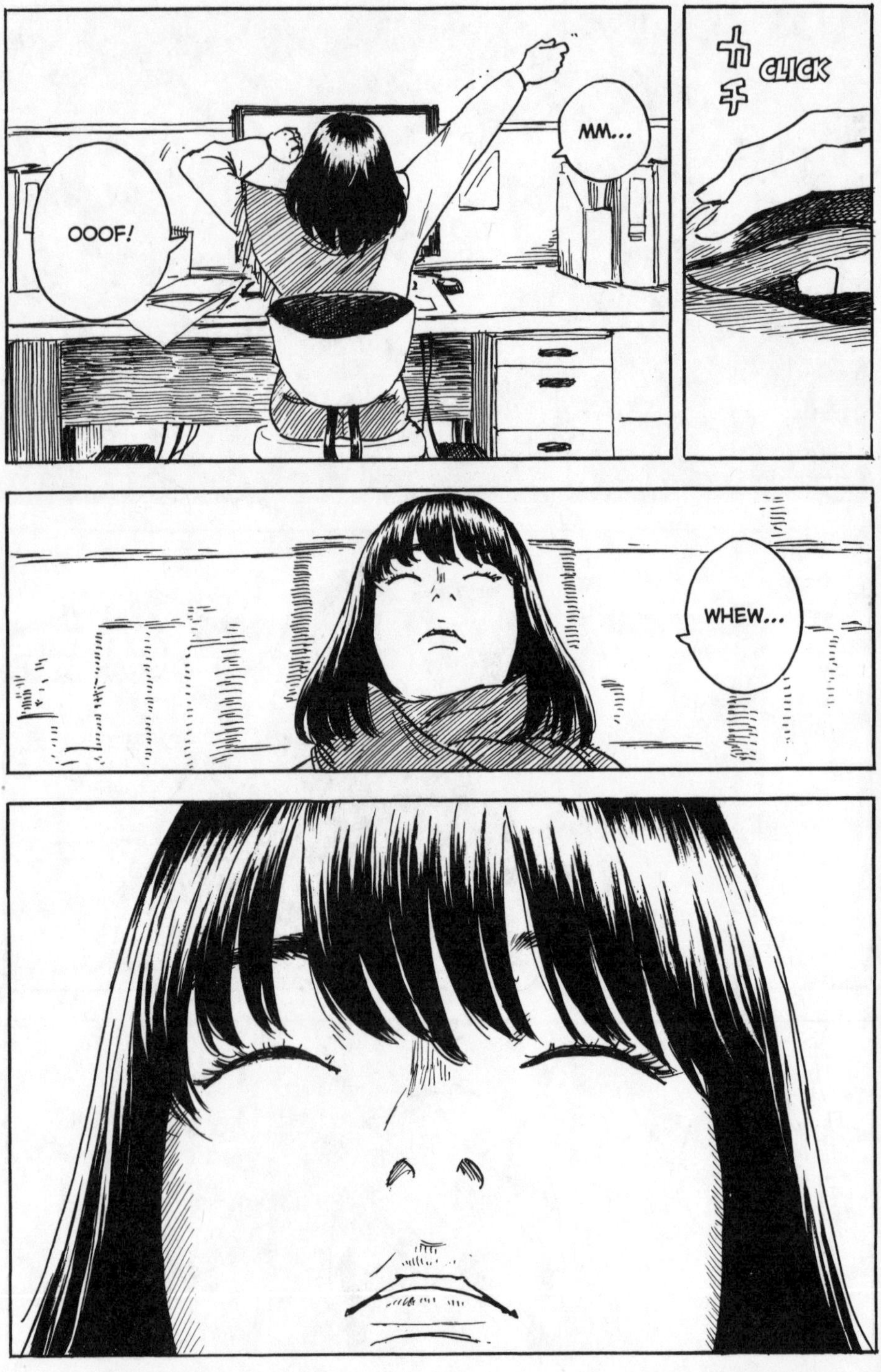
カチ
CLICK
MM...
OOOF!
WHEW...

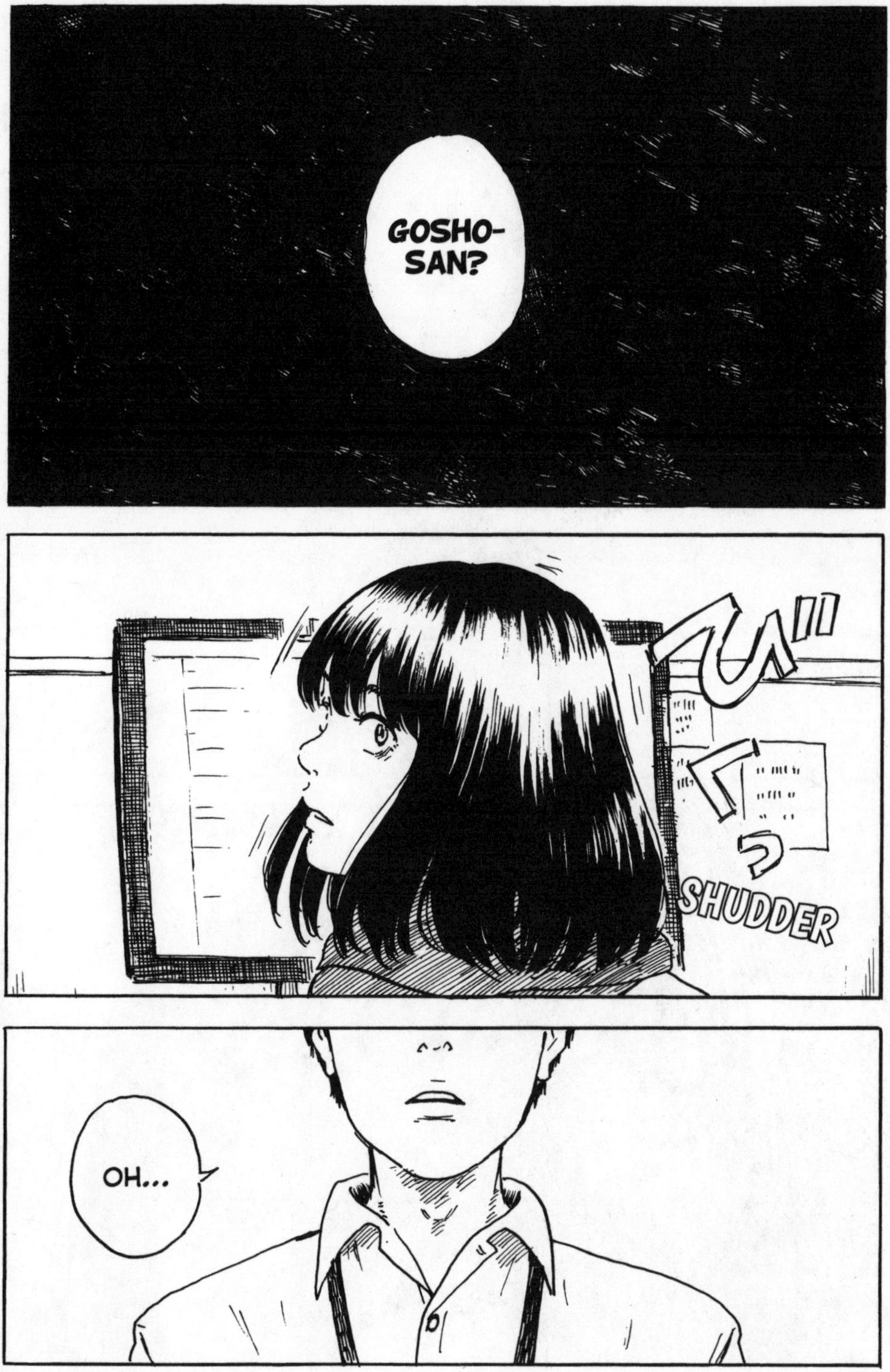
GOSHO-SAN?
びくっ
SHUDDER
OH...

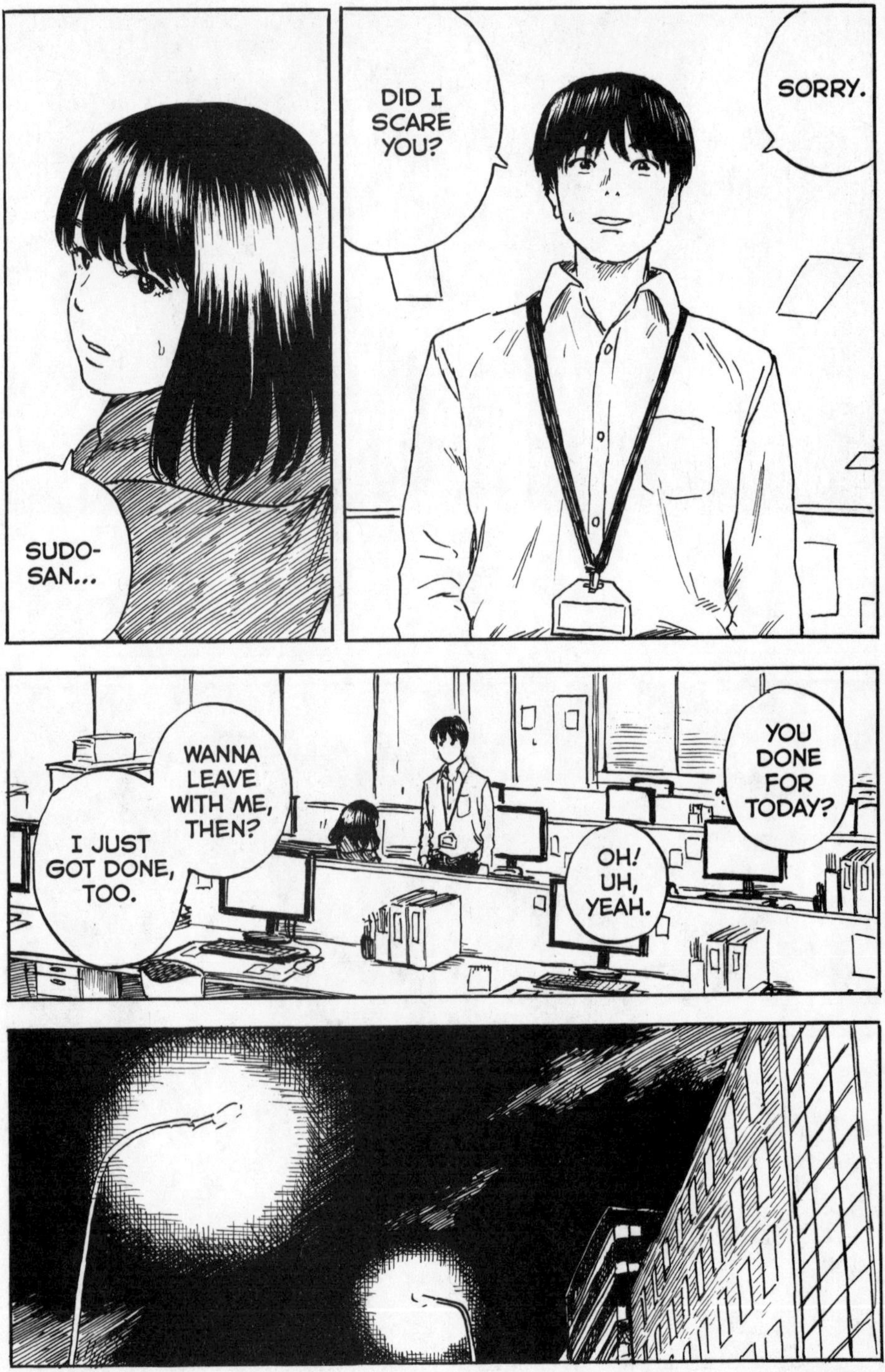
SORRY.
DID I SCARE YOU?
SUDO-SAN...
YOU DONE FOR TODAY?
OH! UH, YEAH.
I JUST GOT DONE, TOO.
WANNA LEAVE WITH ME, THEN?

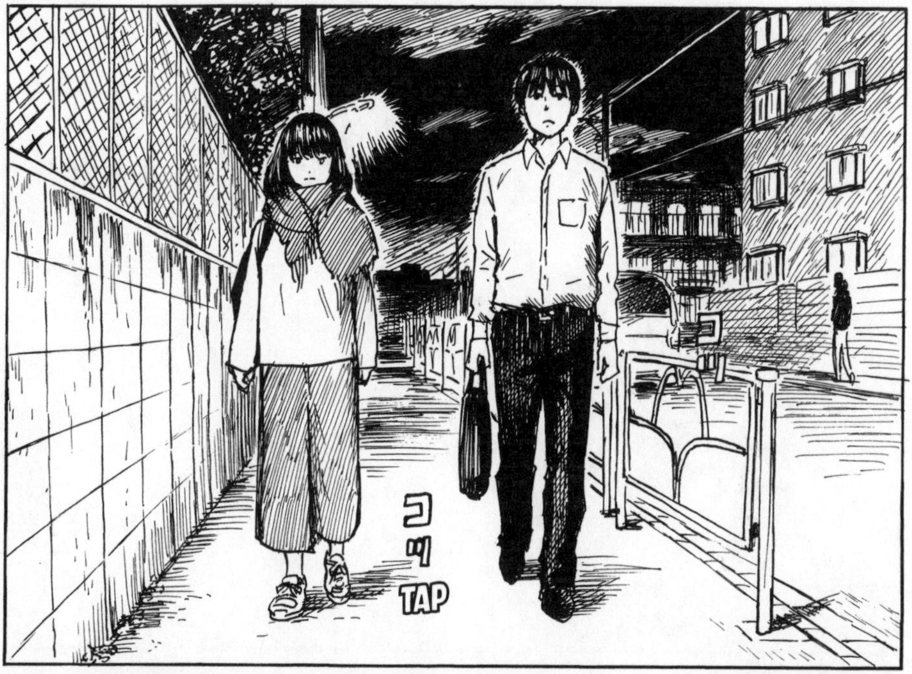
コッ
TAP

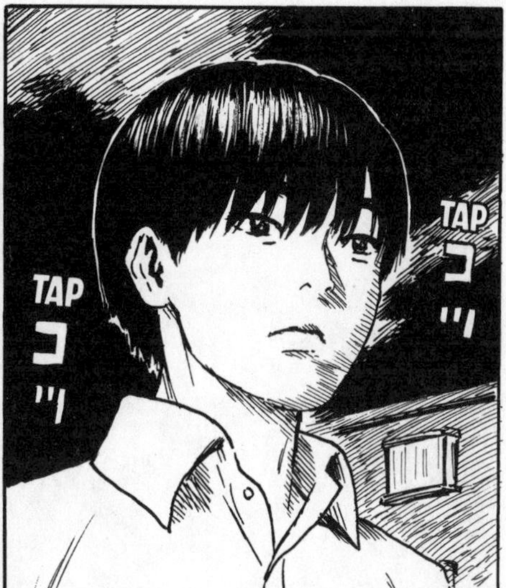
TAP
コッ
TAP
コッ

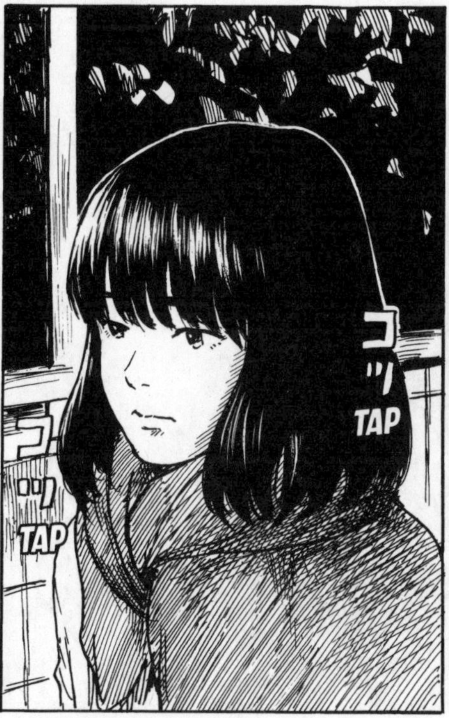
コッ
TAP
コッ
TAP

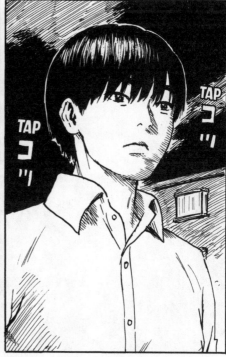

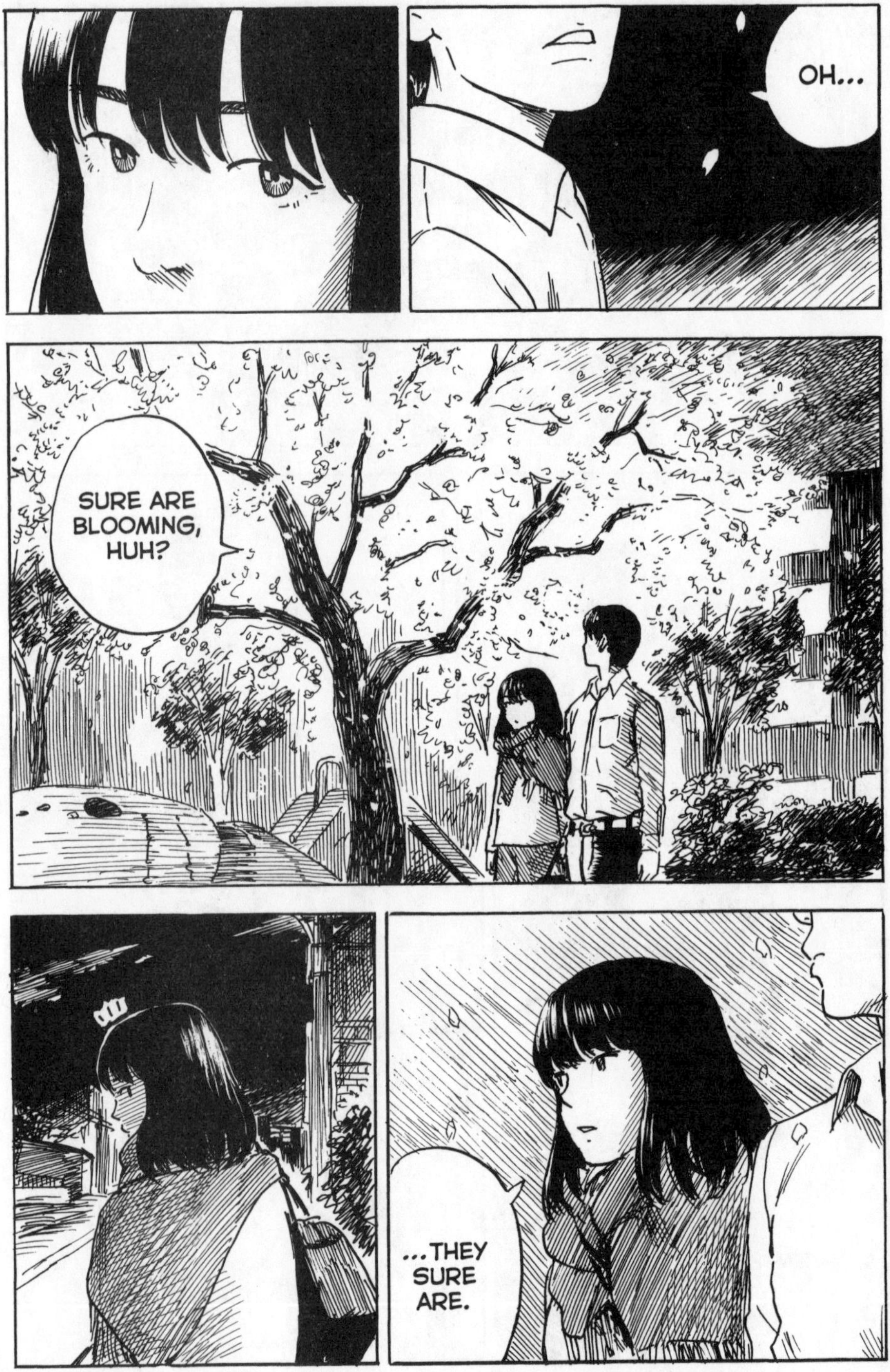
OH...
SURE ARE BLOOMING, HUH?
...THEY SURE ARE.

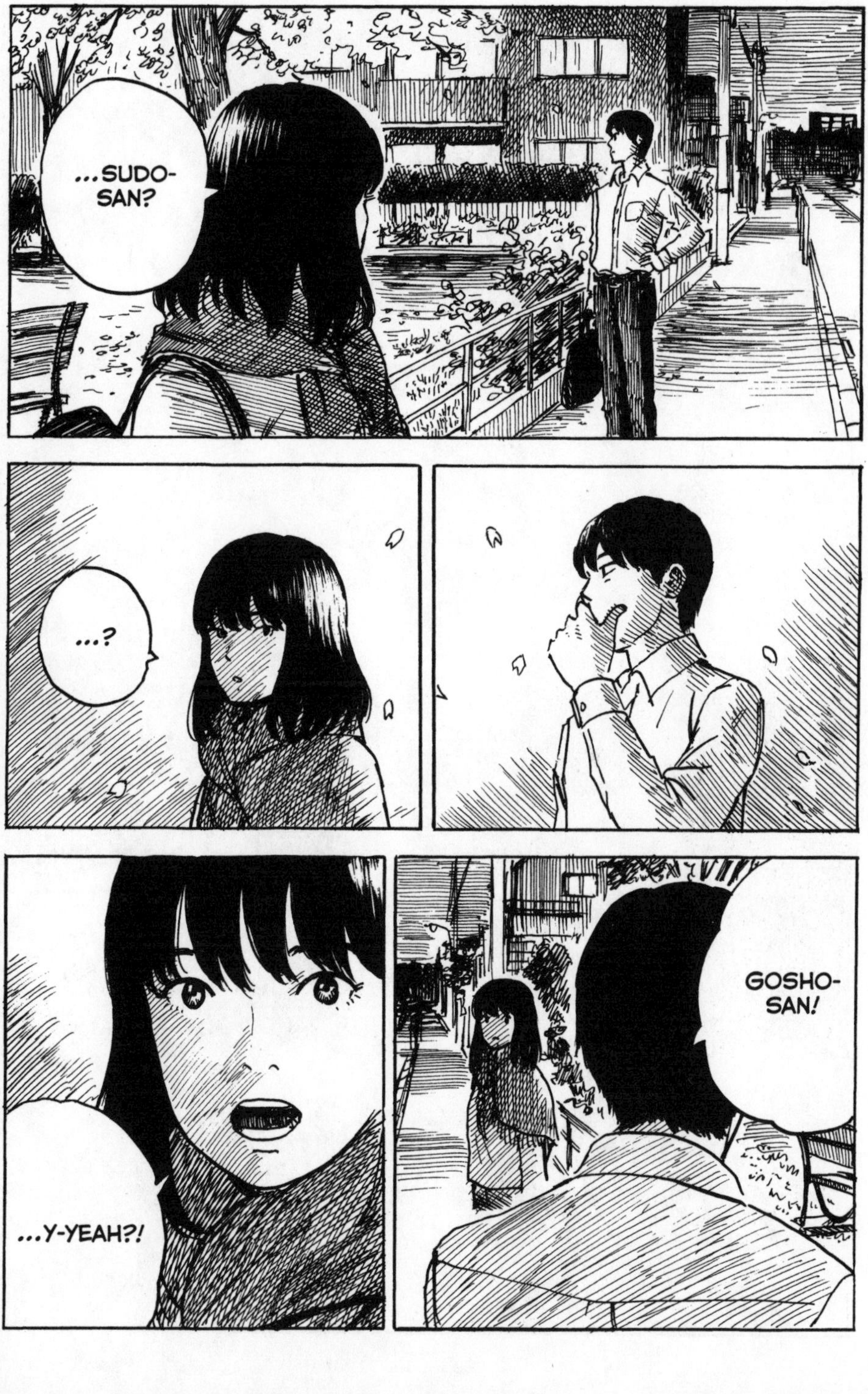
...SUDO-SAN?
...?
GOSHO-SAN!
...Y-YEAH?!

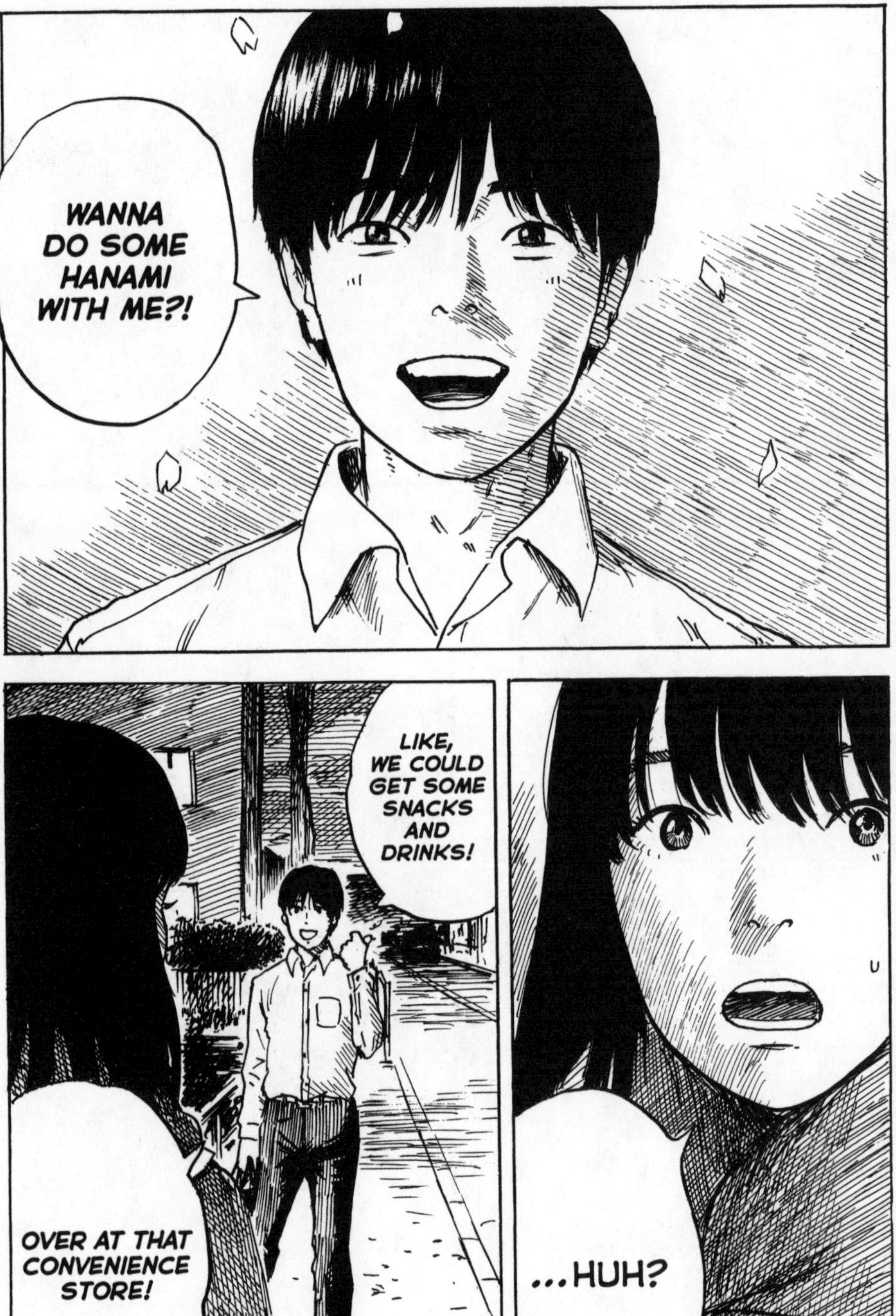
WANNA DO SOME HANAMI WITH ME?!
...HUH?
LIKE, WE COULD GET SOME SNACKS AND DRINKS!
OVER AT THAT CONVENIENCE STORE!

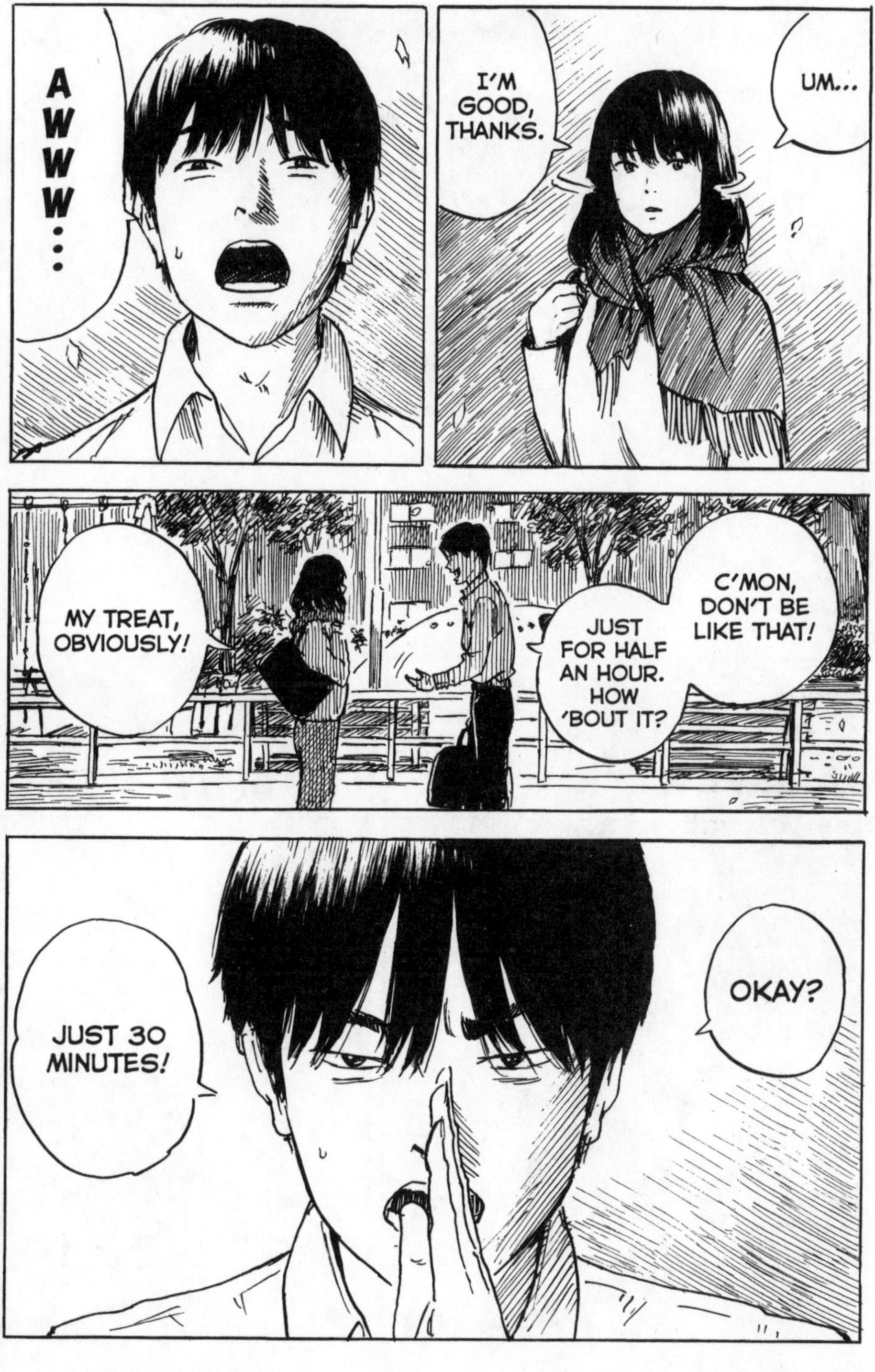
UM...
I'M GOOD, THANKS.
AWWW...
C'MON, DON'T BE LIKE THAT!
JUST FOR HALF AN HOUR. HOW 'BOUT IT?
MY TREAT, OBVIOUSLY!
OKAY?
JUST 30 MINUTES!

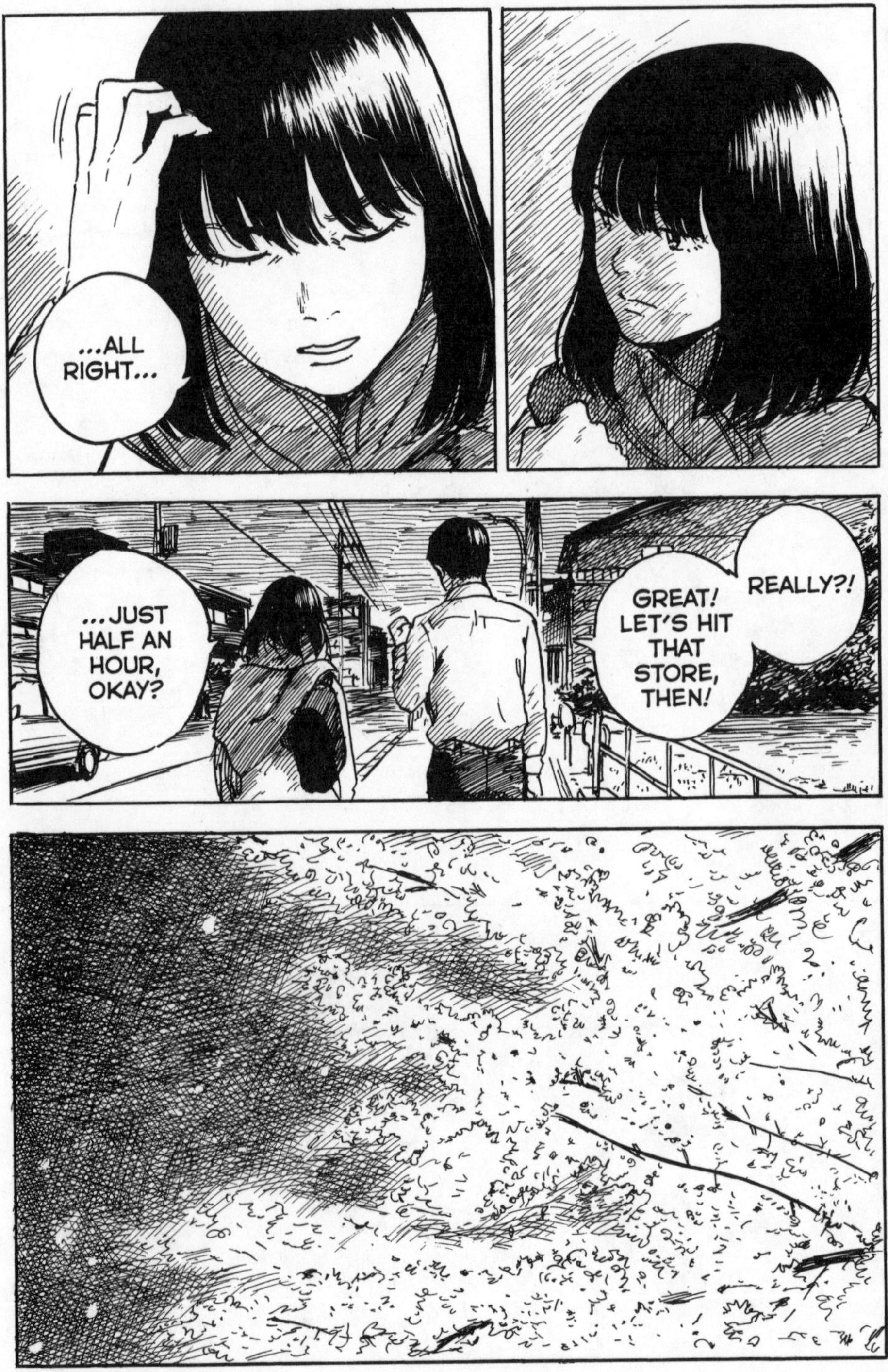
...ALL RIGHT...
REALLY?!
GREAT! LET'S HIT THAT STORE, THEN!
...JUST HALF AN HOUR, OKAY?

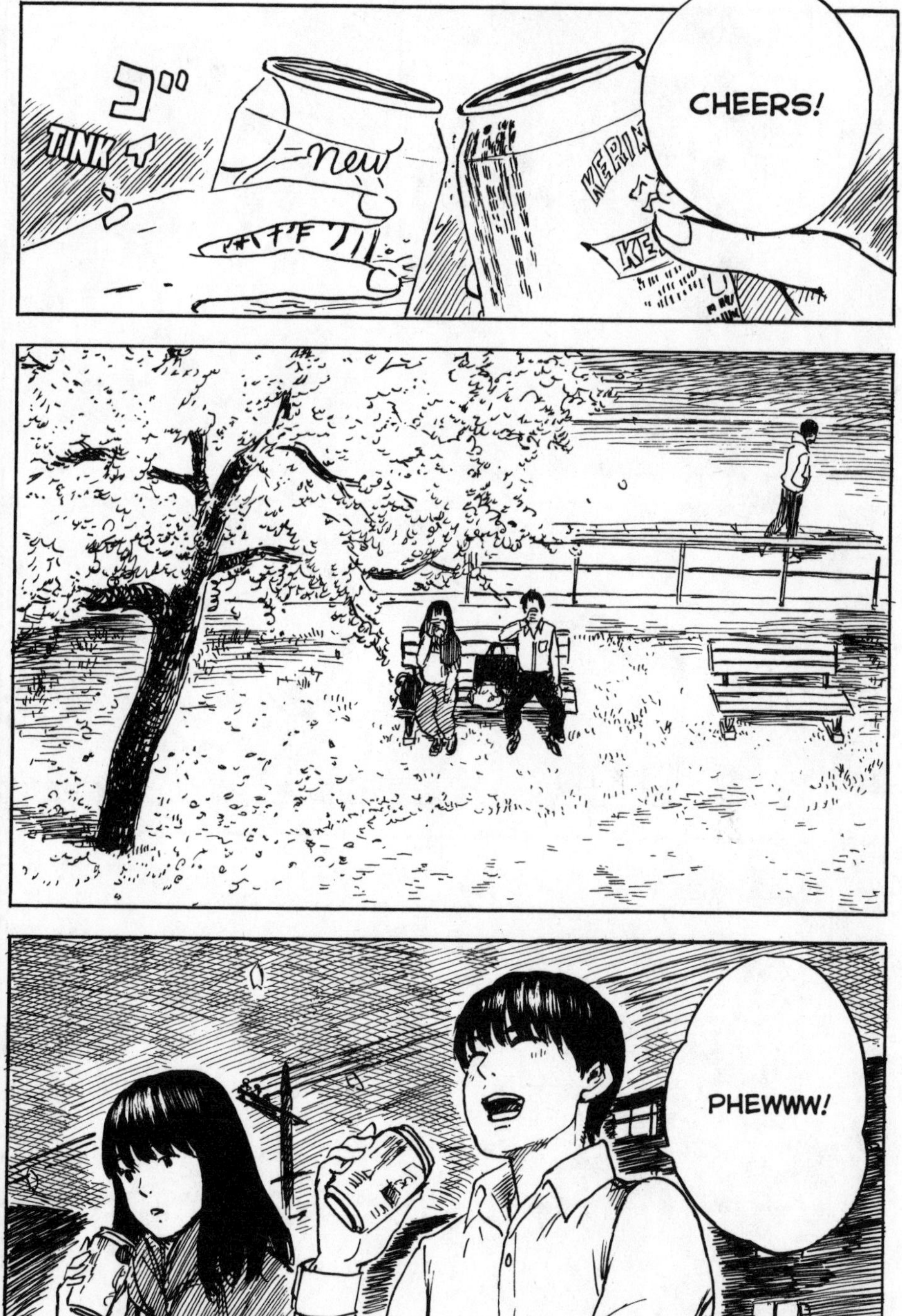
CHEERS!
TINK
PHEWWW!

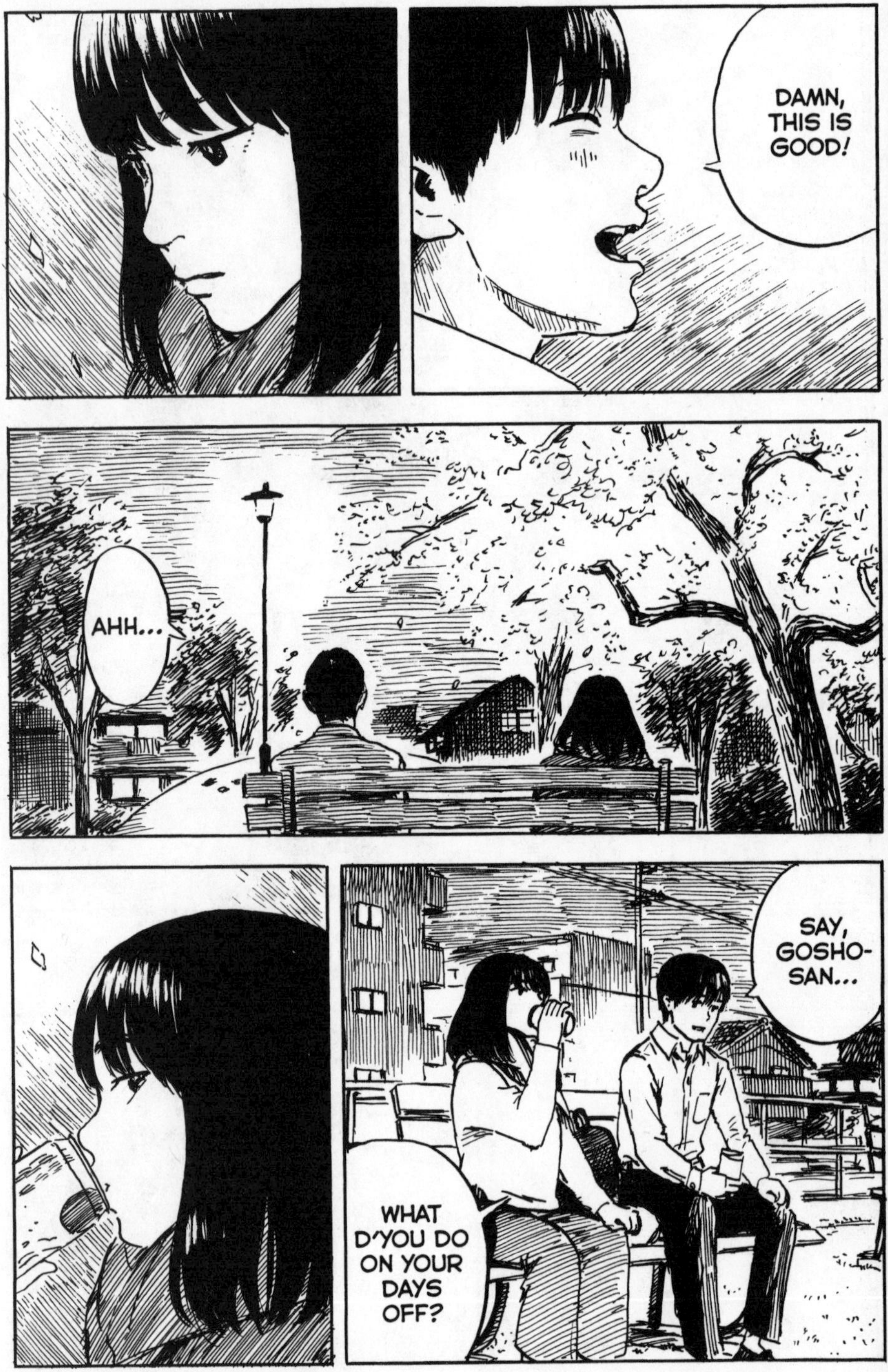
DAMN, THIS IS GOOD!
AHH...
SAY, GOSHO-SAN...
WHAT D'YOU DO ON YOUR DAYS OFF?

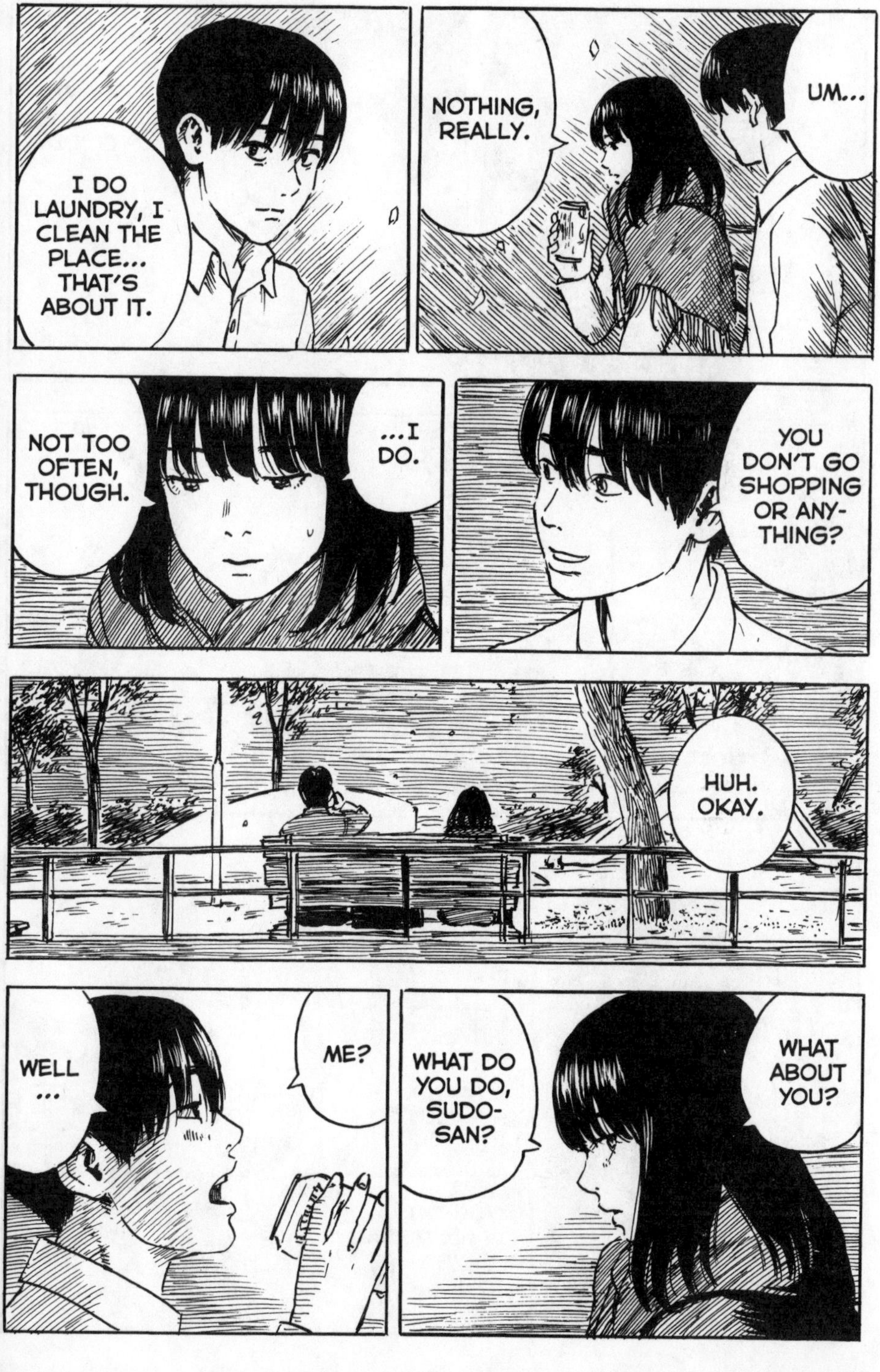
UM...
NOTHING, REALLY.
I DO LAUNDRY, I CLEAN THE PLACE... THAT'S ABOUT IT.
YOU DON'T GO SHOPPING OR ANY-THING?
...I DO.
NOT TOO OFTEN, THOUGH.
HUH. OKAY.
WHAT ABOUT YOU?
WHAT DO YOU DO, SUDO-SAN?
ME?
WELL ...

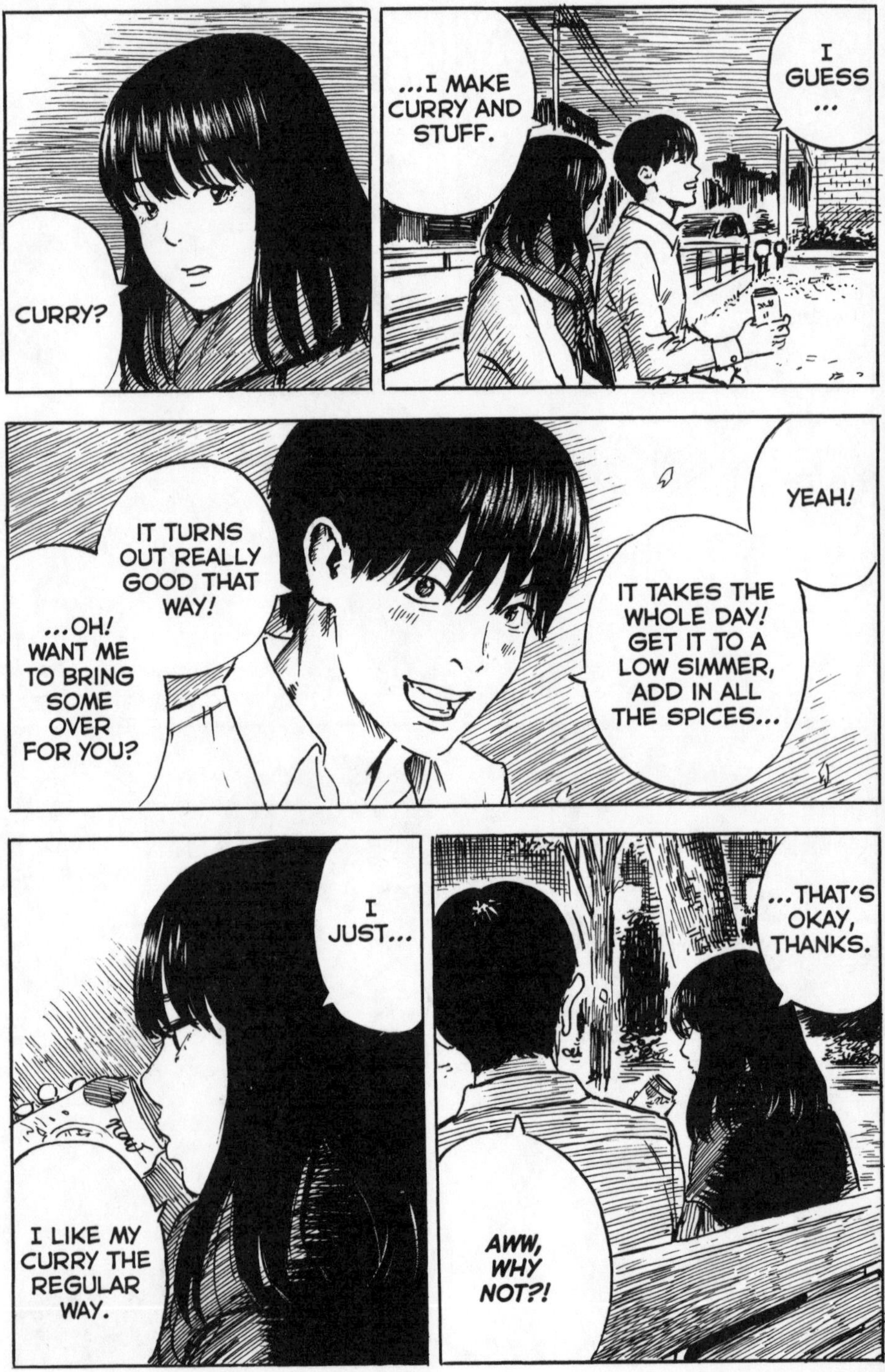
I GUESS...
...I MAKE CURRY AND STUFF.
CURRY?
YEAH!
IT TAKES THE WHOLE DAY! GET IT TO A LOW SIMMER, ADD IN ALL THE SPICES...
IT TURNS OUT REALLY GOOD THAT WAY!
...OH! WANT ME TO BRING SOME OVER FOR YOU?
...THAT'S OKAY, THANKS.
AWW, WHY NOT?!
I JUST...
I LIKE MY CURRY THE REGULAR WAY.

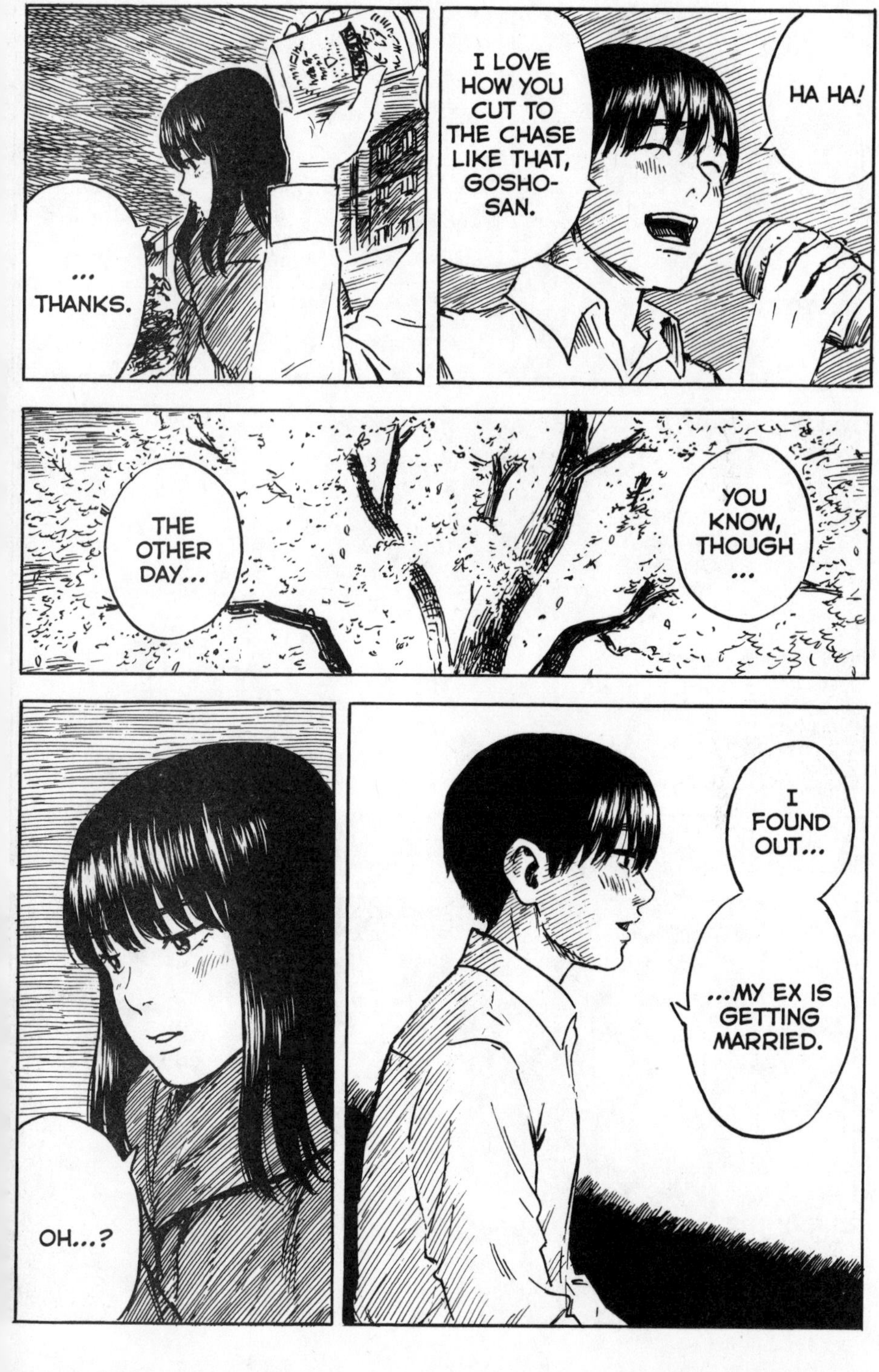
HA HA!
I LOVE HOW YOU CUT TO THE CHASE LIKE THAT, GOSHO-SAN.
... THANKS.
YOU KNOW, THOUGH ...
THE OTHER DAY...
I FOUND OUT...
...MY EX IS GETTING MARRIED.
OH...?

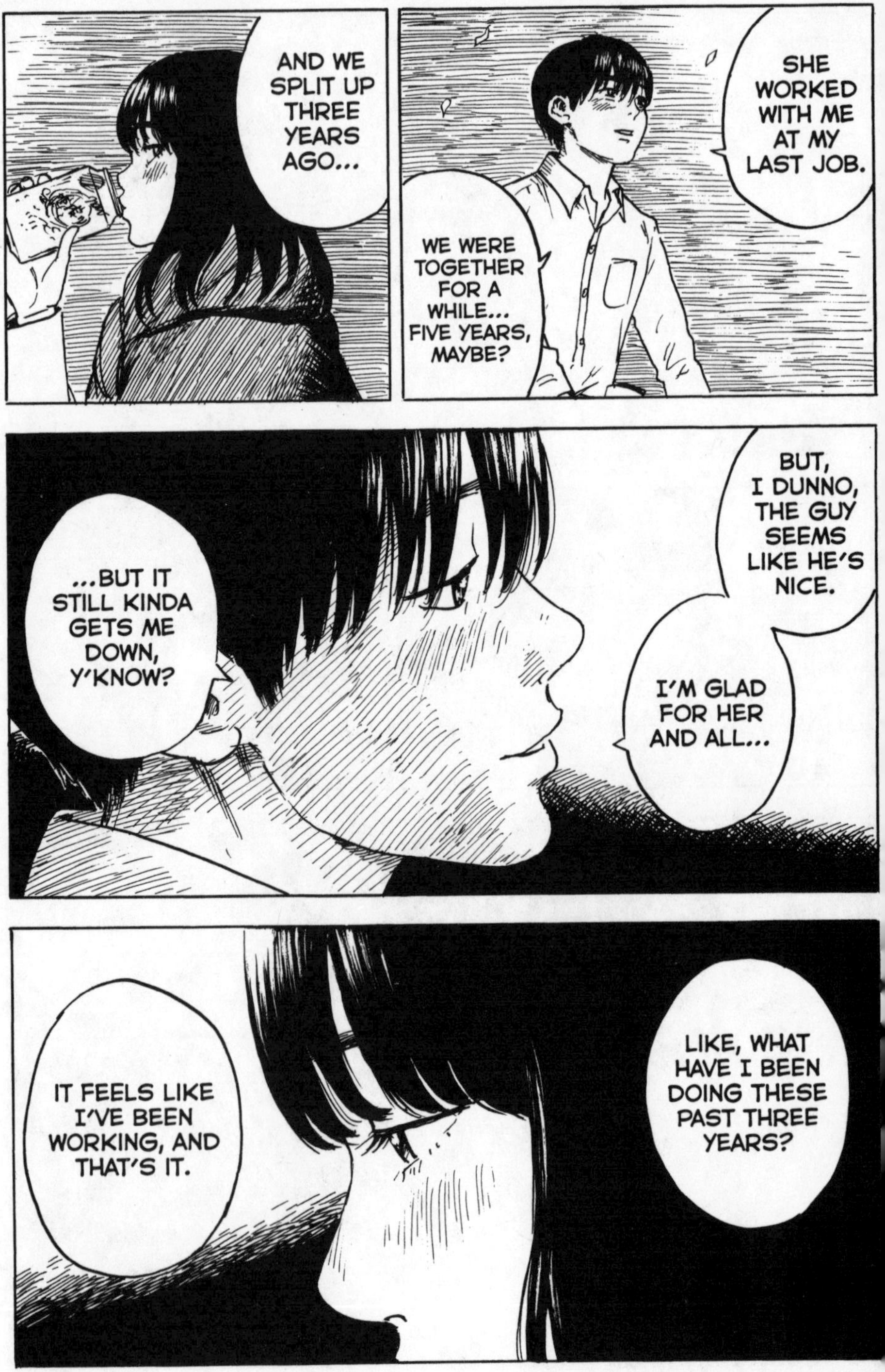
SHE WORKED WITH ME AT MY LAST JOB.
WE WERE TOGETHER FOR A WHILE... FIVE YEARS, MAYBE?
AND WE SPLIT UP THREE YEARS AGO...
BUT, I DUNNO, THE GUY SEEMS LIKE HE'S NICE.
I'M GLAD FOR HER AND ALL...
...BUT IT STILL KINDA GETS ME DOWN, Y'KNOW?
LIKE, WHAT HAVE I BEEN DOING THESE PAST THREE YEARS?
IT FEELS LIKE I'VE BEEN WORKING, AND THAT'S IT.

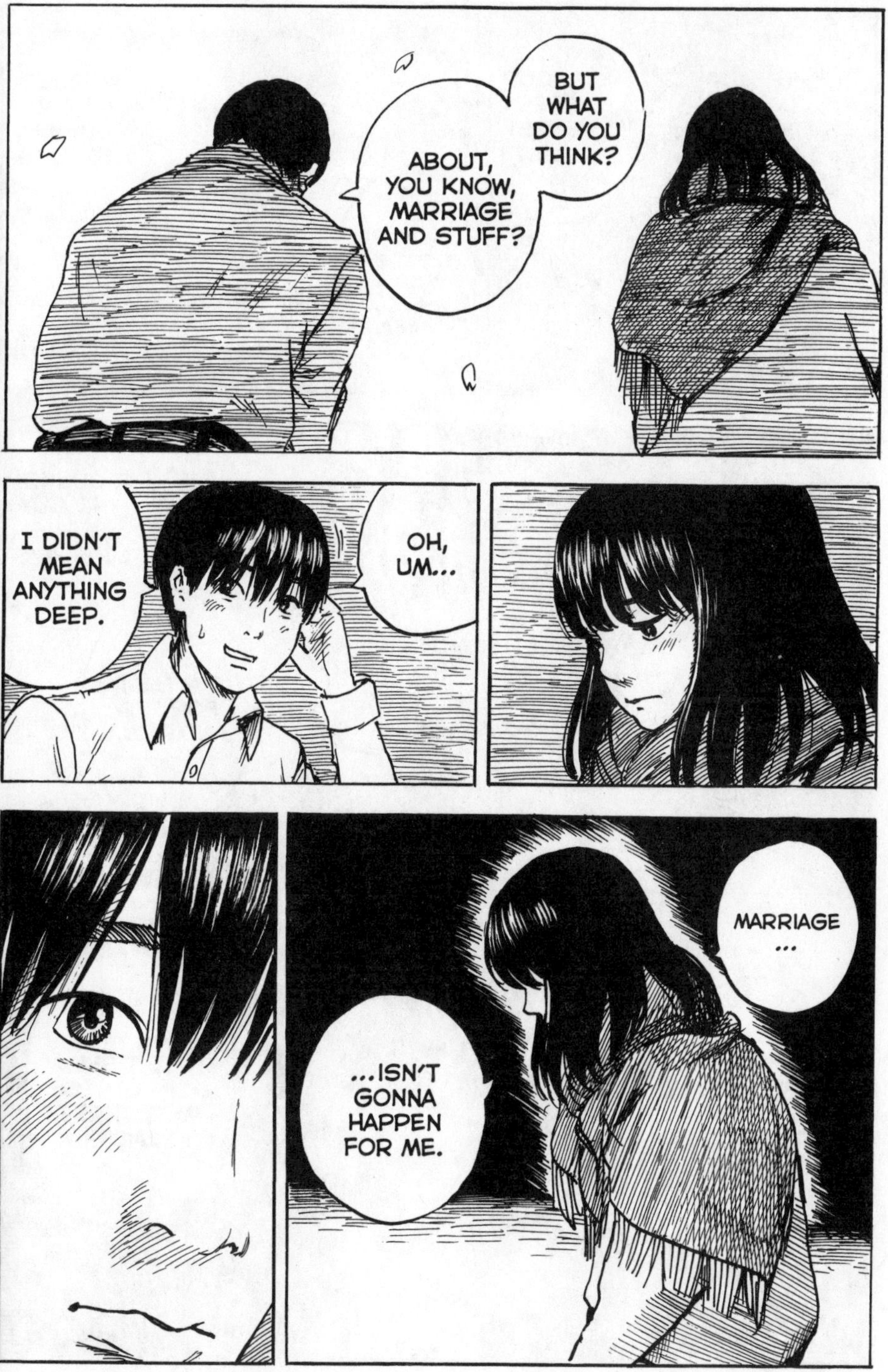
BUT WHAT DO YOU THINK?
ABOUT, YOU KNOW, MARRIAGE AND STUFF?
OH, UM...
I DIDN'T MEAN ANYTHING DEEP.
MARRIAGE...
...ISN'T GONNA HAPPEN FOR ME.

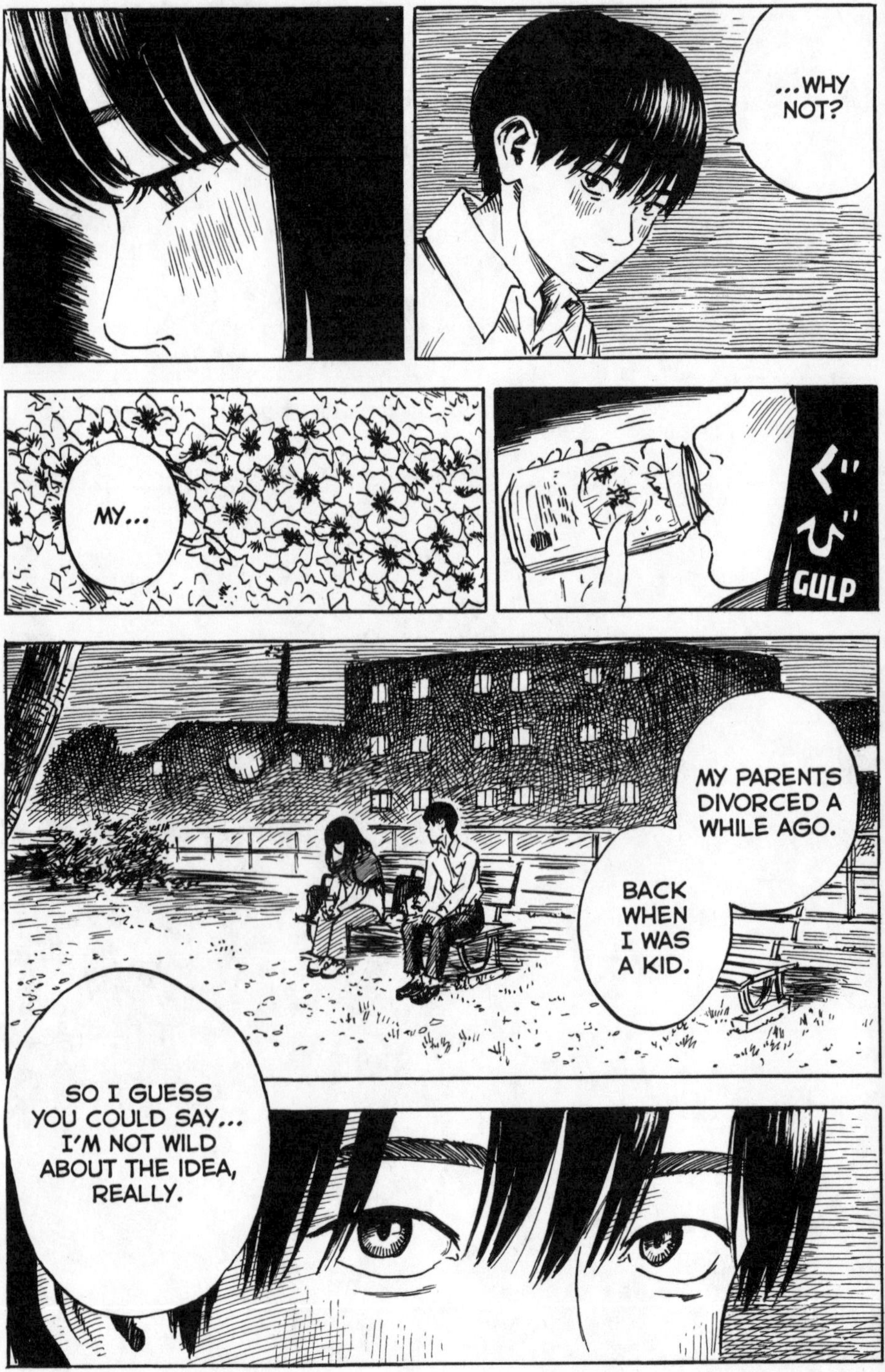
...WHY NOT?
ぐび
GULP
MY...
MY PARENTS DIVORCED A WHILE AGO.
BACK WHEN I WAS A KID.
SO I GUESS YOU COULD SAY... I'M NOT WILD ABOUT THE IDEA, REALLY.

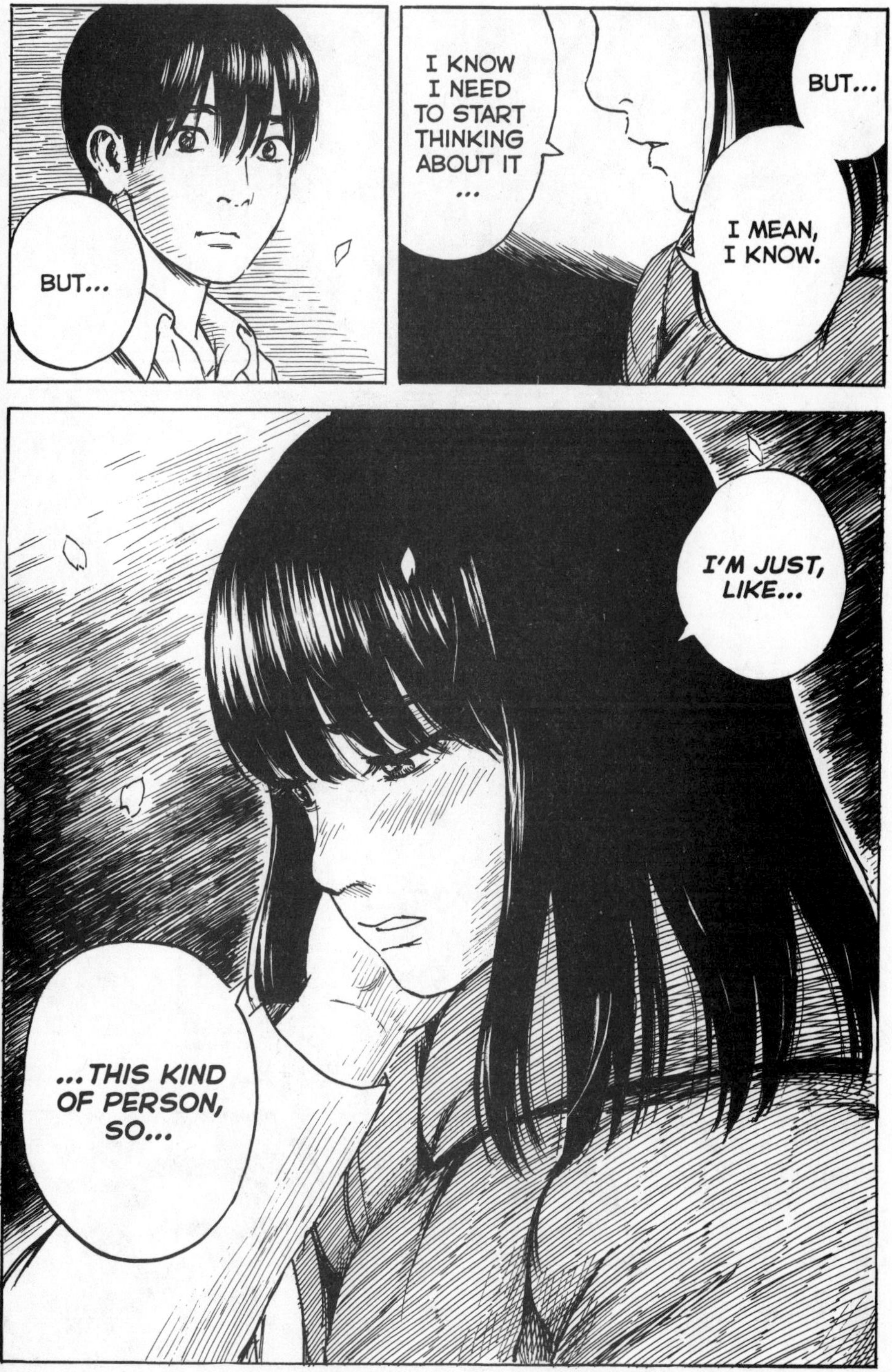
I KNOW I NEED TO START THINKING ABOUT IT ...
I MEAN, I KNOW.
BUT...
BUT...
I'M JUST, LIKE...
...THIS KIND OF PERSON, SO...

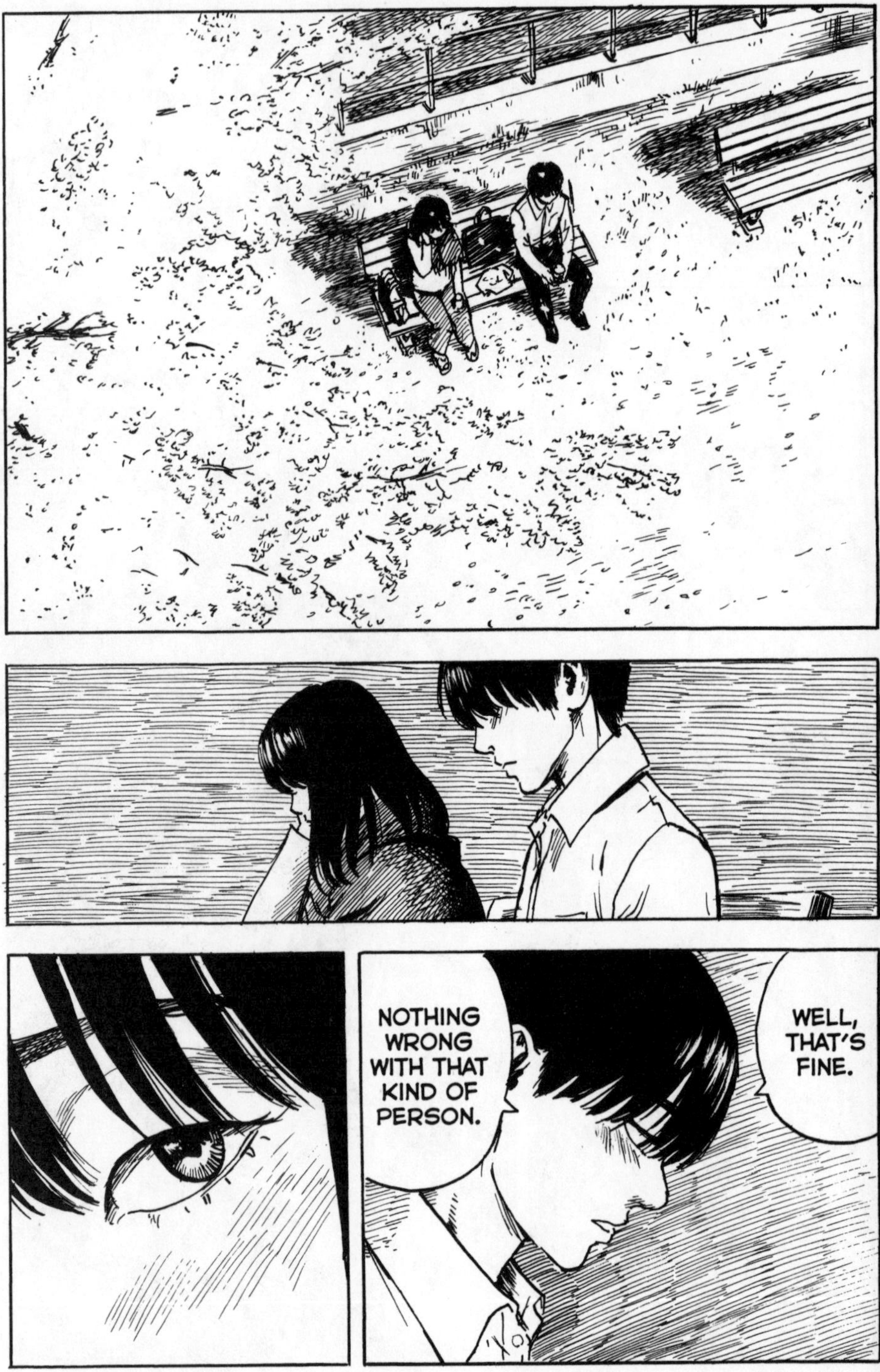
WELL, THAT'S FINE.
NOTHING WRONG WITH THAT KIND OF PERSON.

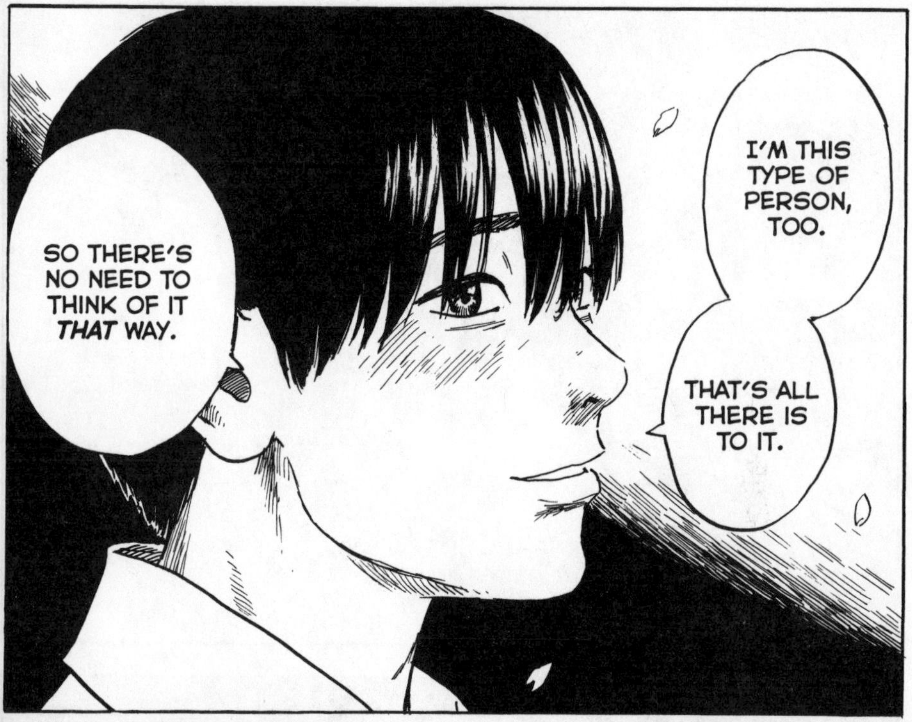
I'M THIS TYPE OF PERSON, TOO.
THAT'S ALL THERE IS TO IT.
SO THERE'S NO NEED TO THINK OF IT *THAT* WAY.

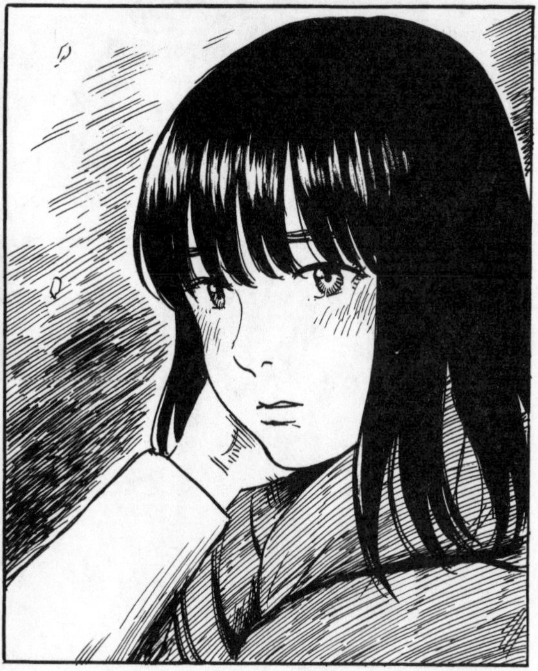

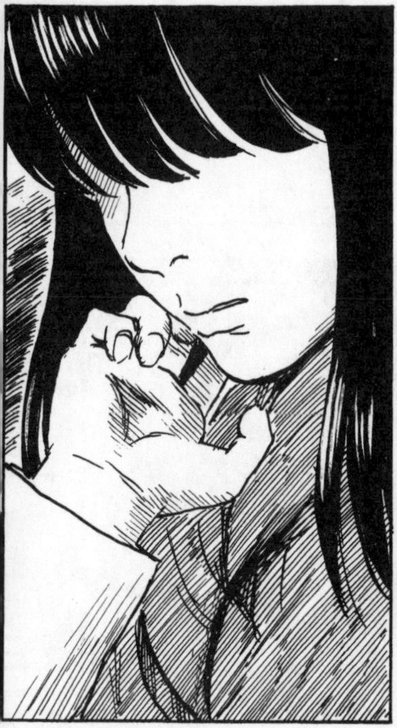

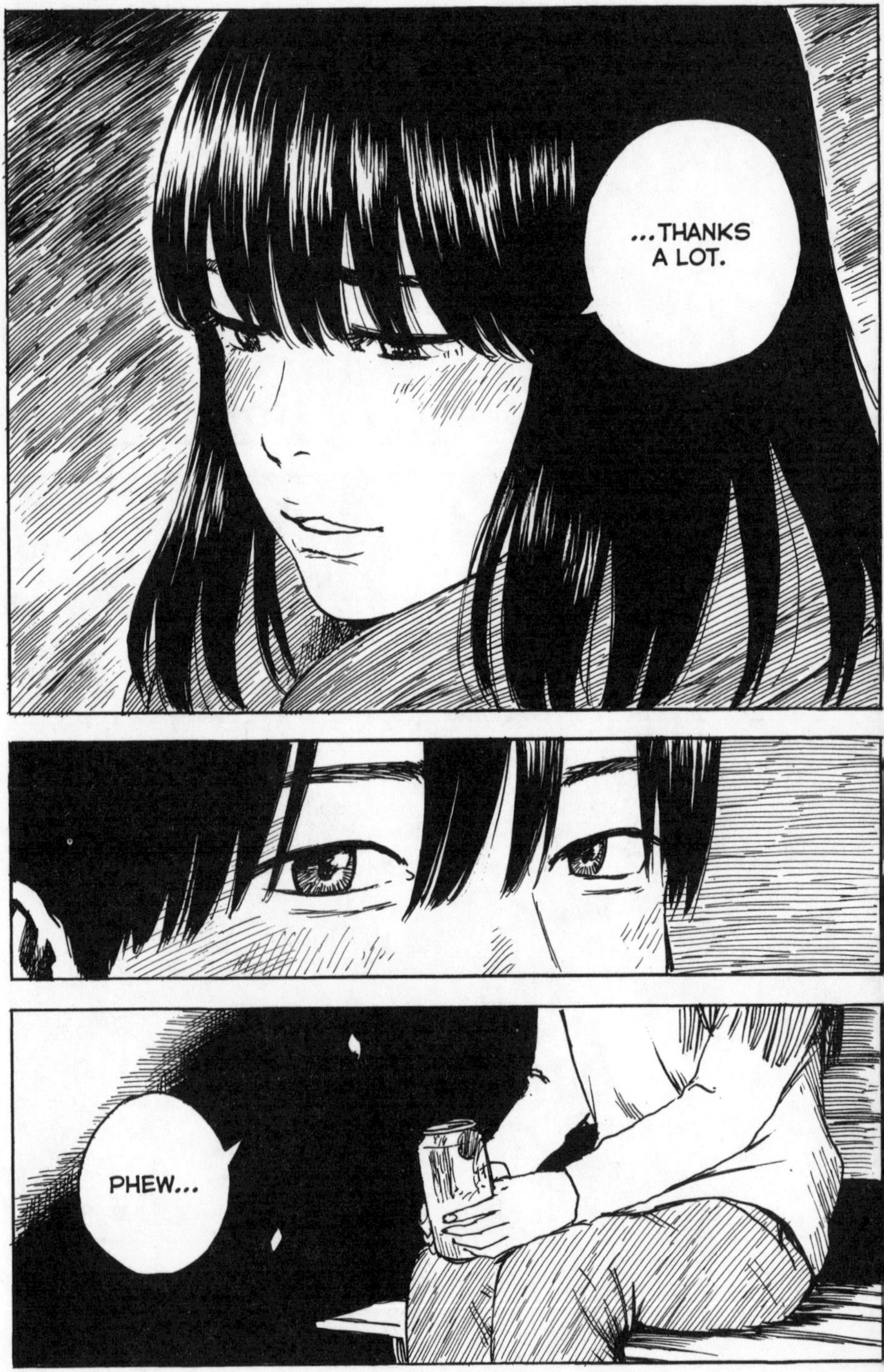
...THANKS A LOT.
PHEW...

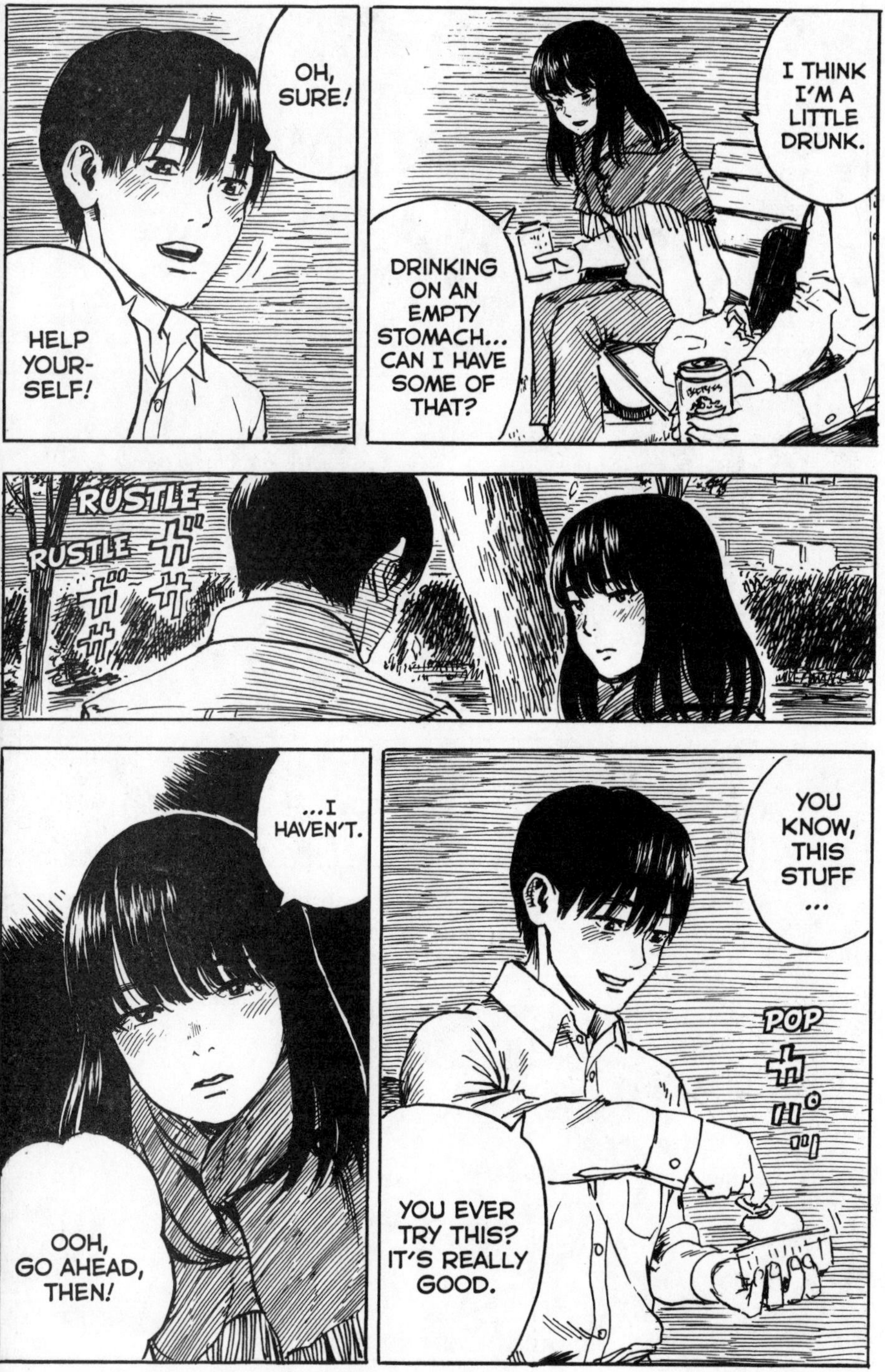
I THINK I'M A LITTLE DRUNK.
DRINKING ON AN EMPTY STOMACH... CAN I HAVE SOME OF THAT?
OH, SURE!
HELP YOURSELF!
RUSTLE
RUSTLE
ガサガサ
YOU KNOW, THIS STUFF ...
POP
YOU EVER TRY THIS? IT'S REALLY GOOD.
...I HAVEN'T.
OOH, GO AHEAD, THEN!

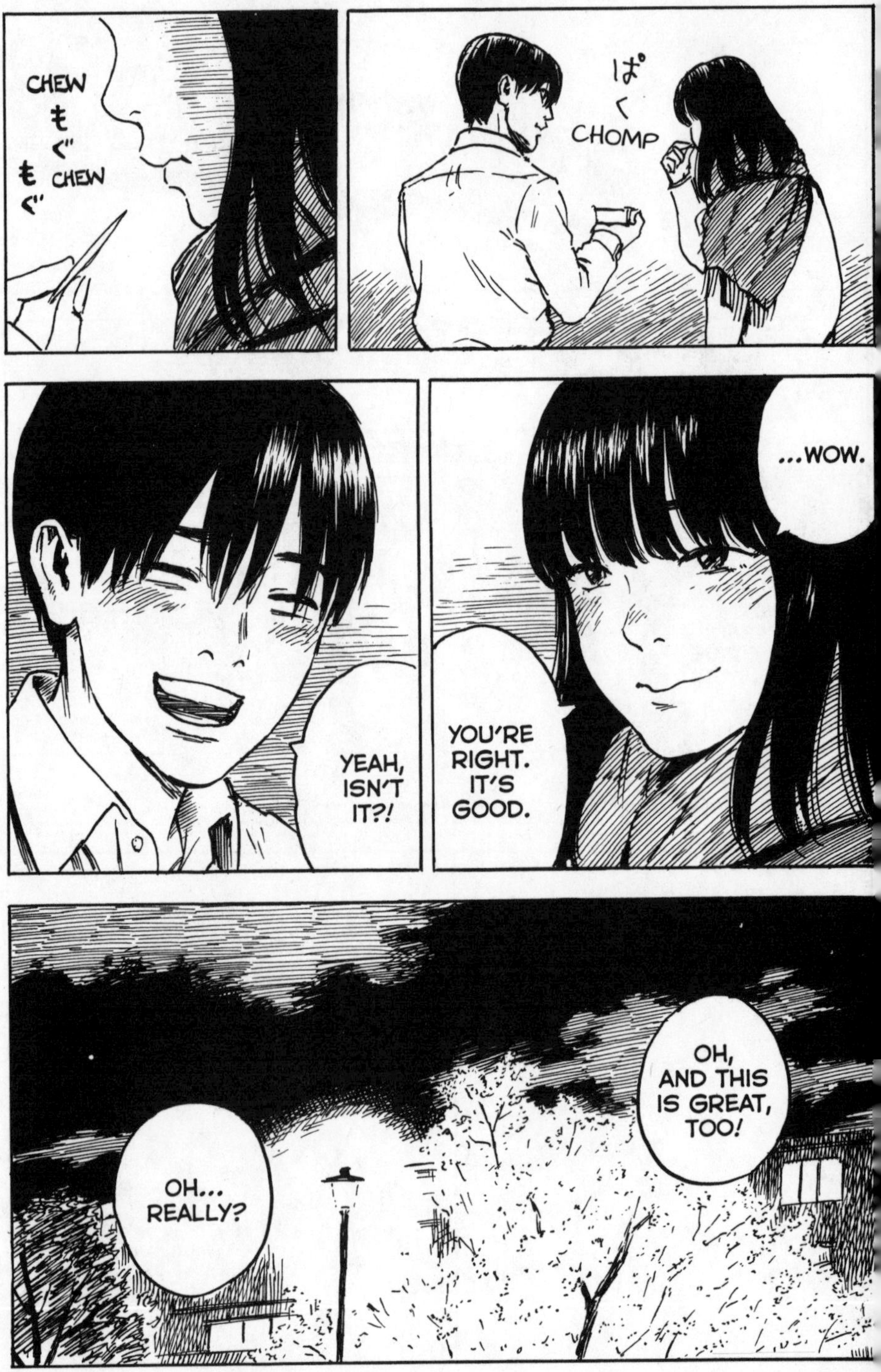
ぱく
CHOMP
CHEW
もぐもぐ
CHEW
...WOW.
YOU'RE RIGHT. IT'S GOOD.
YEAH, ISN'T IT?!
OH, AND THIS IS GREAT, TOO!
OH... REALLY?

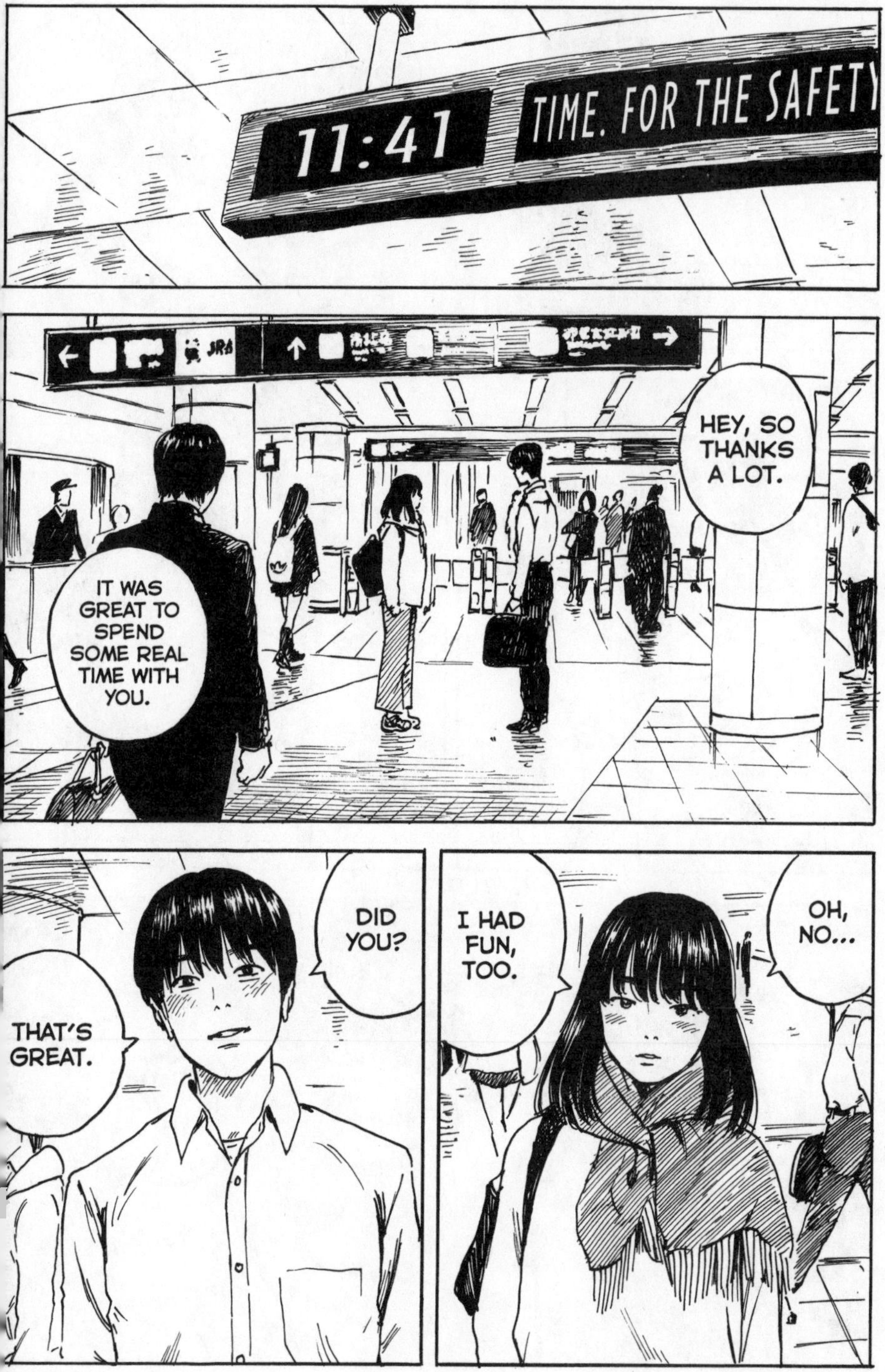
11:41
TIME. FOR THE SAFETY
HEY, SO THANKS A LOT.
IT WAS GREAT TO SPEND SOME REAL TIME WITH YOU.
OH, NO...
I HAD FUN, TOO.
DID YOU?
THAT'S GREAT.

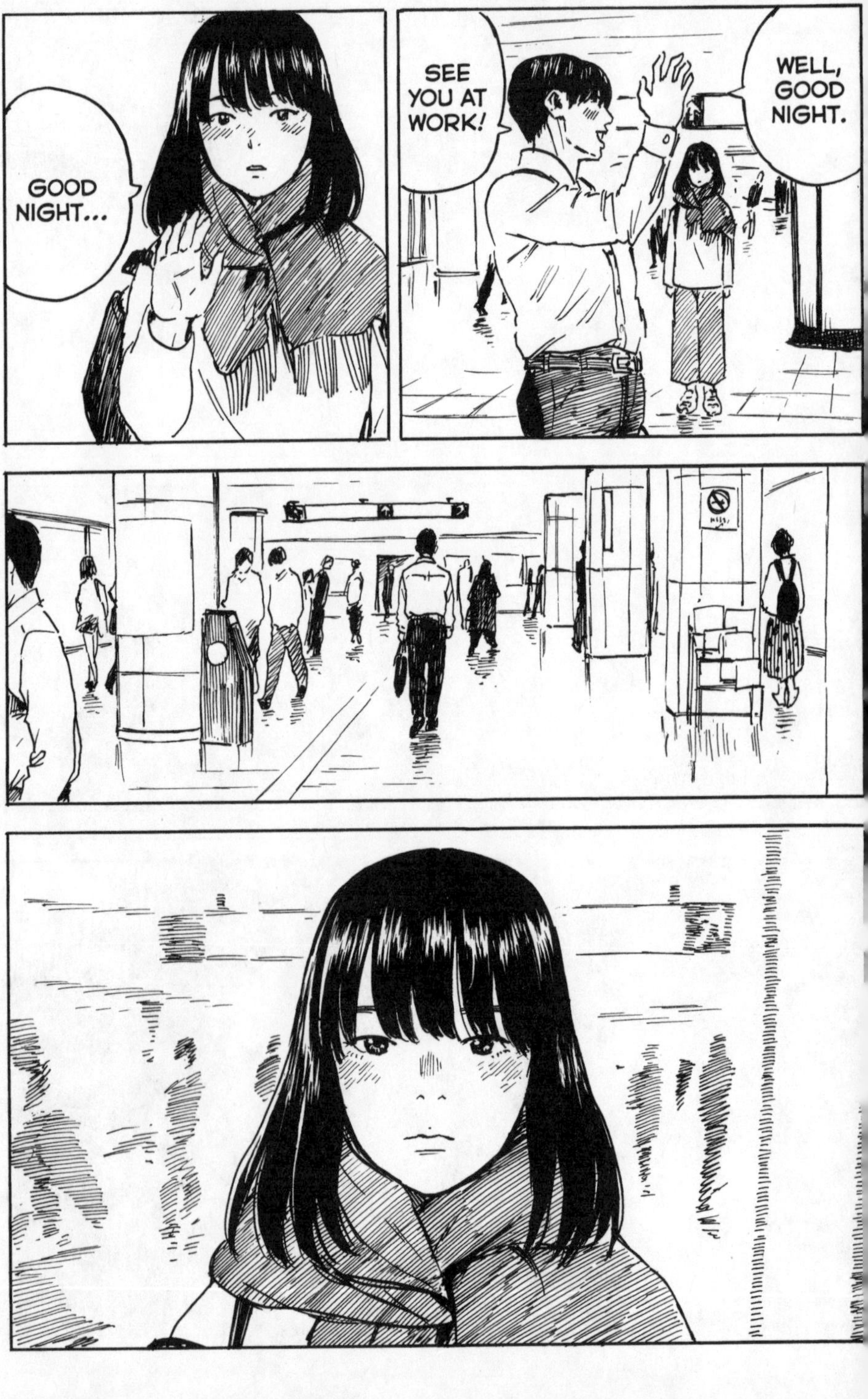
WELL, GOOD NIGHT.
SEE YOU AT WORK!
GOOD NIGHT...

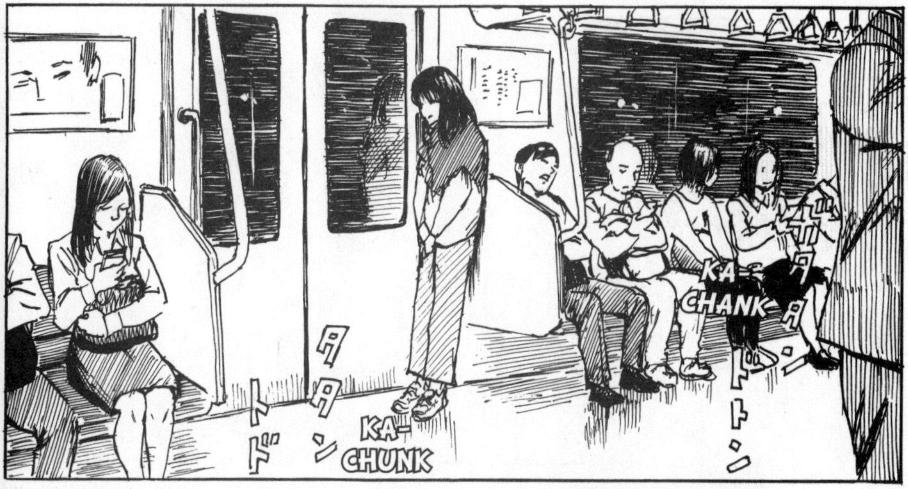
KA-CHANK
KA-CHUNK

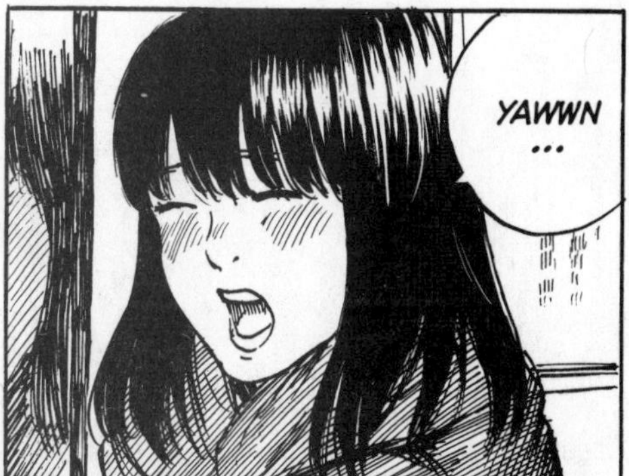
YAWWN ...

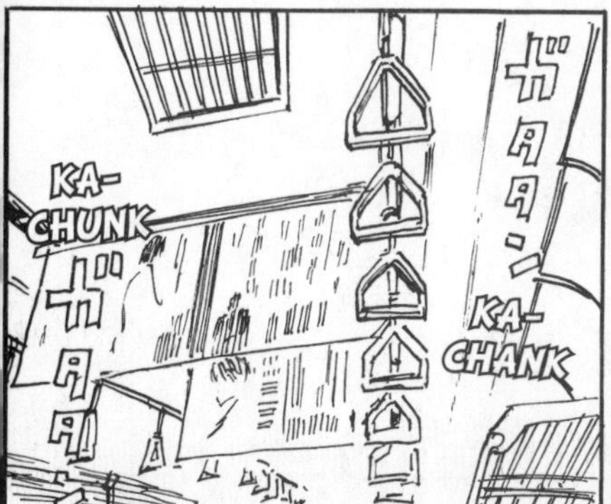
KA-CHANK
KA-CHUNK

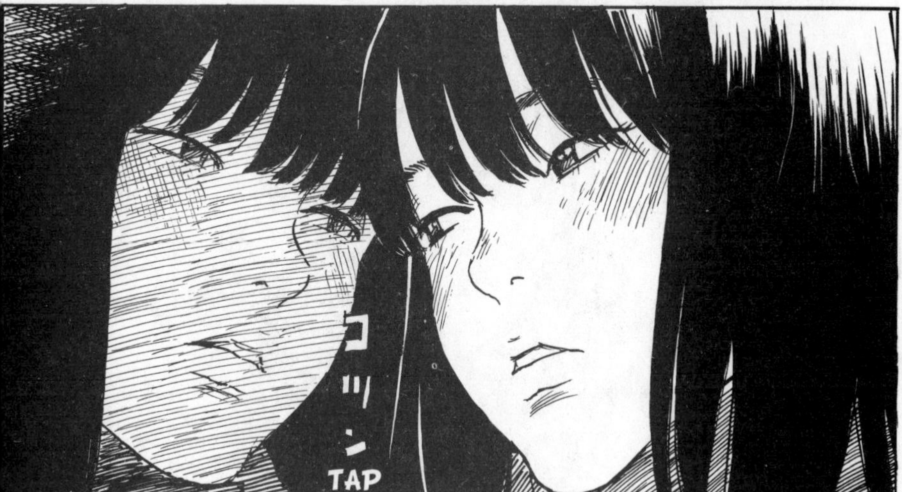
TAP

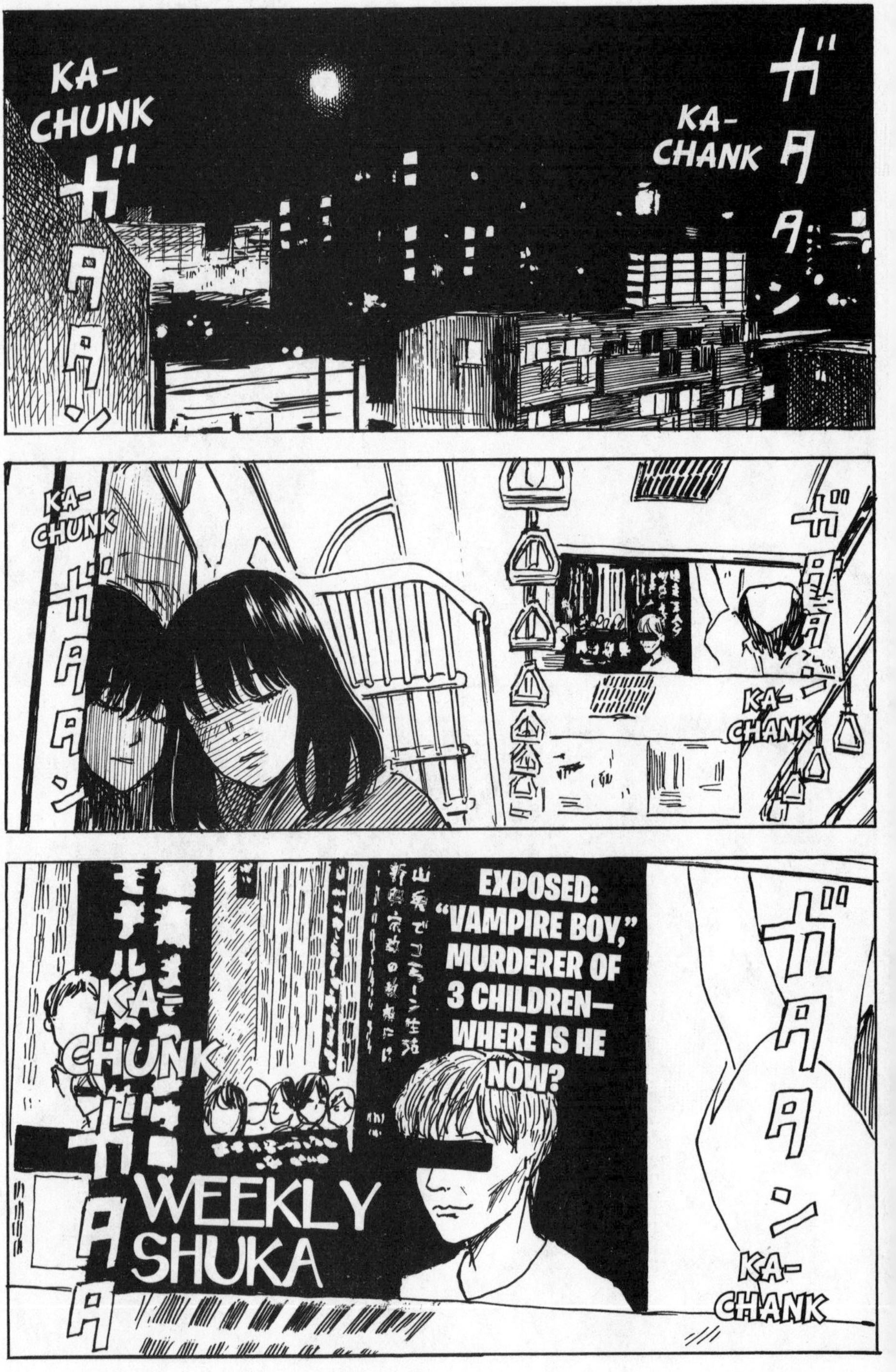
ガタタン
KA-CHANK
KA-CHUNK
ガタタン
ガタタン
KA-CHANK
KA-CHUNK
ガタタン
ガタタン
KA-CHANK
EXPOSED: "VAMPIRE BOY," MURDERER OF 3 CHILDREN— WHERE IS HE NOW?
KA-CHUNK
ガタタ
WEEKLY SHUKA

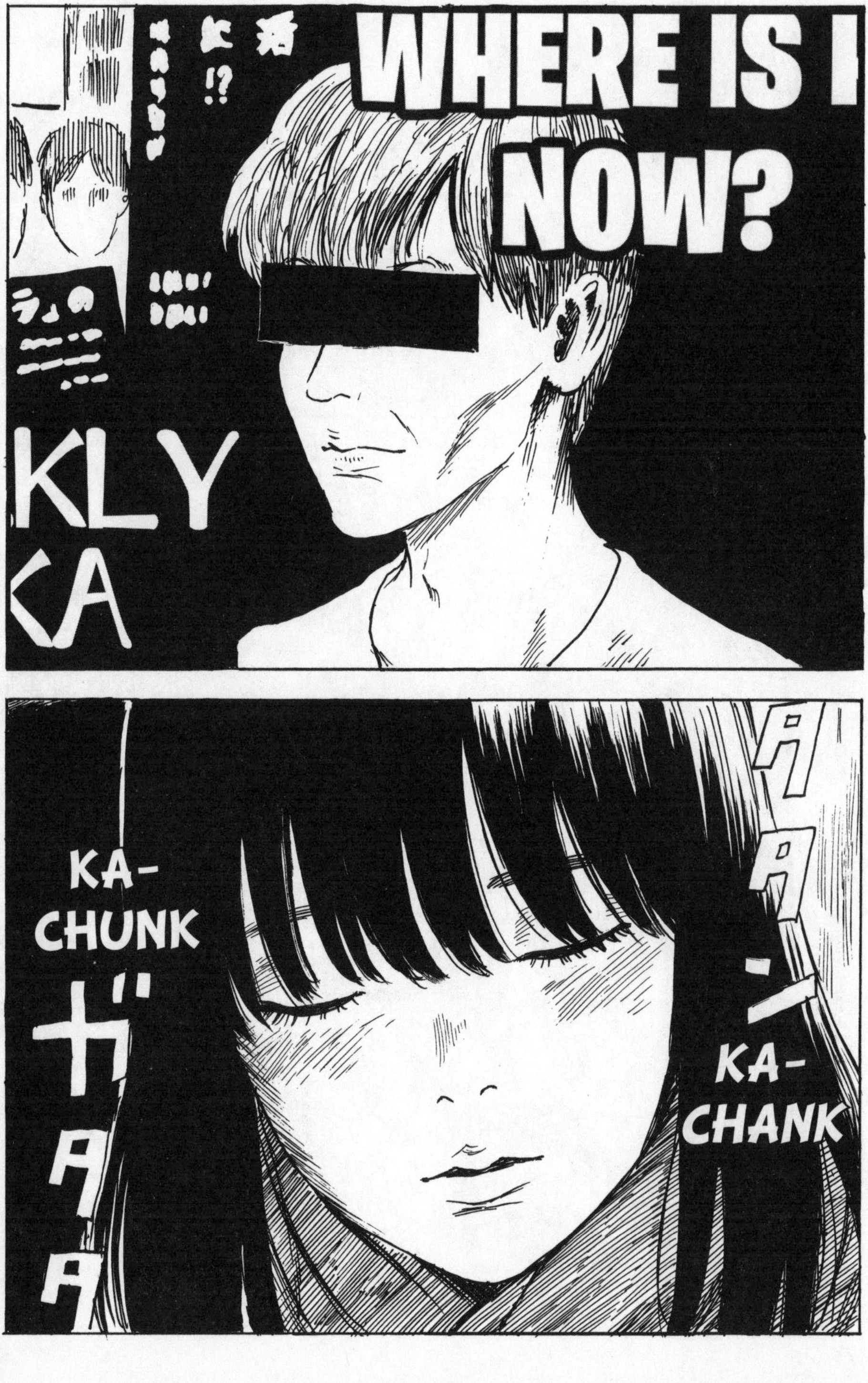
WHERE IS I NOW?
KA-CHANK
KA-CHUNK

Chapter 27: A Wounded Heart

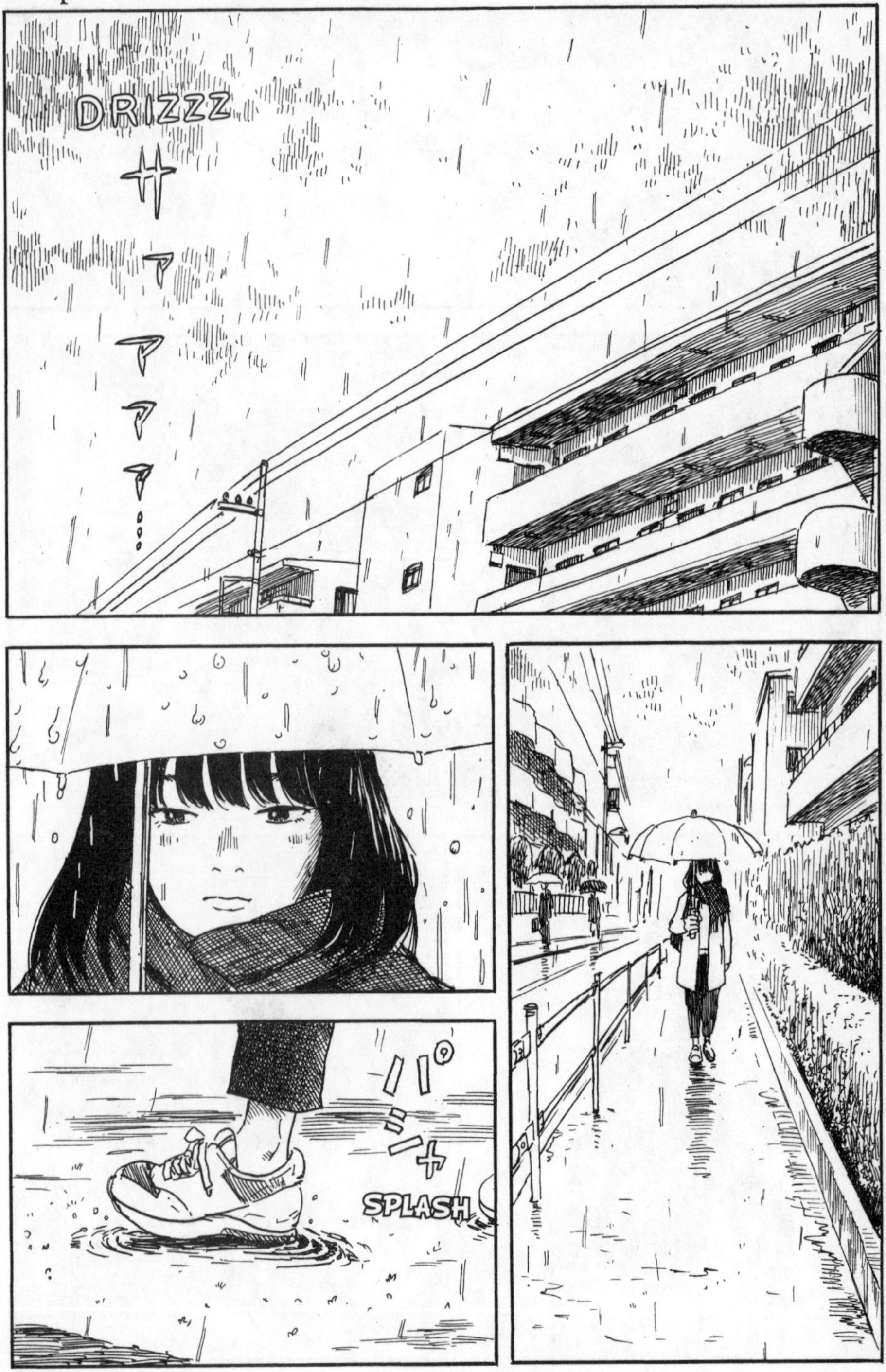
DRIZZZ
サァァァァ…
SPLASH

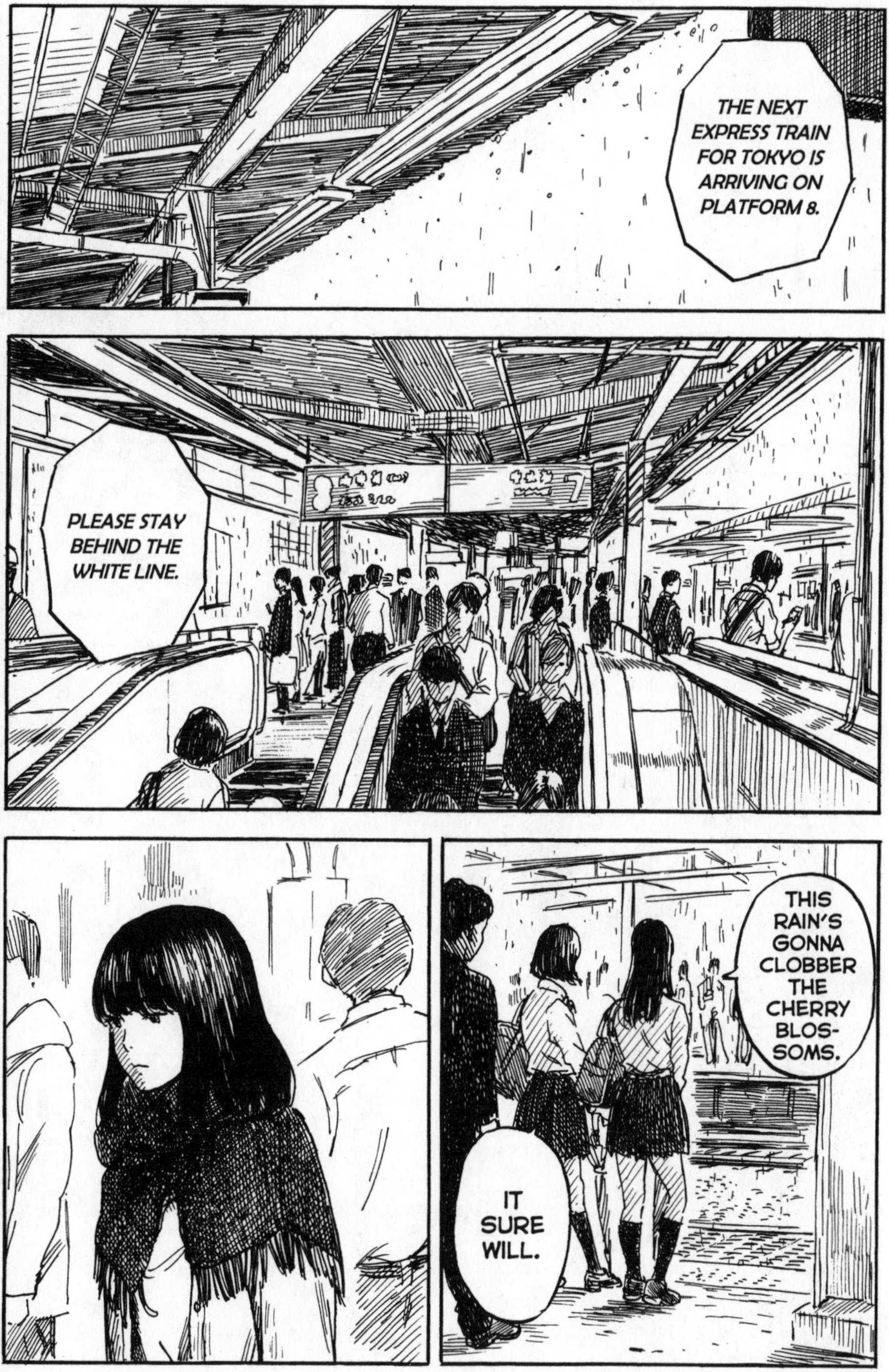
THE NEXT EXPRESS TRAIN FOR TOKYO IS ARRIVING ON PLATFORM 8.
PLEASE STAY BEHIND THE WHITE LINE.
THIS RAIN'S GONNA CLOBBER THE CHERRY BLOS-SOMS.
IT SURE WILL.

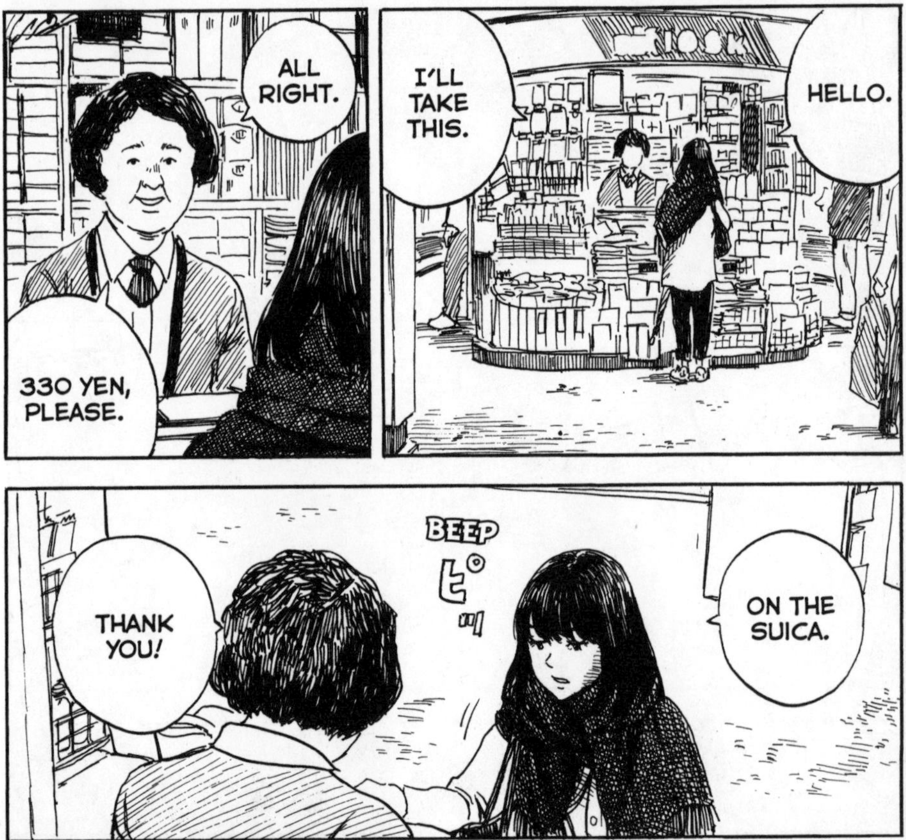
HELLO.
I'LL TAKE THIS.
ALL RIGHT.
330 YEN, PLEASE.
ON THE SUICA.
BEEP
THANK YOU!

*NOTE: SUICA CARDS ARE REFILLABLE ELECTRONIC CASH CARDS, USED PRIMARILY FOR TRANSIT AND AT CONVENIENCE STORES.

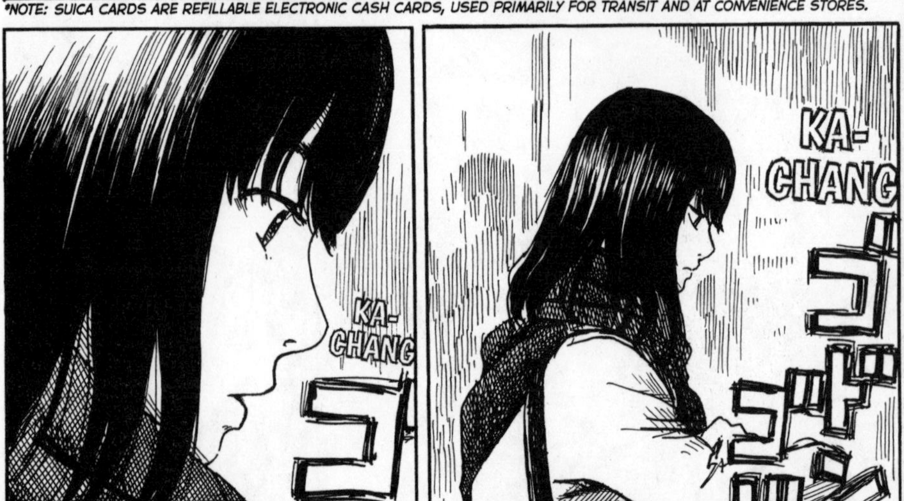
KA-CHANG
KA-CHANG

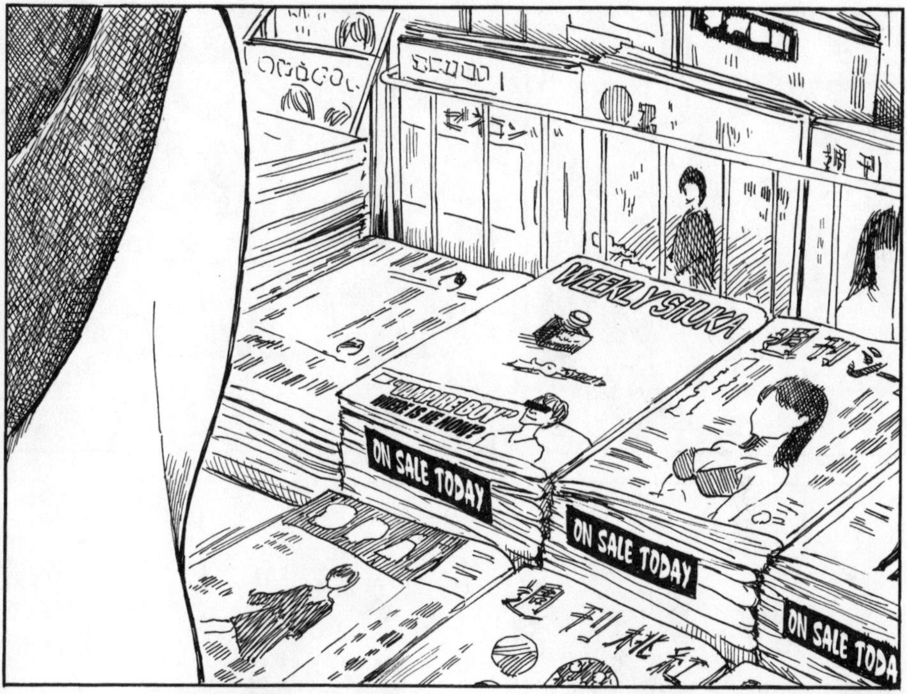
WEEKLY SHUKA
"VAMPIRE BOY"
WHERE IS HE NOW?
ON SALE TODAY
週刊シー
ON SALE TODAY
週刊桃紅
ON SALE TODA
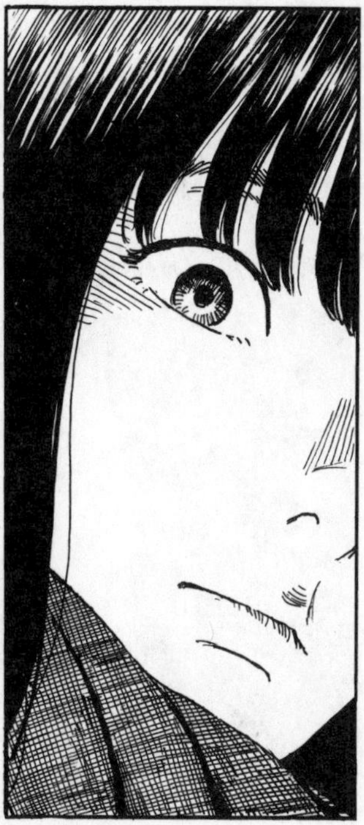
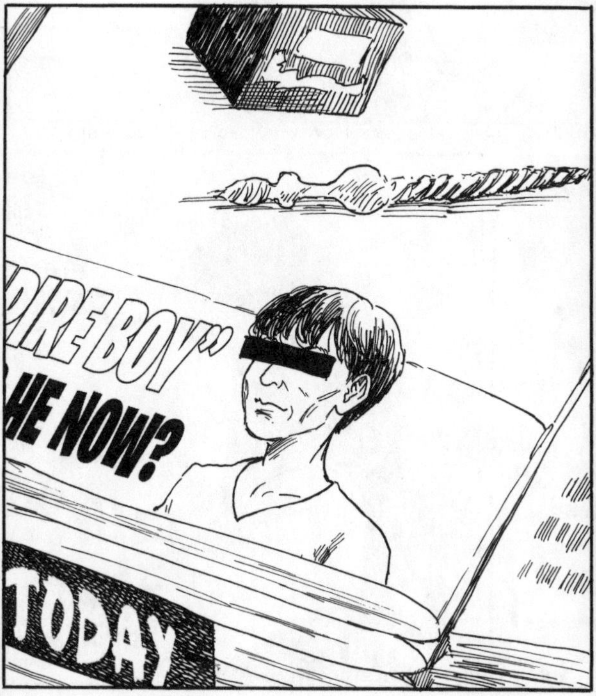
PIRE BOY"
HE NOW?
TODAY

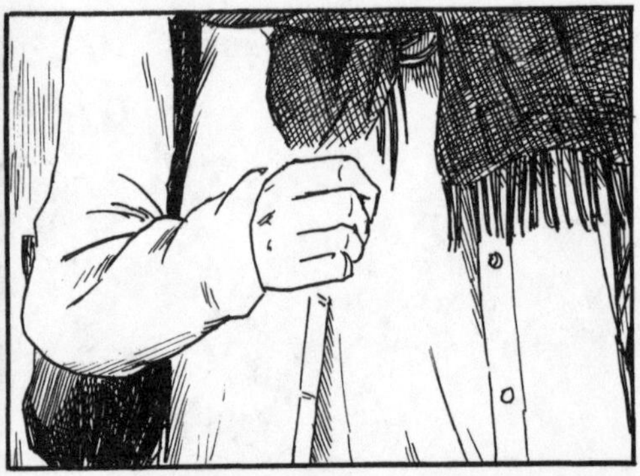
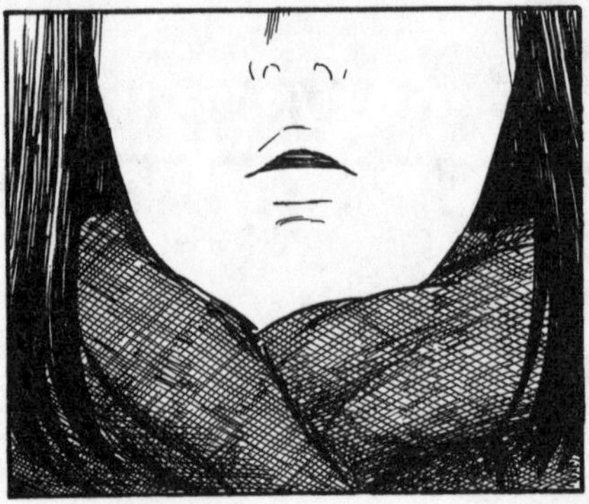
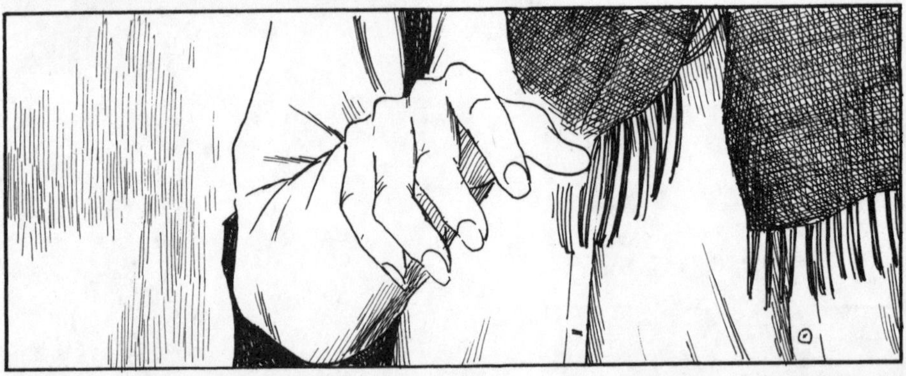
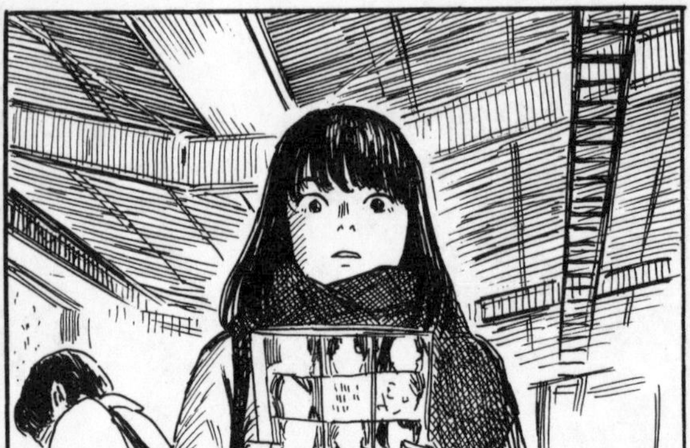
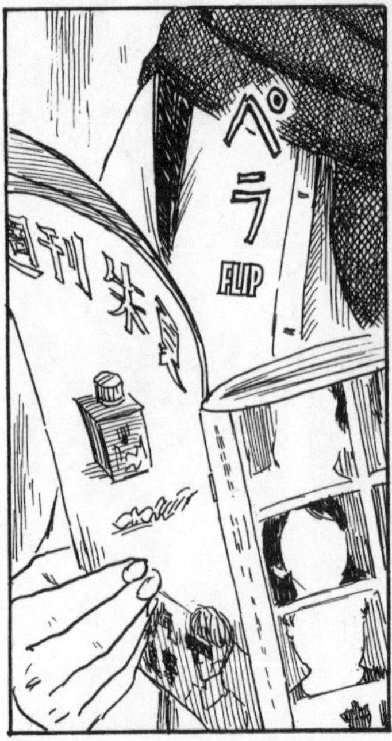
ペラ
FLIP

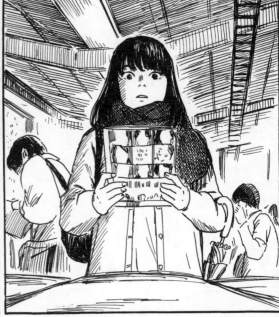

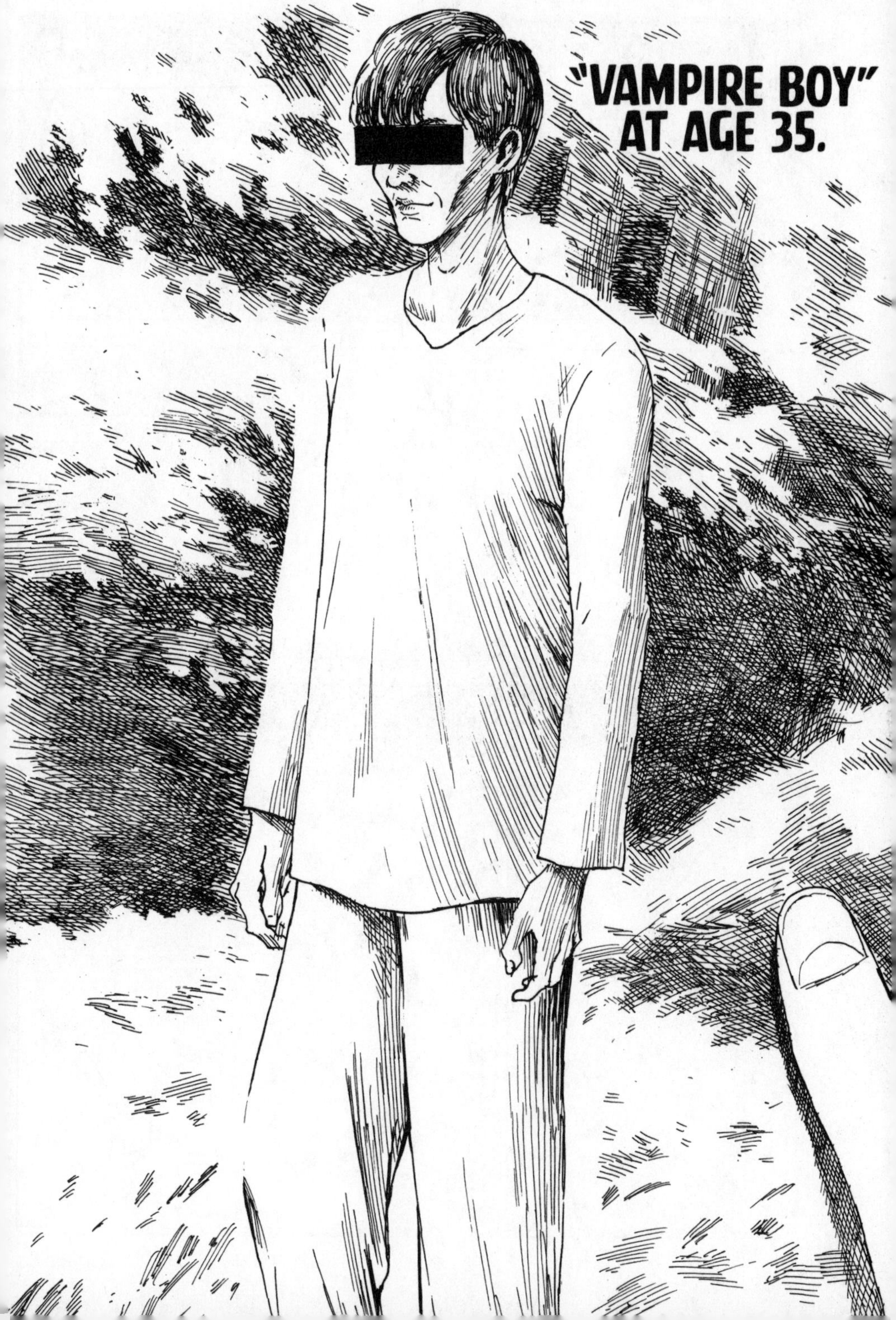
"VAMPIRE BOY" AT AGE 35.

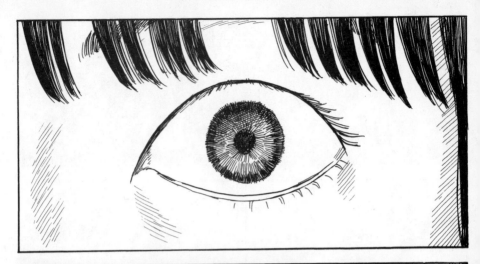

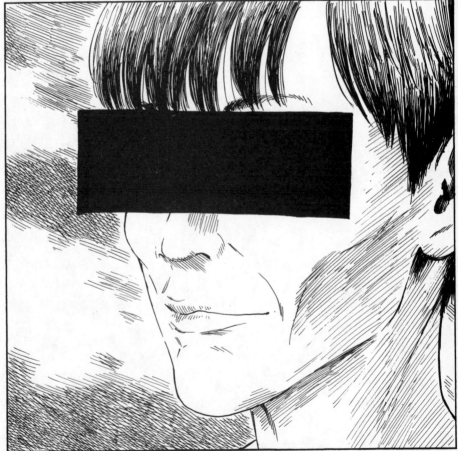

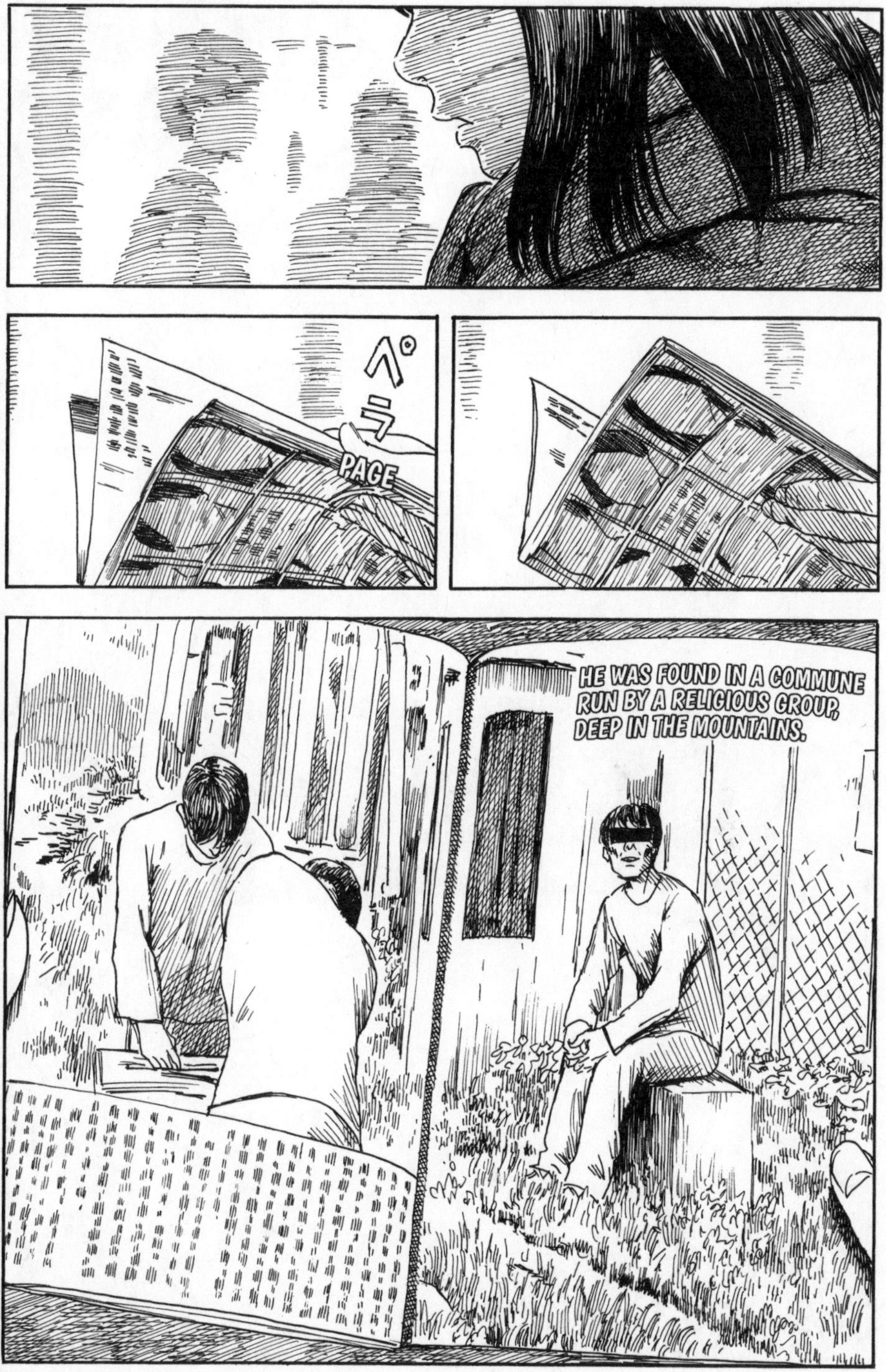
ペラ
PAGE
HE WAS FOUND IN A COMMUNE RUN BY A RELIGIOUS GROUP, DEEP IN THE MOUNTAINS.

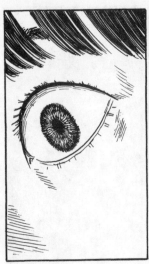

le was once the
ause of public
outrage, the
"vampire boy"
who murdered
three children
and drained th
blood from th
bodies.
He has yet to
offer a word of
apology to the
public, but now
he lives a quiet
peaceful life in
religious
community.

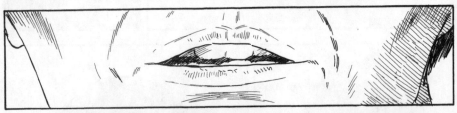

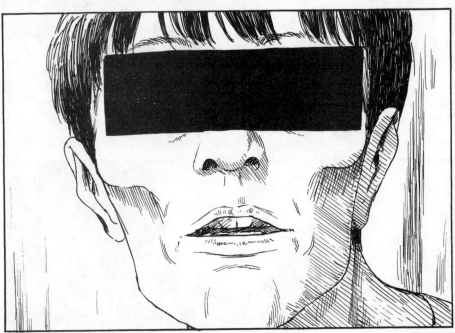

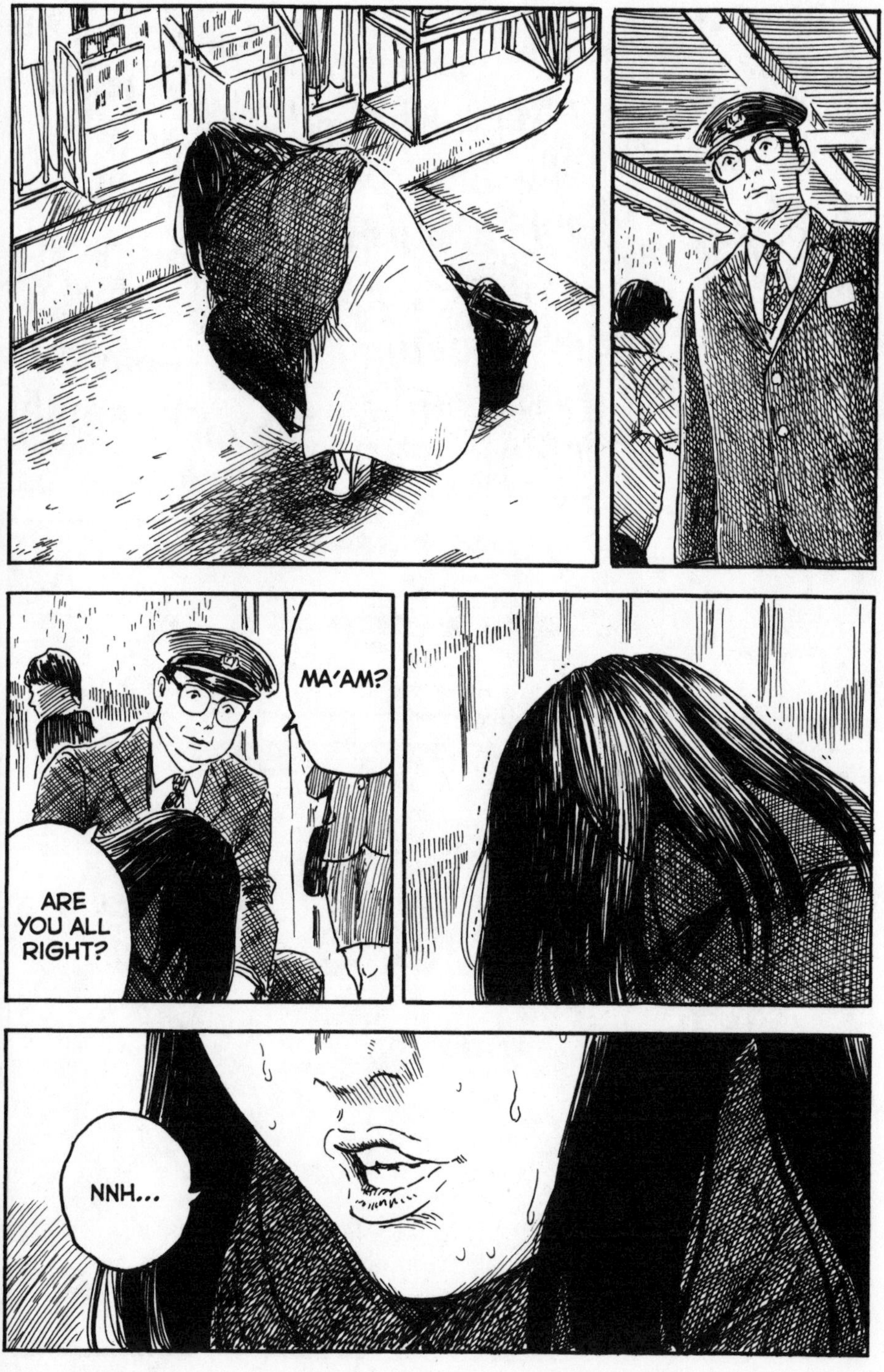
MA'AM?
ARE YOU ALL RIGHT?
NNH...

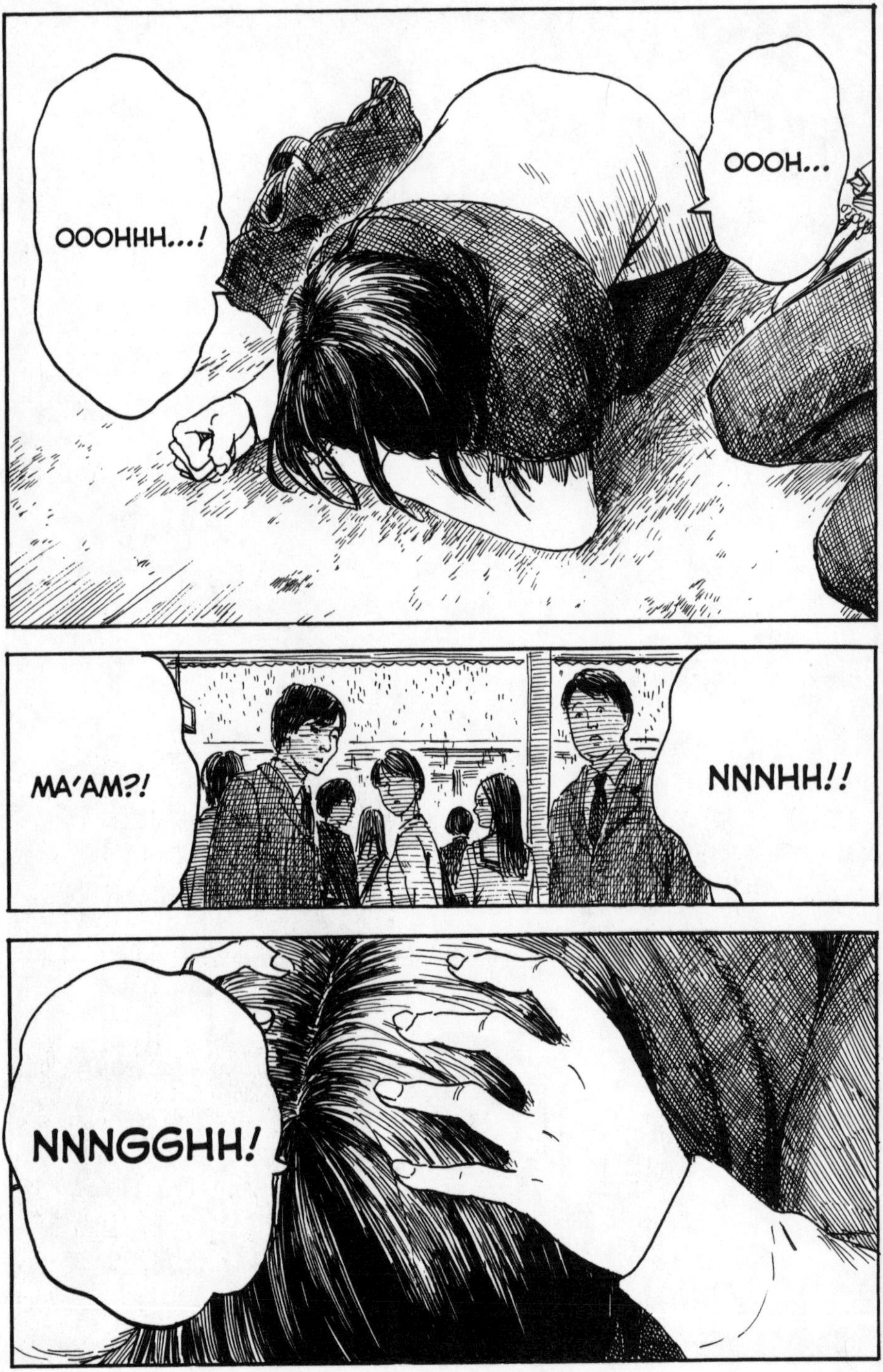
OOOH...
OOOHHH...!
NNNHH!!
MA'AM?!
NNNGGHH!

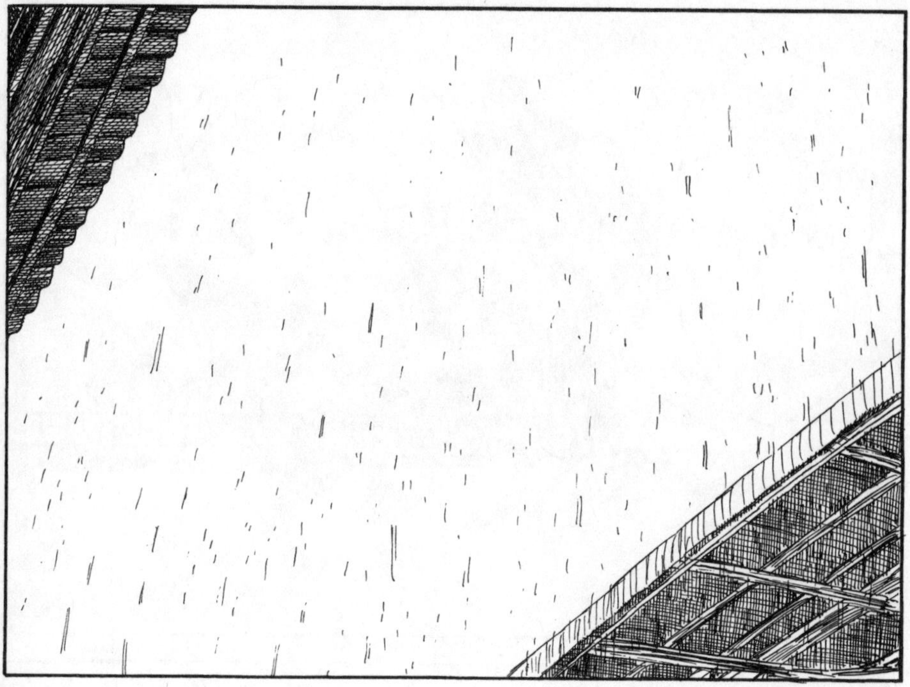
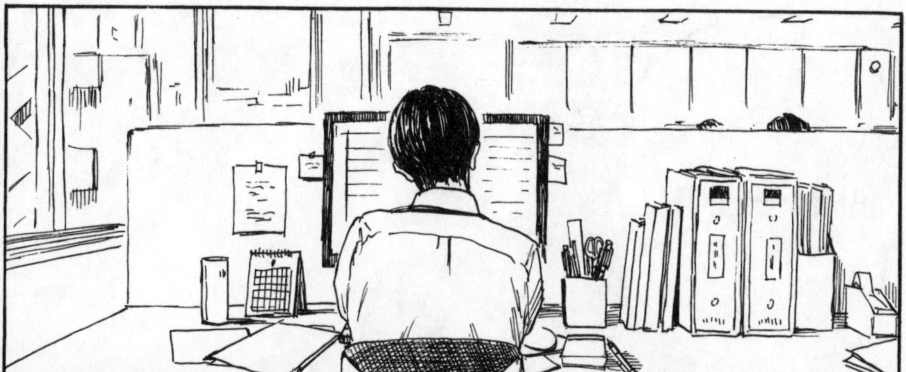

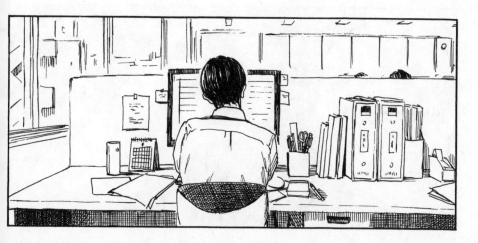

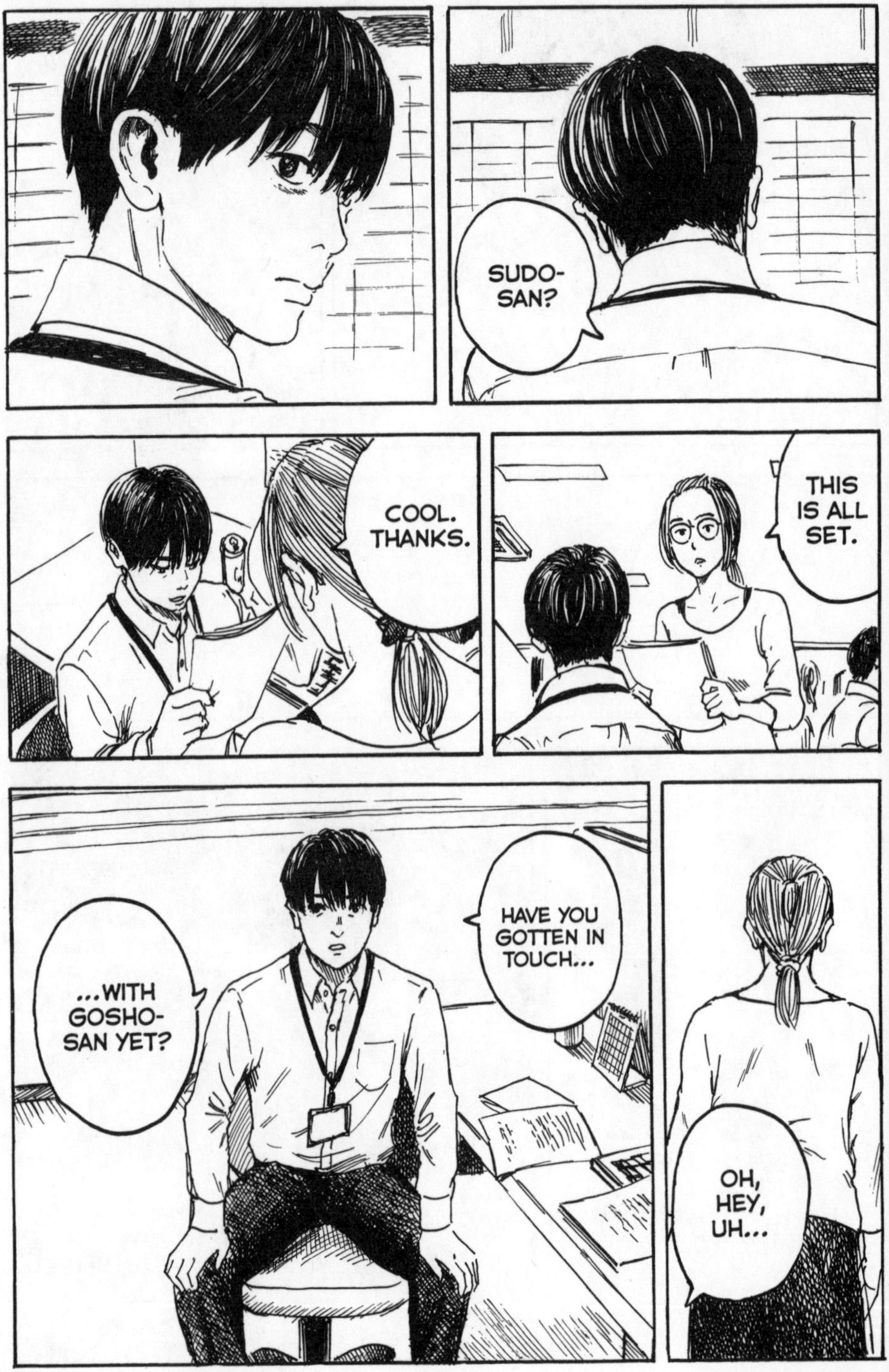
SUDO-SAN?
THIS IS ALL SET.
COOL. THANKS.
OH, HEY, UH...
HAVE YOU GOTTEN IN TOUCH...
...WITH GOSHO-SAN YET?

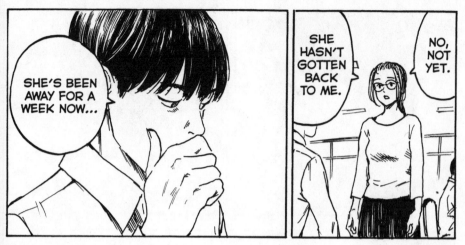

NO, NOT YET.
SHE HASN'T GOTTEN BACK TO ME.
SHE'S BEEN AWAY FOR A WEEK NOW...
YOU KNOW...
I THINK I BETTER CHECK ON HER.
TAP
コッ
TAP
コッ

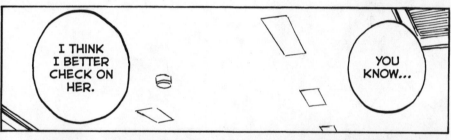

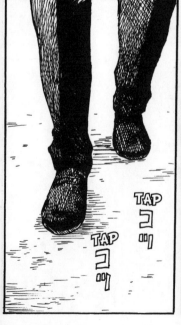

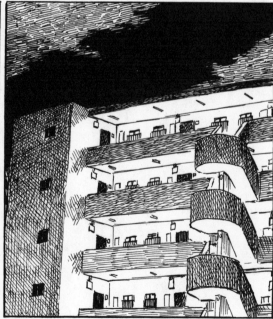

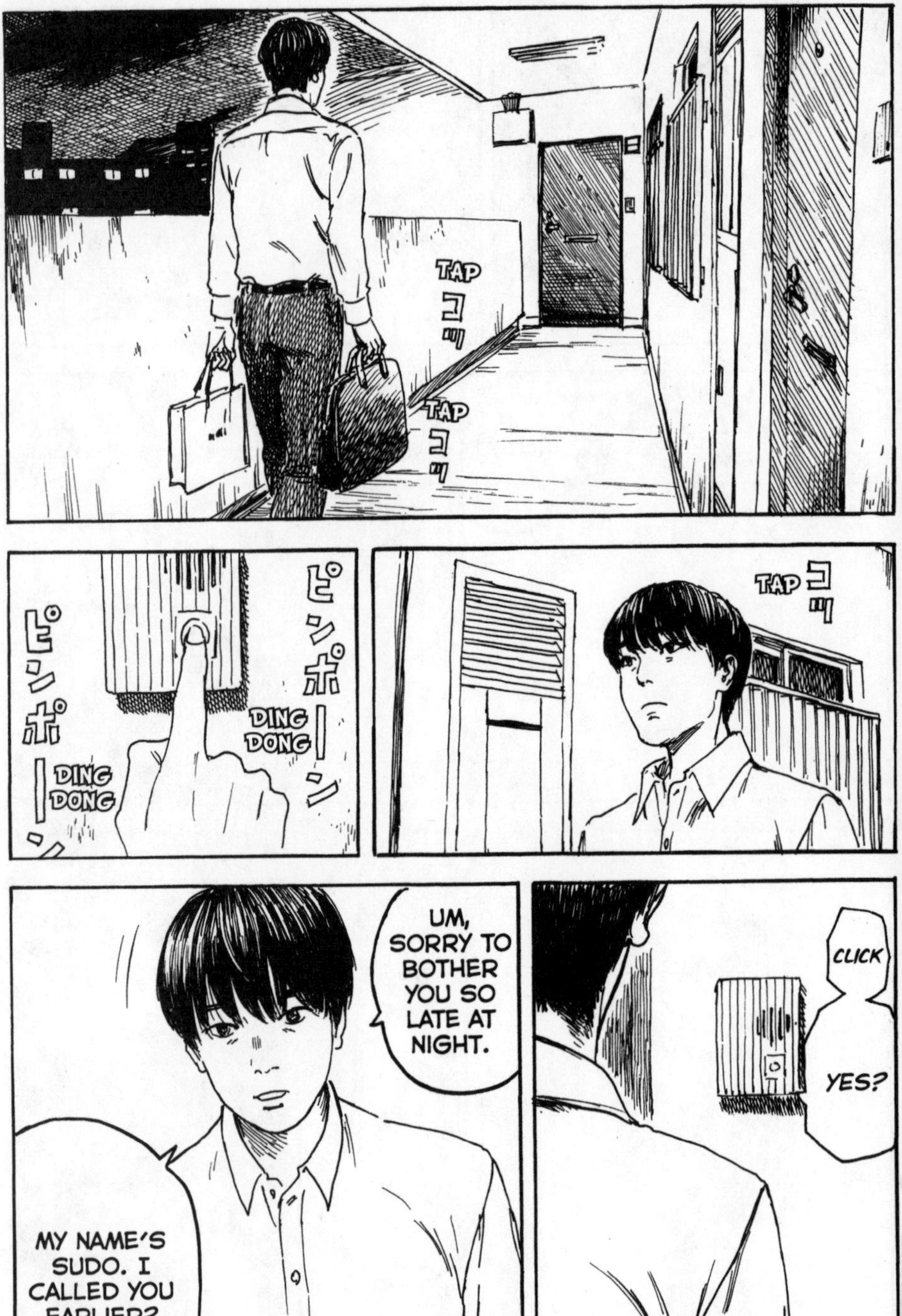
TAP
コッ
TAP
コッ
TAP
コッ
ピンポーン
DING DONG
ピンポーン
DING DONG
CLICK
YES?
UM, SORRY TO BOTHER YOU SO LATE AT NIGHT.
MY NAME'S SUDO. I CALLED YOU EARLIER?

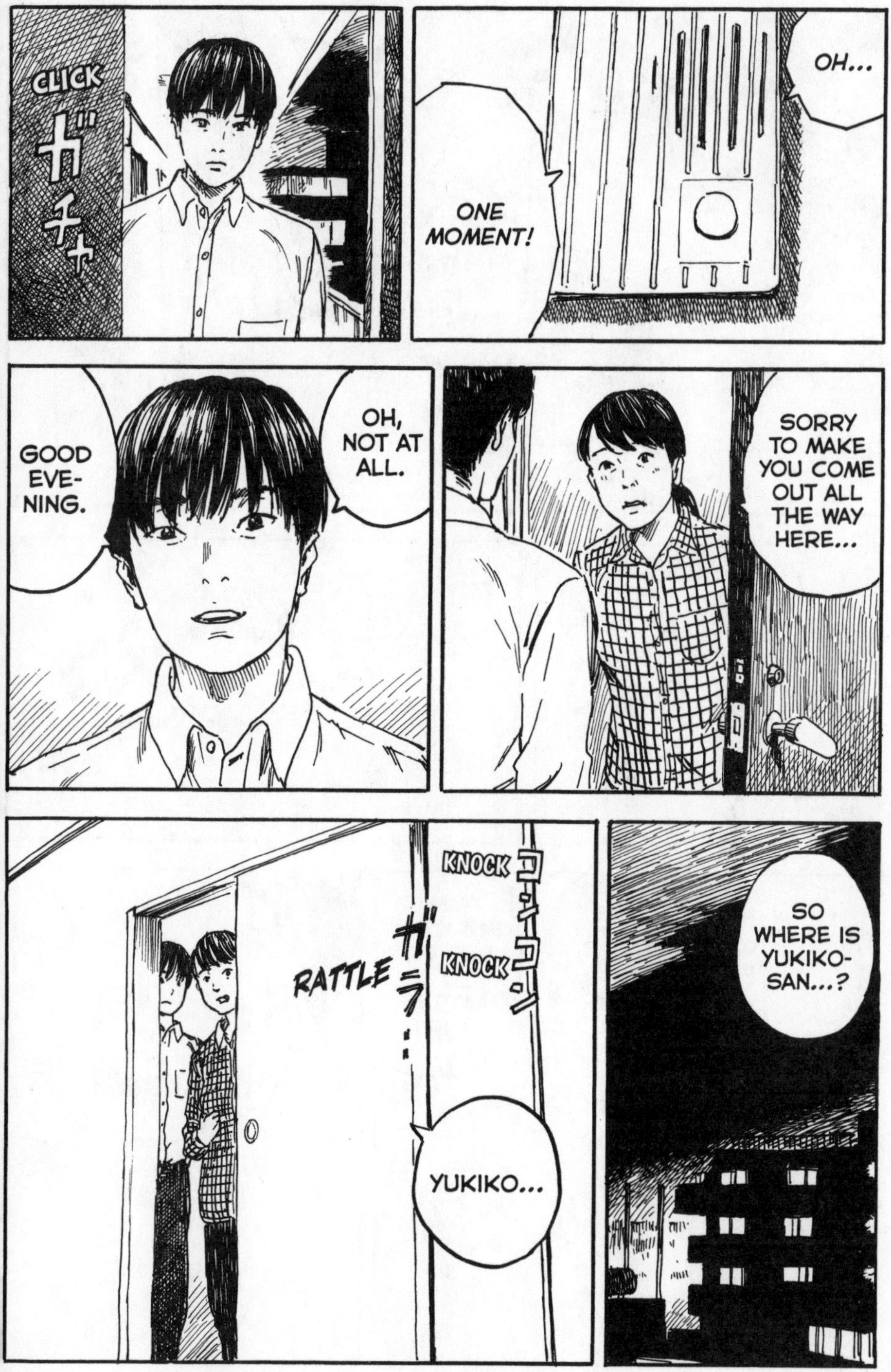
OH...
ONE MOMENT!
CLICK
ガチャ
SORRY TO MAKE YOU COME OUT ALL THE WAY HERE...
OH, NOT AT ALL.
GOOD EVE-NING.
SO WHERE IS YUKIKO-SAN...?
KNOCK
コンコン
KNOCK
RATTLE
ガラ...
YUKIKO...

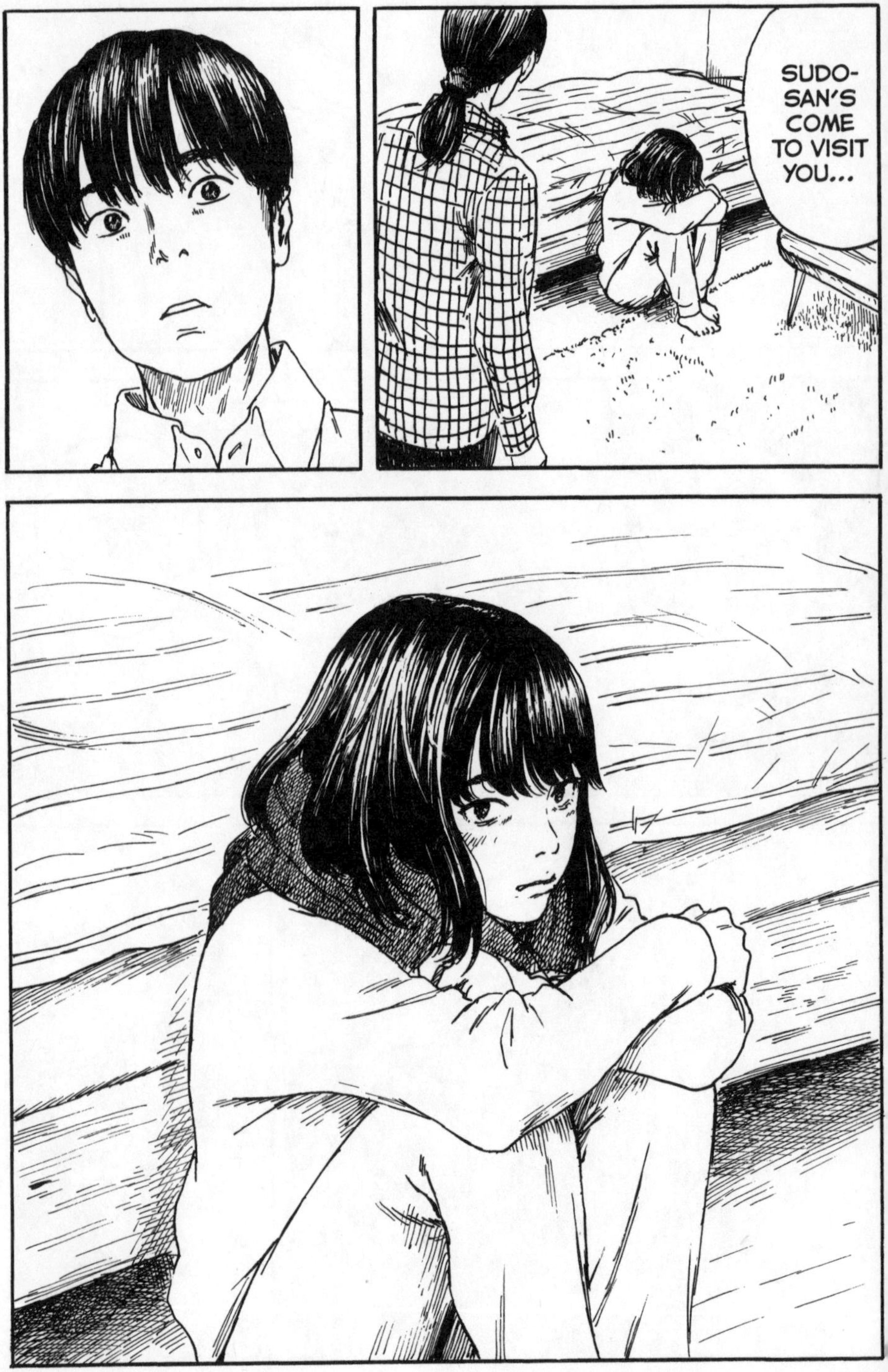
SUDO-SAN'S COME TO VISIT YOU...

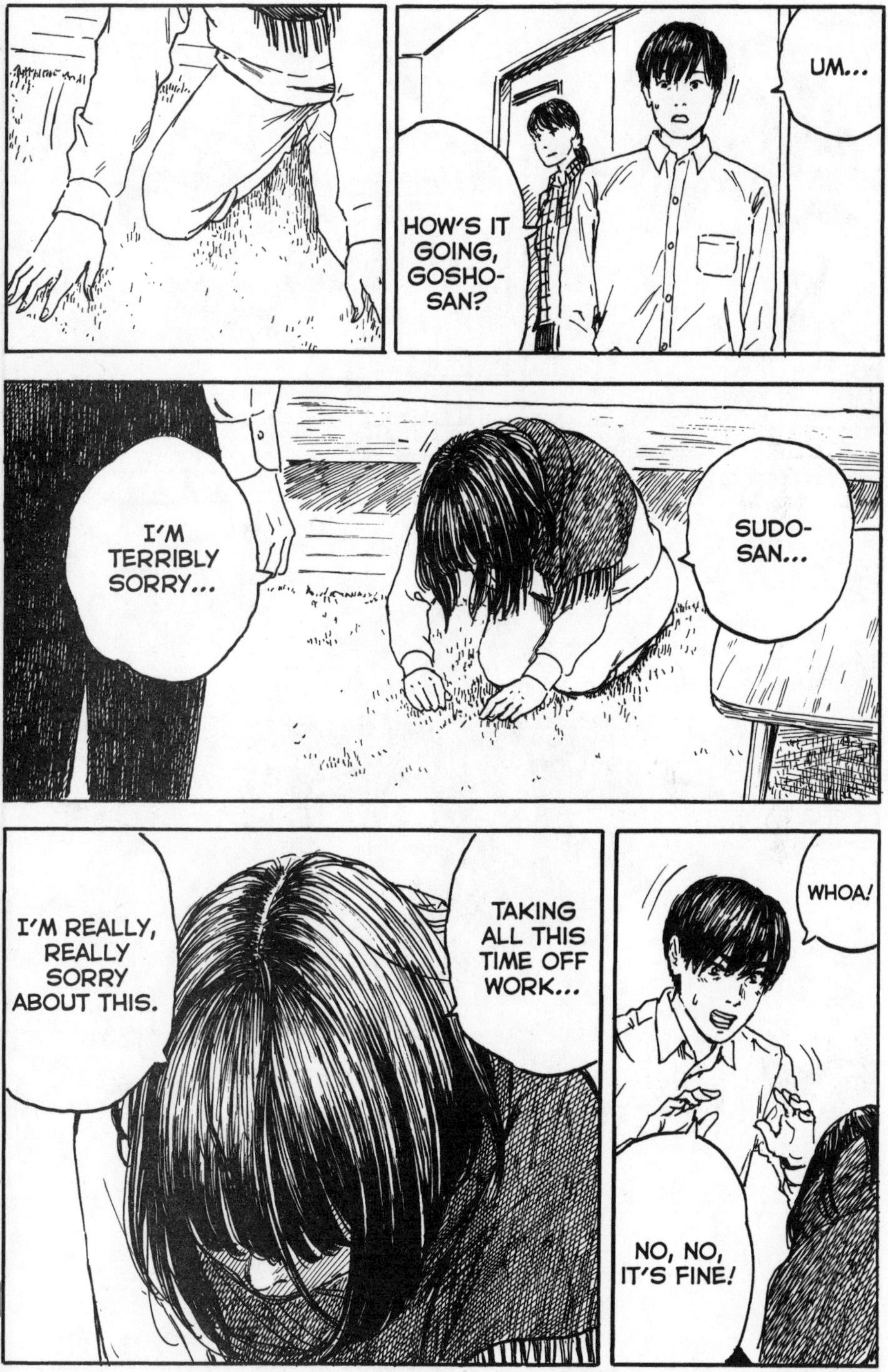
UM...
HOW'S IT GOING, GOSHO-SAN?
SUDO-SAN...
I'M TERRIBLY SORRY...
WHOA!
NO, NO, IT'S FINE!
TAKING ALL THIS TIME OFF WORK...
I'M REALLY, REALLY SORRY ABOUT THIS.

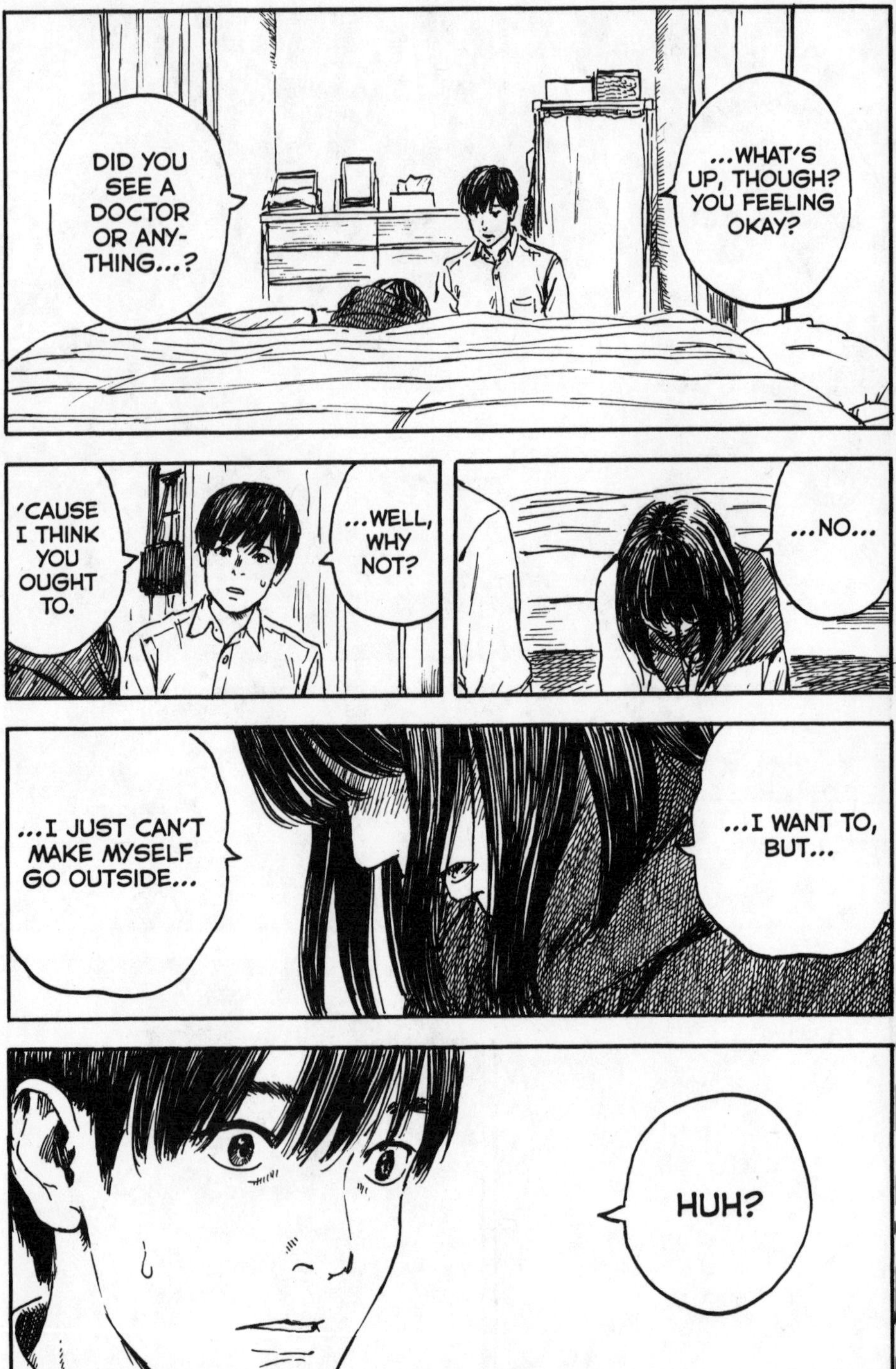
...WHAT'S UP, THOUGH? YOU FEELING OKAY?
DID YOU SEE A DOCTOR OR ANY-THING...?
...NO...
...WELL, WHY NOT?
'CAUSE I THINK YOU OUGHT TO.
...I WANT TO, BUT...
...I JUST CAN'T MAKE MYSELF GO OUTSIDE...
HUH?

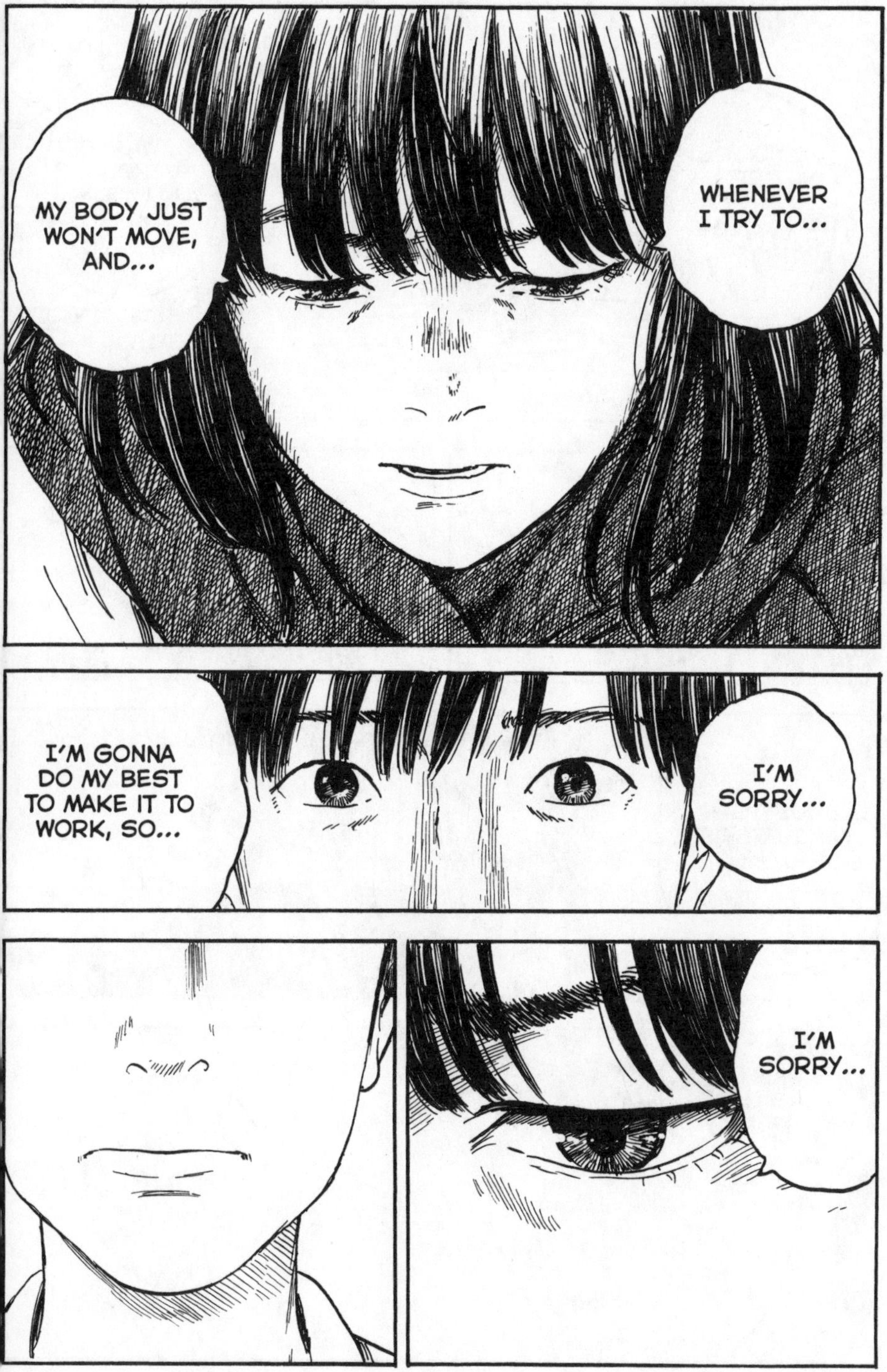
WHENEVER I TRY TO...
MY BODY JUST WON'T MOVE, AND...
I'M SORRY...
I'M GONNA DO MY BEST TO MAKE IT TO WORK, SO...
I'M SORRY...

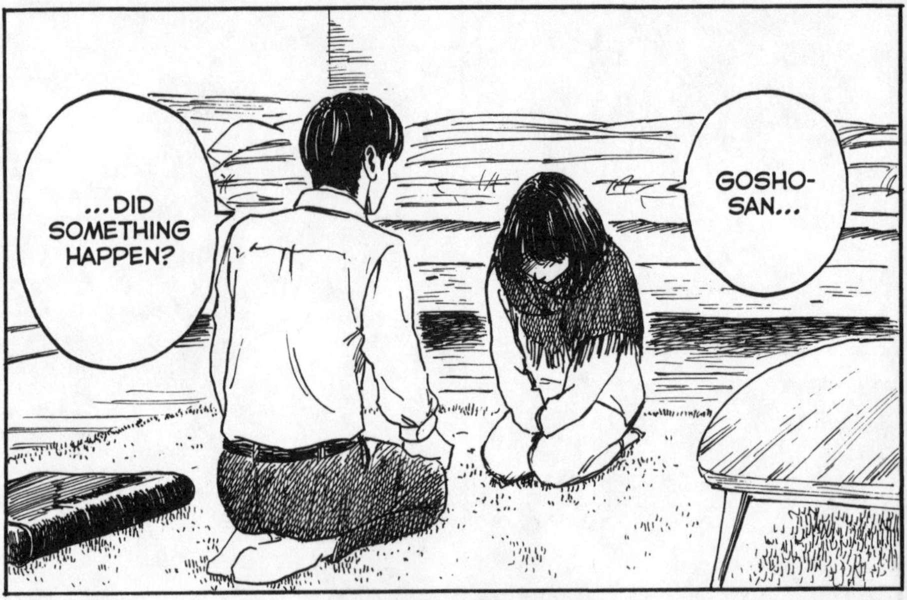
GOSHO-SAN...
...DID SOMETHING HAPPEN?

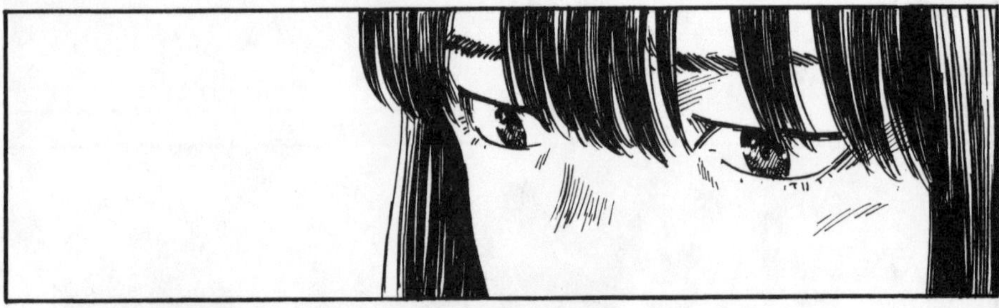

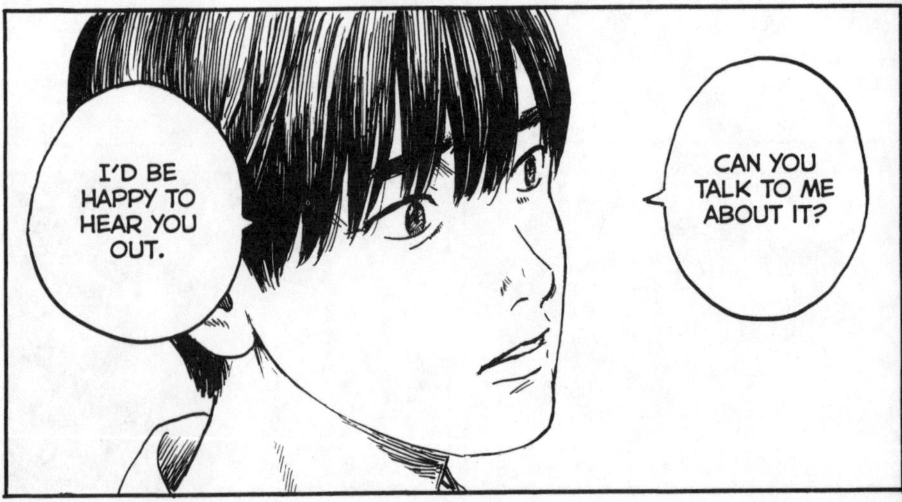
CAN YOU TALK TO ME ABOUT IT?
I'D BE HAPPY TO HEAR YOU OUT.

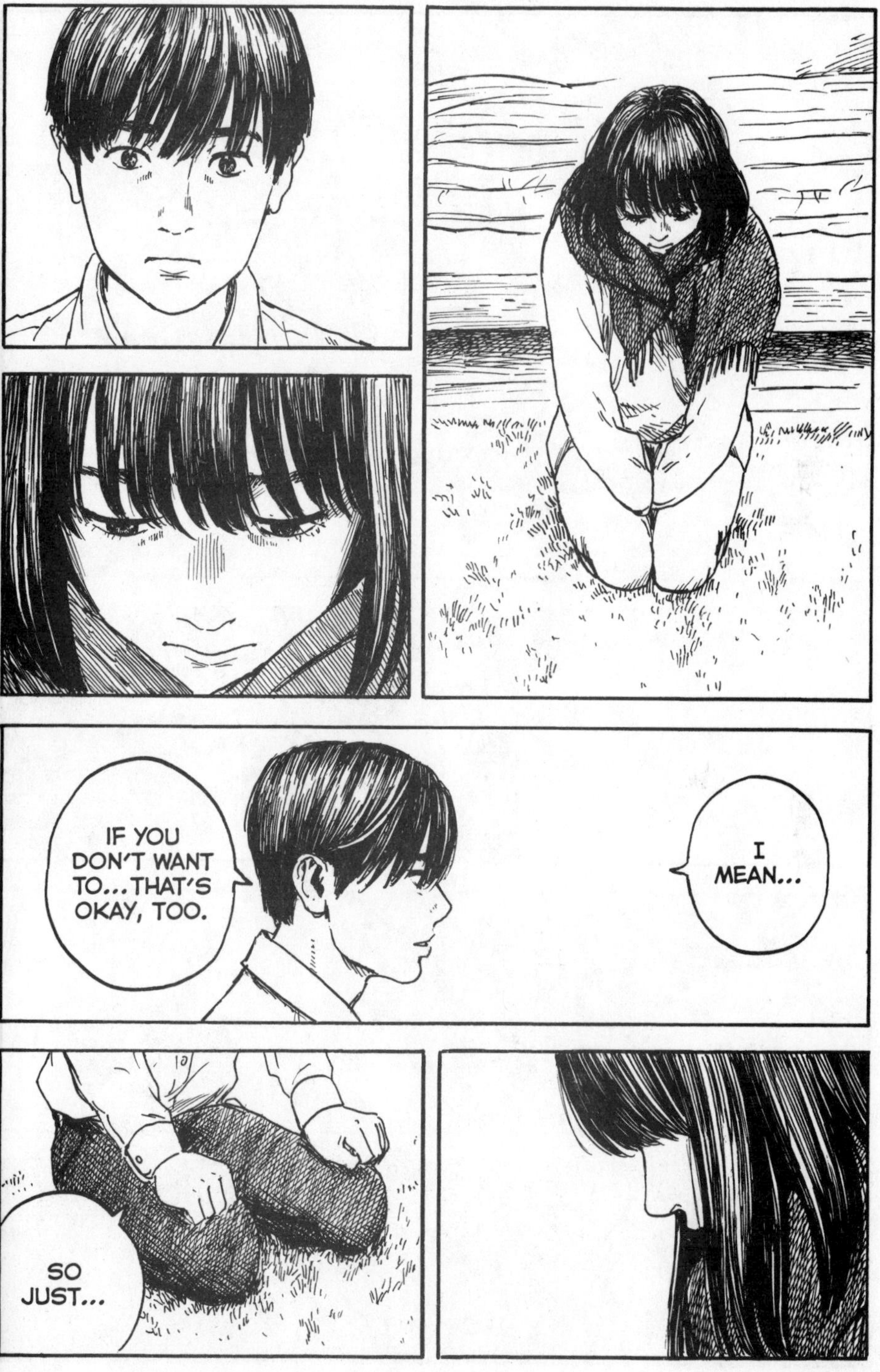
I MEAN...
IF YOU DON'T WANT TO...THAT'S OKAY, TOO.
SO JUST...

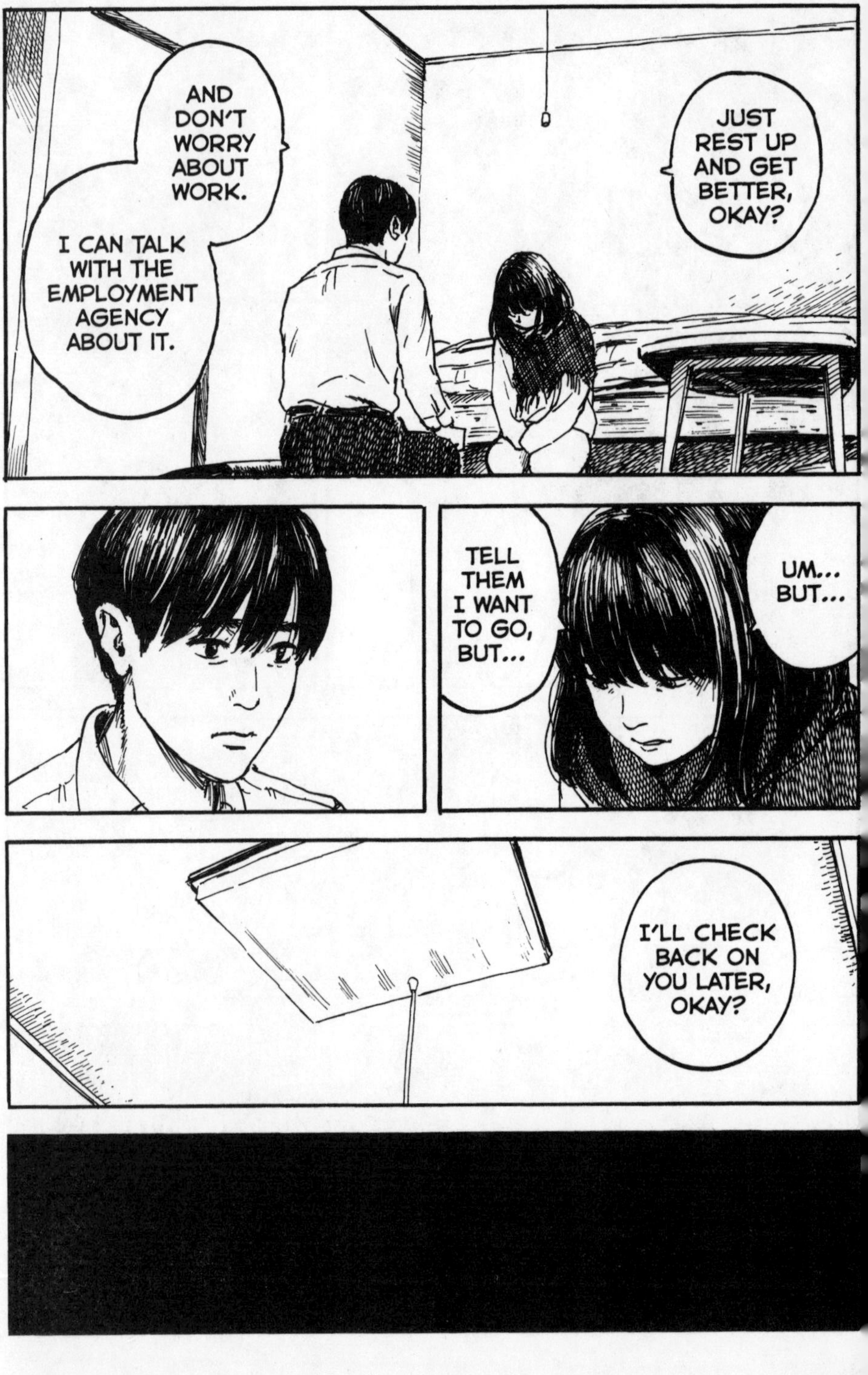
JUST REST UP AND GET BETTER, OKAY?
AND DON'T WORRY ABOUT WORK.
I CAN TALK WITH THE EMPLOYMENT AGENCY ABOUT IT.
UM... BUT...
TELL THEM I WANT TO GO, BUT...
I'LL CHECK BACK ON YOU LATER, OKAY?

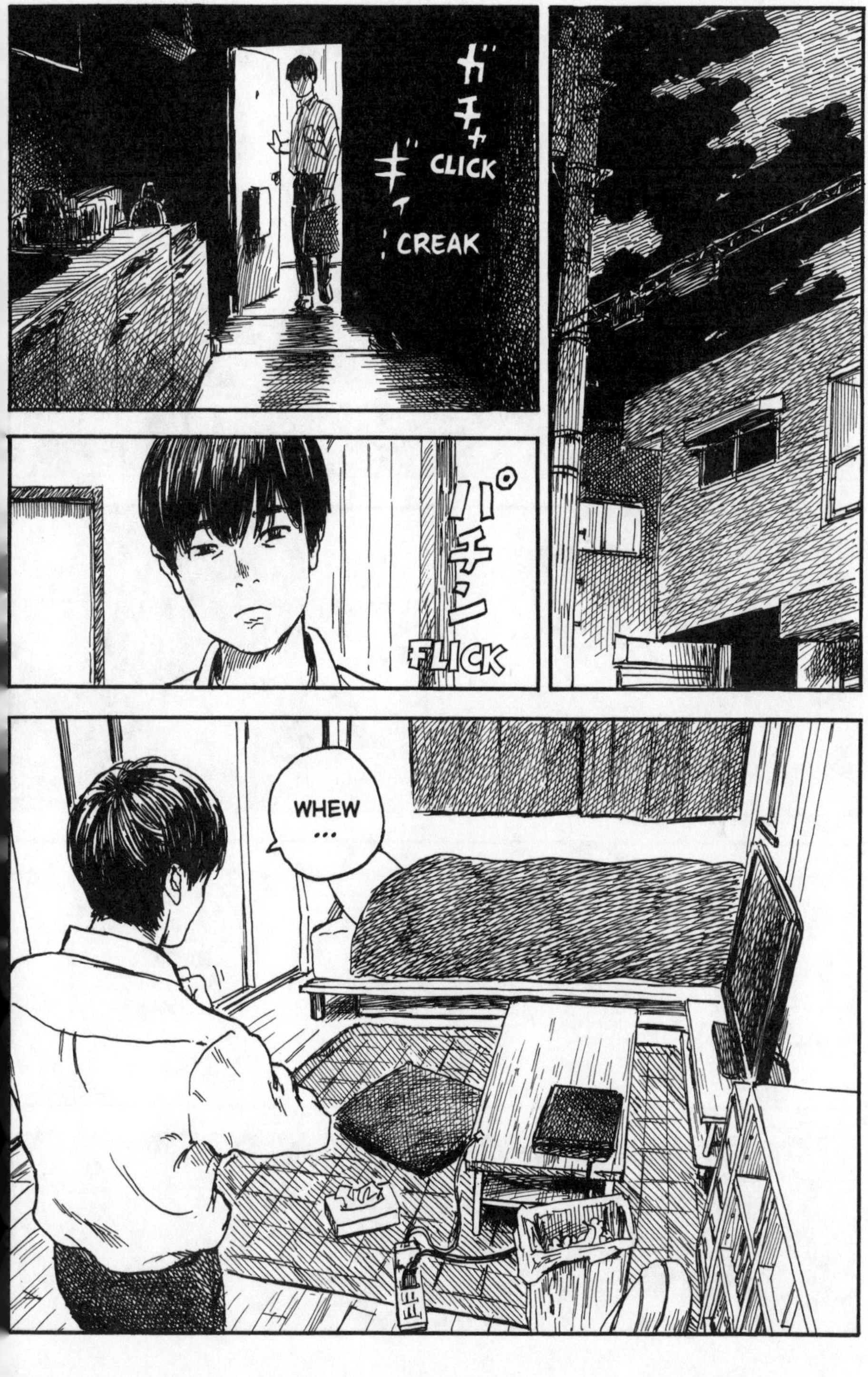
ガチャ
CLICK
ギィ
CREAK
パチン
FLICK
WHEW ...

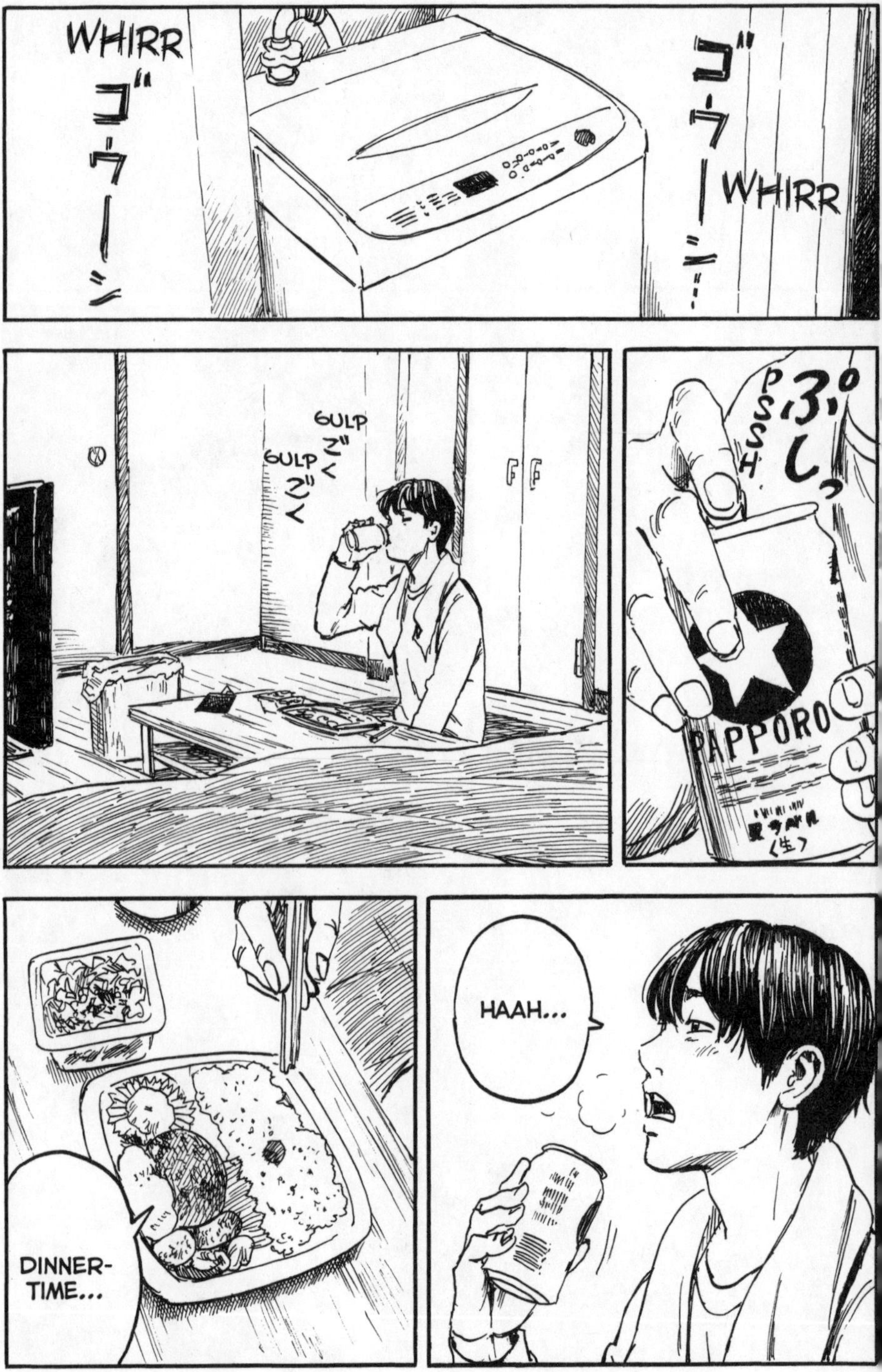
ゴウーーン…
WHIRR
WHIRR
ゴウーーン
PSSH
ぷしっ
PAPPORO
GULP
ごく
GULP
ごく
HAAH...
DINNER-TIME...

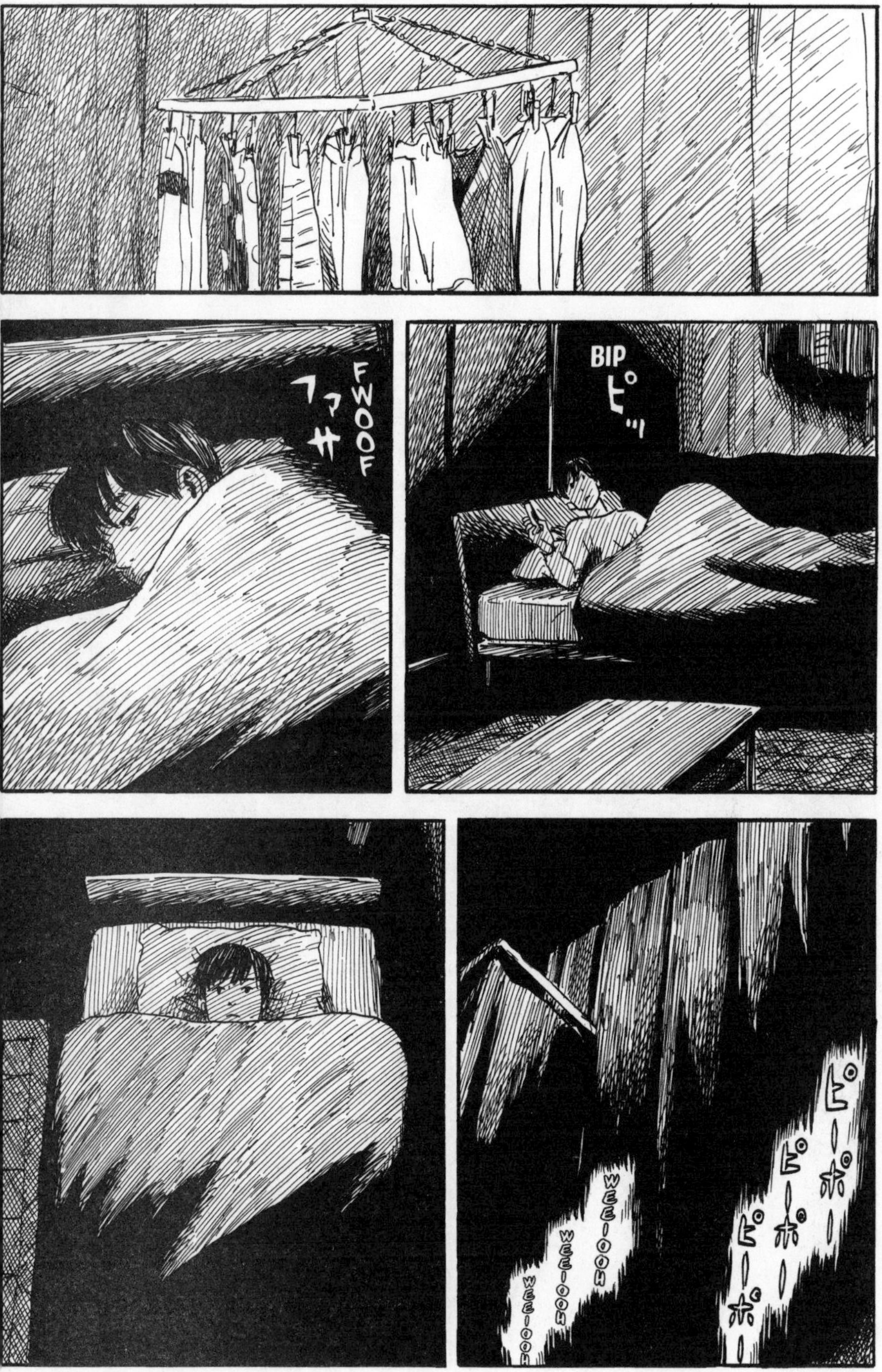
BIP
ピッ
FWOOF
ファサ
WEEIOOH
WEEIOOH
WEEIOOH
ピーポーピーポーピーポー

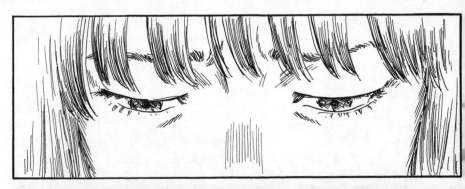

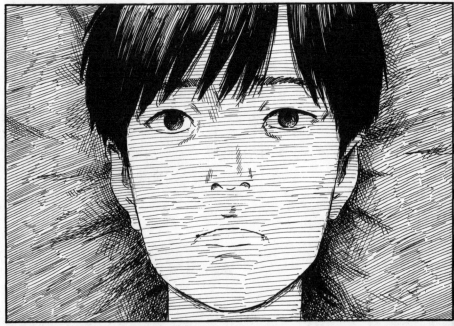

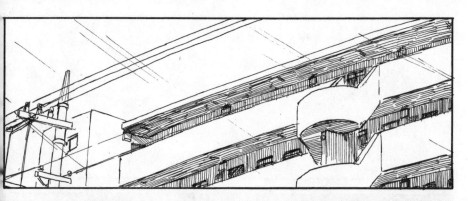

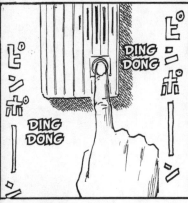

DING
DONG

ピ
ン
ポ
ー
ン

DING
DONG

ピ
ン
ポ
ー
ン

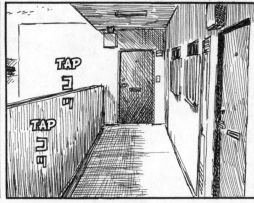

TAP
コ
ツ

TAP
コ
ツ

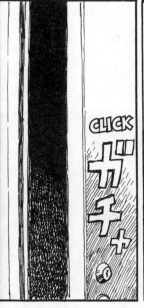

CLICK

ガ
チ
ャ

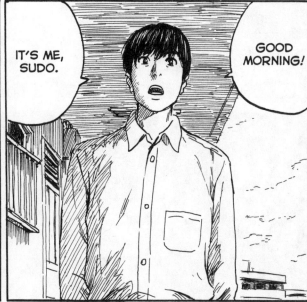

IT'S ME,
SUDO.

GOOD
MORNING!

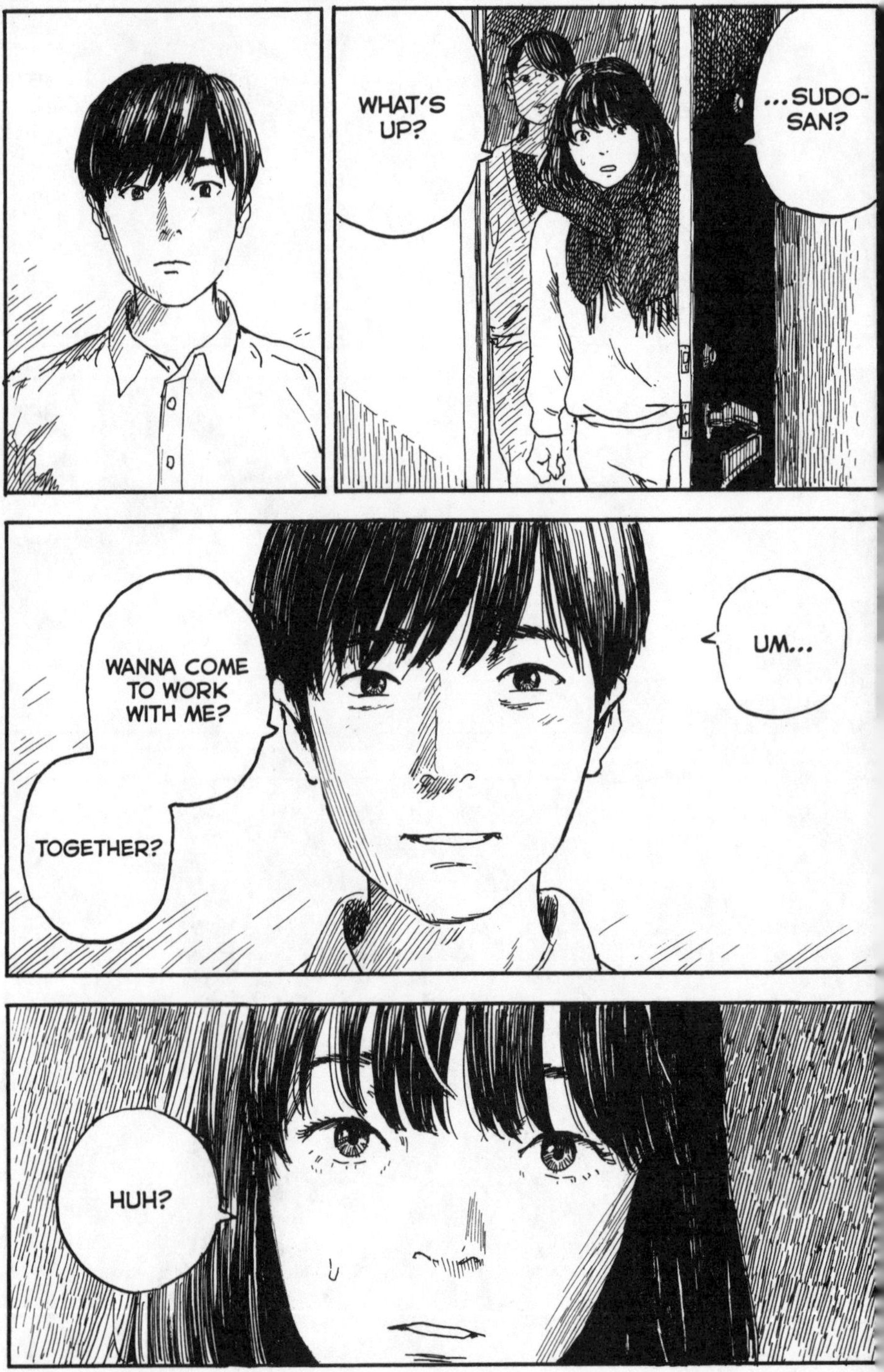
...SUDO-SAN?
WHAT'S UP?
UM...
WANNA COME TO WORK WITH ME?
TOGETHER?
HUH?

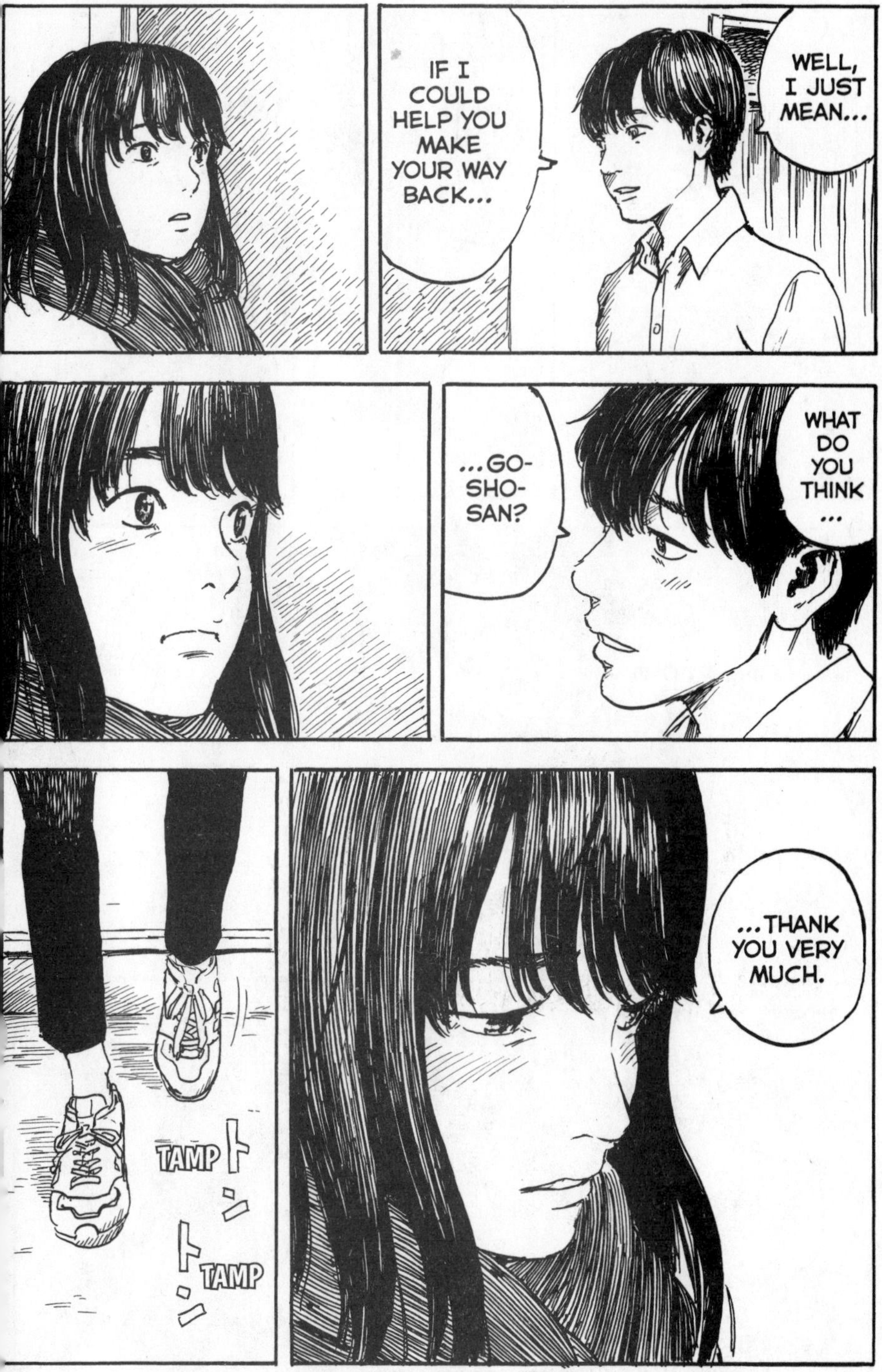
WELL, I JUST MEAN...
IF I COULD HELP YOU MAKE YOUR WAY BACK...
WHAT DO YOU THINK ...
...GO-SHO-SAN?
...THANK YOU VERY MUCH.
TAMP
TAMP

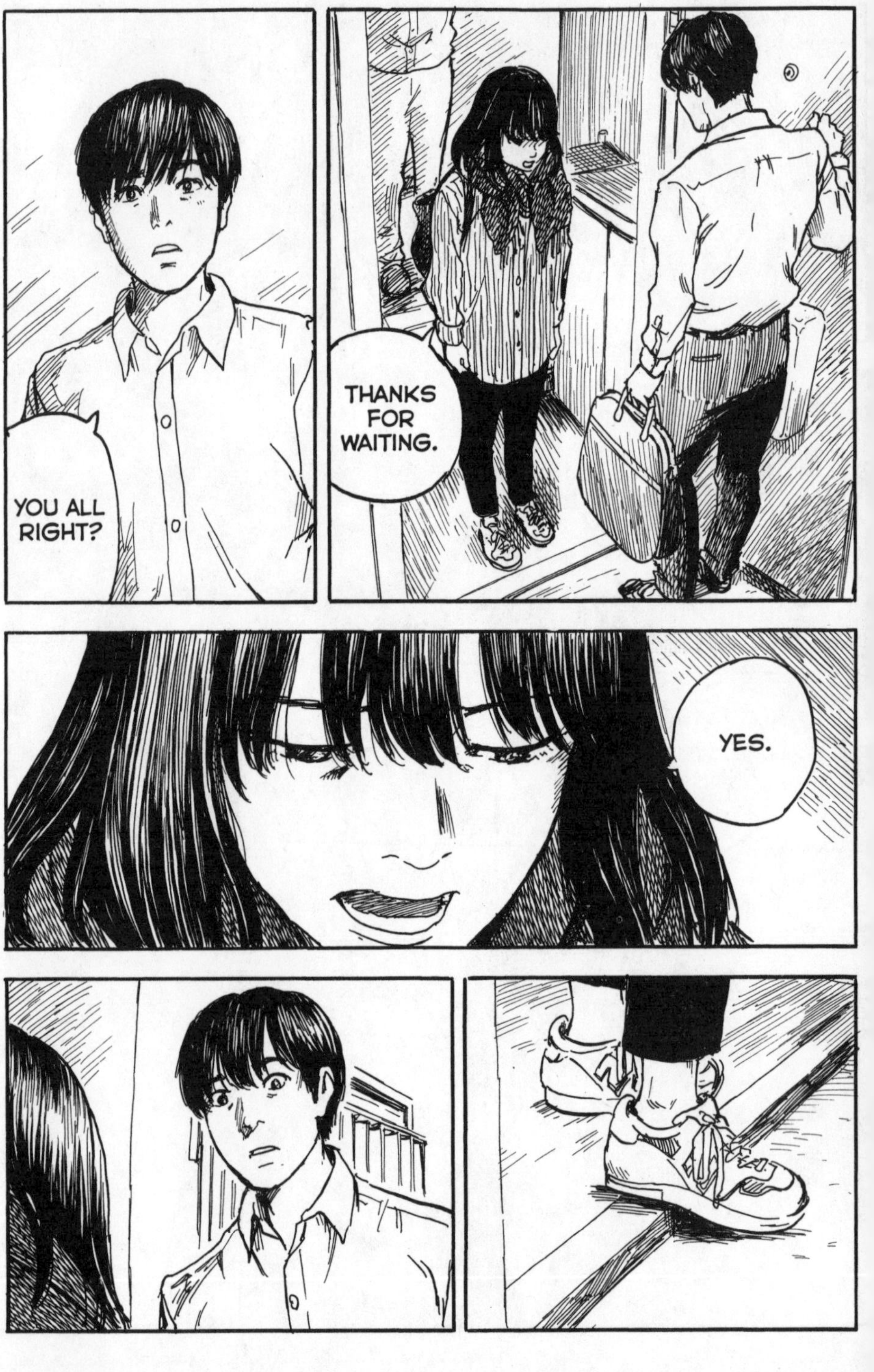
THANKS FOR WAITING.
YOU ALL RIGHT?
YES.

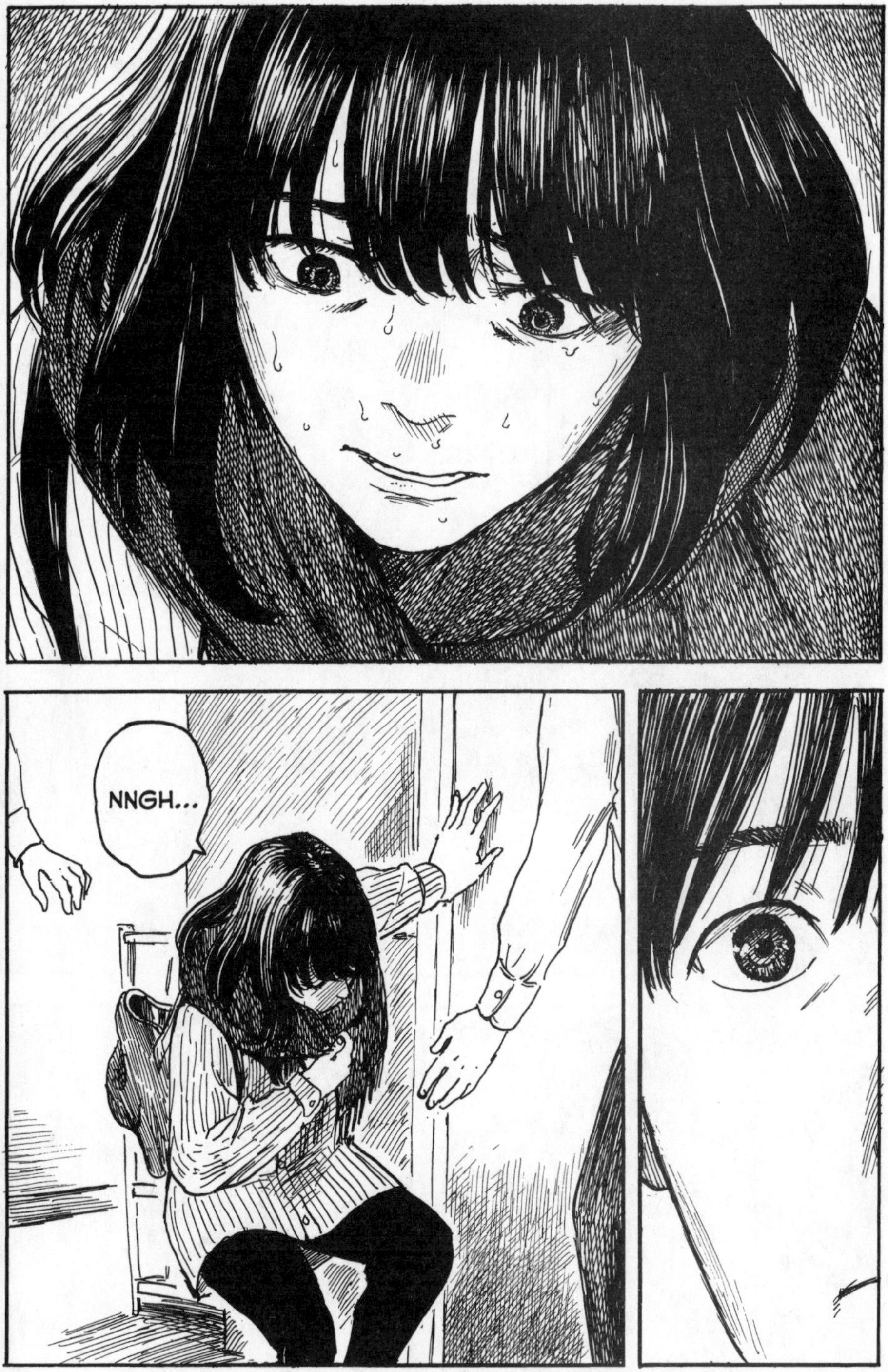
NNGH...

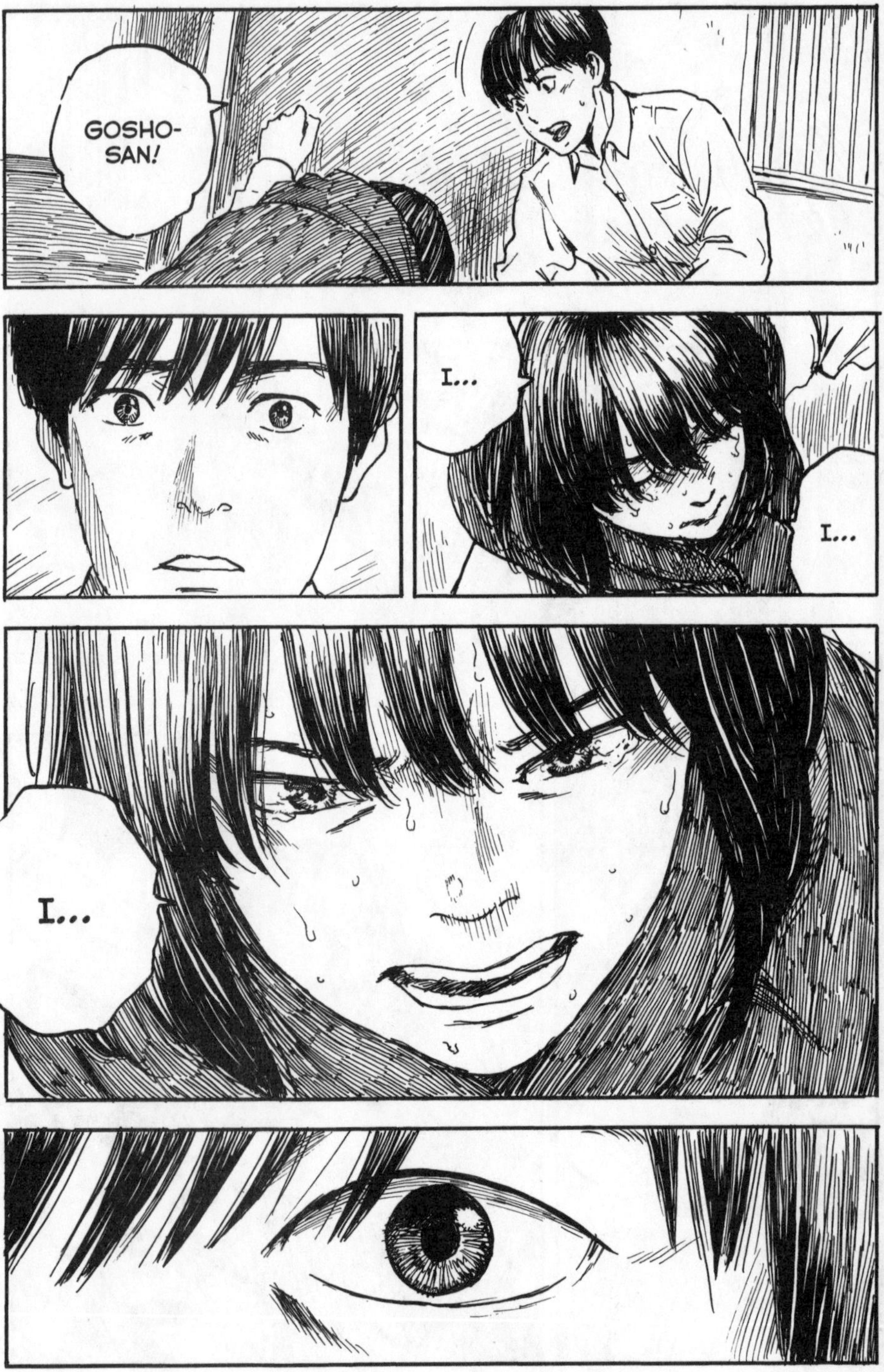
GOSHO-SAN!
I...
I...
I...

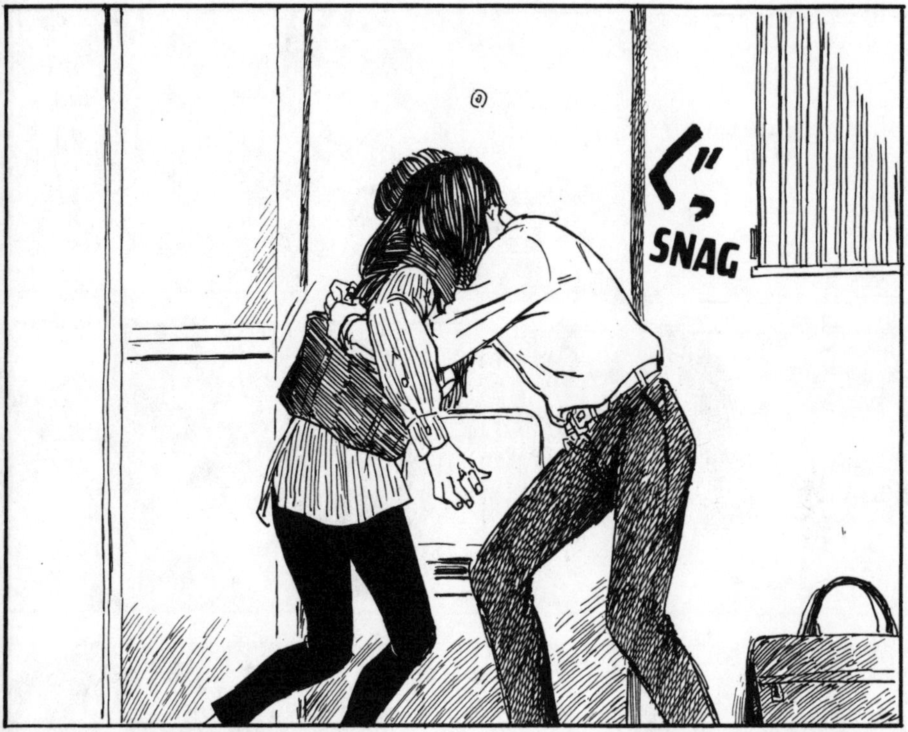
ぐっ
SNAG
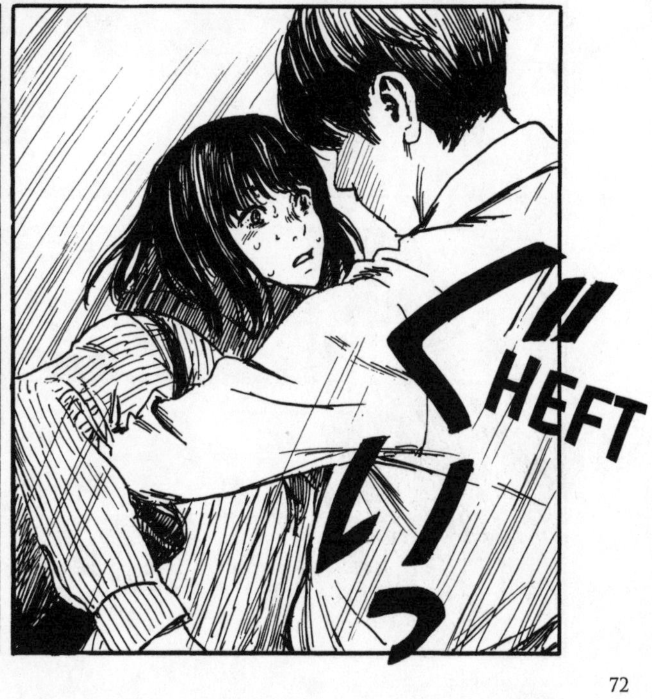
ぐいっ
HEFT
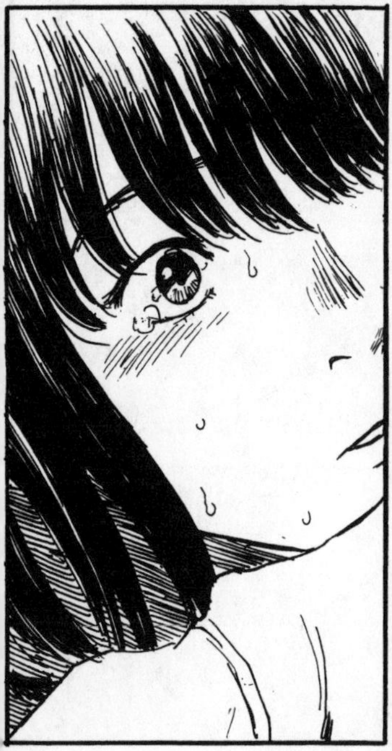

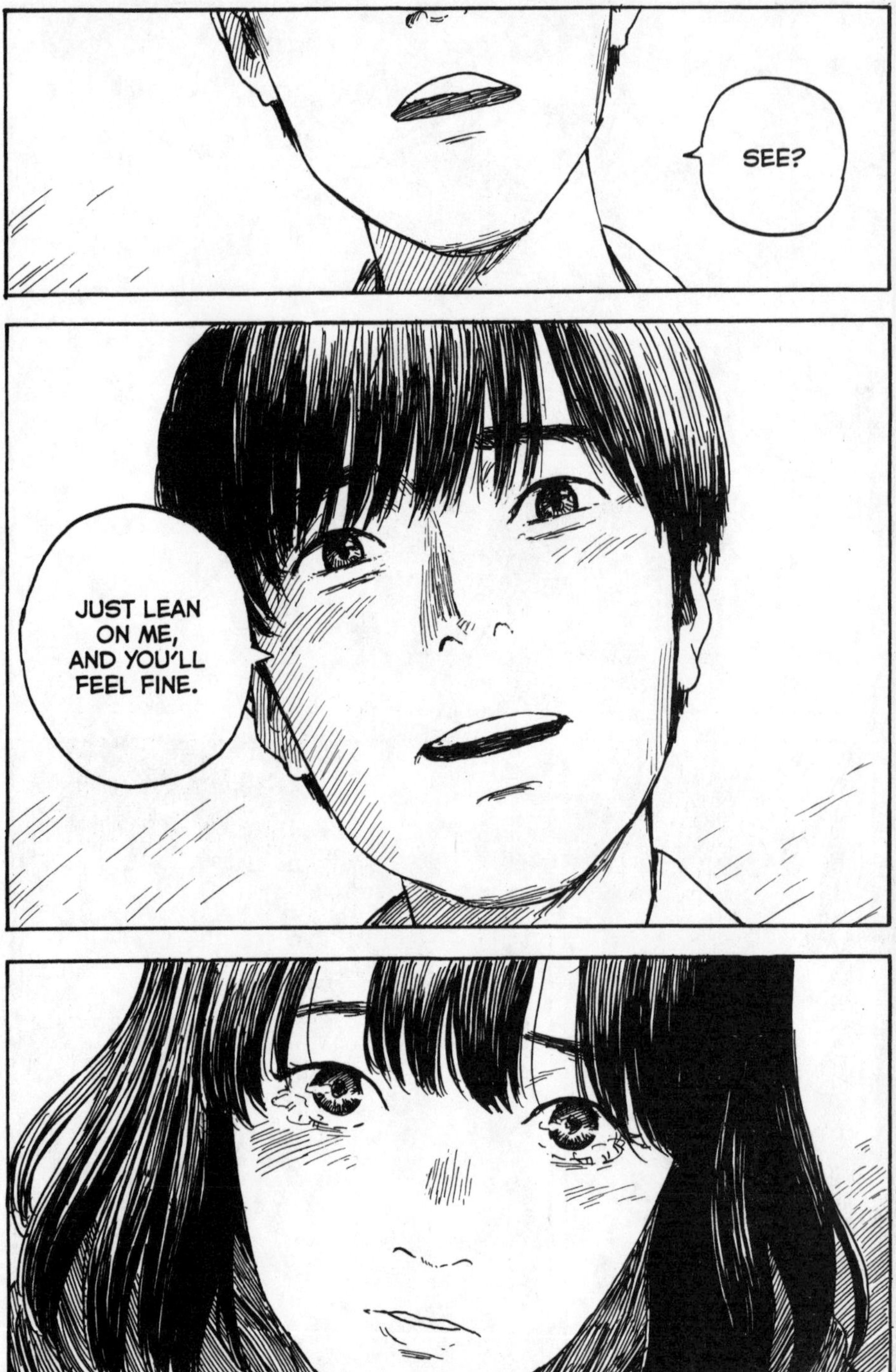
SEE?
JUST LEAN ON ME, AND YOU'LL FEEL FINE.

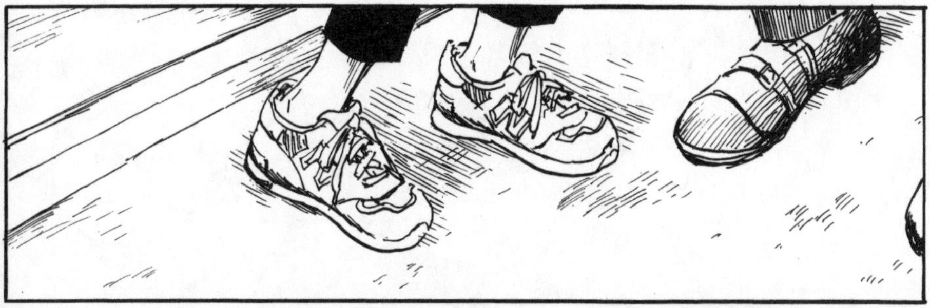

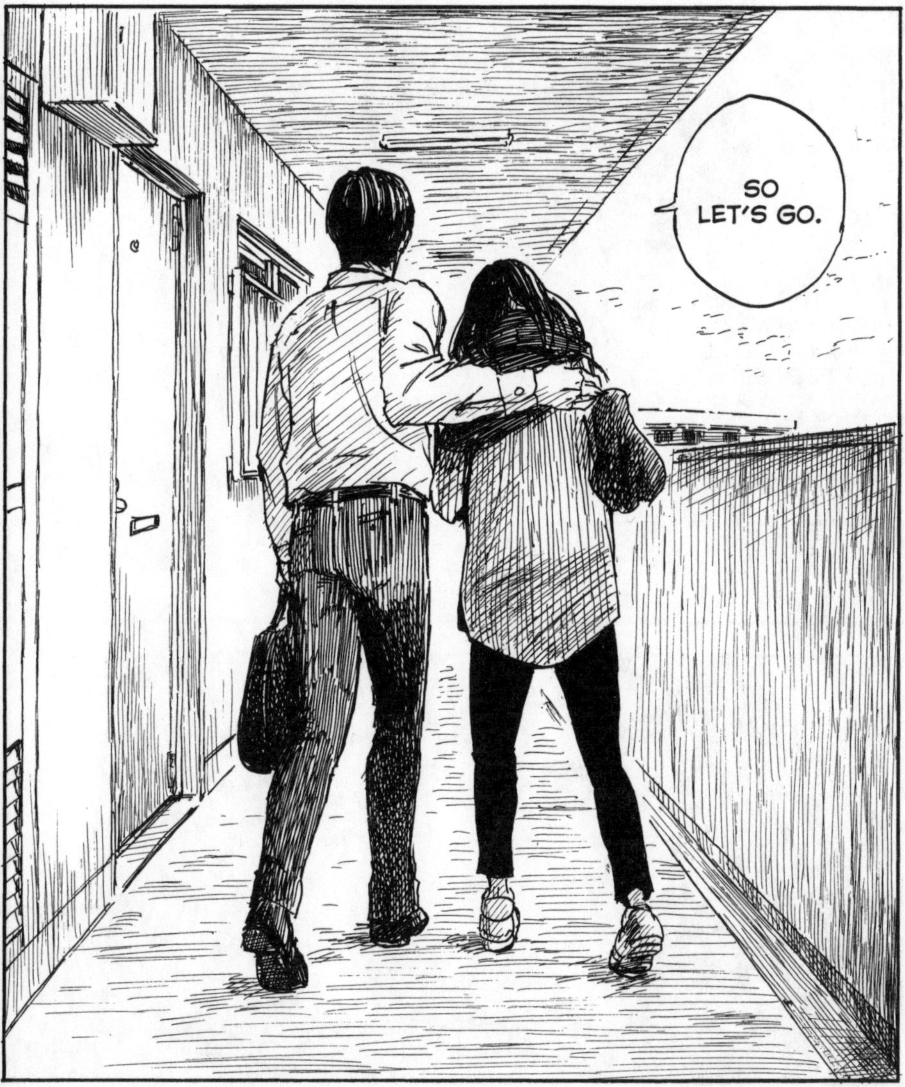
SO LET'S GO.

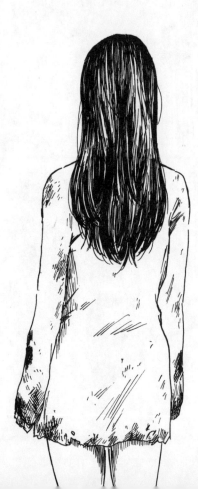
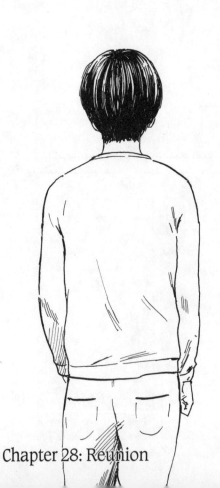

Chapter 28: Reunion

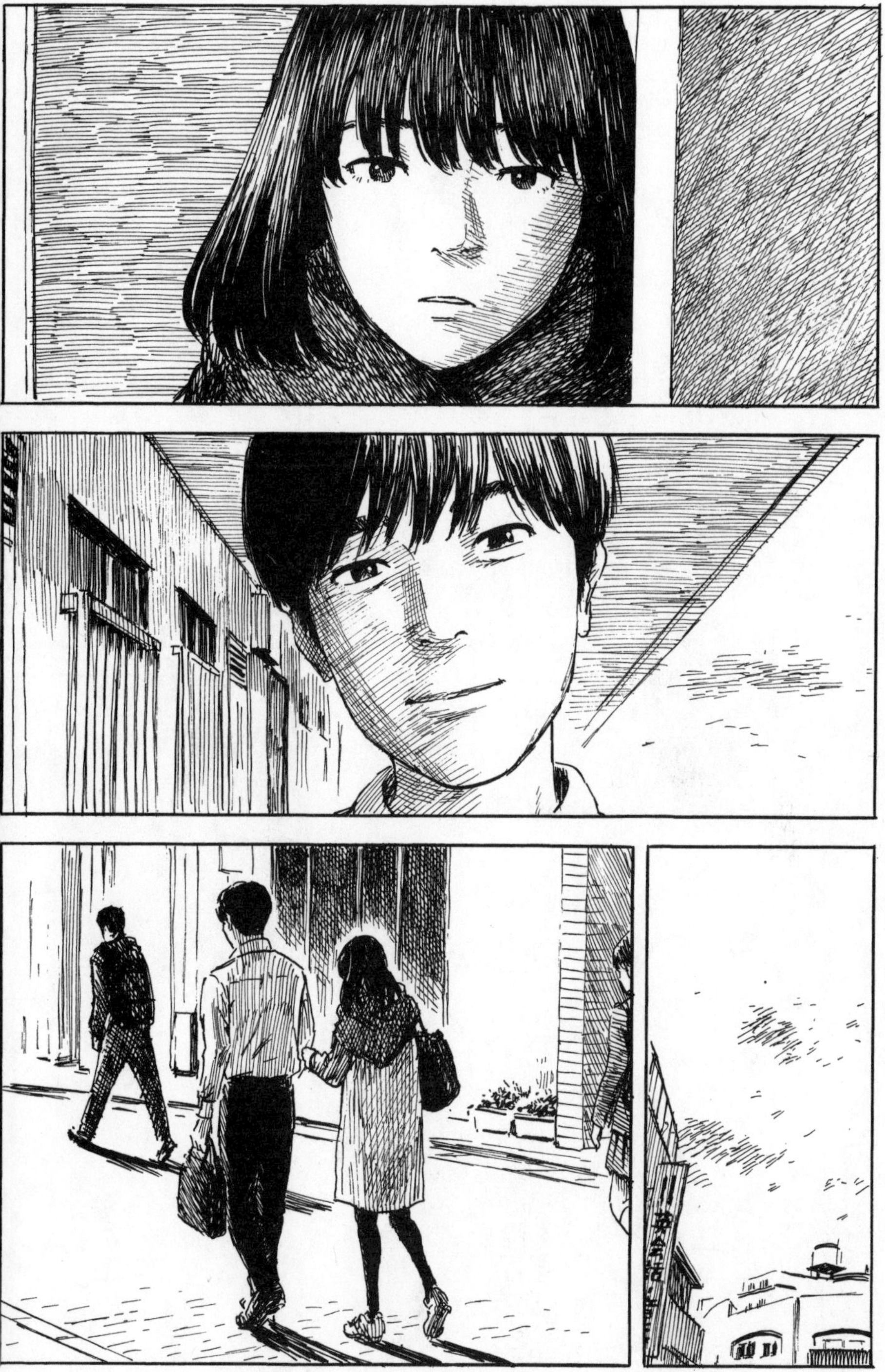

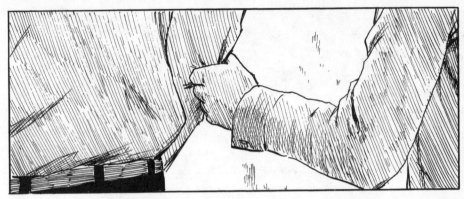

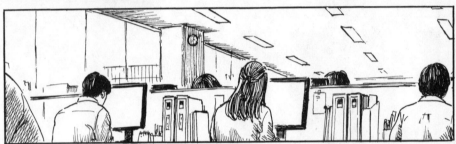

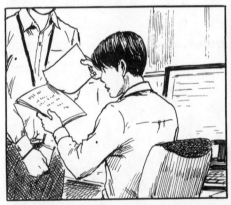

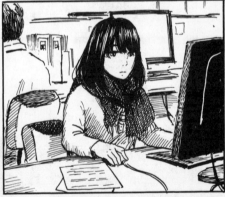

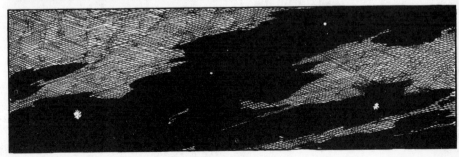

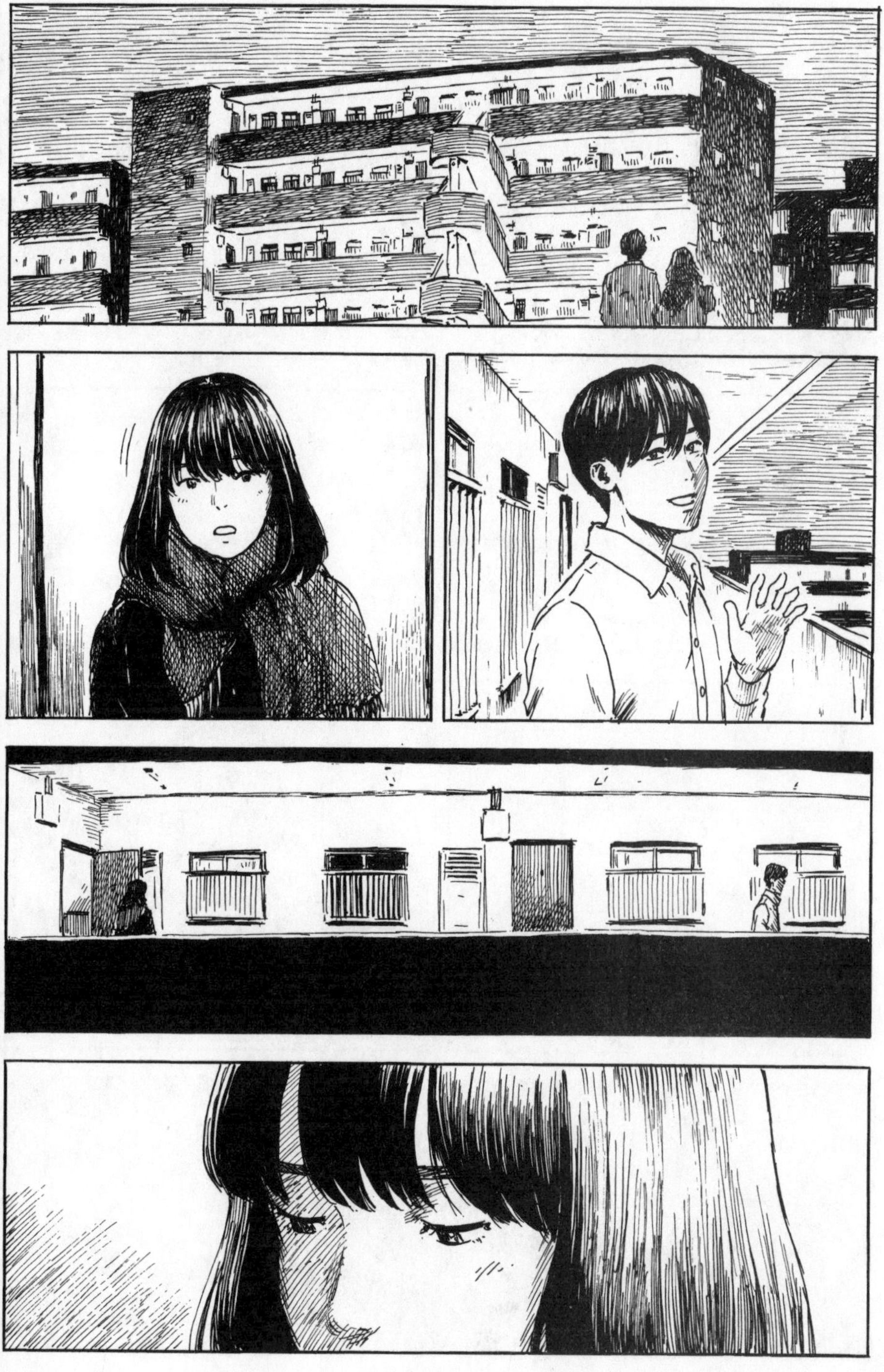

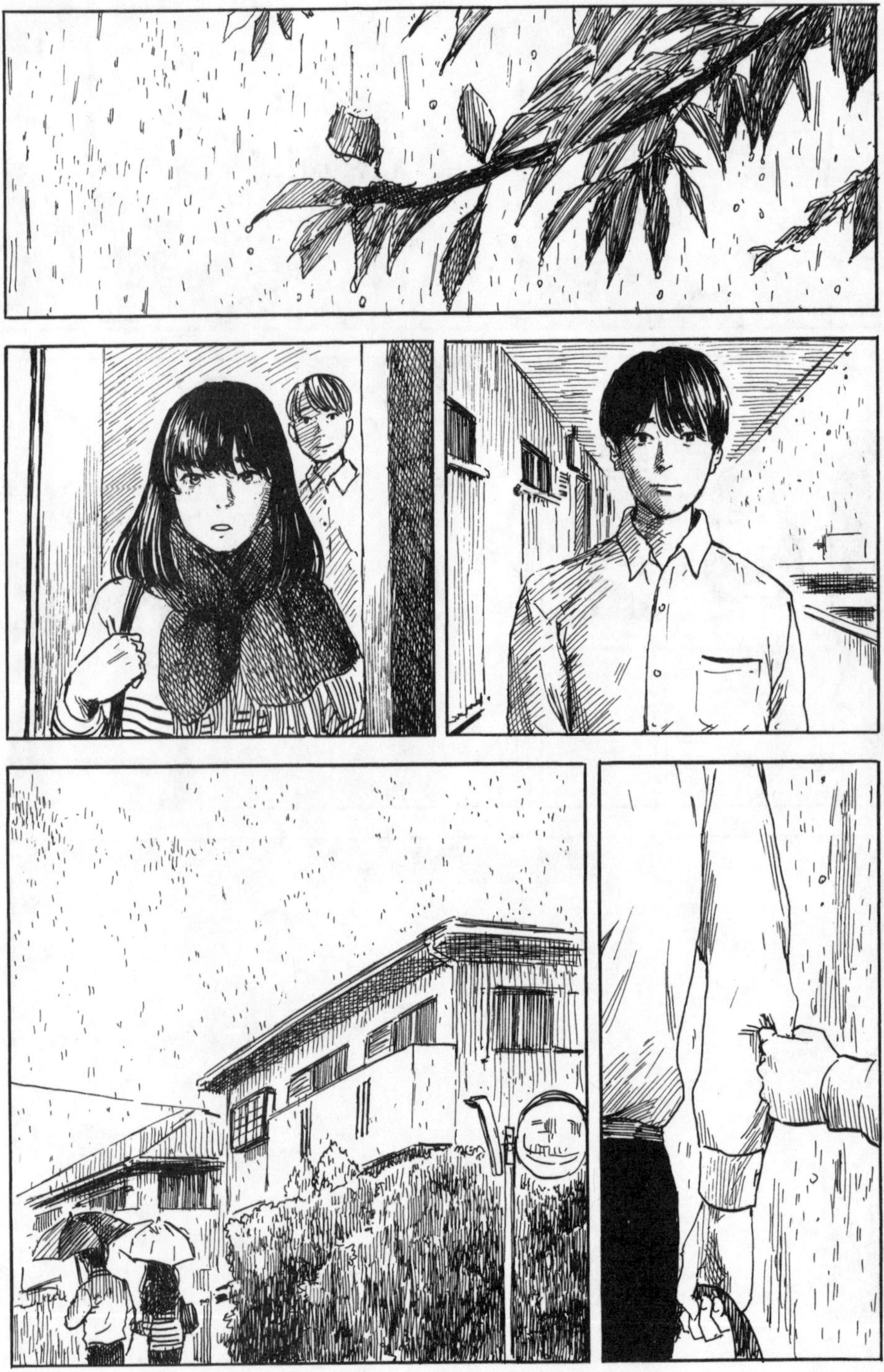

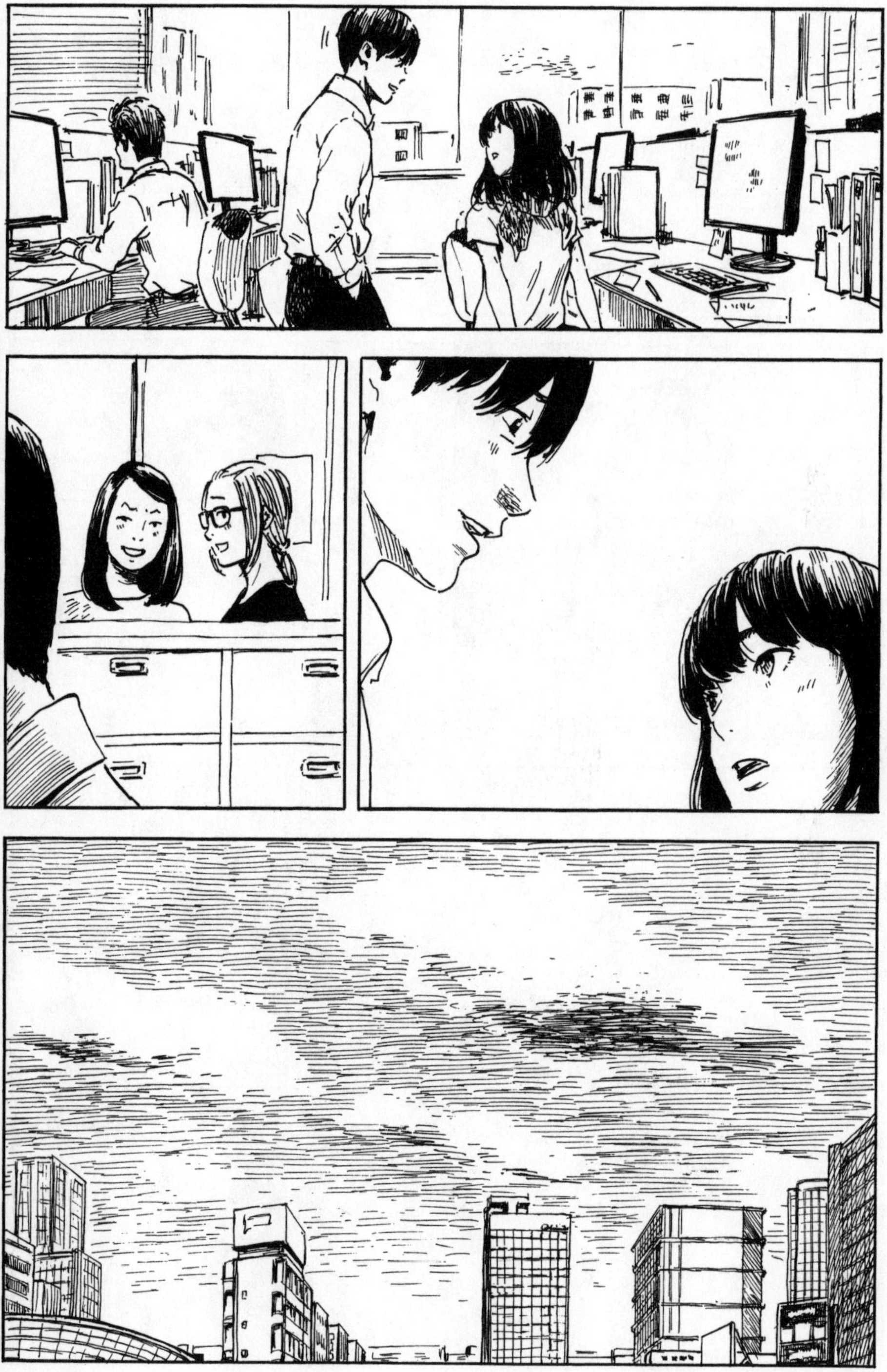

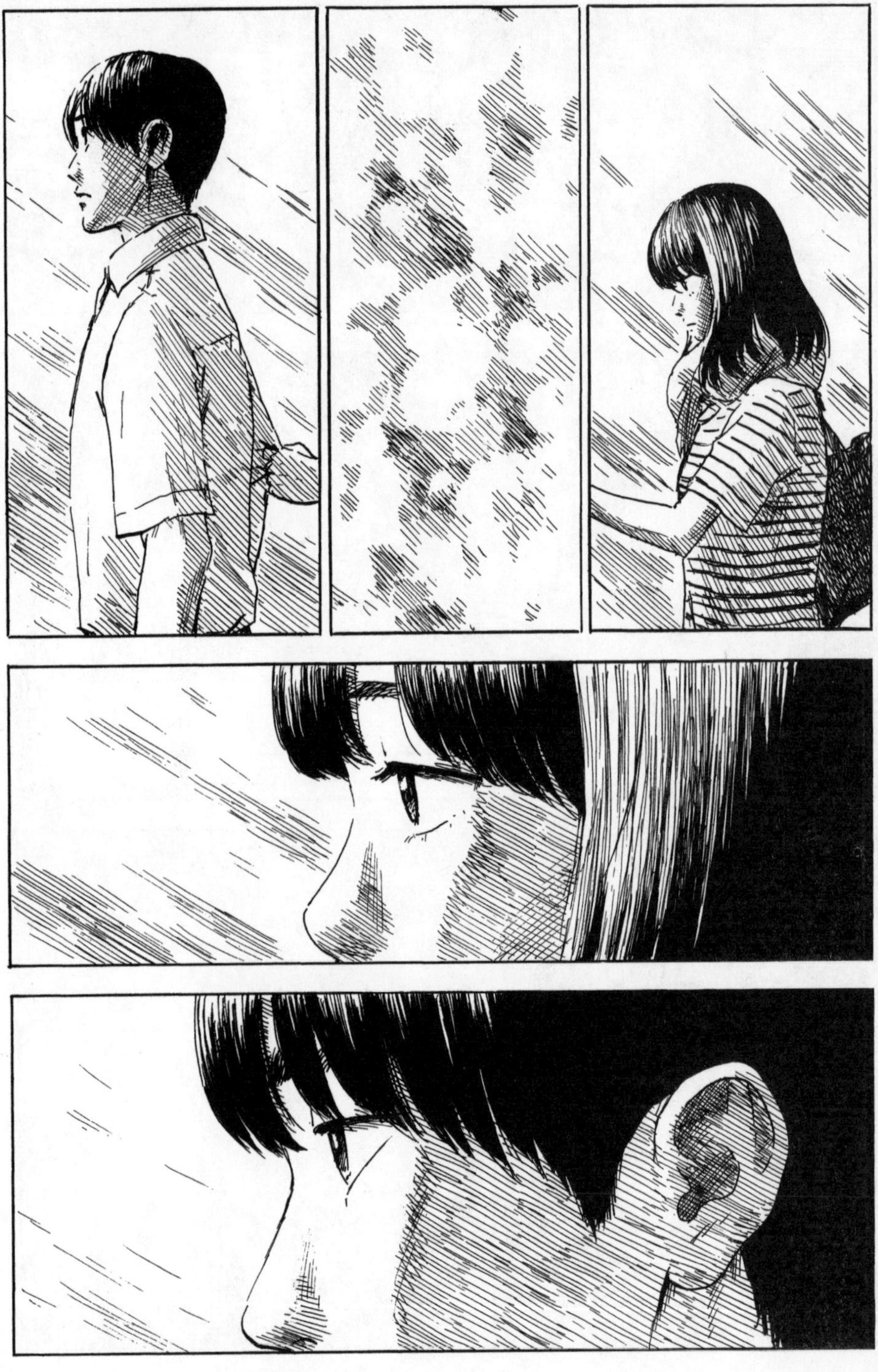

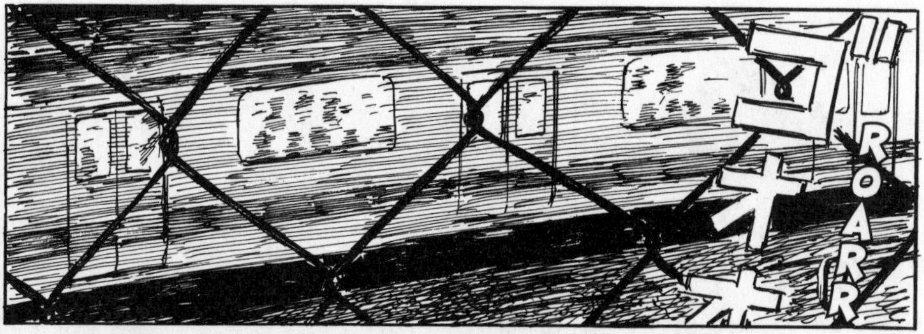
ROARR
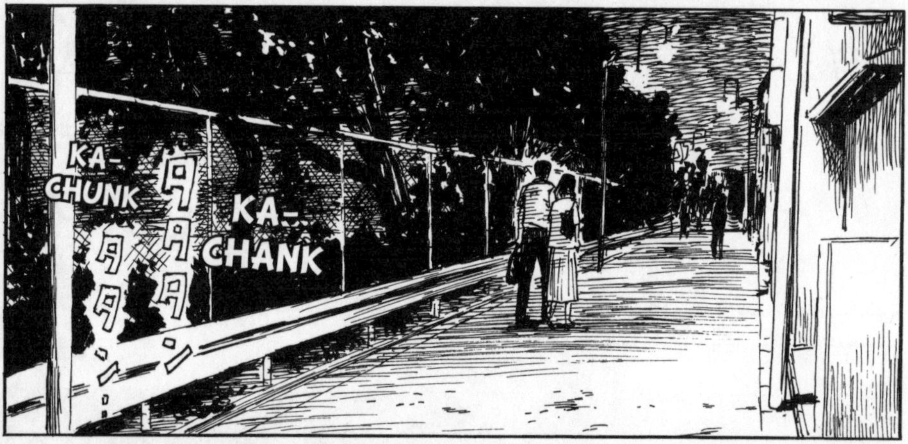
KA-CHUNK
KA-CHANK
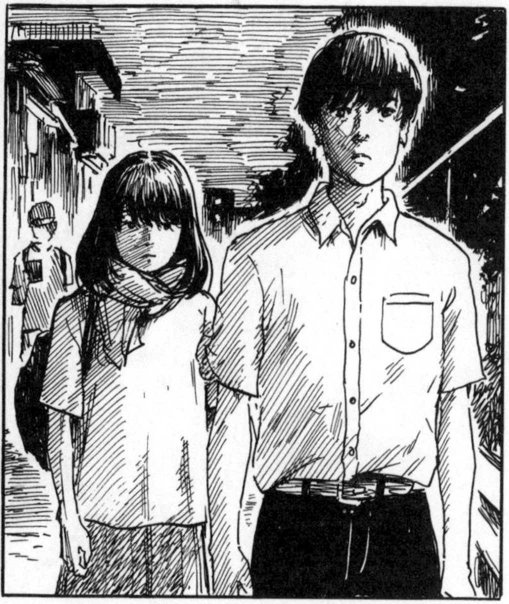
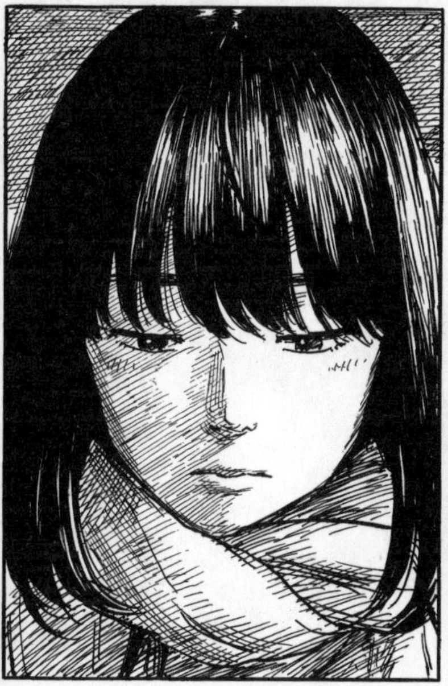

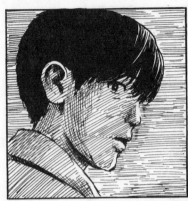

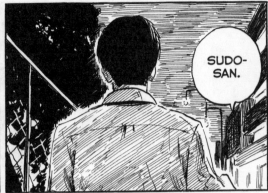

SUDO-SAN.

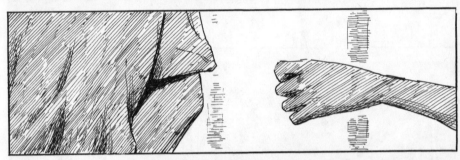

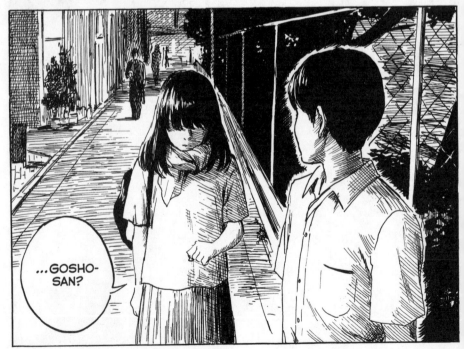

...GOSHO-SAN?

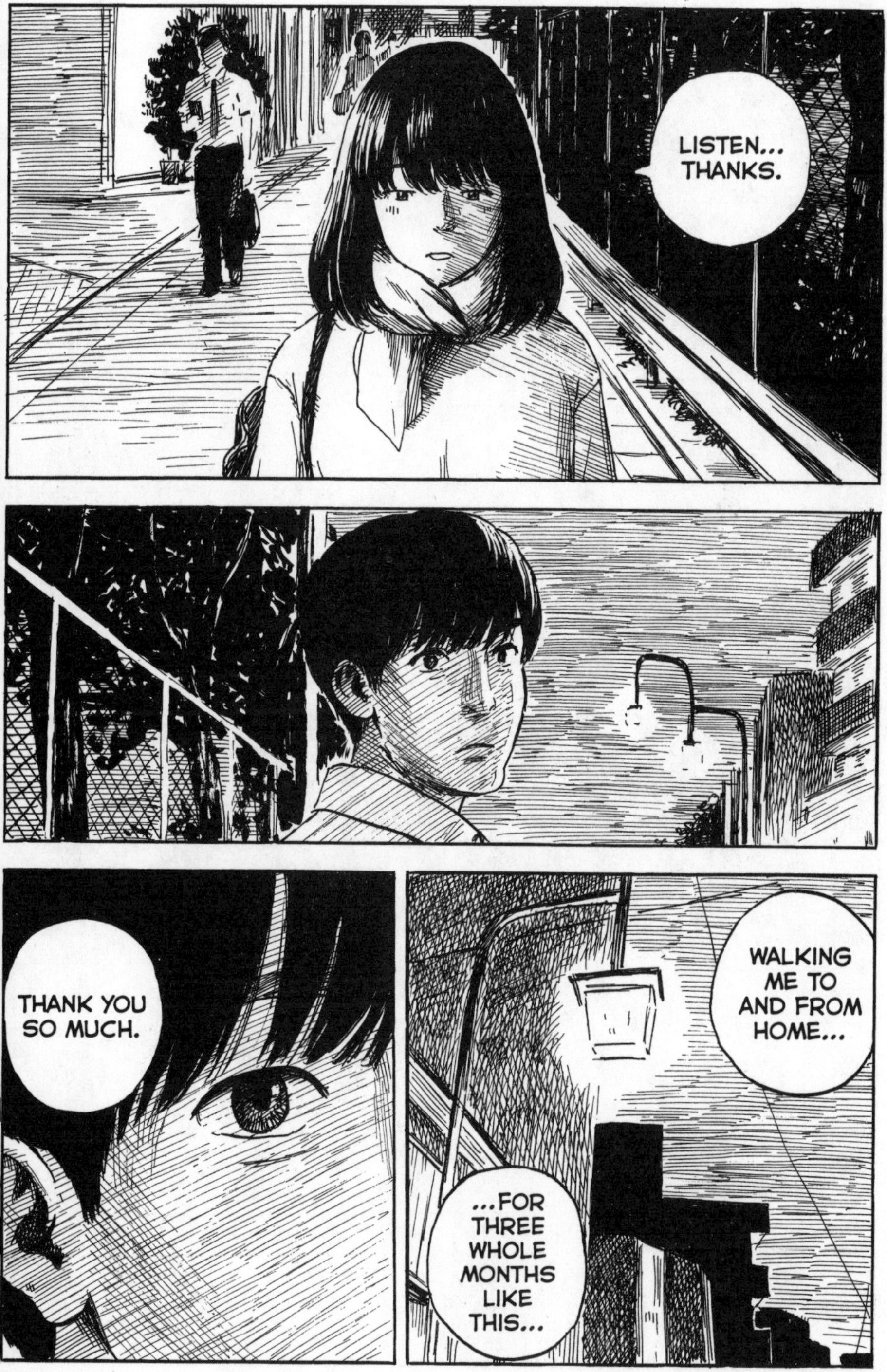
LISTEN... THANKS.
WALKING ME TO AND FROM HOME...
...FOR THREE WHOLE MONTHS LIKE THIS...
THANK YOU SO MUCH.

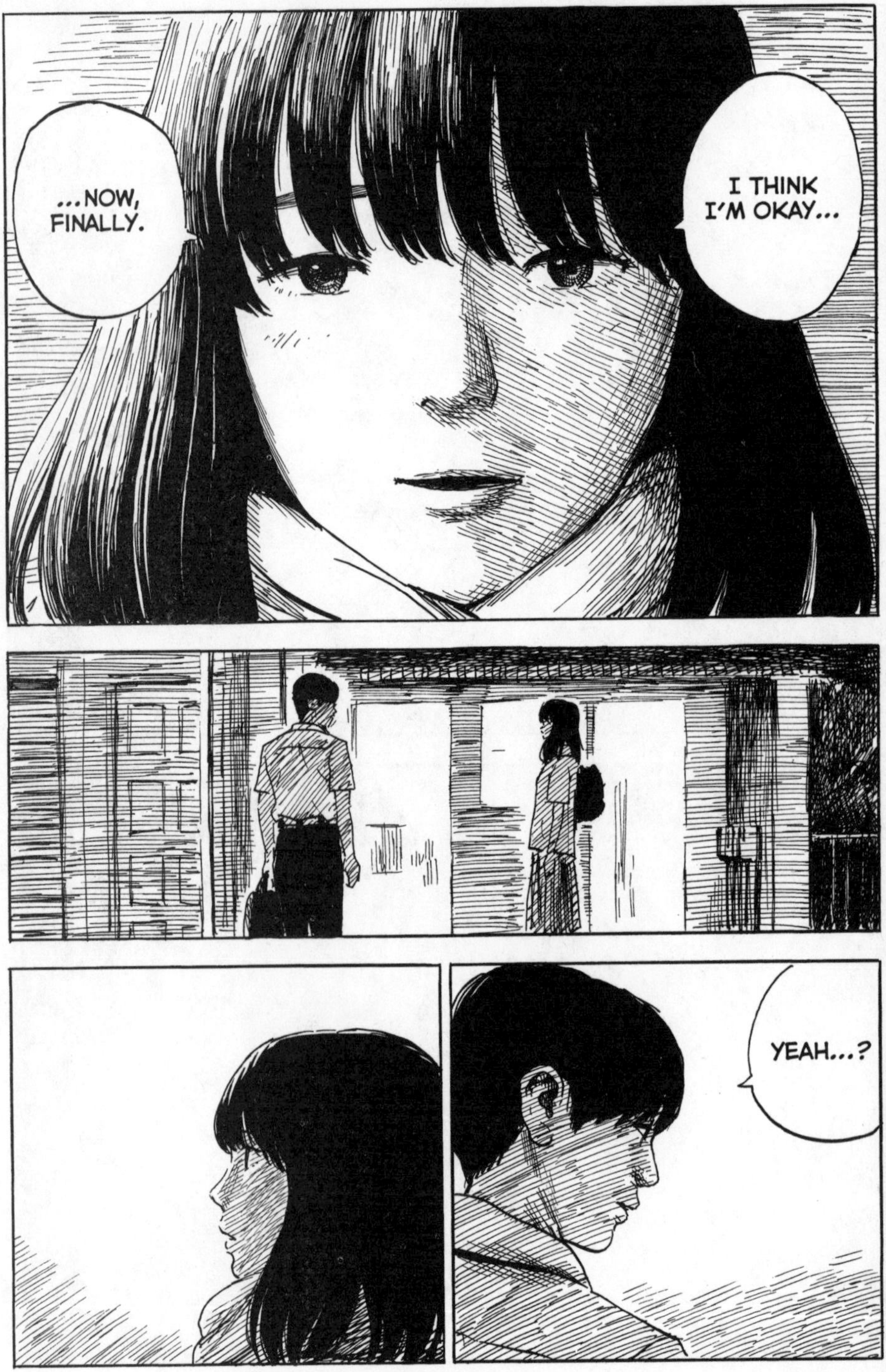
I THINK I'M OKAY...
...NOW, FINALLY.
YEAH...?

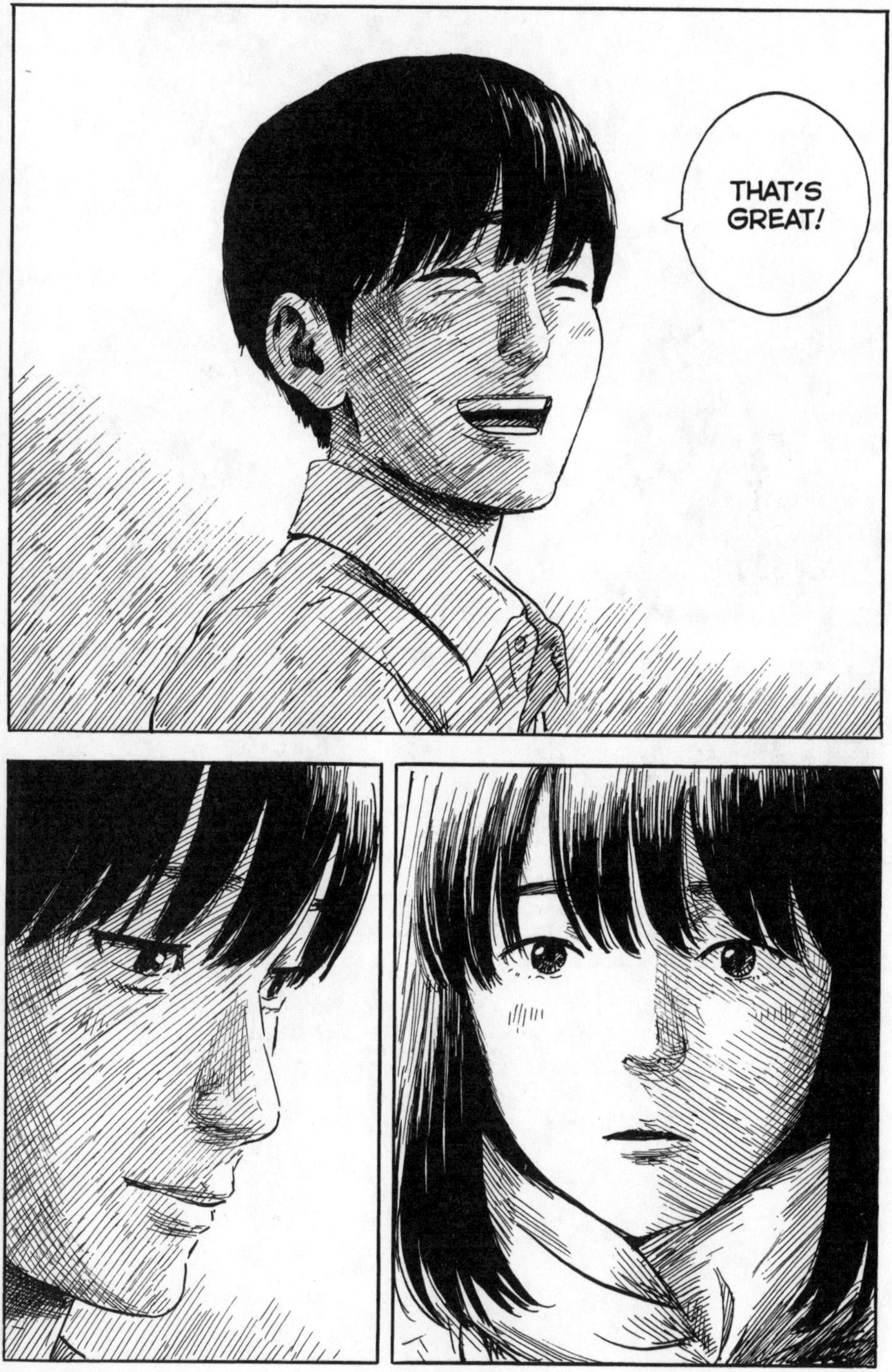
THAT'S GREAT!

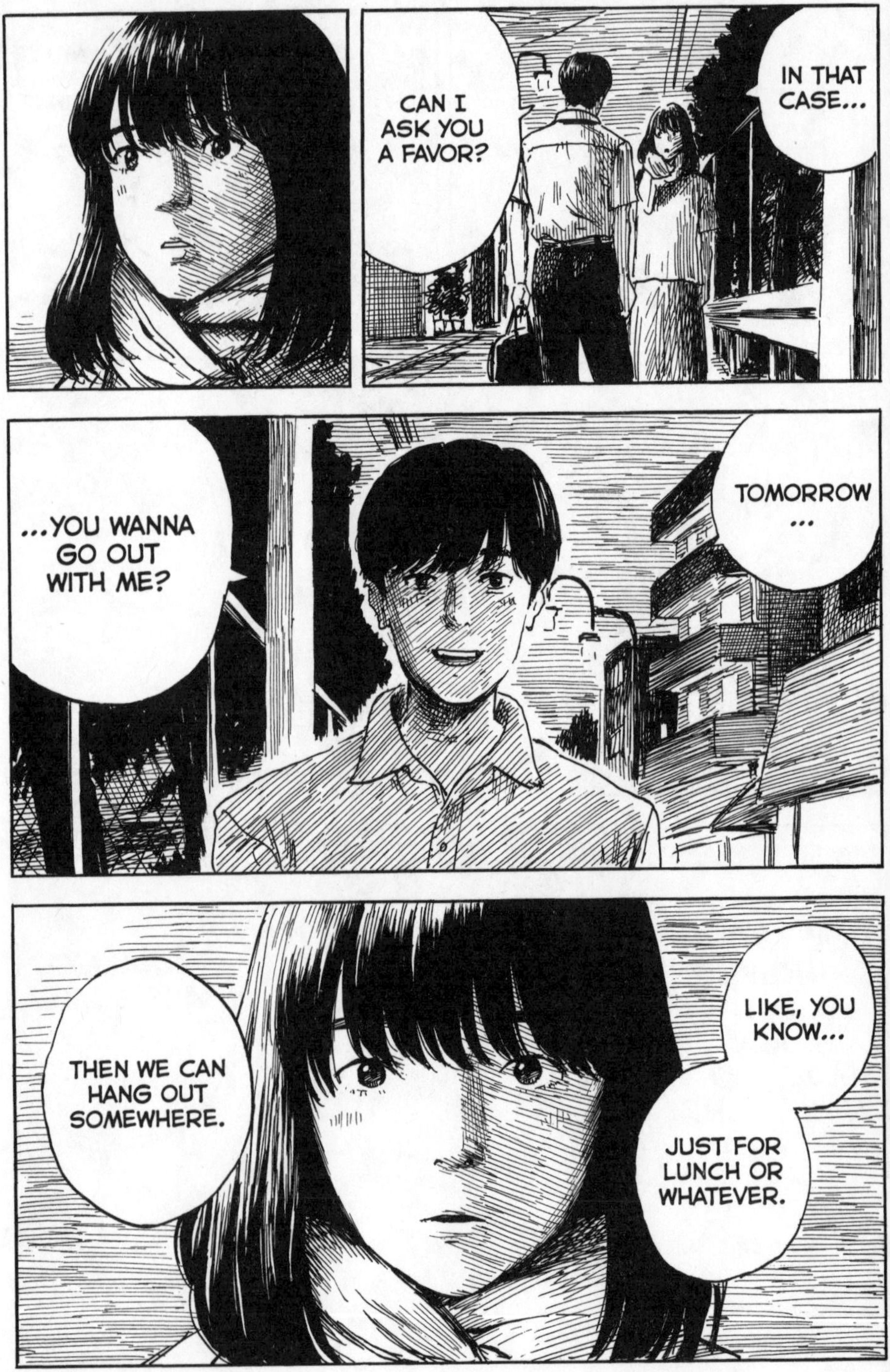
IN THAT CASE...
CAN I ASK YOU A FAVOR?
TOMORROW ...
...YOU WANNA GO OUT WITH ME?
LIKE, YOU KNOW...
JUST FOR LUNCH OR WHATEVER.
THEN WE CAN HANG OUT SOMEWHERE.

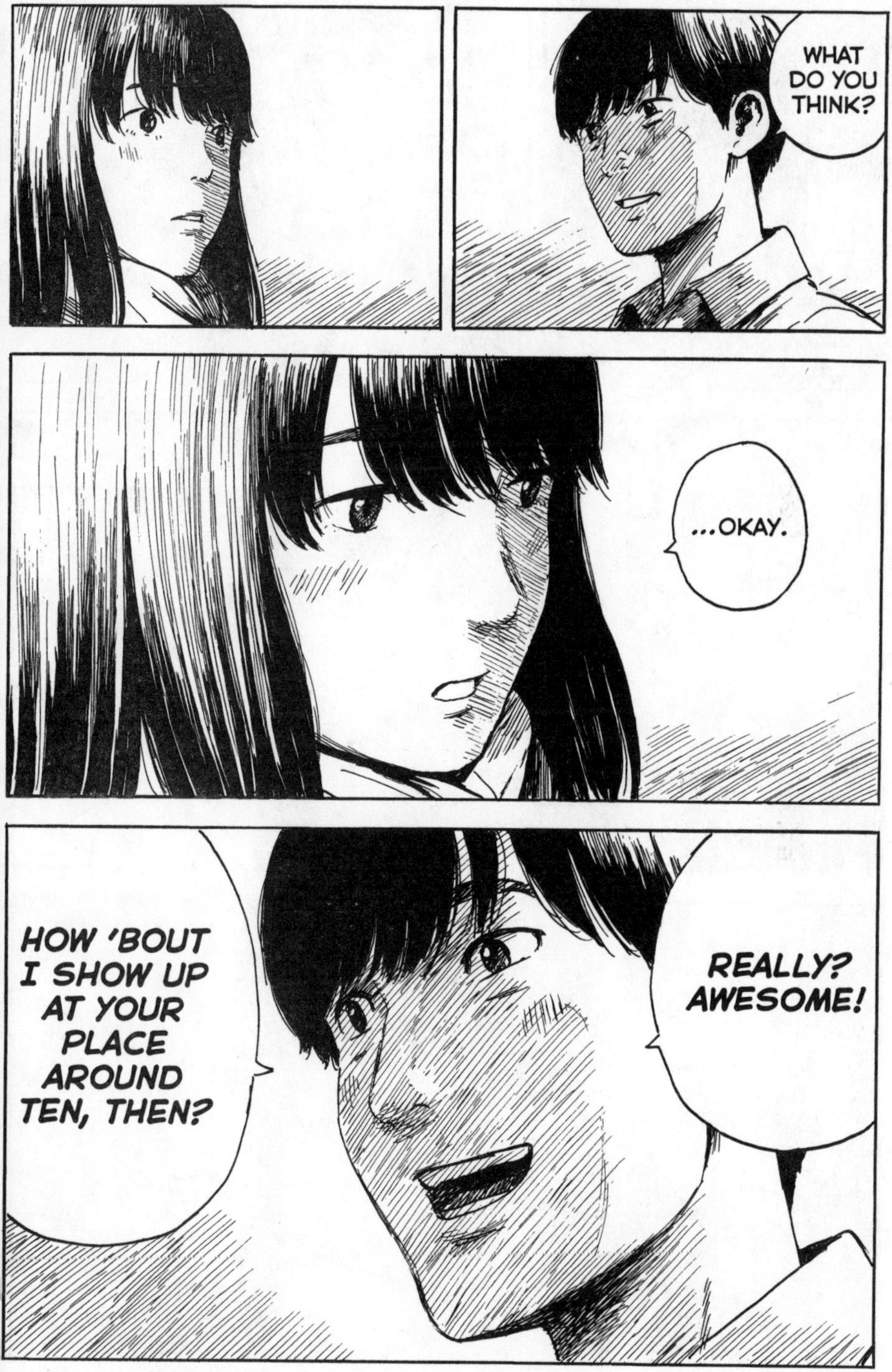
WHAT DO YOU THINK?
...OKAY.
REALLY? AWESOME!
HOW 'BOUT I SHOW UP AT YOUR PLACE AROUND TEN, THEN?

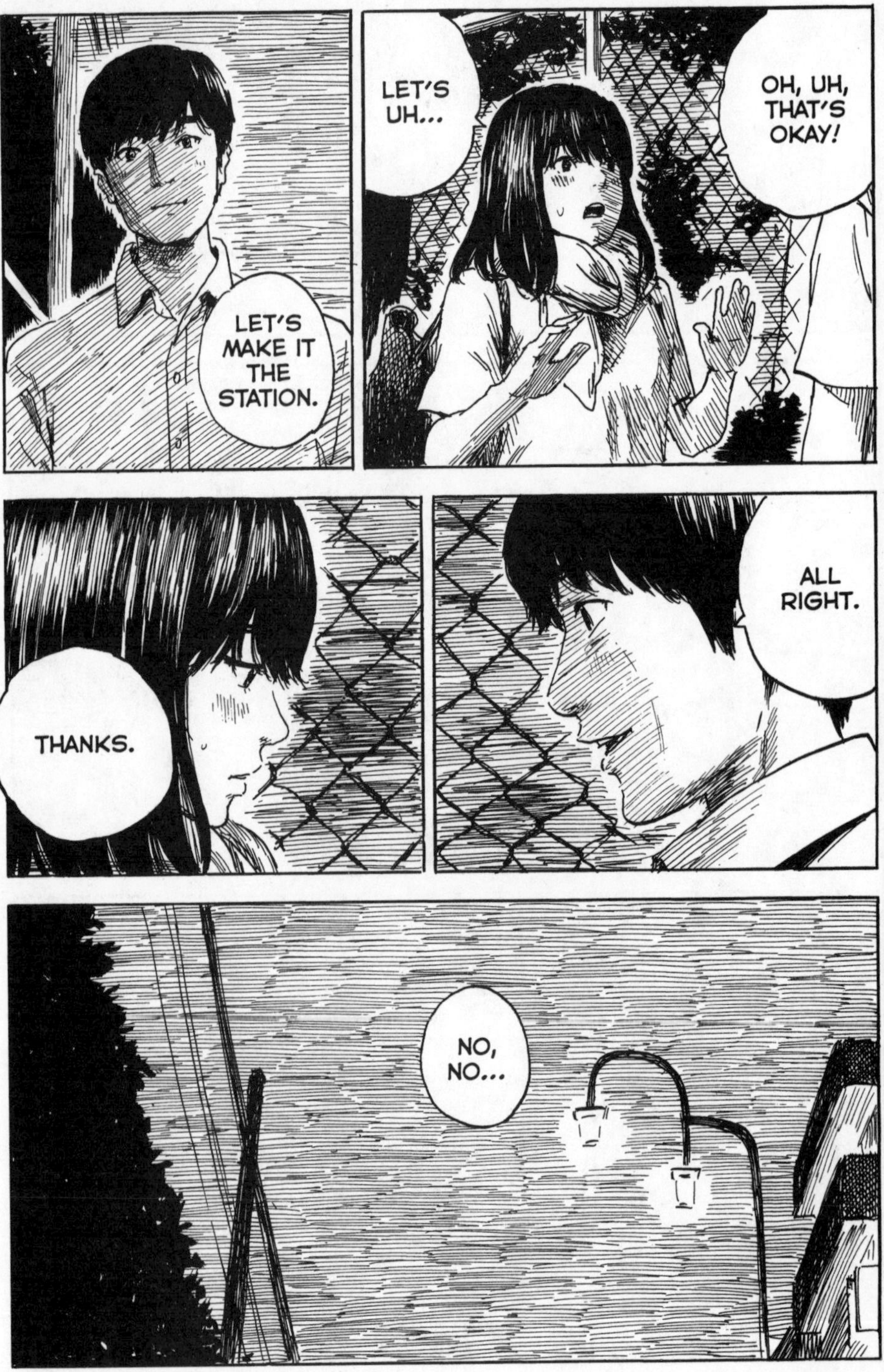
OH, UH, THAT'S OKAY!
LET'S UH...
LET'S MAKE IT THE STATION.
ALL RIGHT.
THANKS.
NO, NO...

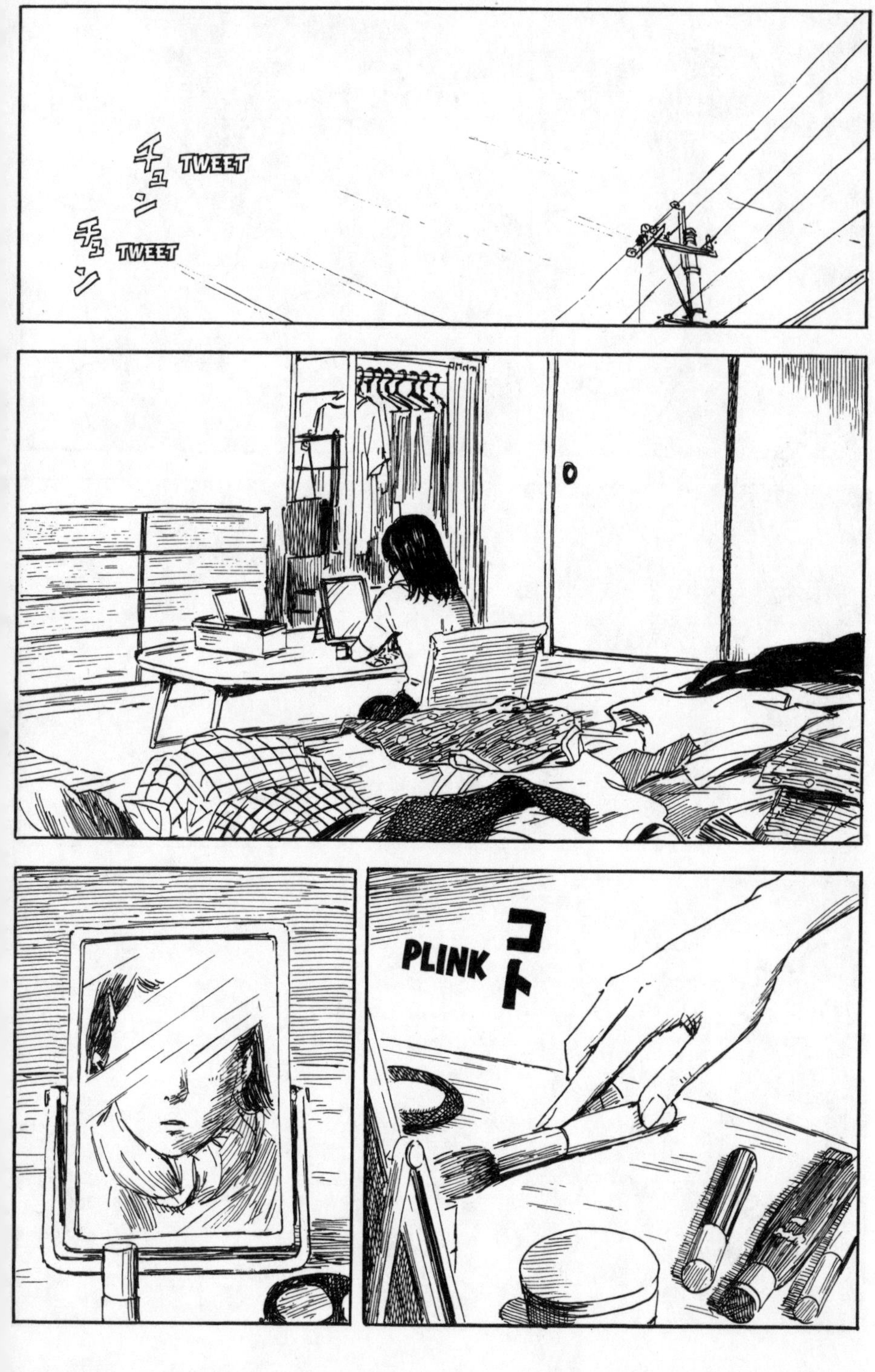
チュン
TWEET
チュン
TWEET
コト
PLINK

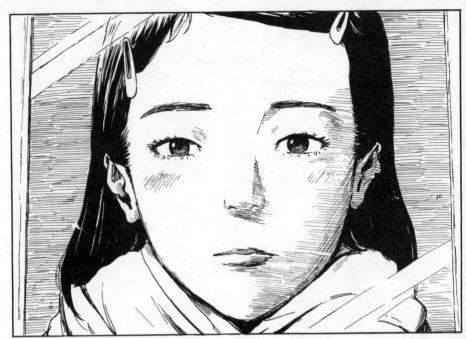

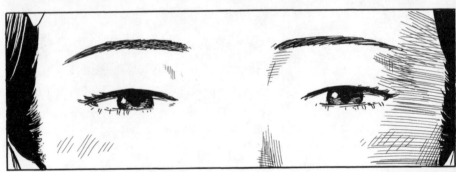

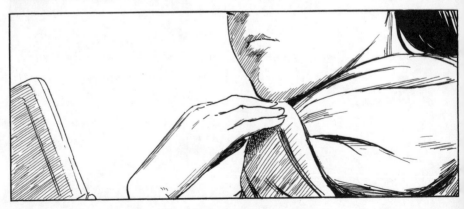

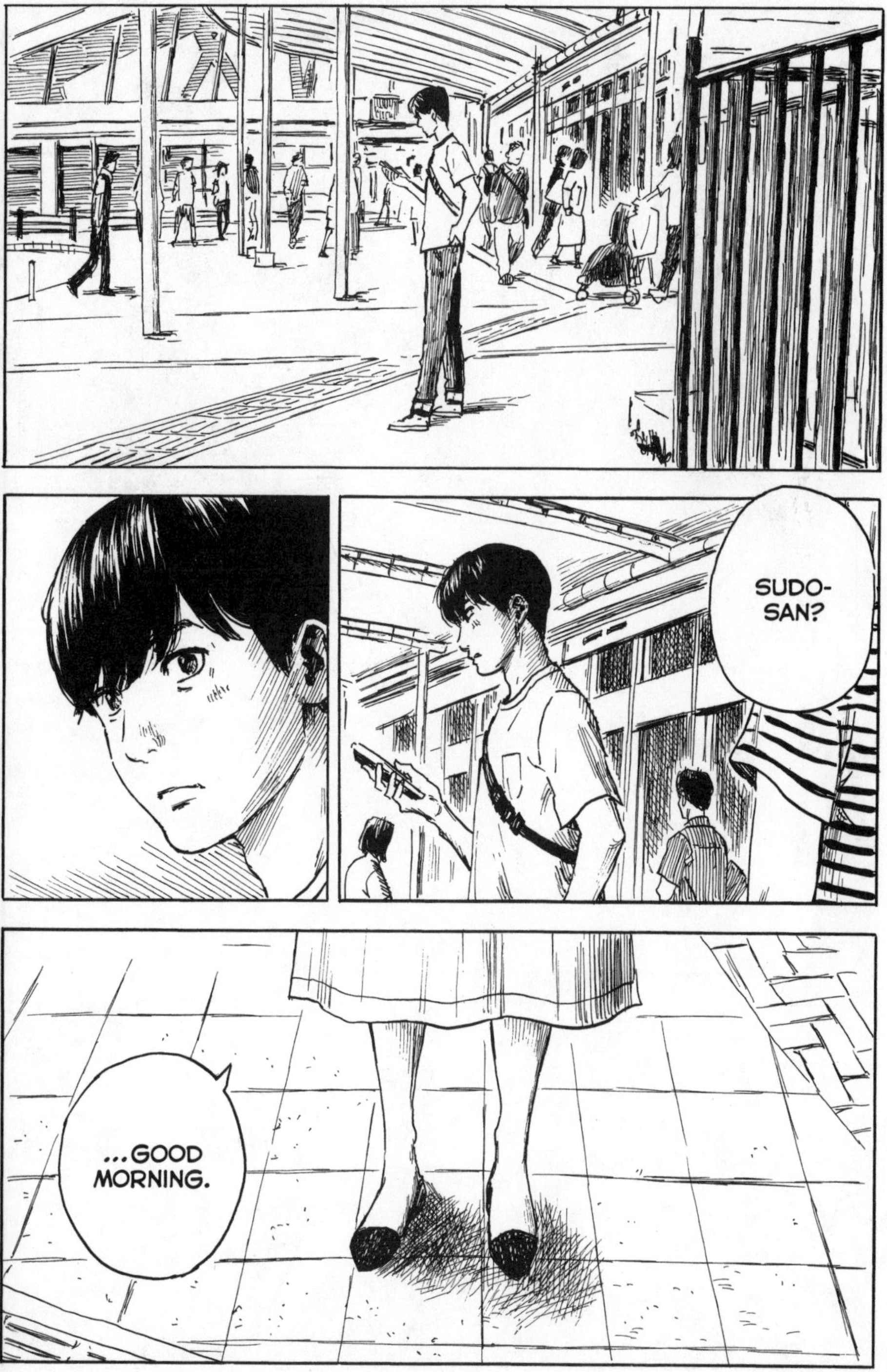
SUDO-SAN?
...GOOD MORNING.

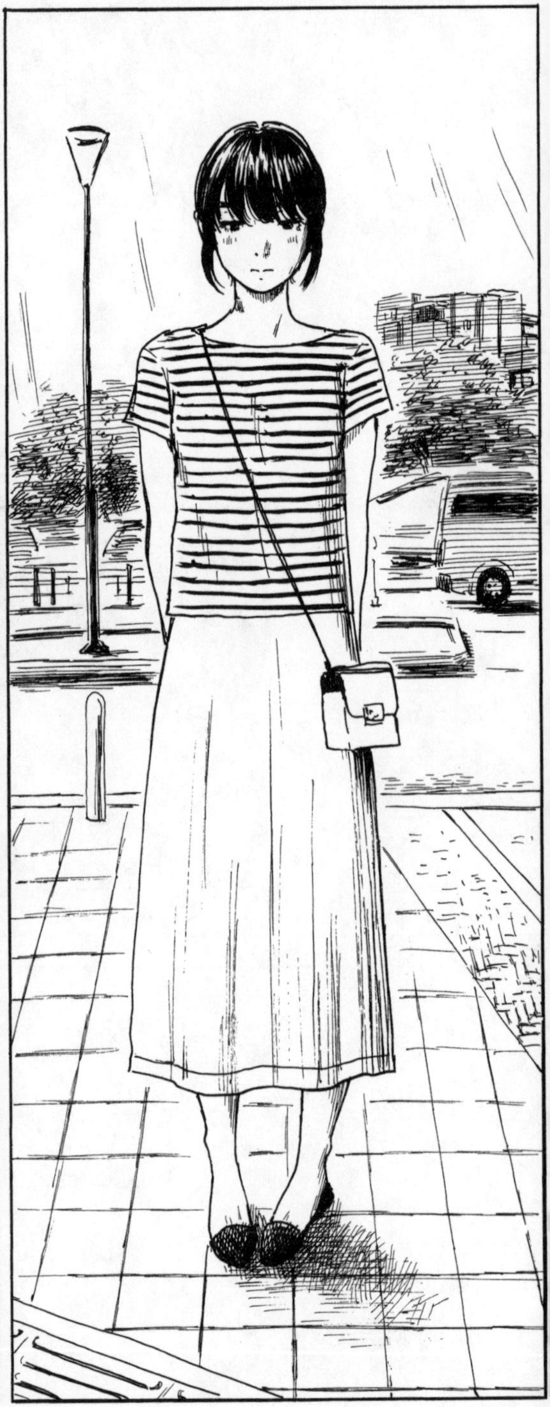

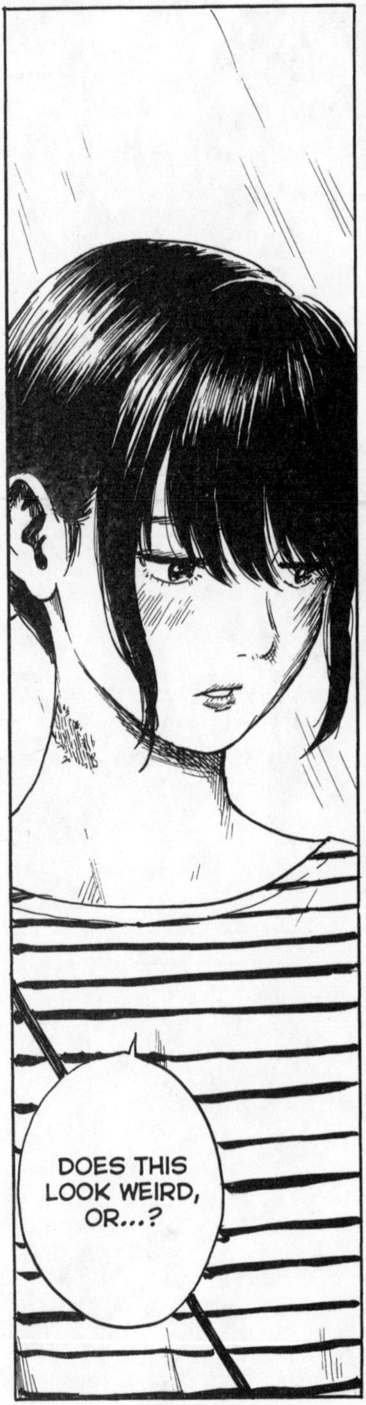
DOES THIS LOOK WEIRD, OR...?

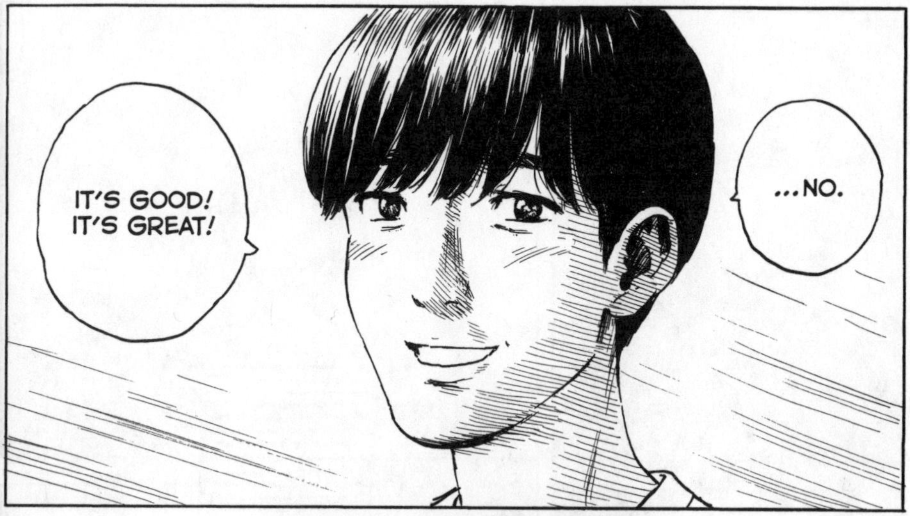
...NO.
IT'S GOOD! IT'S GREAT!
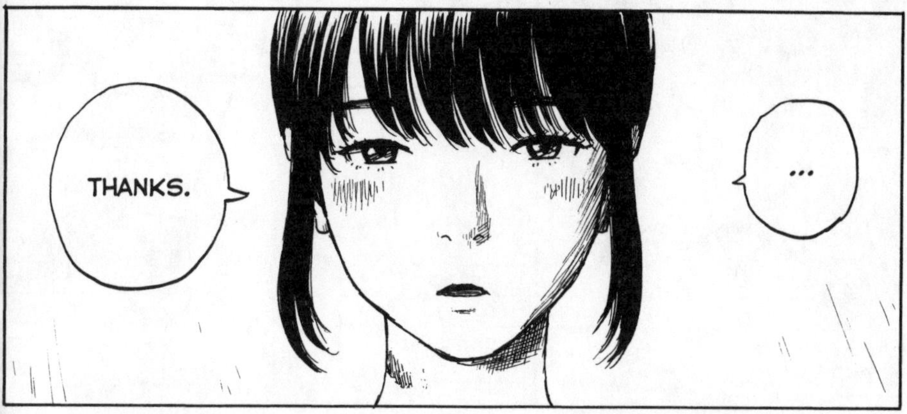
...
THANKS.
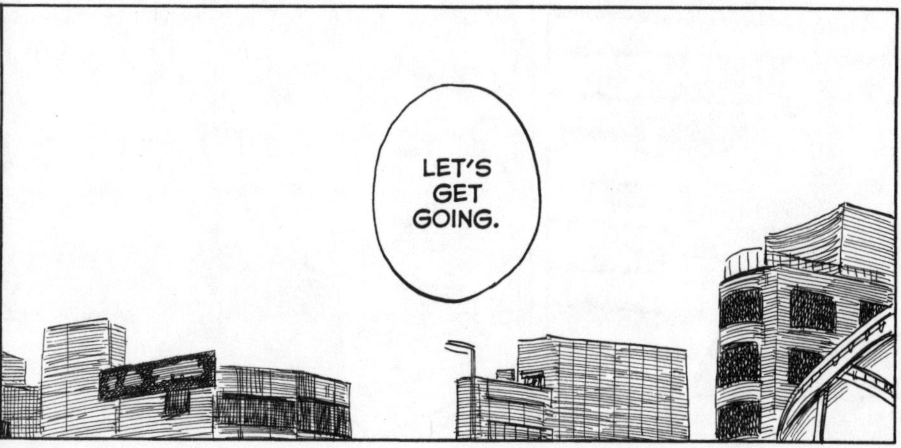
LET'S GET GOING.

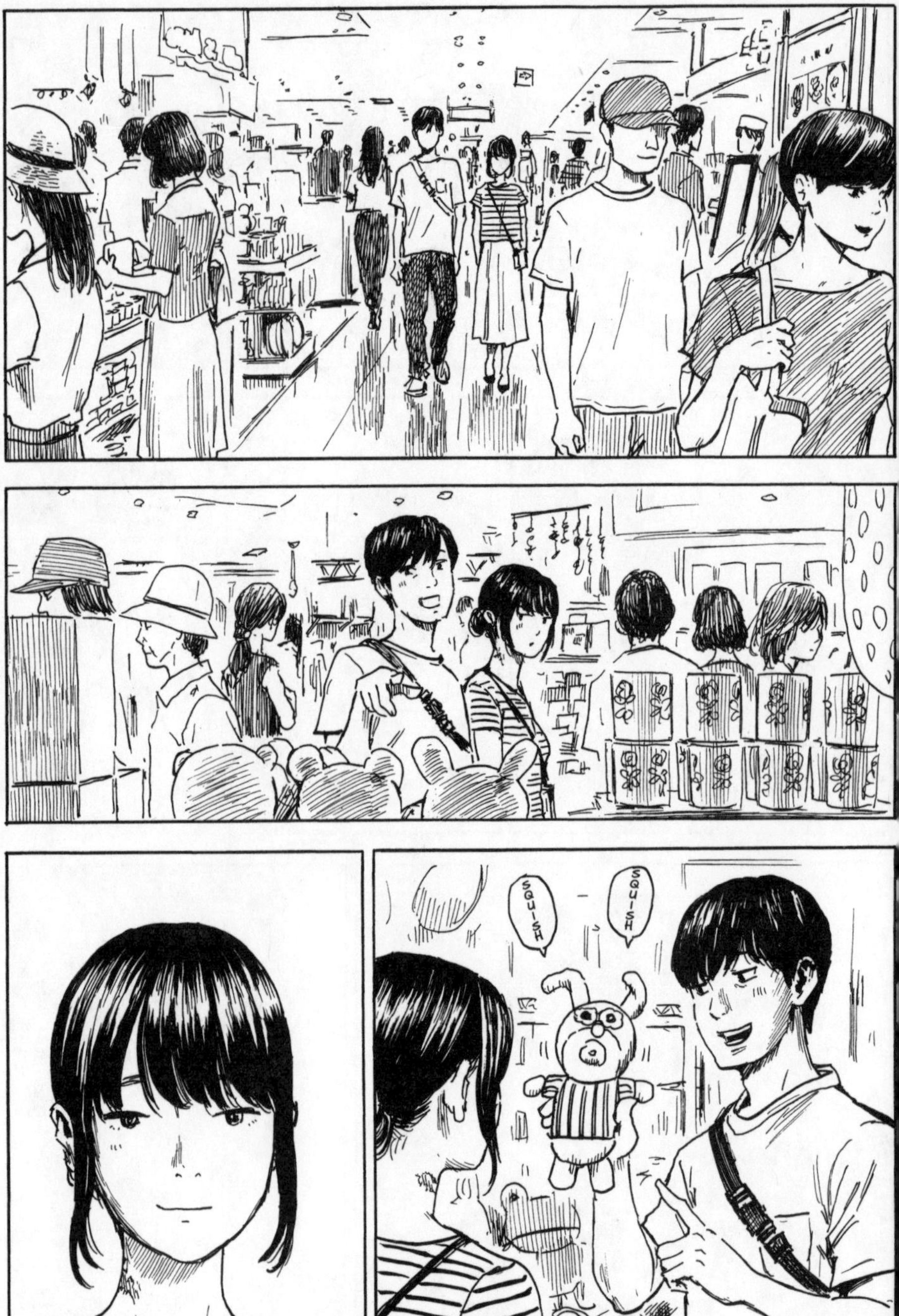
SQUISH
SQUISH

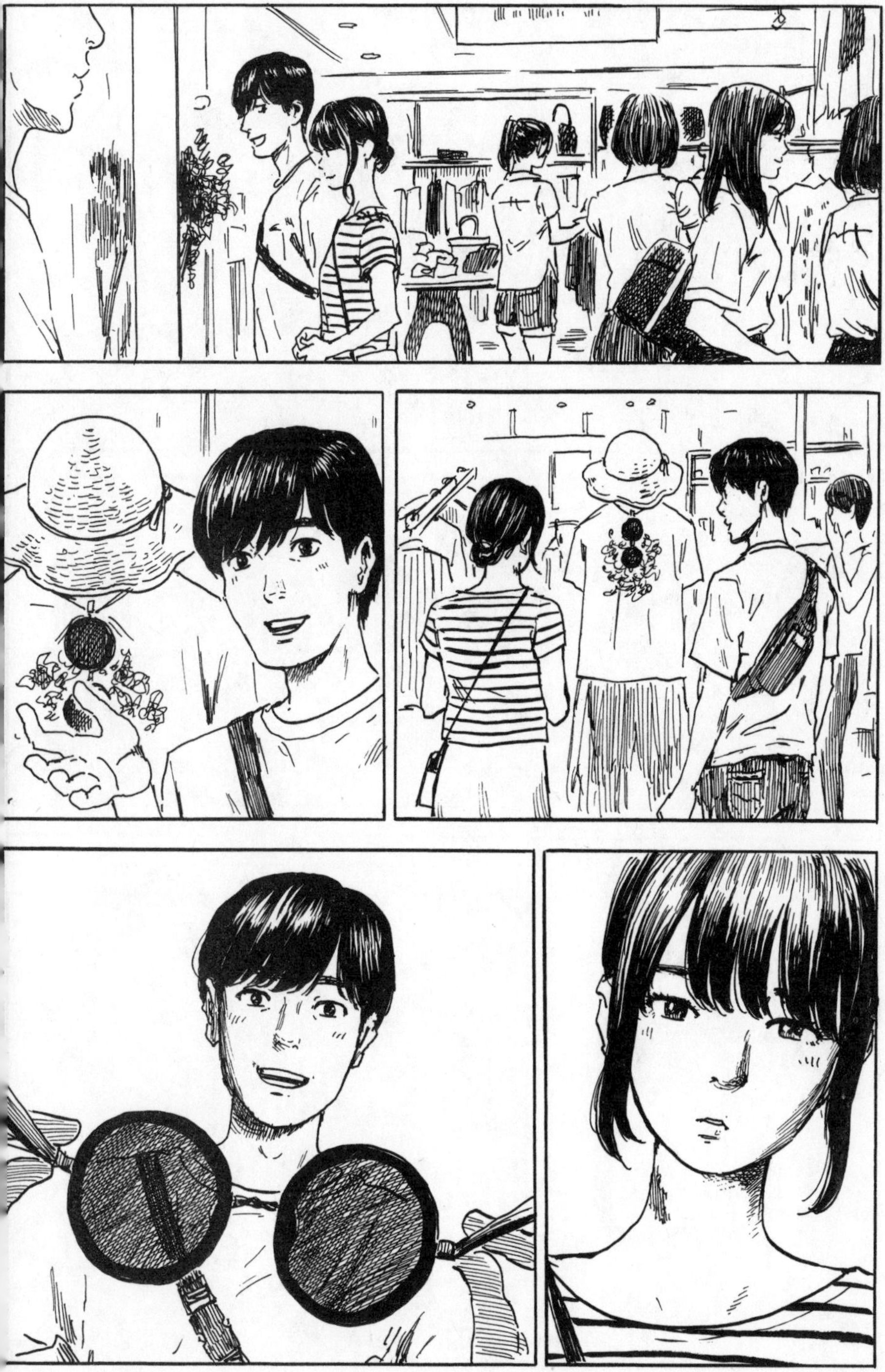

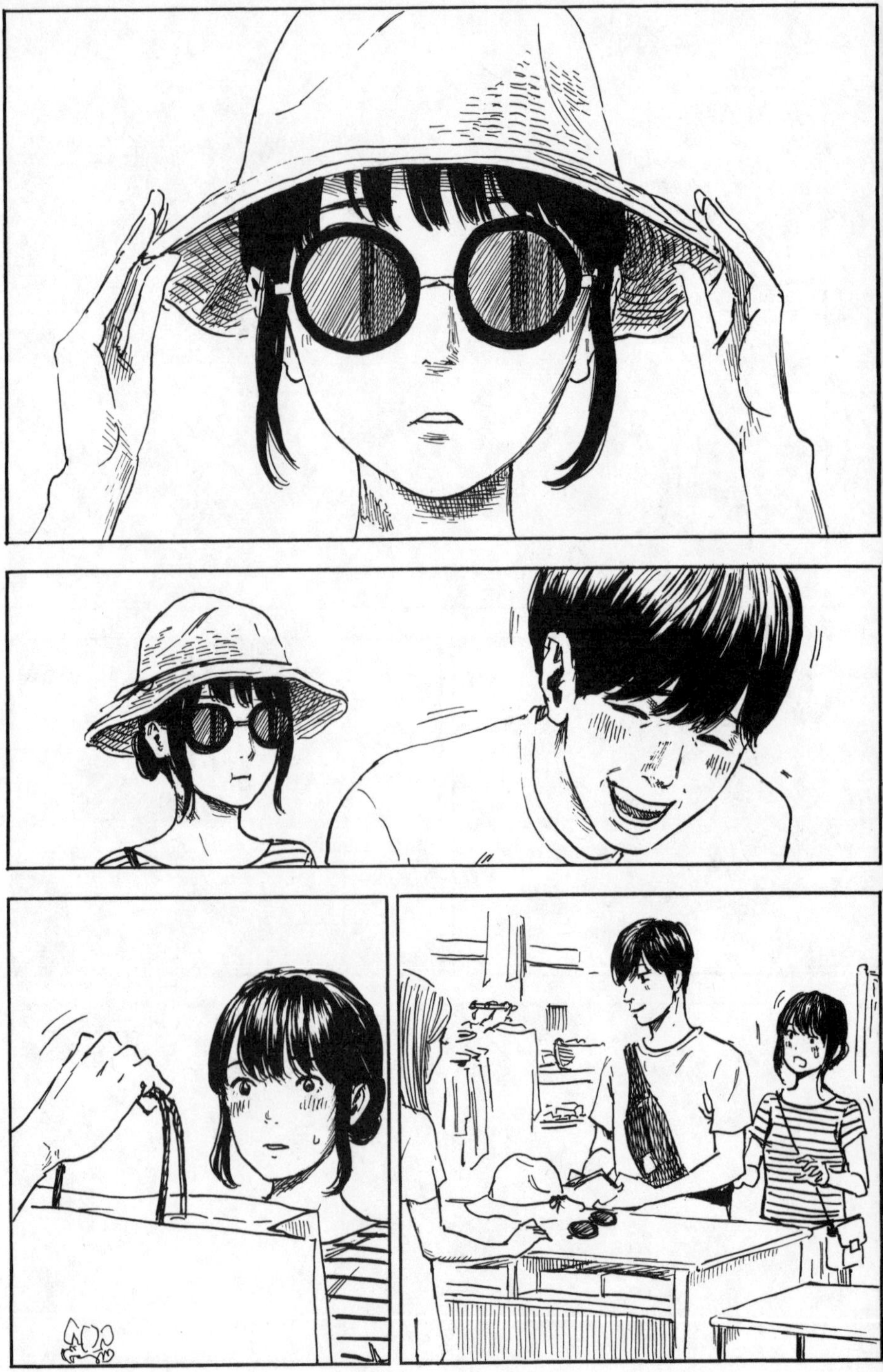

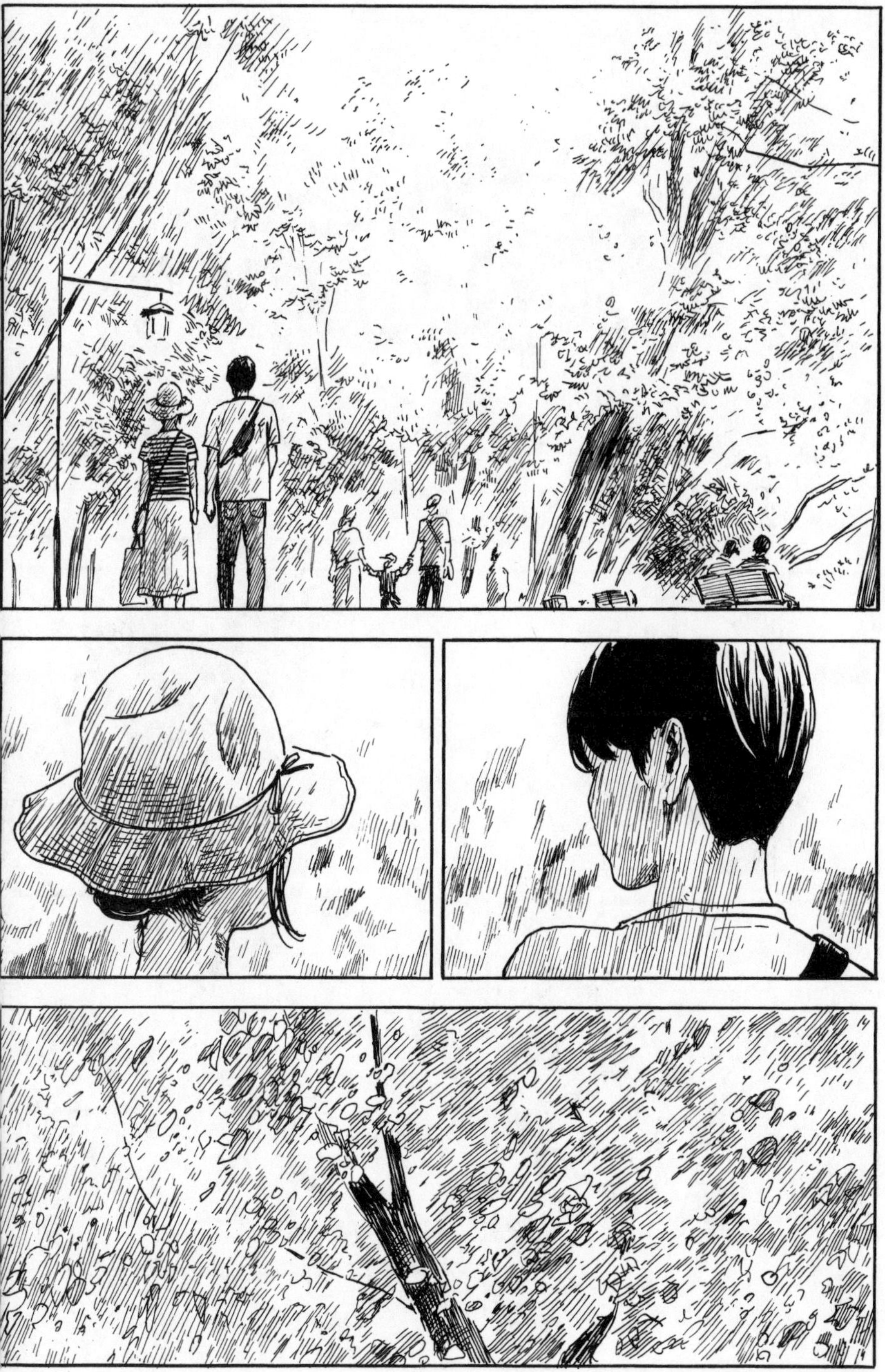

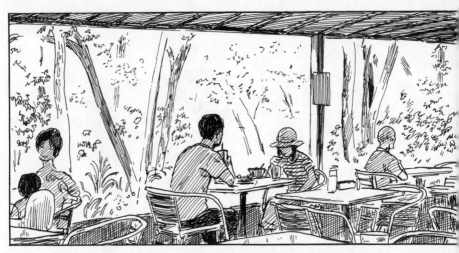

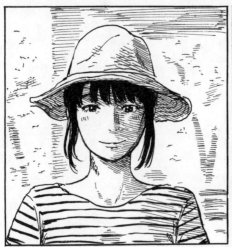

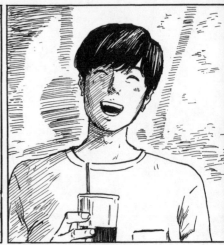

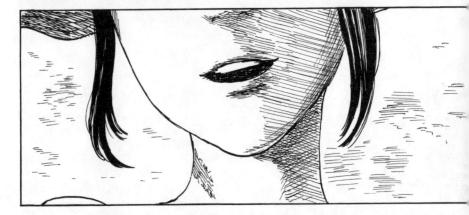

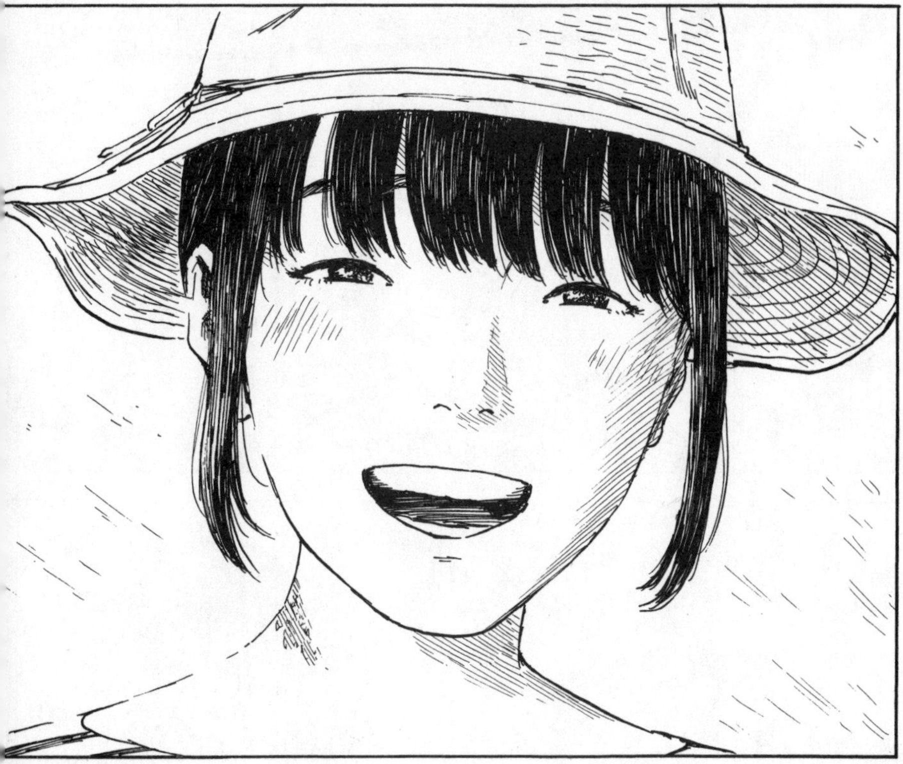

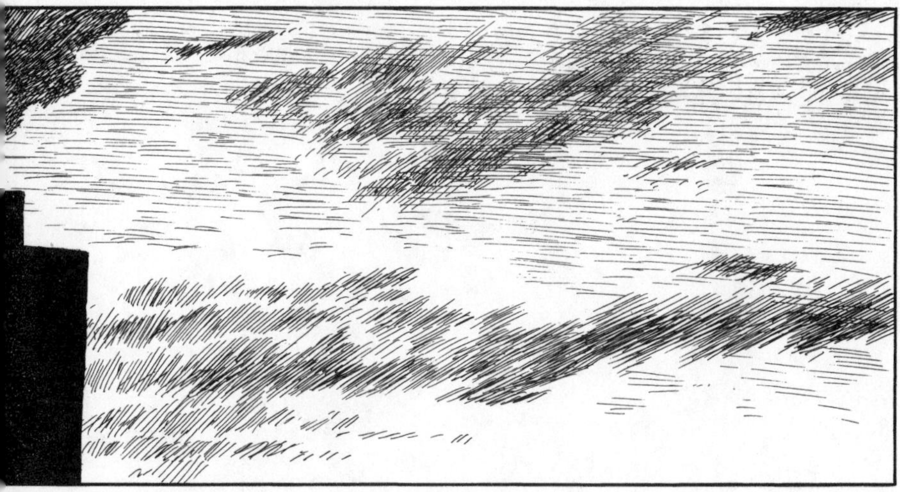

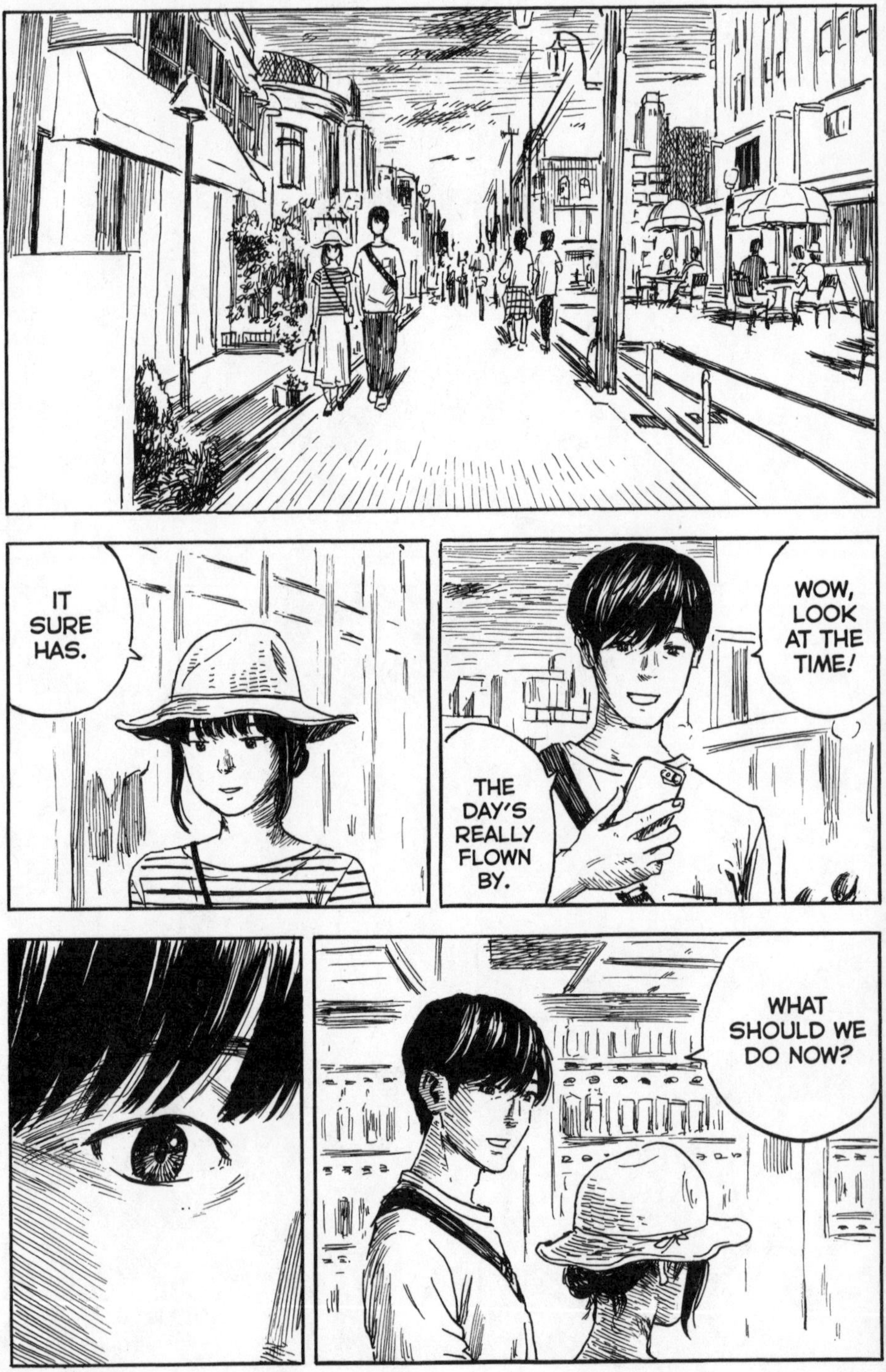
WOW, LOOK AT THE TIME!
THE DAY'S REALLY FLOWN BY.
IT SURE HAS.
WHAT SHOULD WE DO NOW?

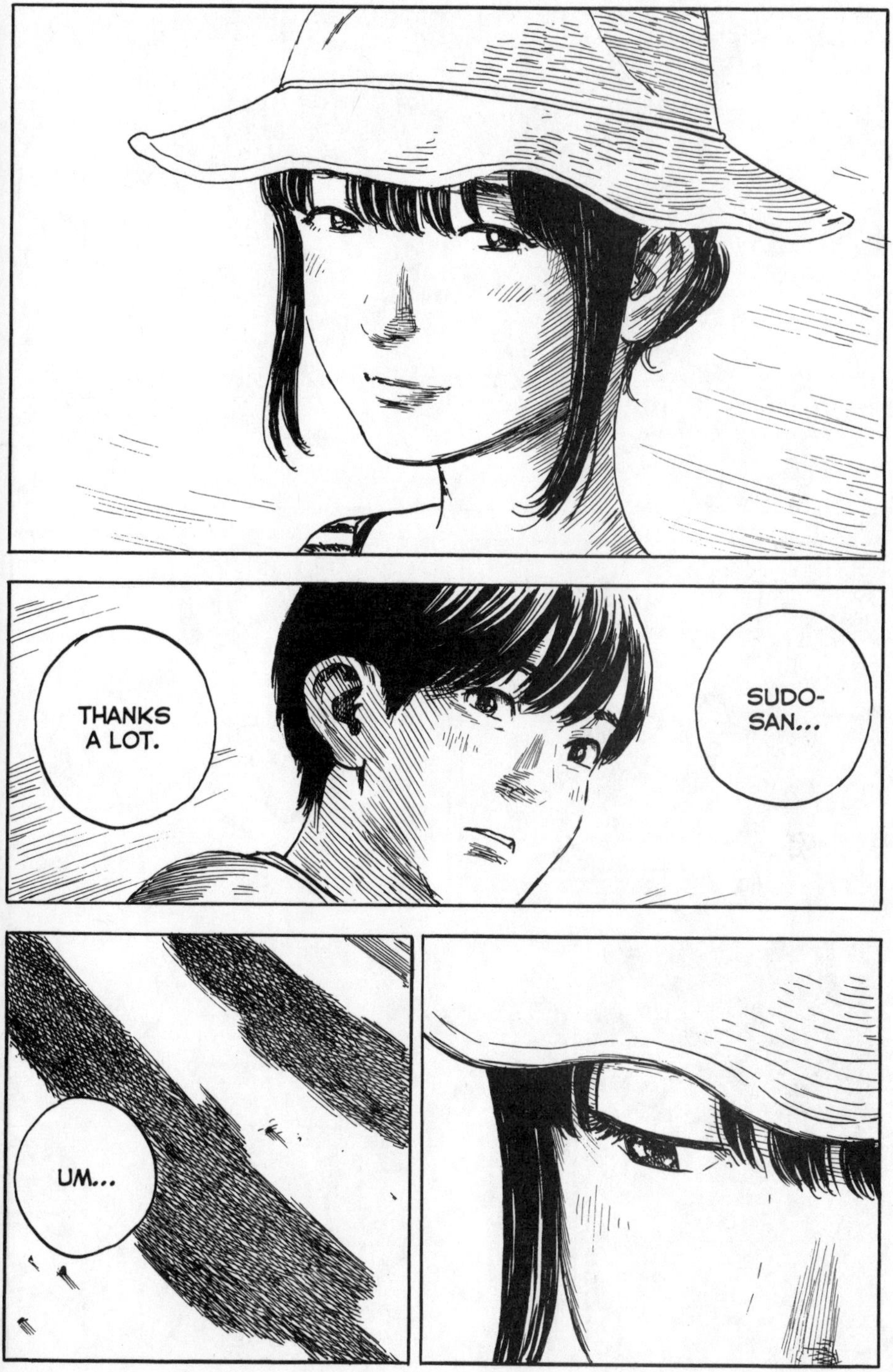
SUDO-SAN...
THANKS A LOT.
UM...

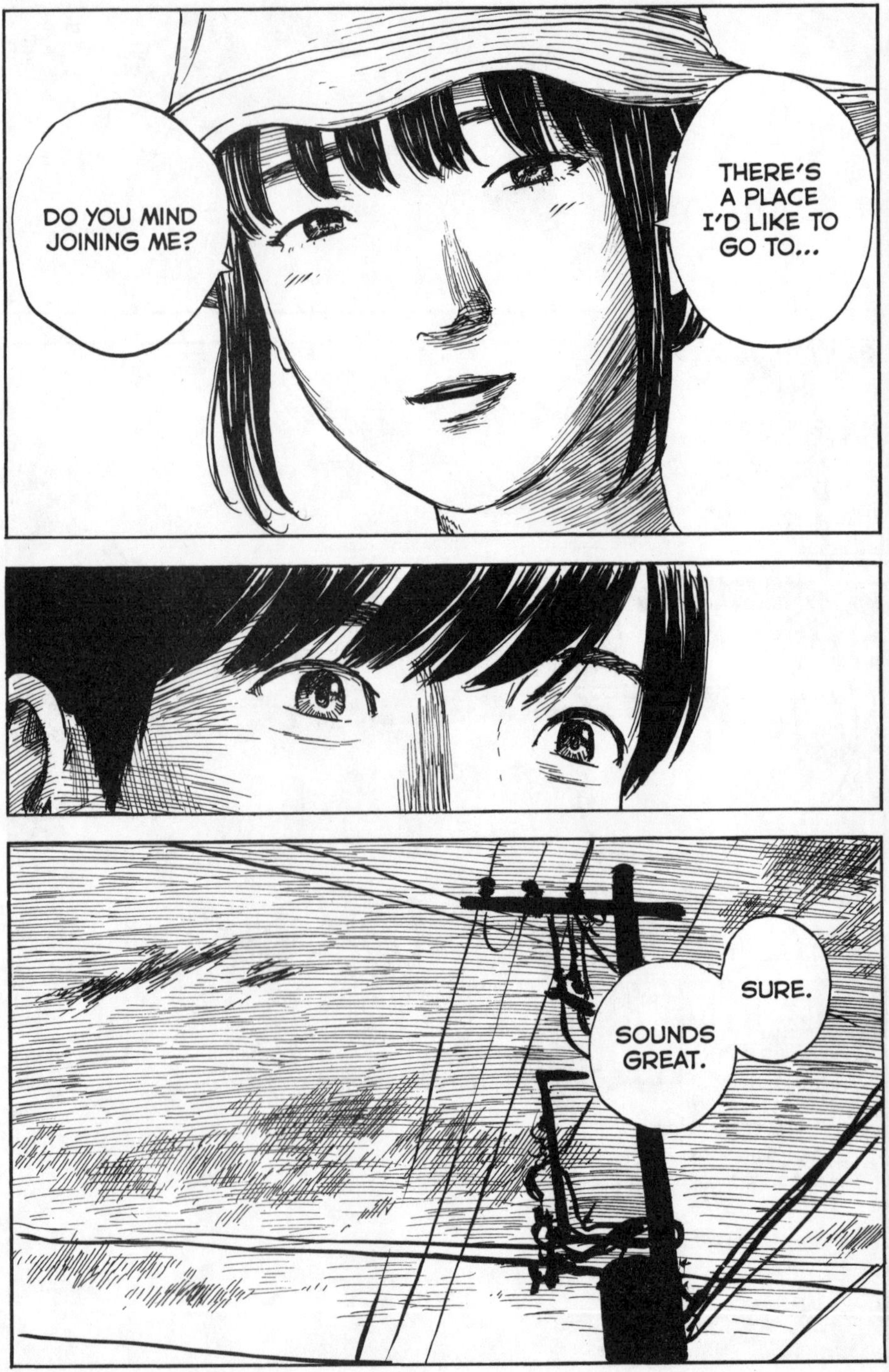
THERE'S A PLACE I'D LIKE TO GO TO...
DO YOU MIND JOINING ME?
SURE.
SOUNDS GREAT.

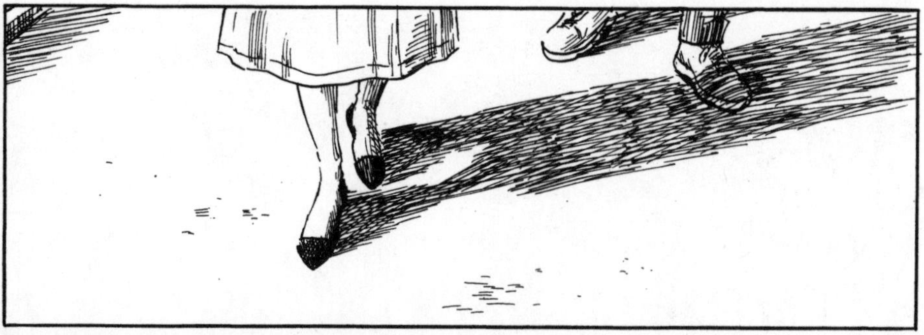
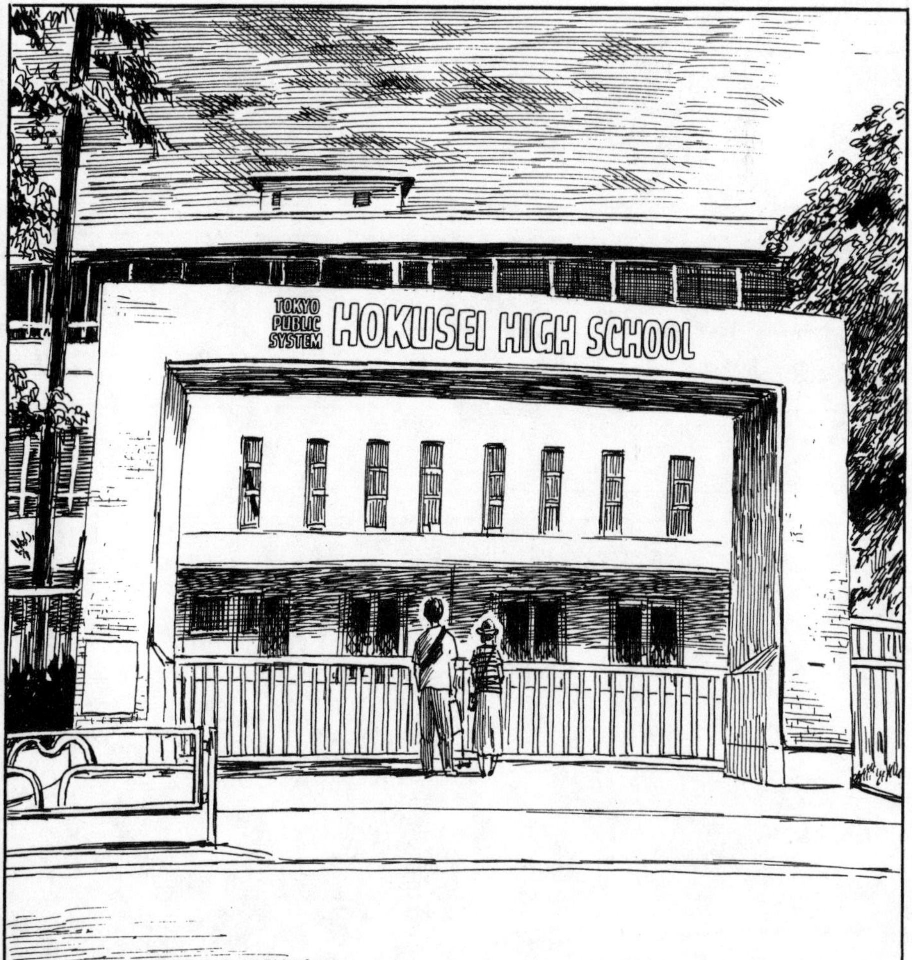
TOKYO PUBLIC SYSTEM
HOKUSEI HIGH SCHOOL

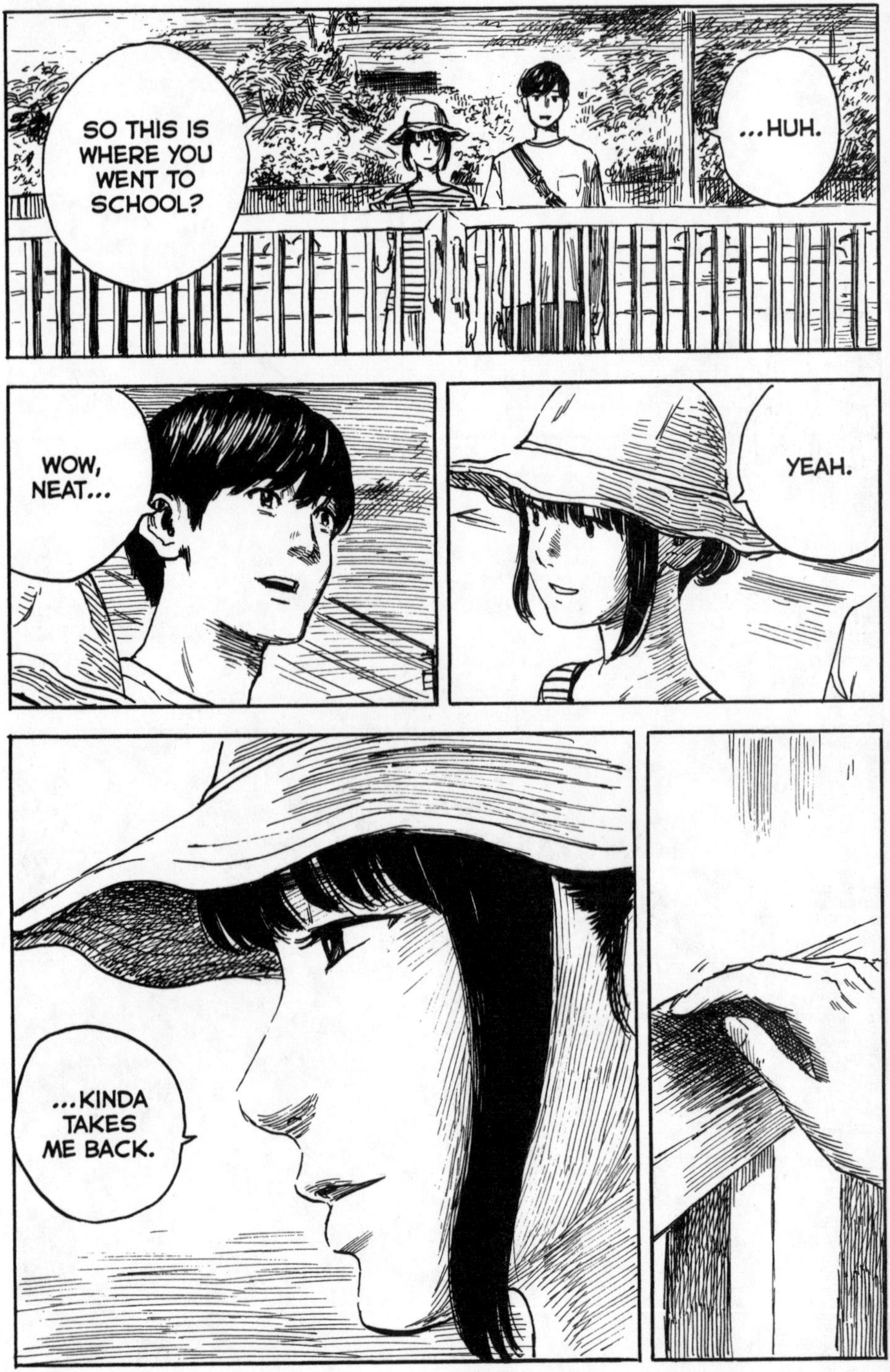
...HUH.
SO THIS IS WHERE YOU WENT TO SCHOOL?
YEAH.
WOW, NEAT...
...KINDA TAKES ME BACK.

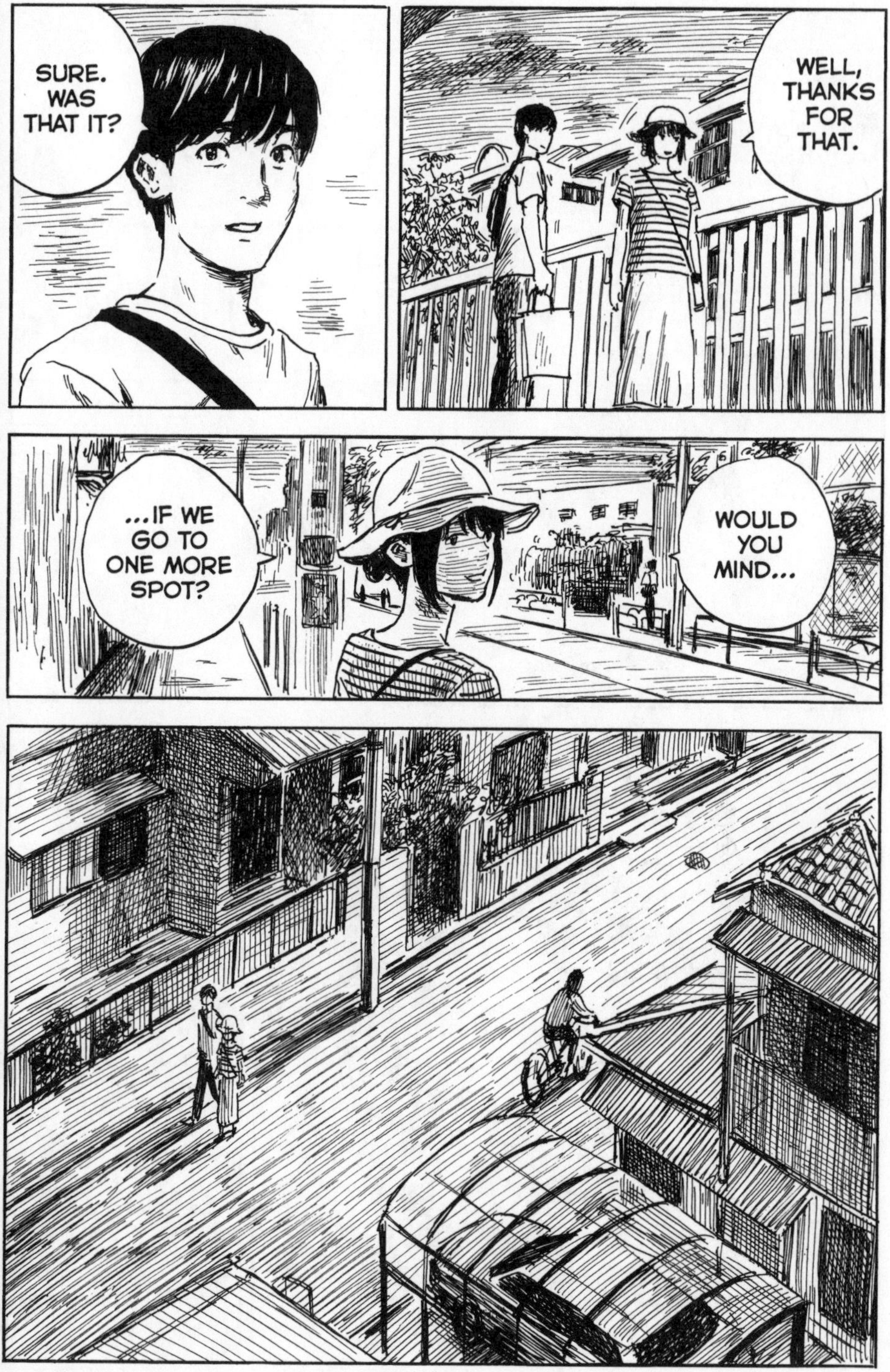
WELL, THANKS FOR THAT.
SURE. WAS THAT IT?
WOULD YOU MIND...
...IF WE GO TO ONE MORE SPOT?

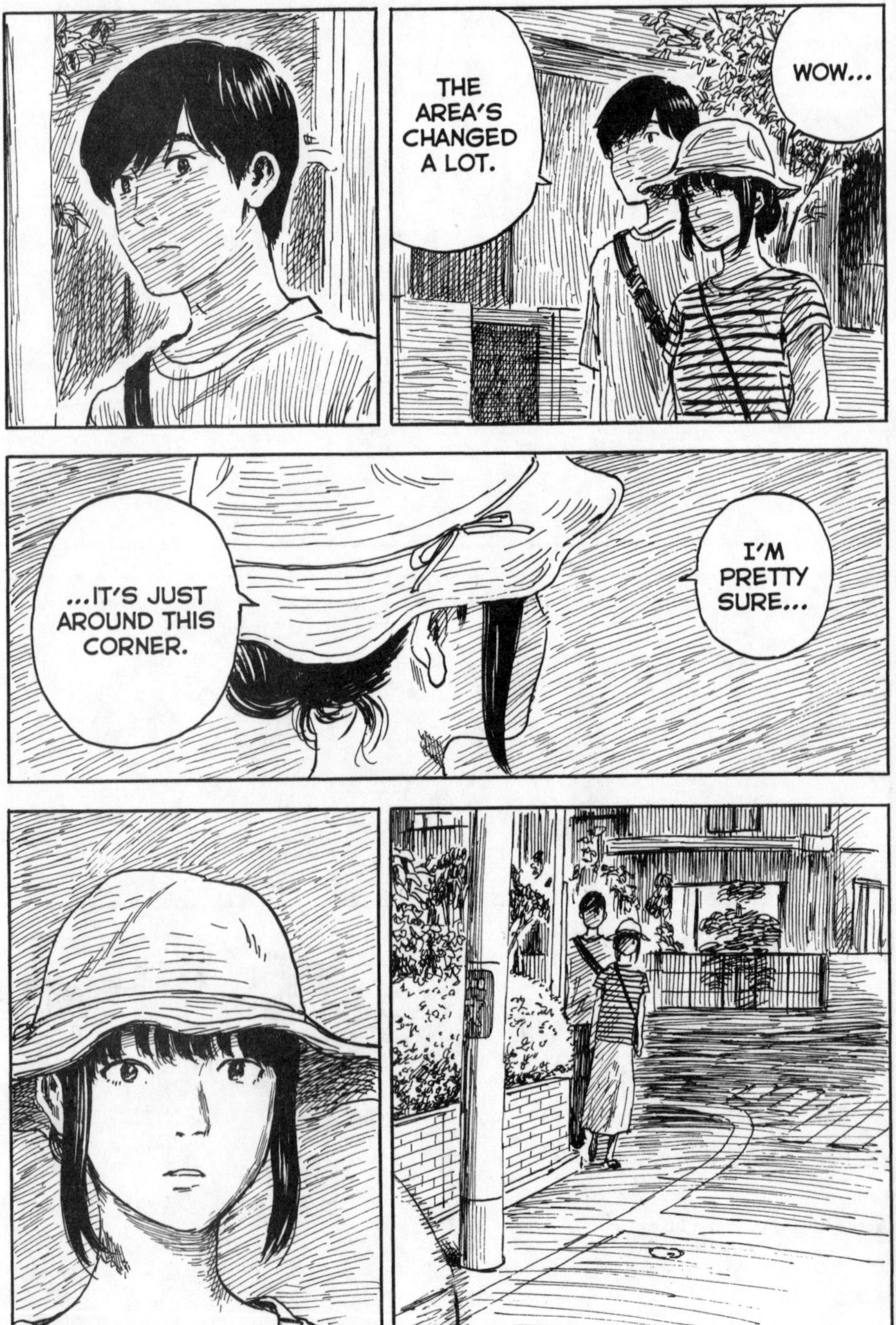
WOW...
THE AREA'S CHANGED A LOT.
I'M PRETTY SURE...
...IT'S JUST AROUND THIS CORNER.

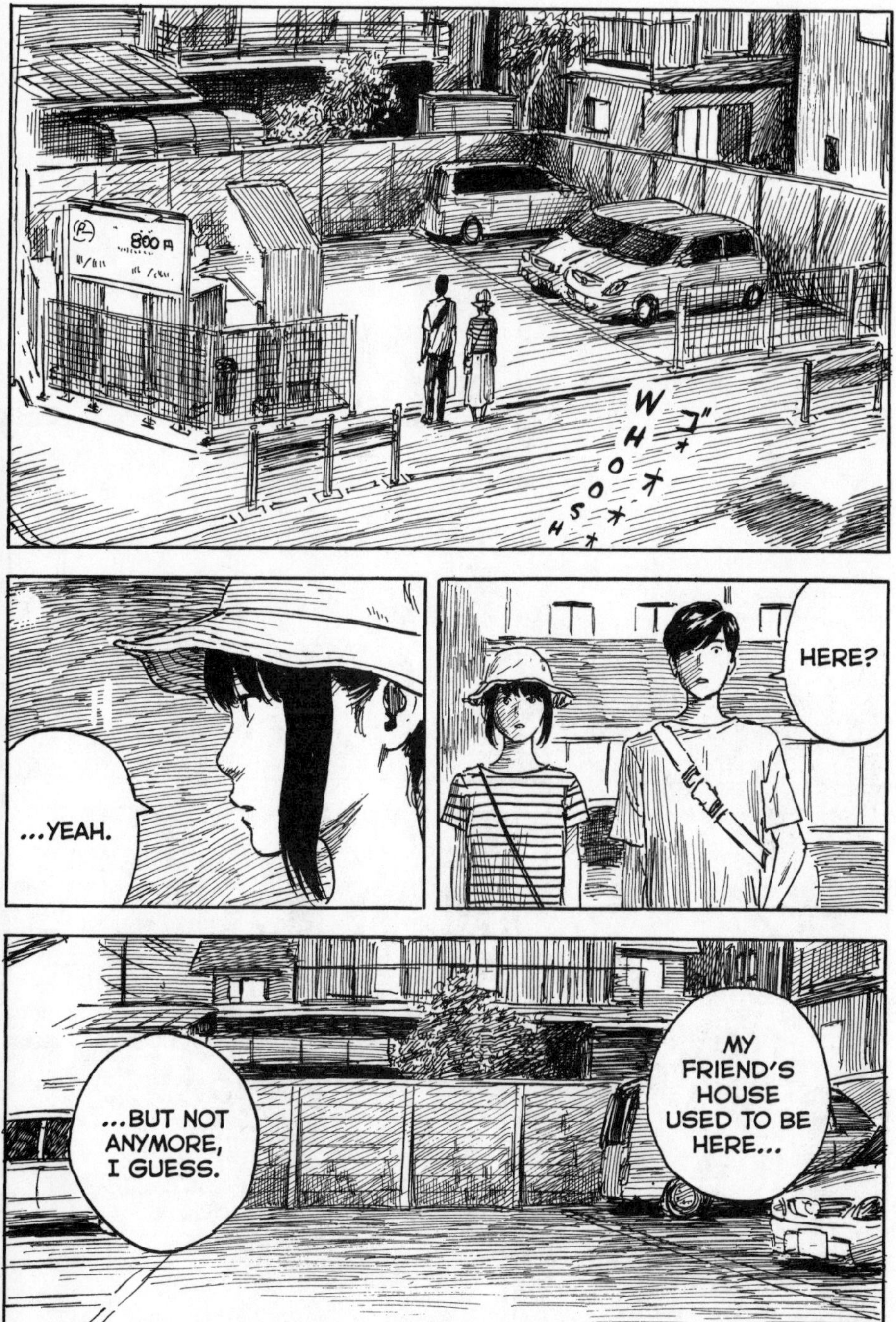
WHOOSH
HERE?
...YEAH.
MY FRIEND'S HOUSE USED TO BE HERE...
...BUT NOT ANYMORE, I GUESS.

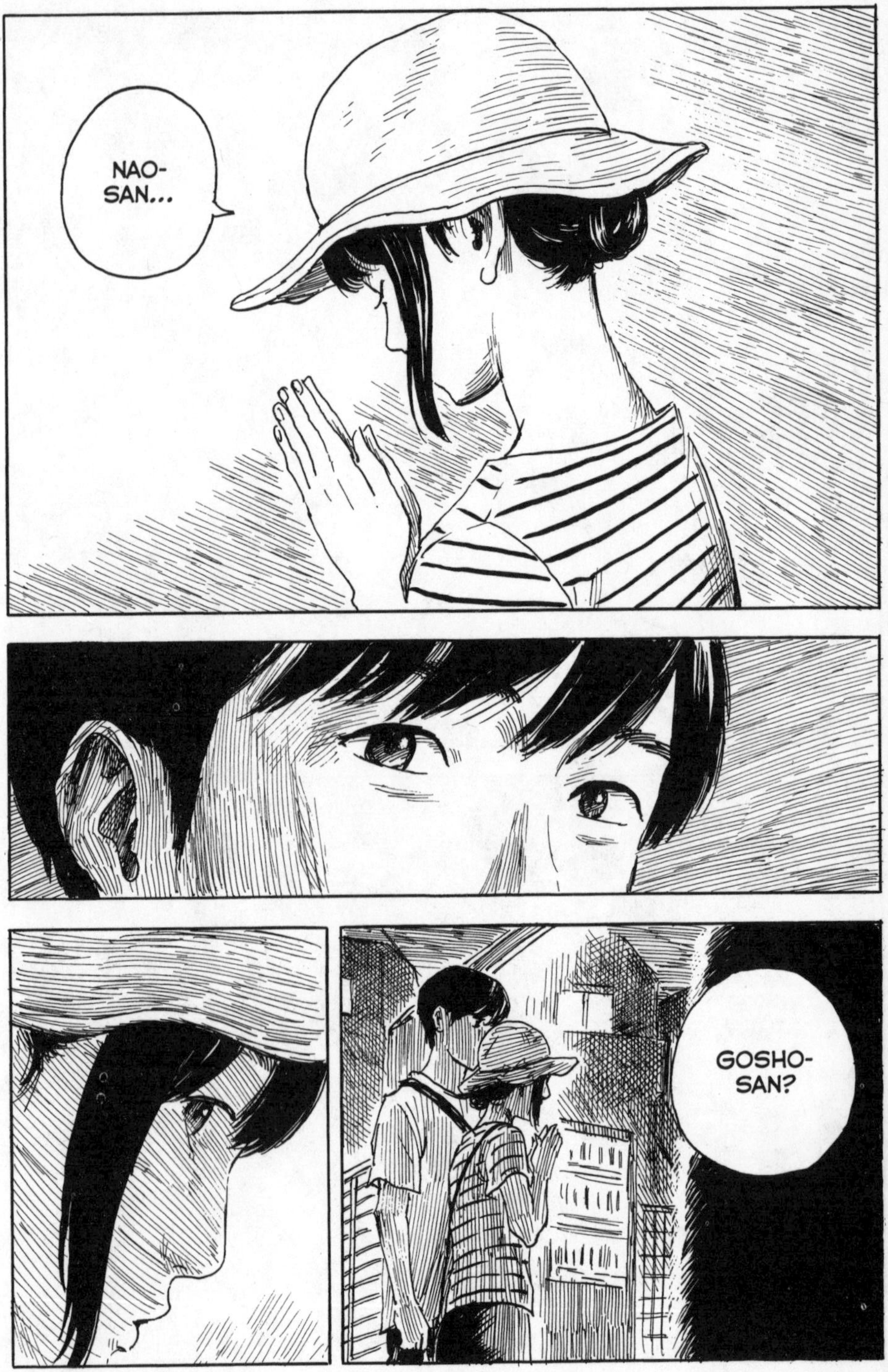
NAO-SAN...
GOSHO-SAN?

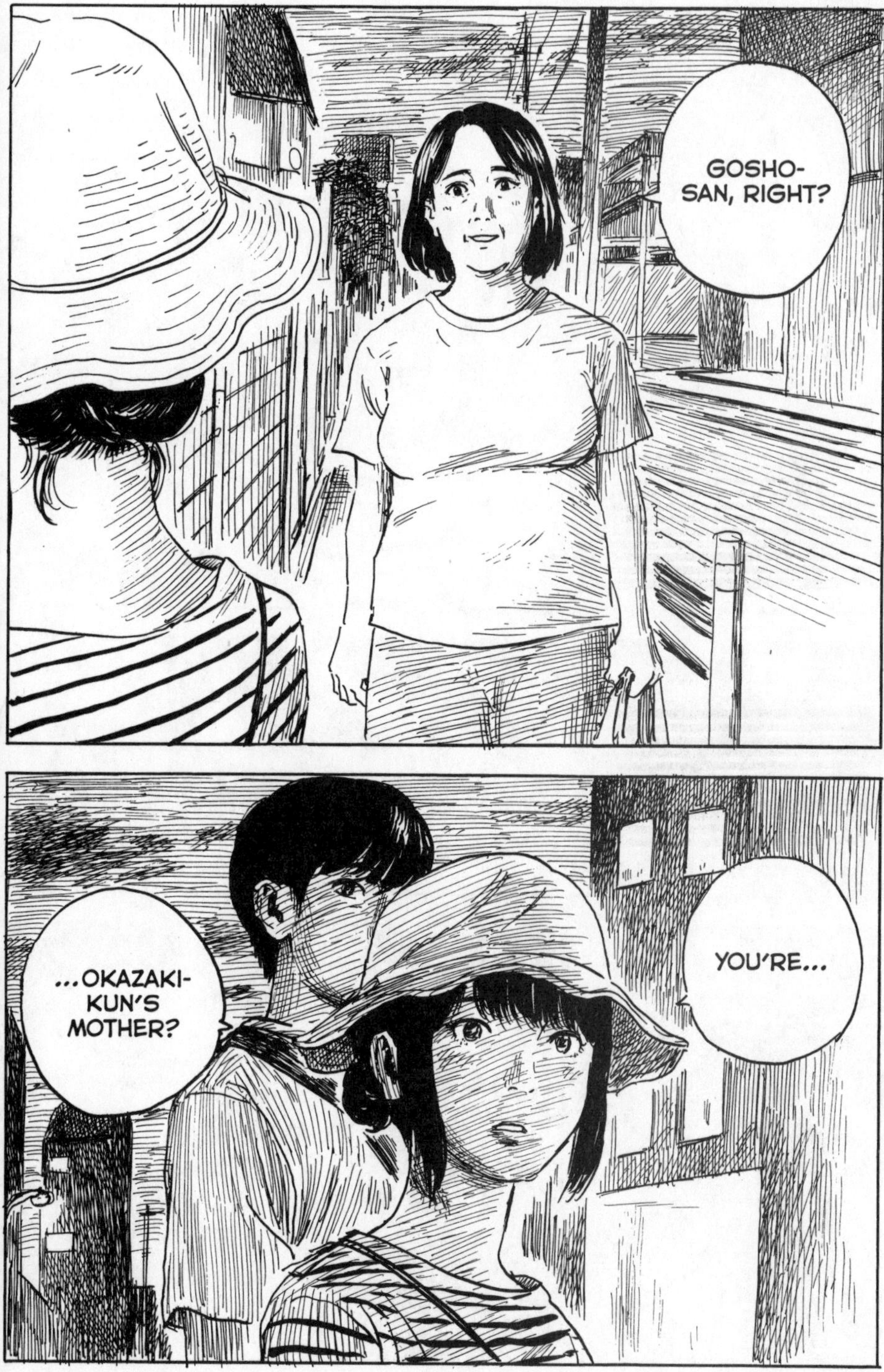
GOSHO-SAN, RIGHT?
YOU'RE...
...OKAZAKI-KUN'S MOTHER?

Chapter 29: Looking Back

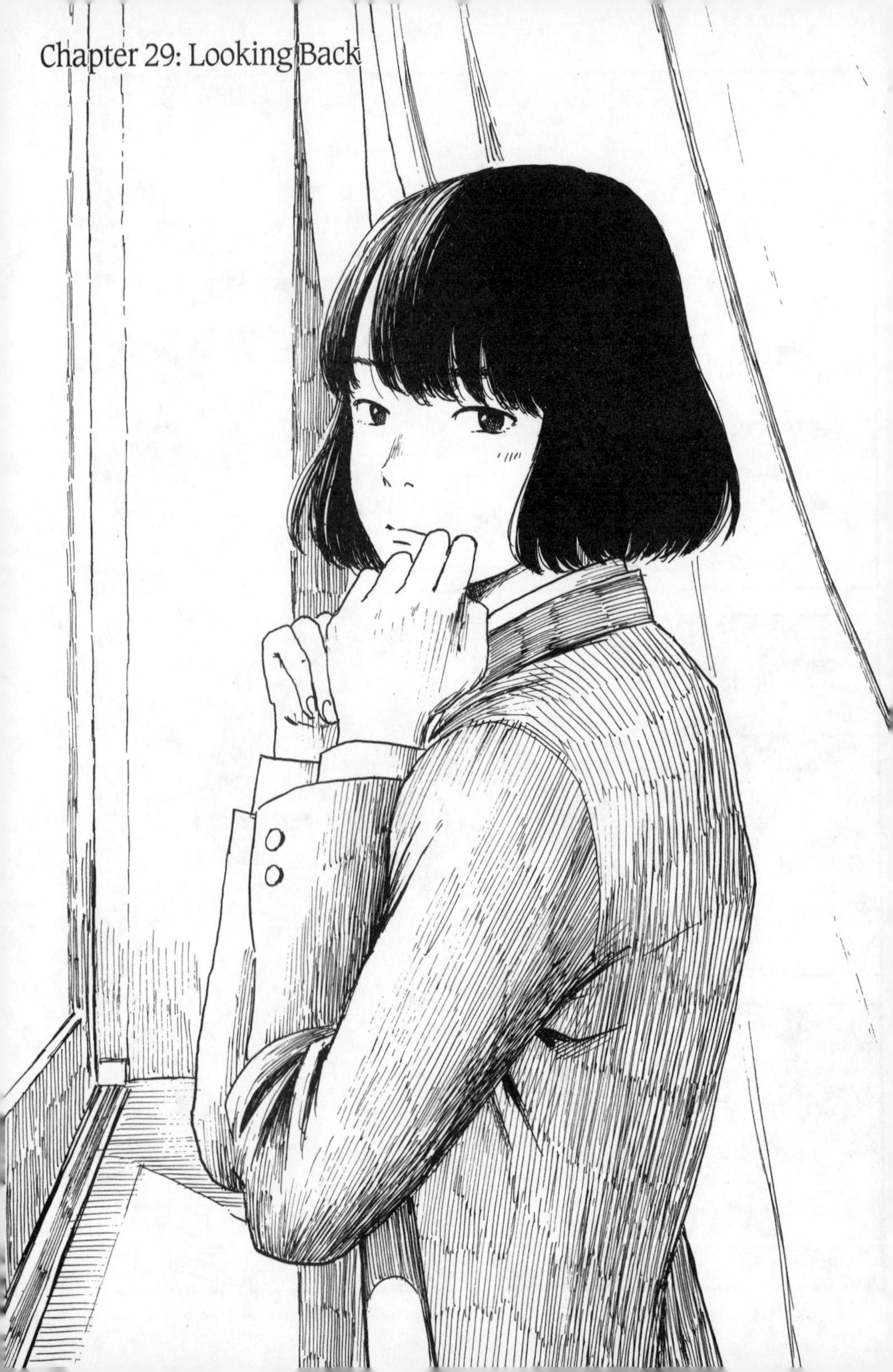

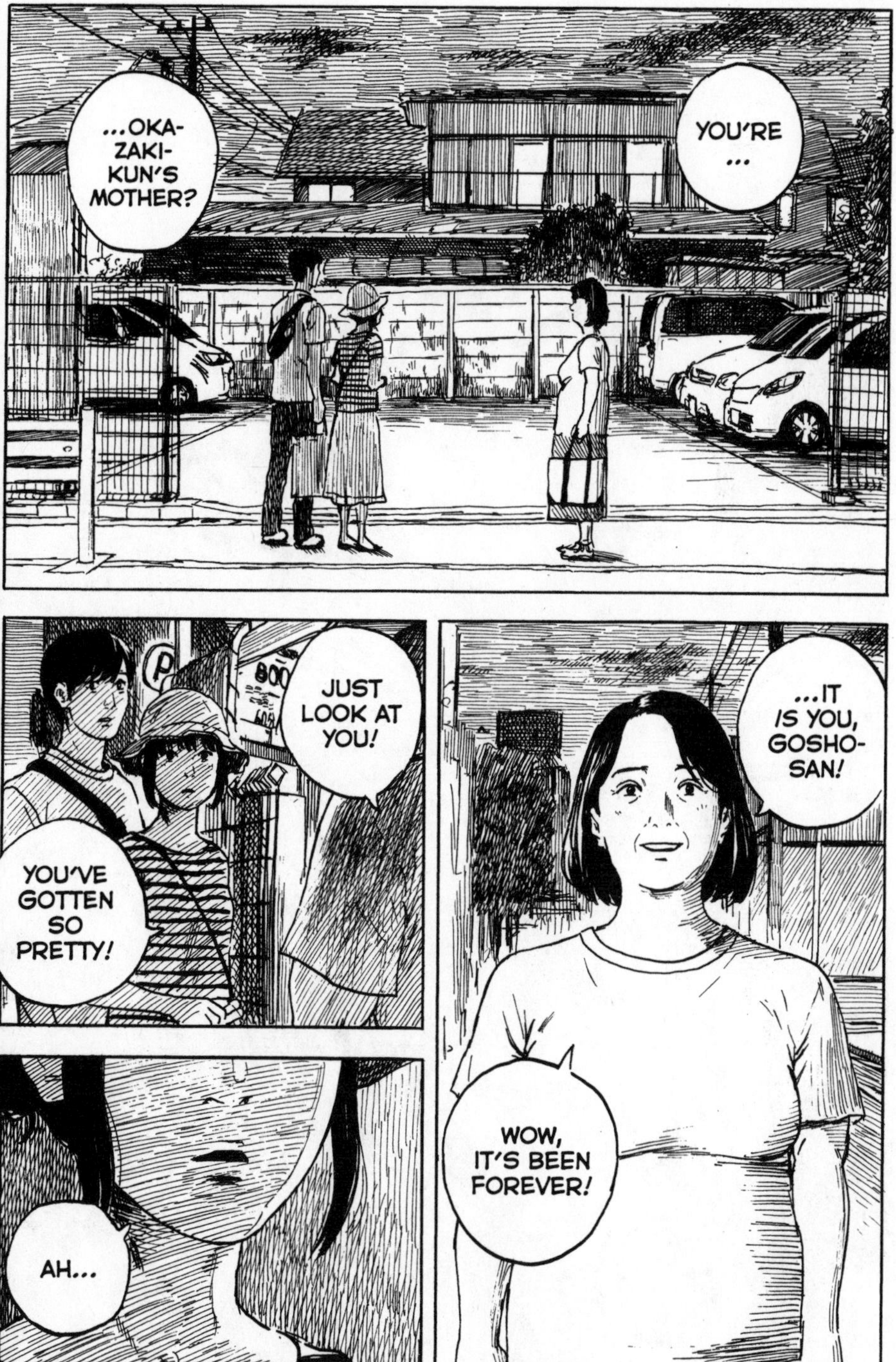
YOU'RE ...
...OKAZAKI-KUN'S MOTHER?
...IT IS YOU, GOSHO-SAN!
WOW, IT'S BEEN FOREVER!
JUST LOOK AT YOU!
YOU'VE GOTTEN SO PRETTY!
AH...

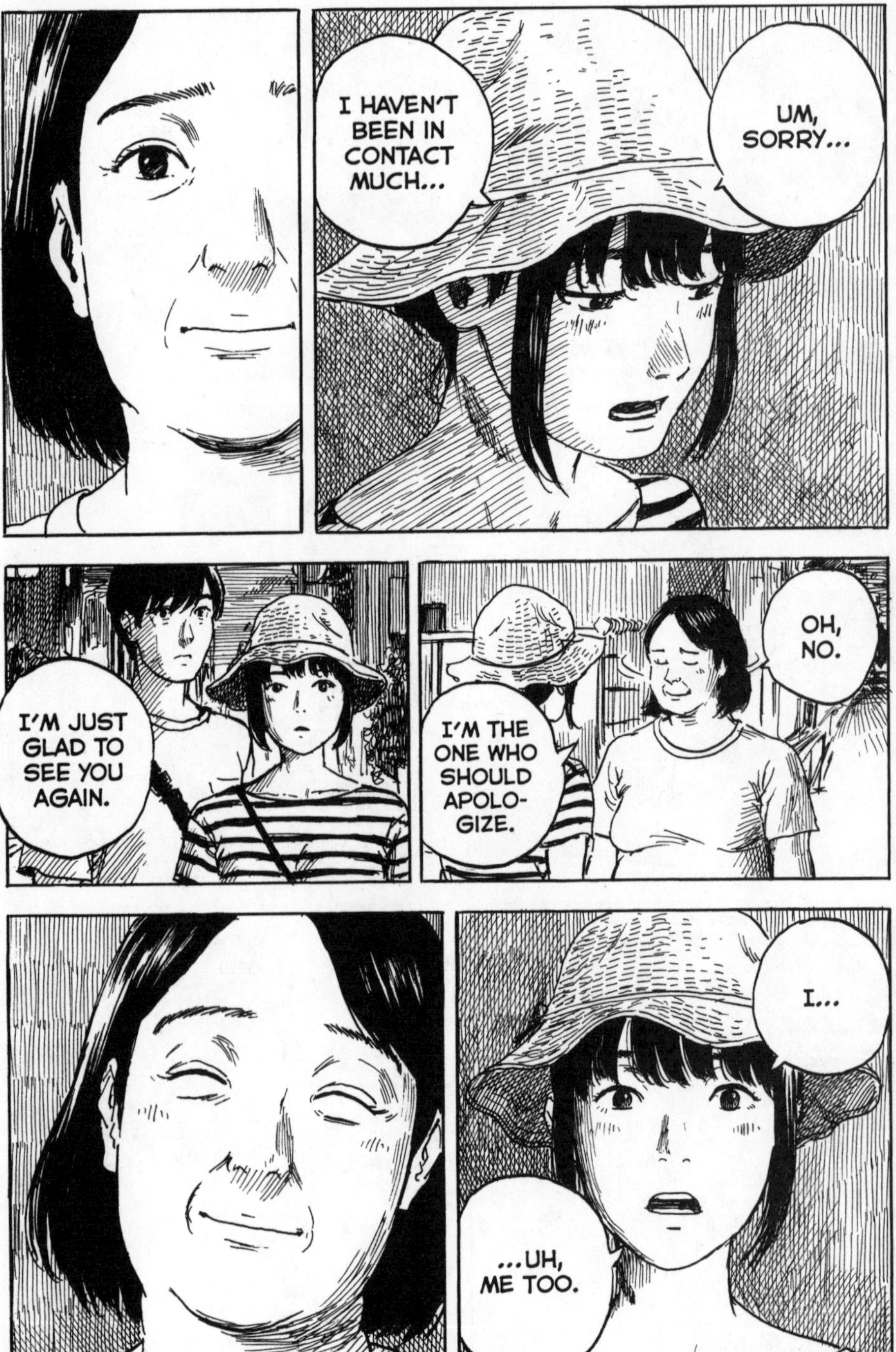
UM, SORRY...
I HAVEN'T BEEN IN CONTACT MUCH...
OH, NO.
I'M THE ONE WHO SHOULD APOLO-GIZE.
I'M JUST GLAD TO SEE YOU AGAIN.
I...
...UH, ME TOO.

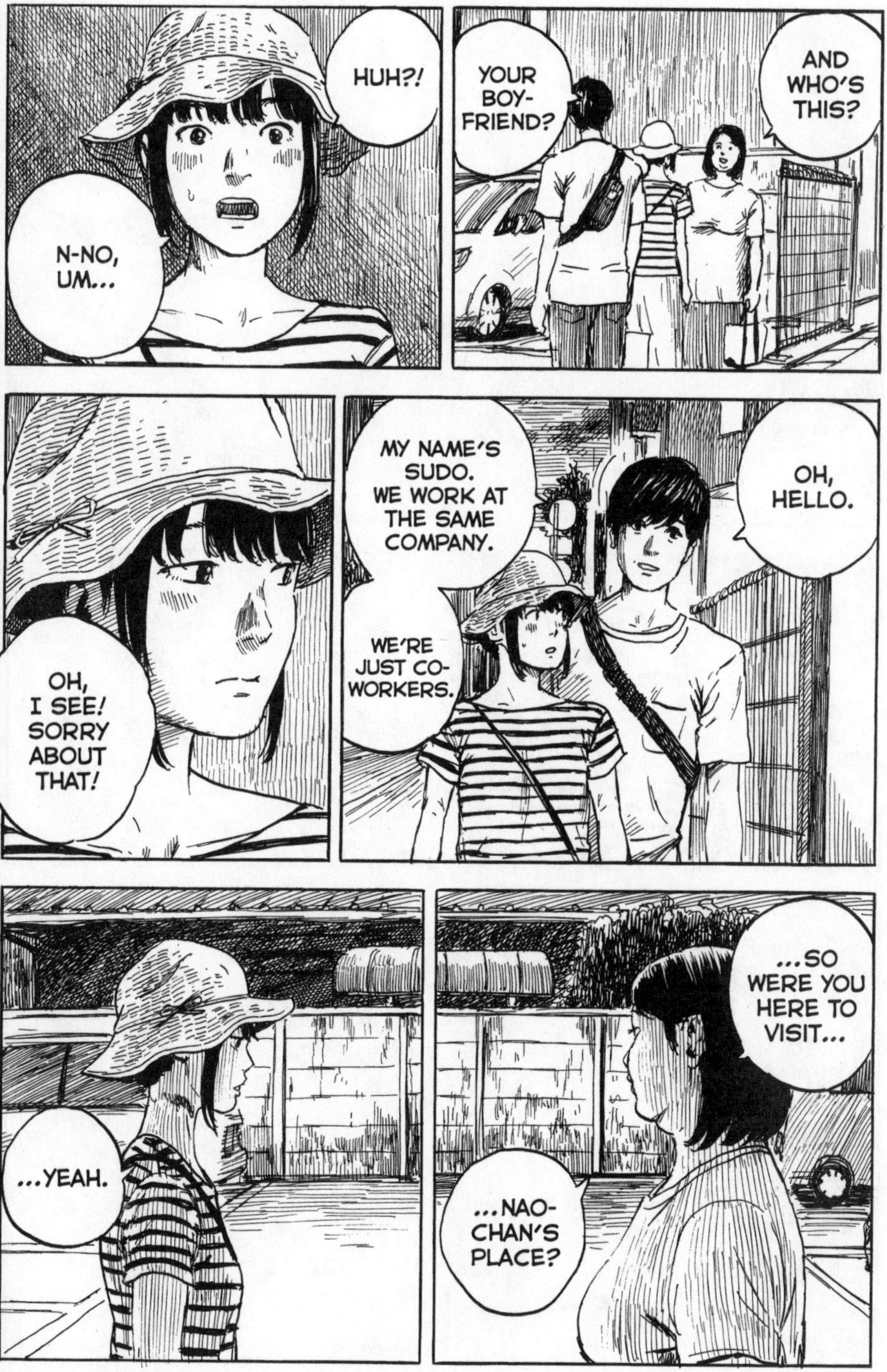
AND WHO'S THIS?
YOUR BOY-FRIEND?
HUH?!
N-NO, UM...
OH, HELLO.
MY NAME'S SUDO. WE WORK AT THE SAME COMPANY.
WE'RE JUST CO-WORKERS.
OH, I SEE! SORRY ABOUT THAT!
...SO WERE YOU HERE TO VISIT...
...NAO-CHAN'S PLACE?
...YEAH.

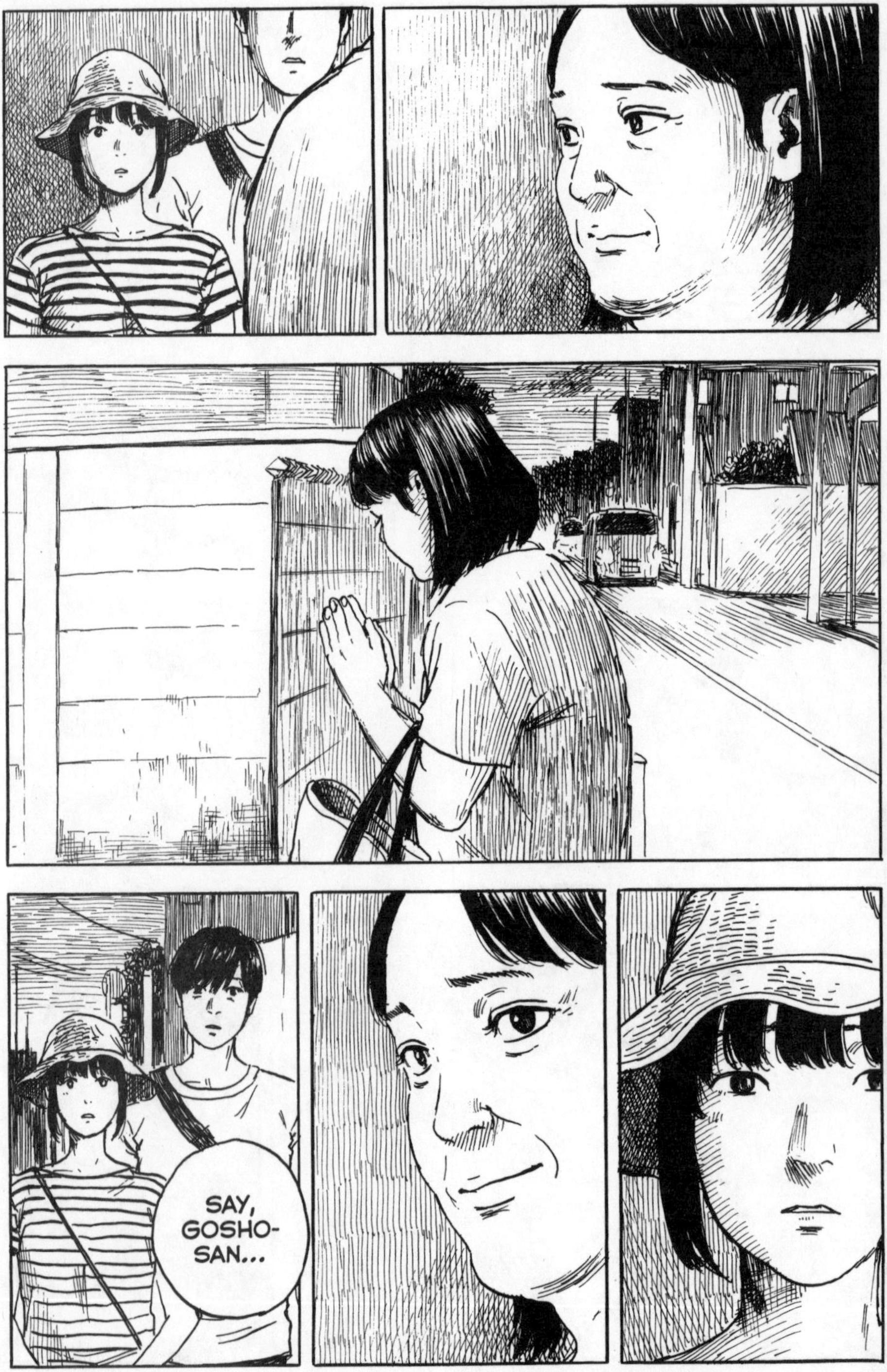
SAY, GOSHO-SAN...

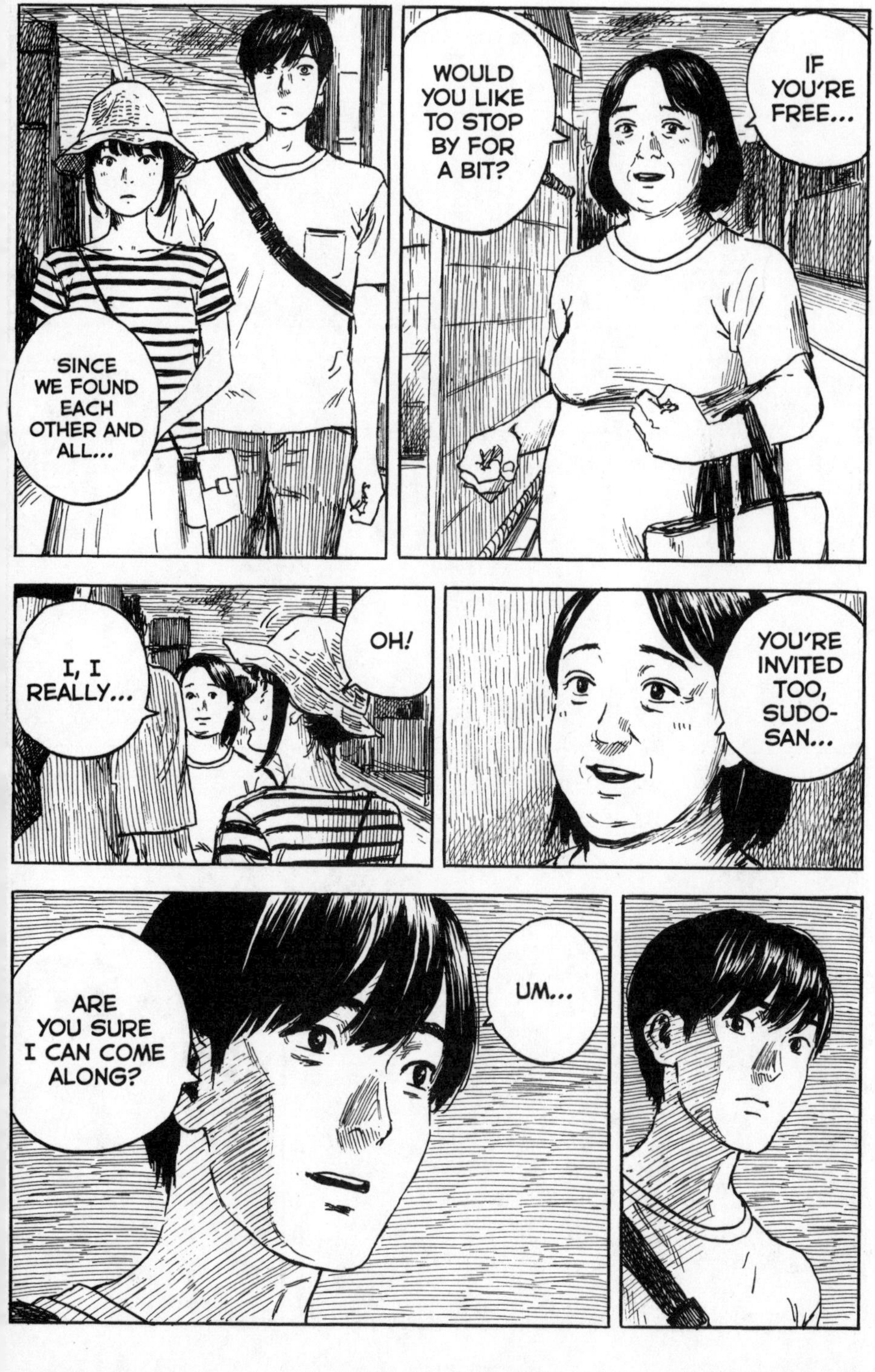
IF YOU'RE FREE...
WOULD YOU LIKE TO STOP BY FOR A BIT?
SINCE WE FOUND EACH OTHER AND ALL...
YOU'RE INVITED TOO, SUDO-SAN...
OH!
I, I REALLY...
UM...
ARE YOU SURE I CAN COME ALONG?

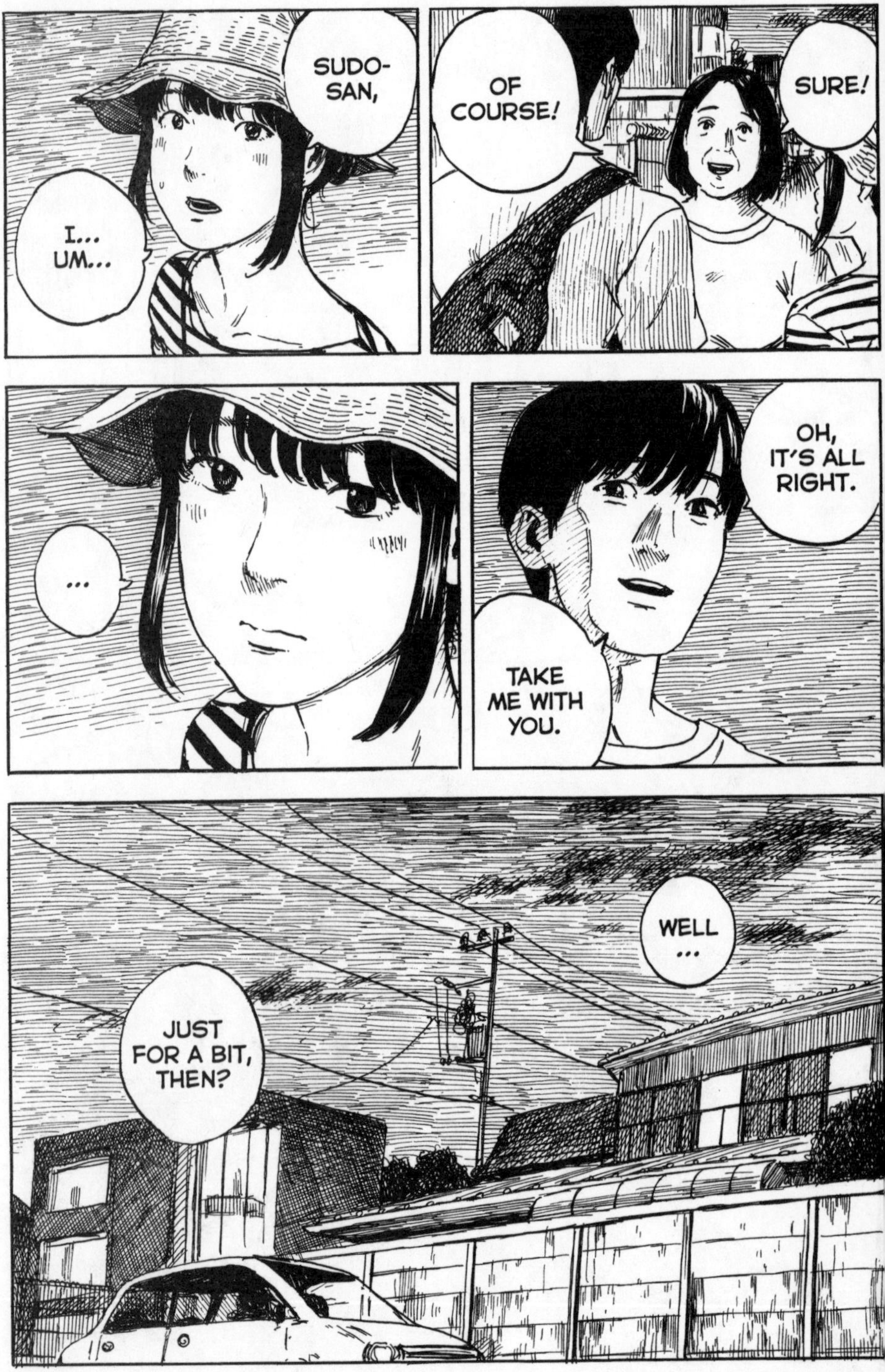
SURE!
OF COURSE!
SUDO-SAN,
I... UM...
OH, IT'S ALL RIGHT.
TAKE ME WITH YOU.
...
WELL ...
JUST FOR A BIT, THEN?

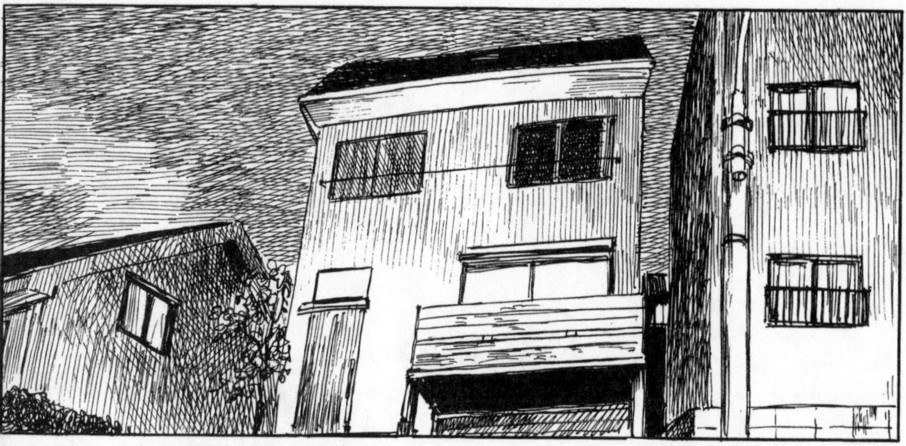

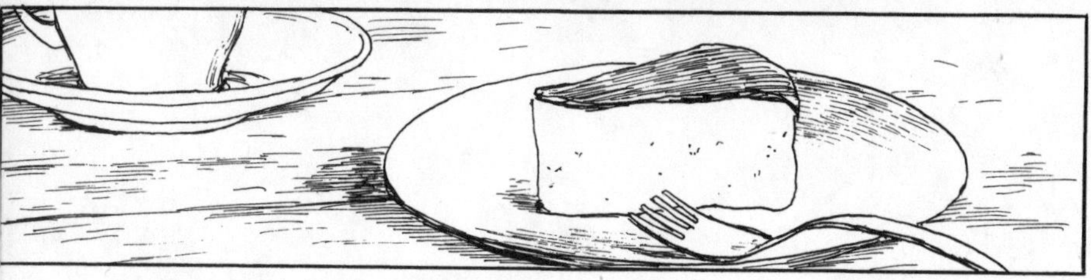

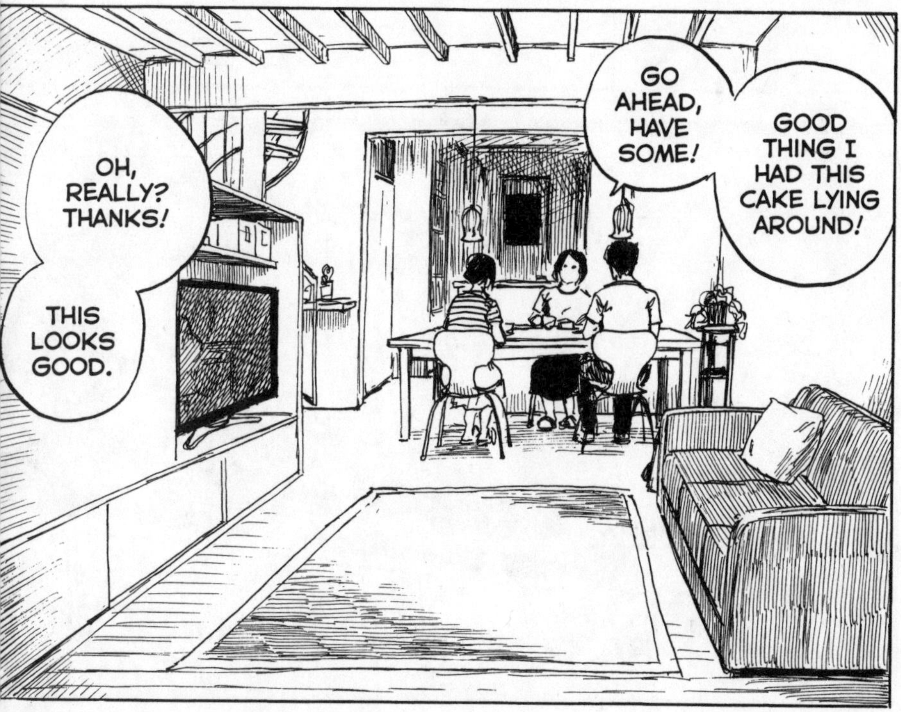
GOOD THING I HAD THIS CAKE LYING AROUND!
GO AHEAD, HAVE SOME!
OH, REALLY? THANKS!
THIS LOOKS GOOD.

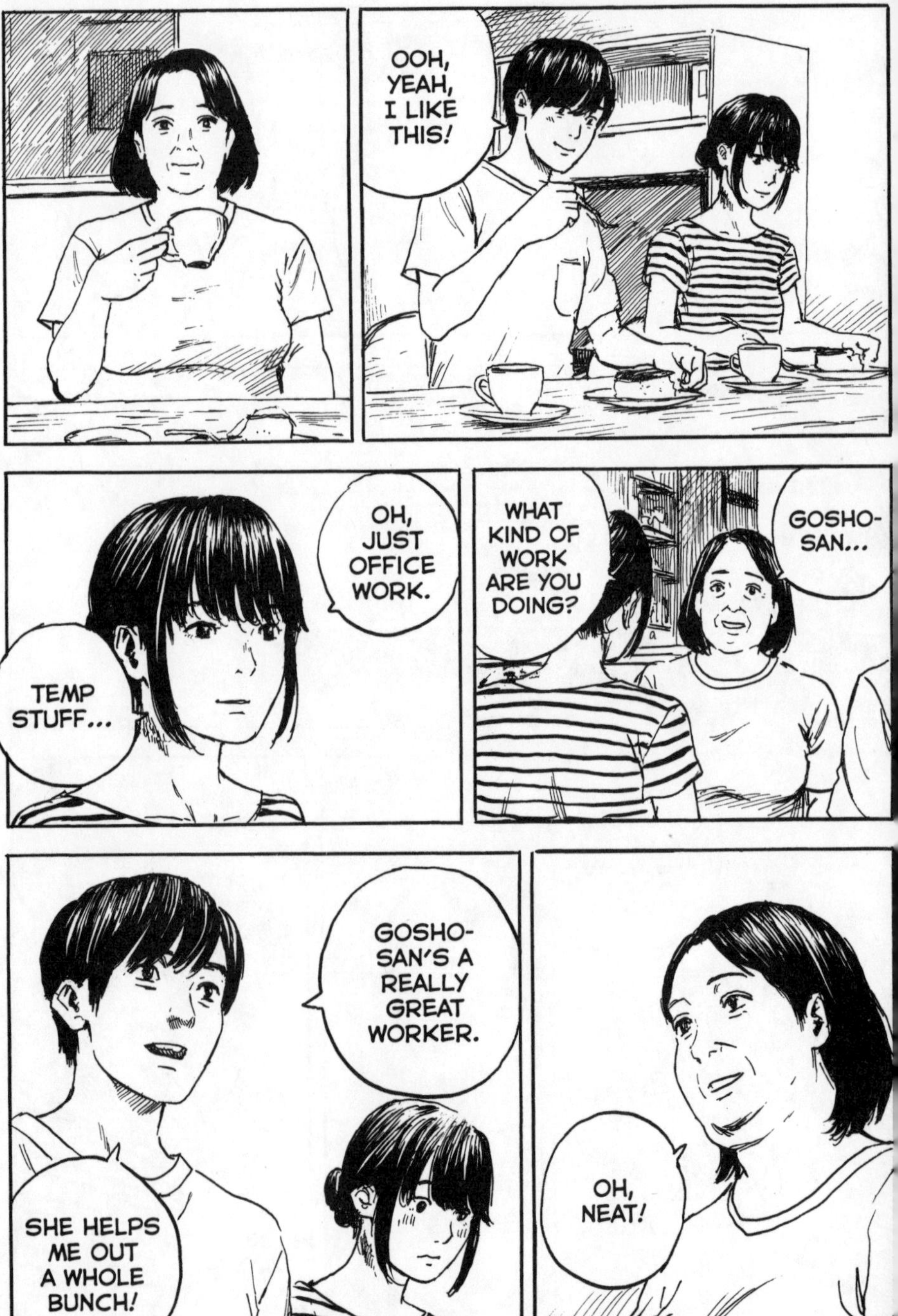
OOH, YEAH, I LIKE THIS!
GOSHO-SAN...
WHAT KIND OF WORK ARE YOU DOING?
OH, JUST OFFICE WORK.
TEMP STUFF...
OH, NEAT!
GOSHO-SAN'S A REALLY GREAT WORKER.
SHE HELPS ME OUT A WHOLE BUNCH!

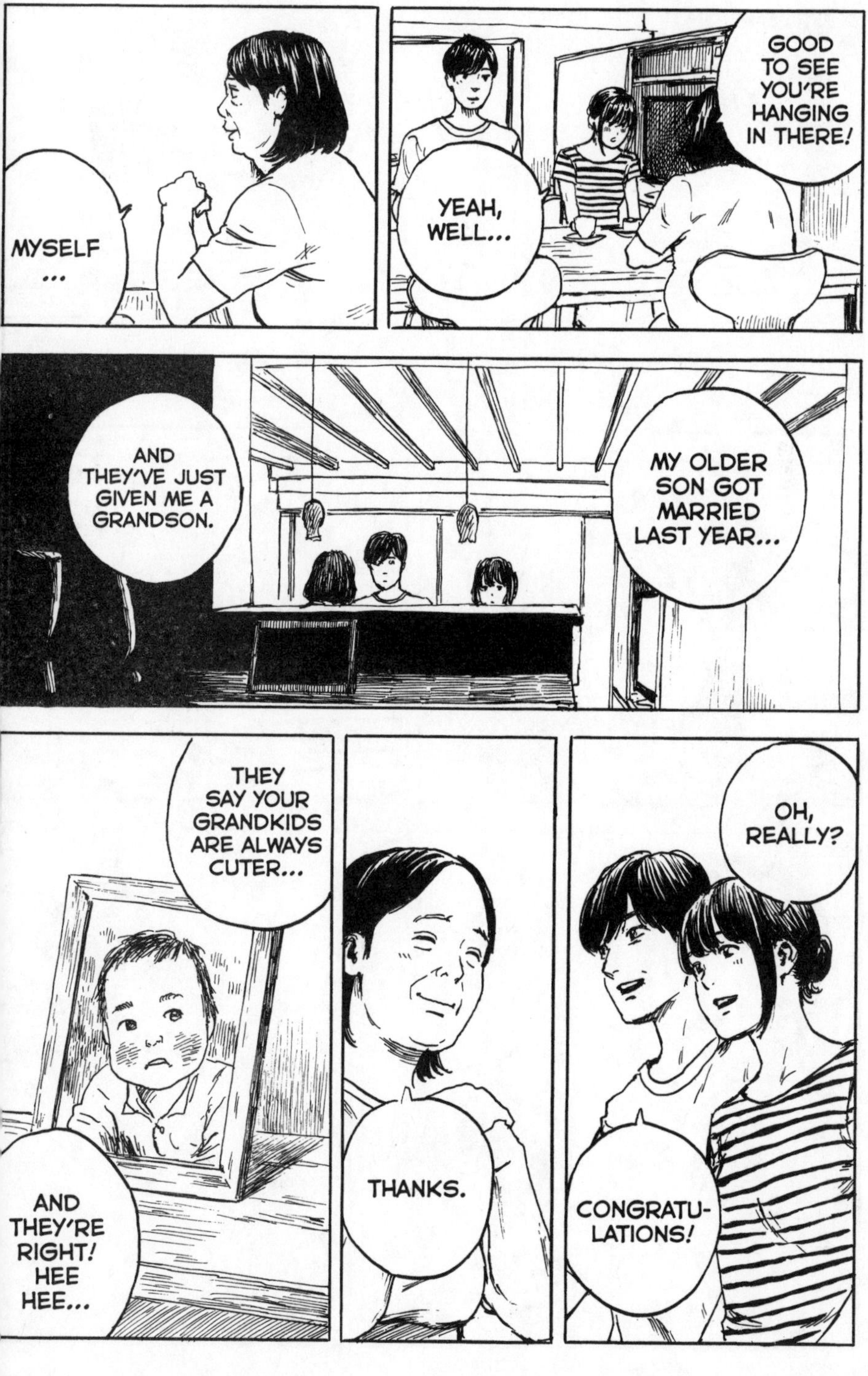
GOOD TO SEE YOU'RE HANGING IN THERE!
YEAH, WELL...
MYSELF ...
MY OLDER SON GOT MARRIED LAST YEAR...
AND THEY'VE JUST GIVEN ME A GRANDSON.
OH, REALLY?
CONGRATULATIONS!
THANKS.
THEY SAY YOUR GRANDKIDS ARE ALWAYS CUTER...
AND THEY'RE RIGHT! HEE HEE...

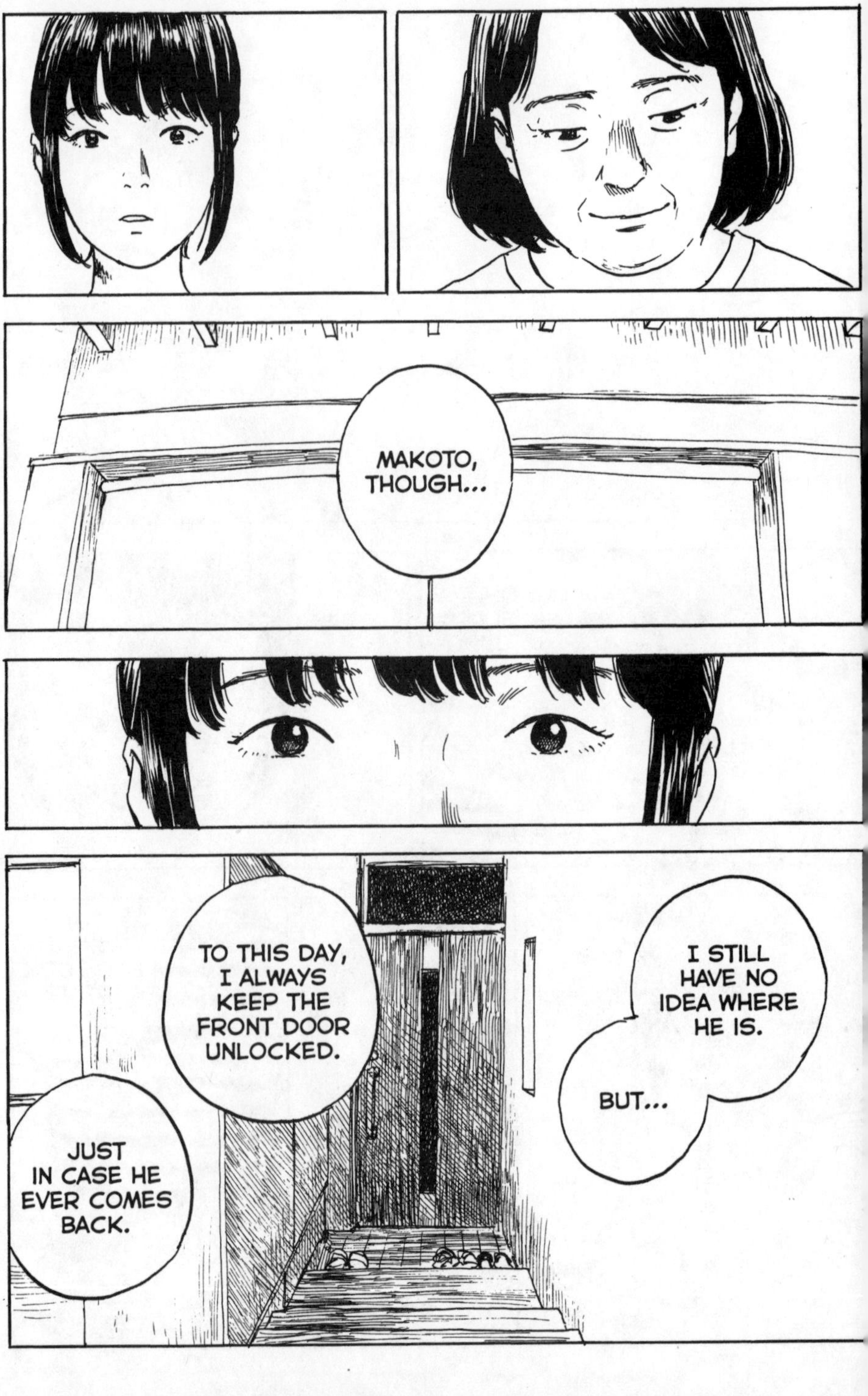
MAKOTO, THOUGH...
I STILL HAVE NO IDEA WHERE HE IS.
BUT...
TO THIS DAY, I ALWAYS KEEP THE FRONT DOOR UNLOCKED.
JUST IN CASE HE EVER COMES BACK.

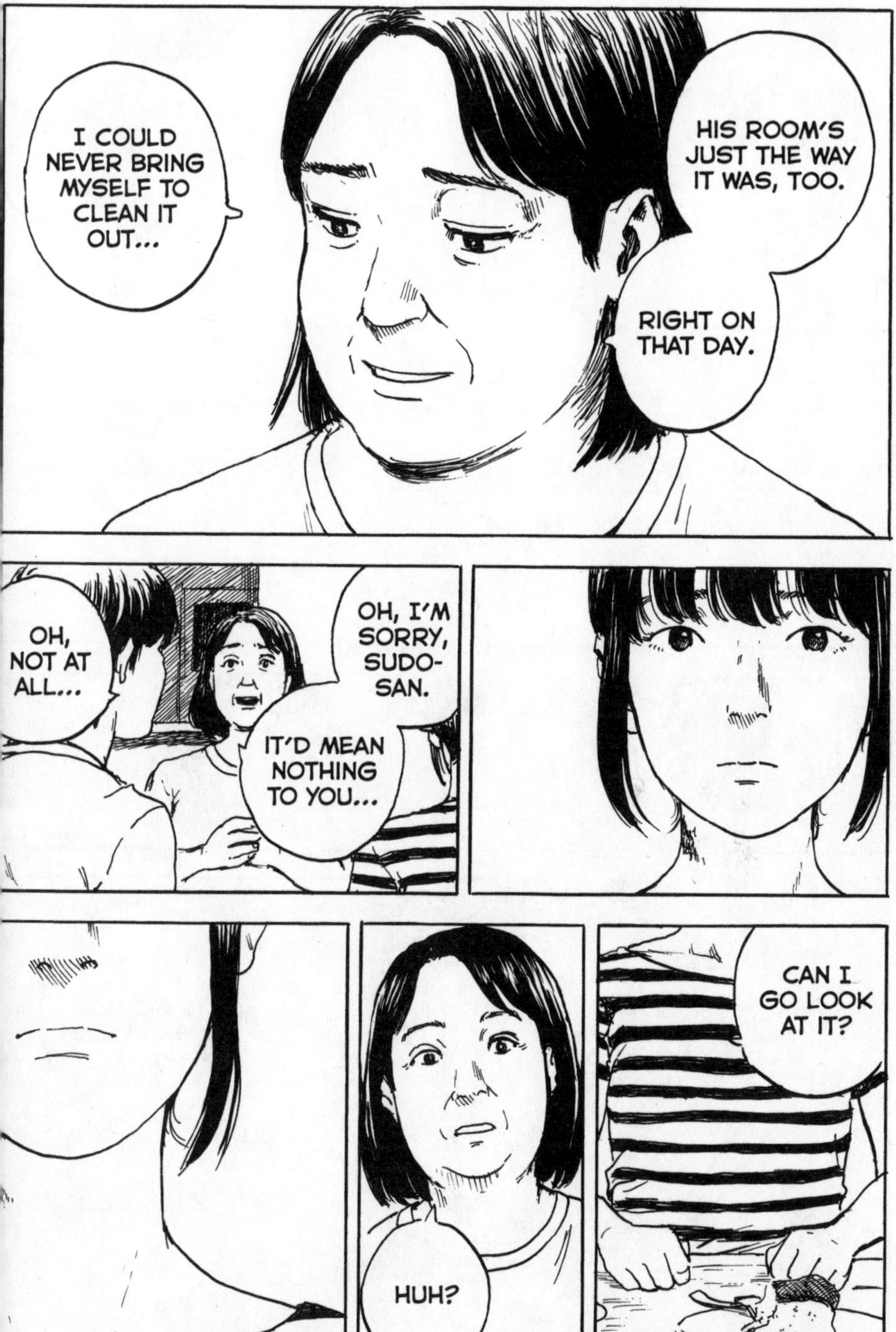
HIS ROOM'S JUST THE WAY IT WAS, TOO.
RIGHT ON THAT DAY.
I COULD NEVER BRING MYSELF TO CLEAN IT OUT...
OH, I'M SORRY, SUDO-SAN.
IT'D MEAN NOTHING TO YOU...
OH, NOT AT ALL...
CAN I GO LOOK AT IT?
HUH?

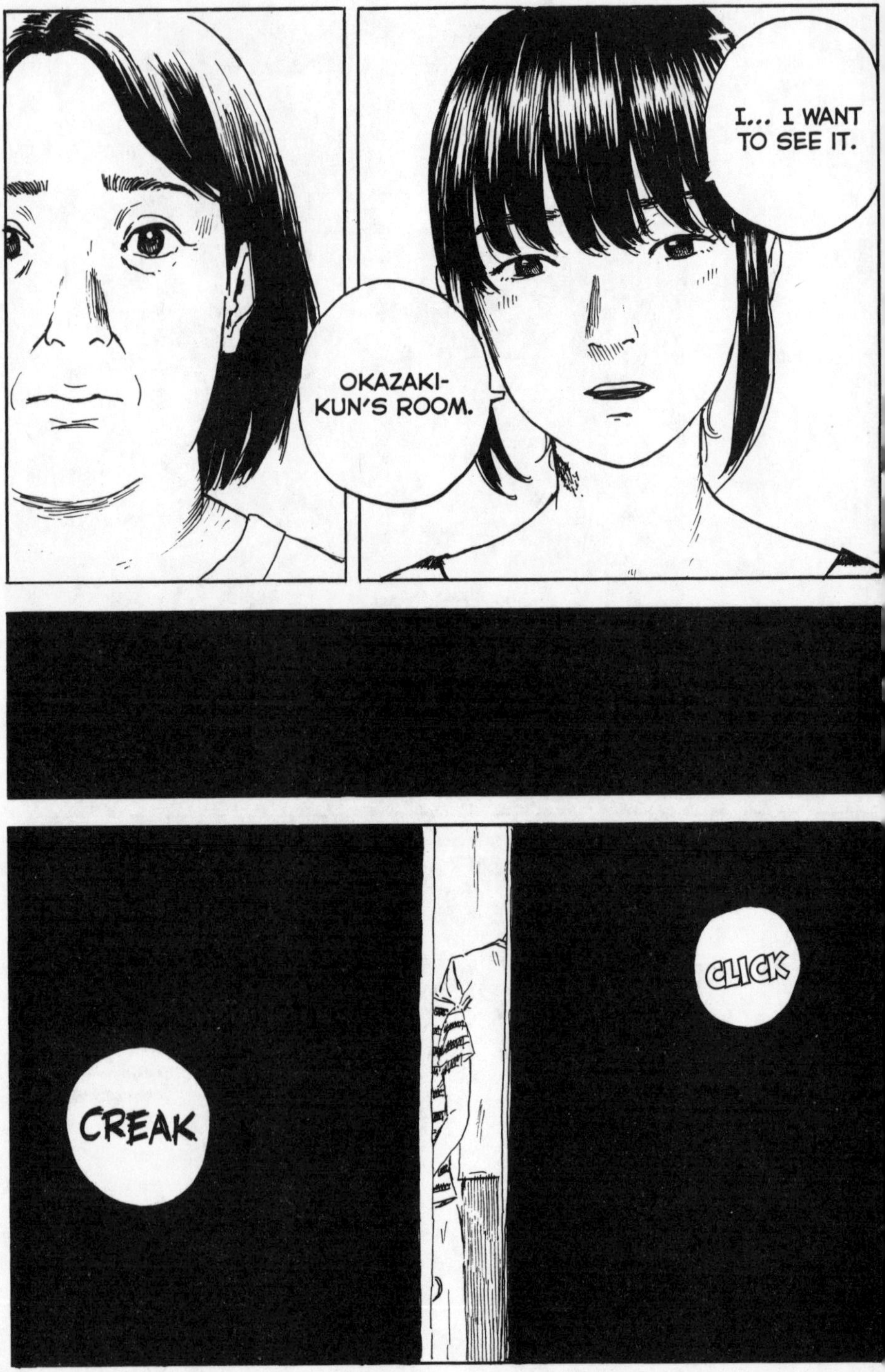
I... I WANT TO SEE IT.
OKAZAKI-KUN'S ROOM.
CLICK
CREAK

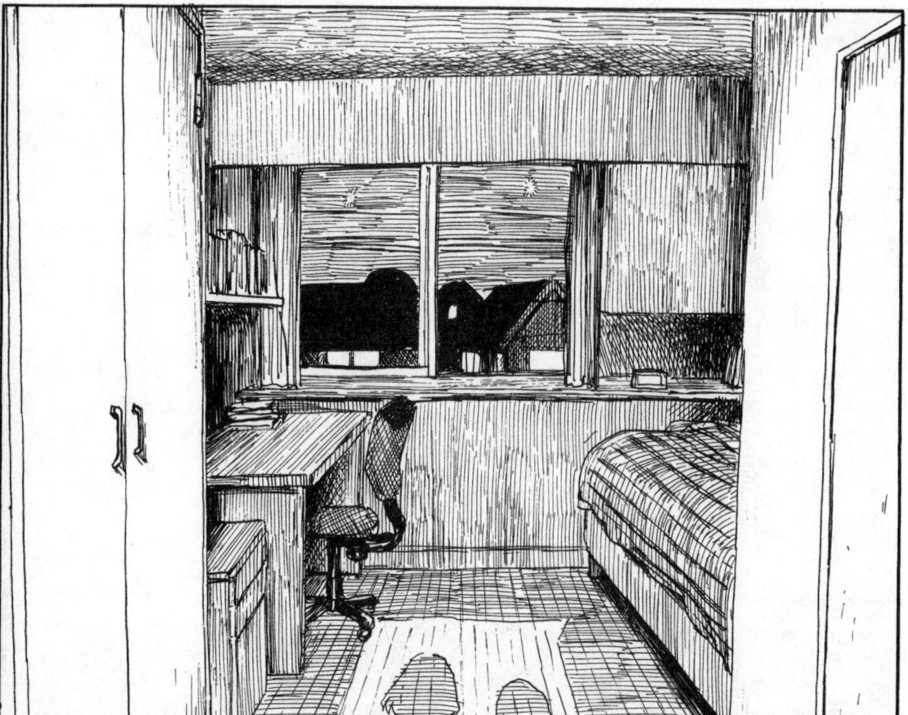

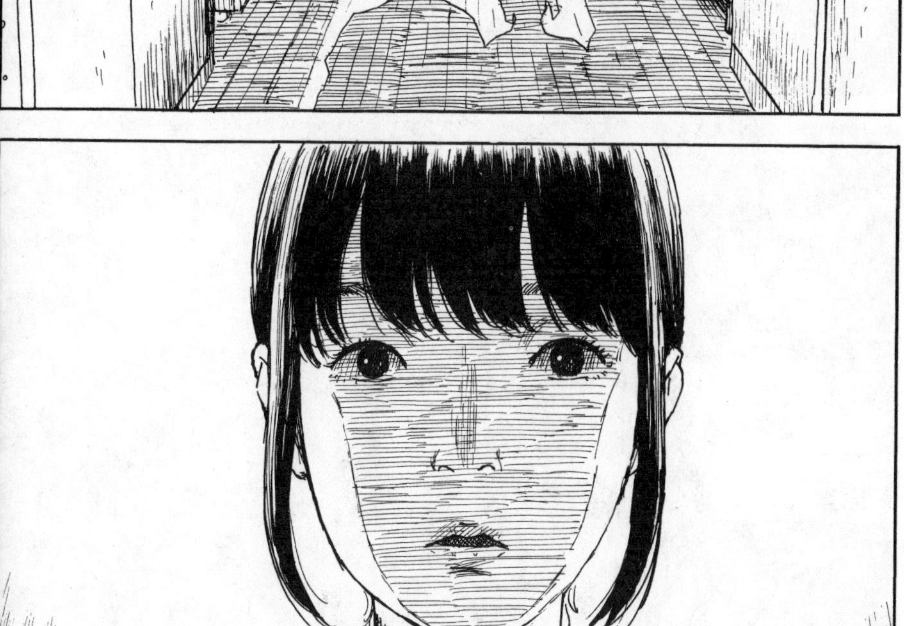

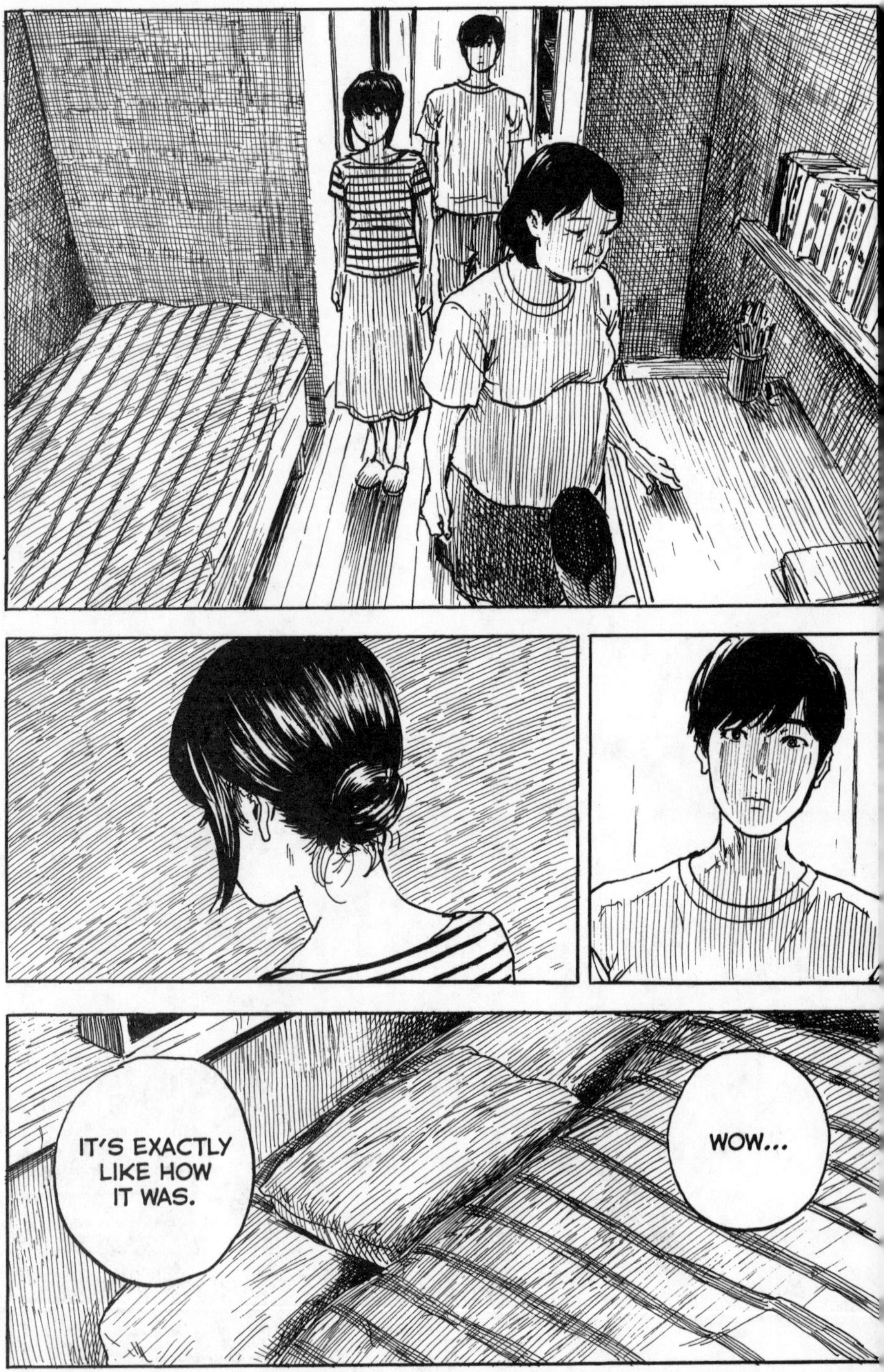
WOW...
IT'S EXACTLY LIKE HOW IT WAS.

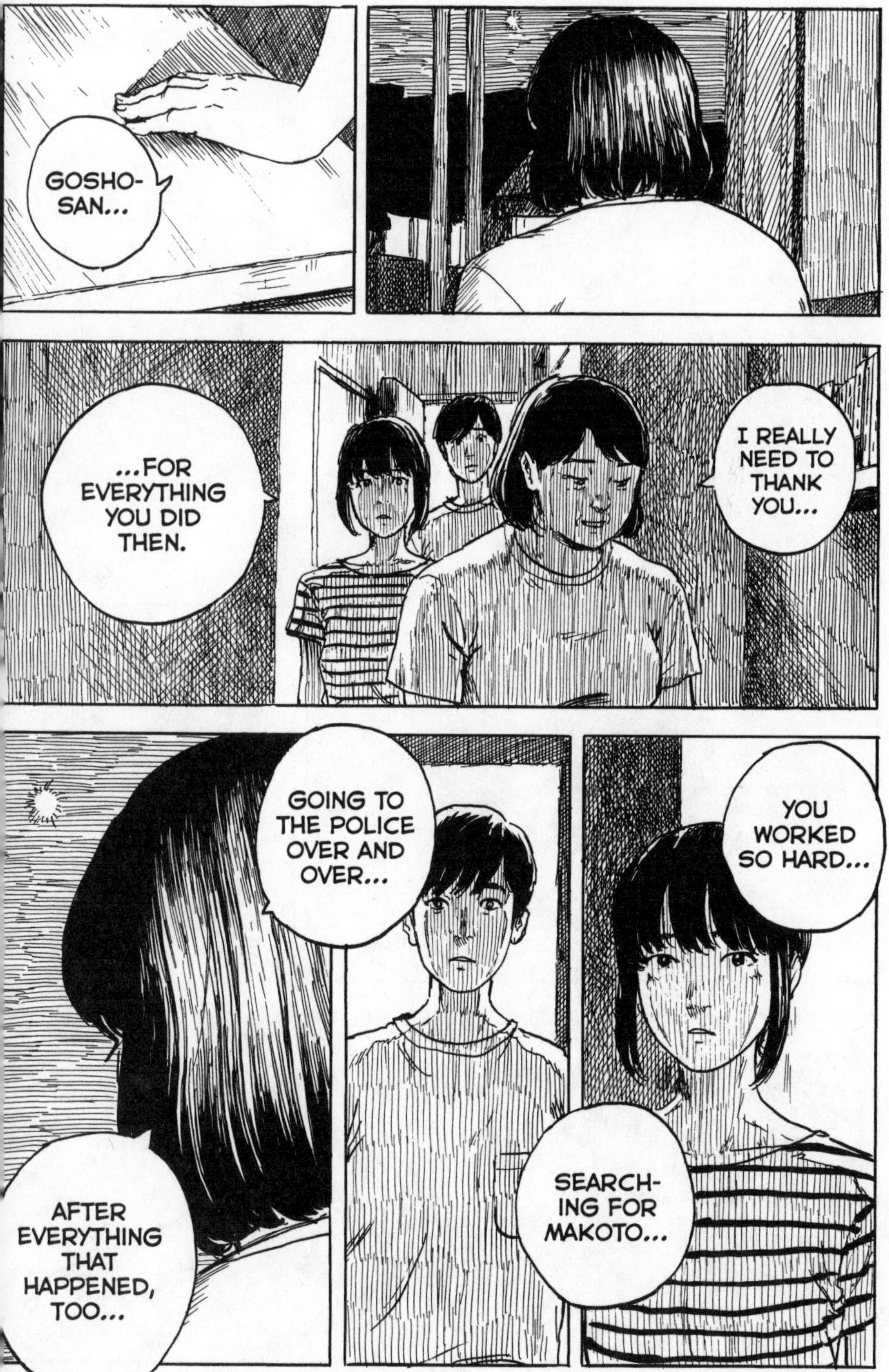
GOSHO-SAN...
I REALLY NEED TO THANK YOU...
...FOR EVERYTHING YOU DID THEN.
YOU WORKED SO HARD...
SEARCHING FOR MAKOTO...
GOING TO THE POLICE OVER AND OVER...
AFTER EVERYTHING THAT HAPPENED, TOO...

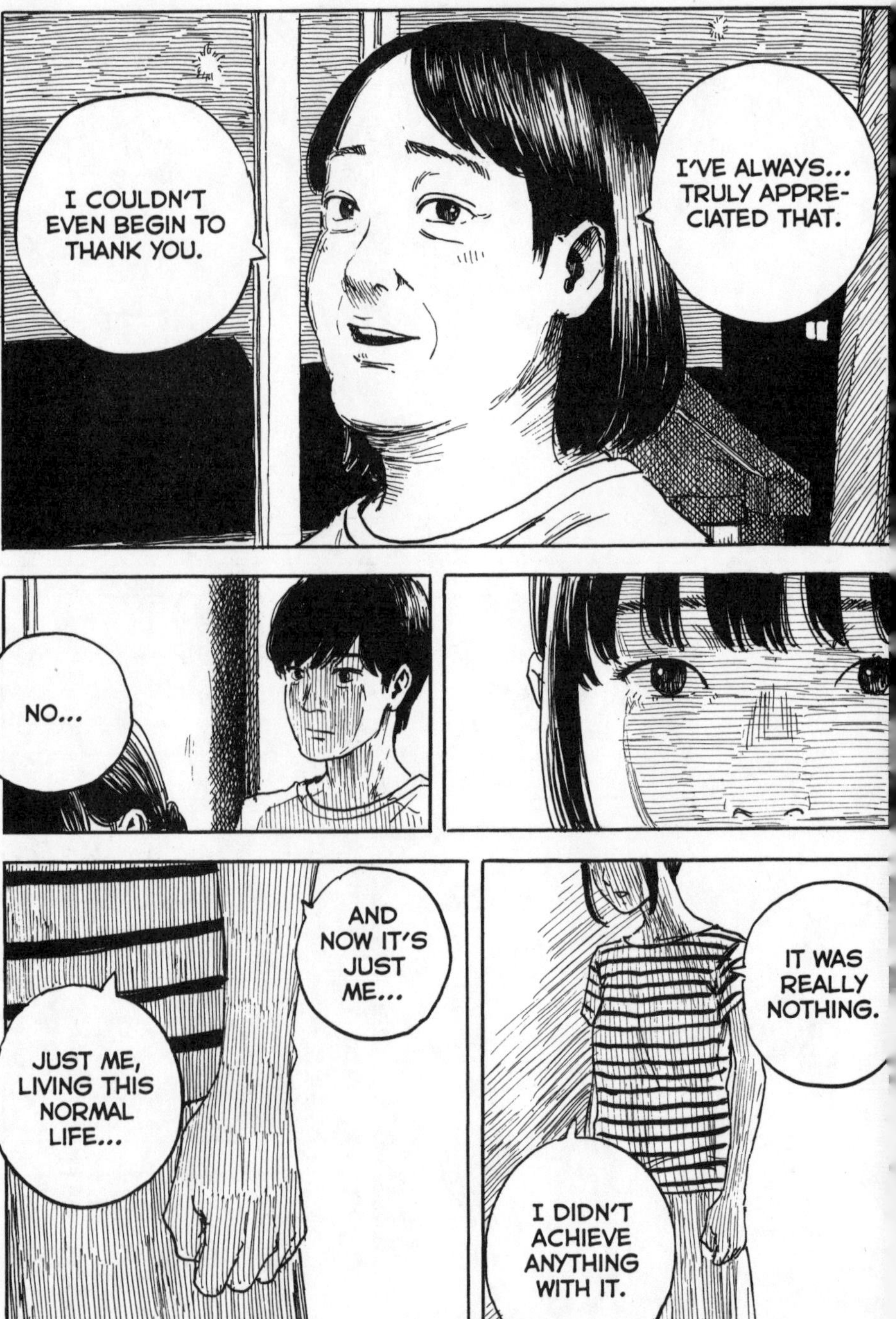
I'VE ALWAYS... TRULY APPRECIATED THAT.
I COULDN'T EVEN BEGIN TO THANK YOU.
NO...
IT WAS REALLY NOTHING.
I DIDN'T ACHIEVE ANYTHING WITH IT.
AND NOW IT'S JUST ME...
JUST ME, LIVING THIS NORMAL LIFE...

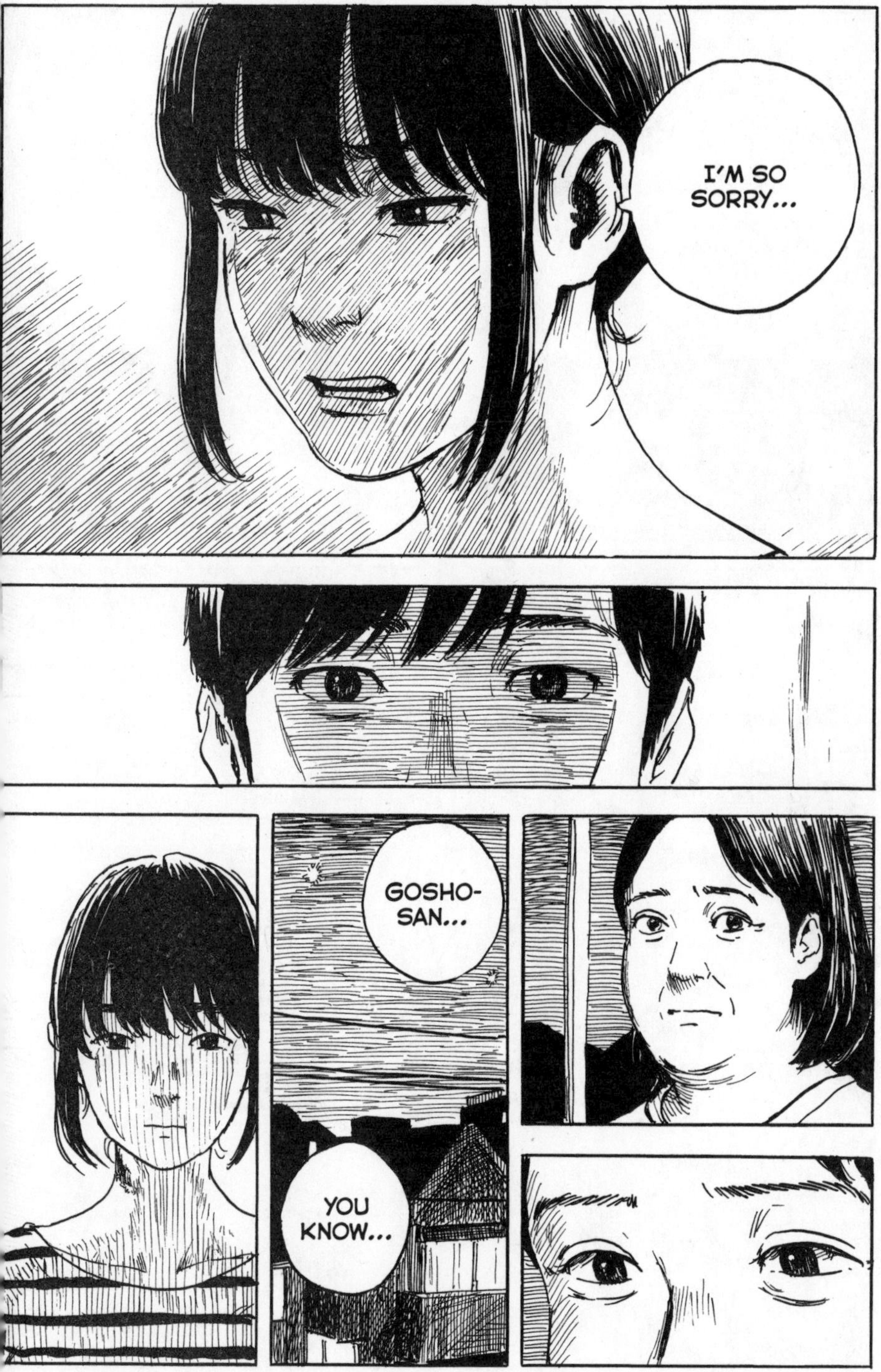
I'M SO SORRY...
GOSHO-SAN...
YOU KNOW...

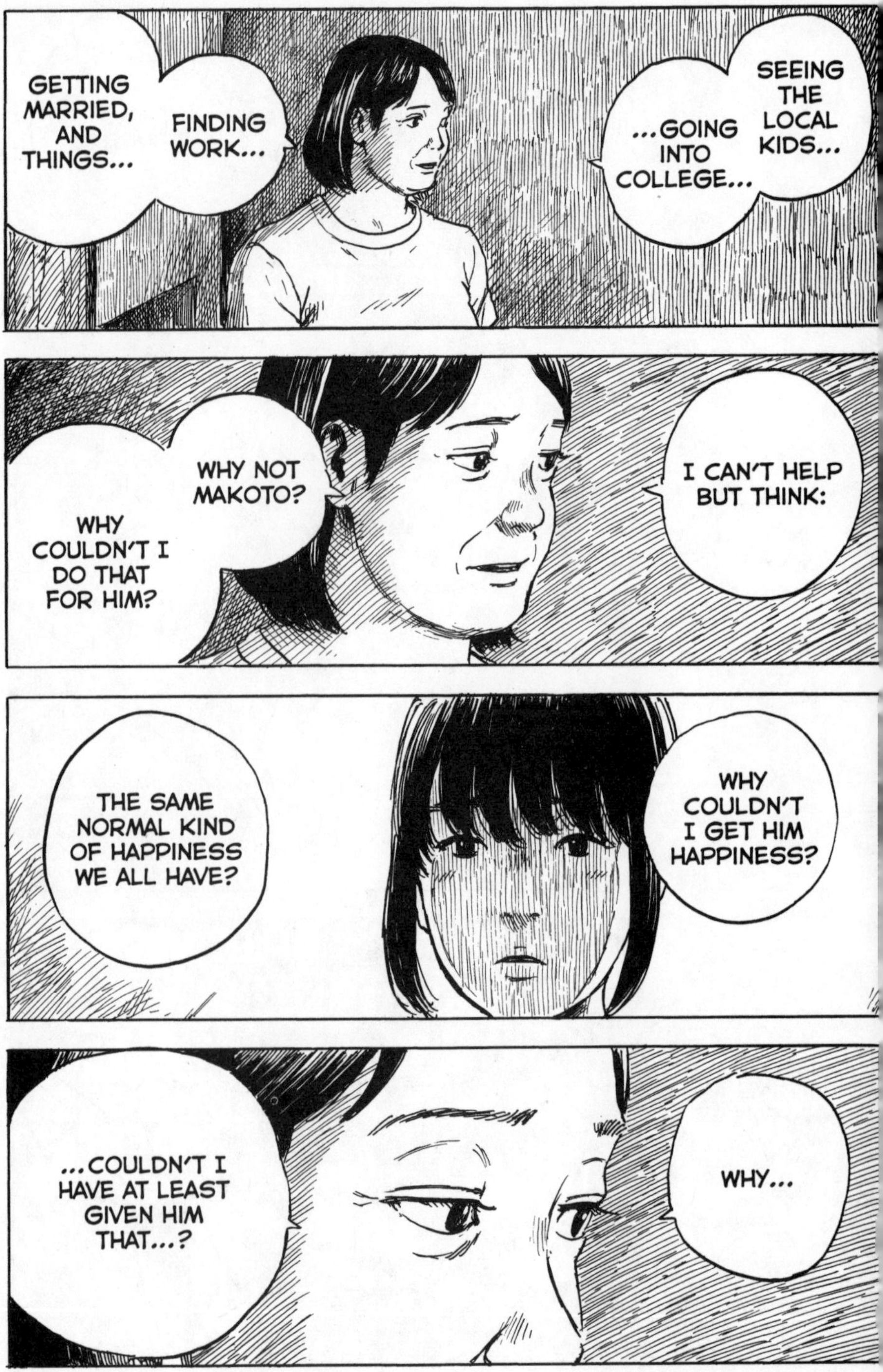
SEEING THE LOCAL KIDS...
...GOING INTO COLLEGE...
FINDING WORK...
GETTING MARRIED, AND THINGS...
I CAN'T HELP BUT THINK:
WHY NOT MAKOTO?
WHY COULDN'T I DO THAT FOR HIM?
WHY COULDN'T I GET HIM HAPPINESS?
THE SAME NORMAL KIND OF HAPPINESS WE ALL HAVE?
WHY...
...COULDN'T I HAVE AT LEAST GIVEN HIM THAT...?

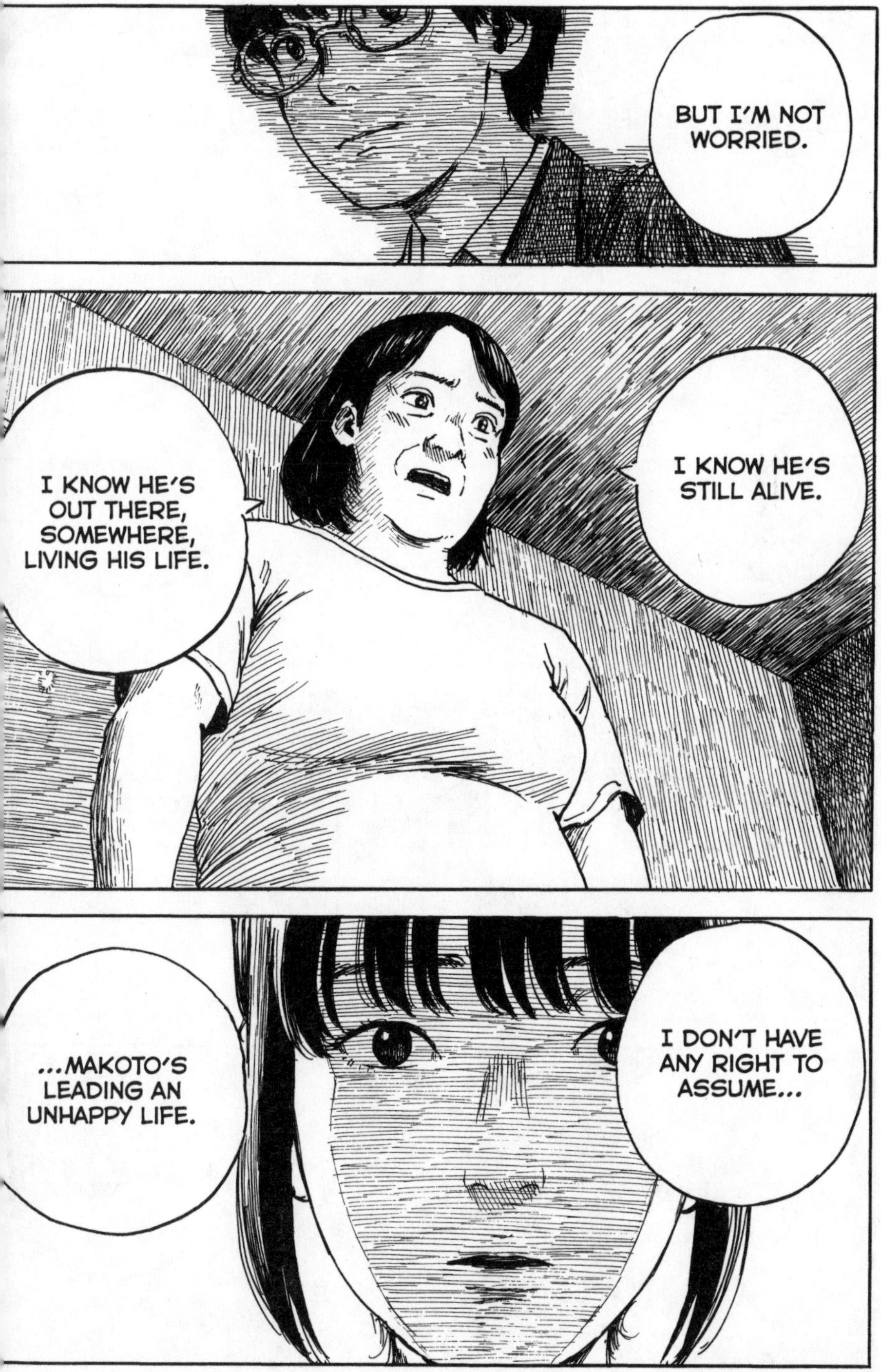
BUT I'M NOT WORRIED.
I KNOW HE'S STILL ALIVE.
I KNOW HE'S OUT THERE, SOMEWHERE, LIVING HIS LIFE.
I DON'T HAVE ANY RIGHT TO ASSUME...
...MAKOTO'S LEADING AN UNHAPPY LIFE.

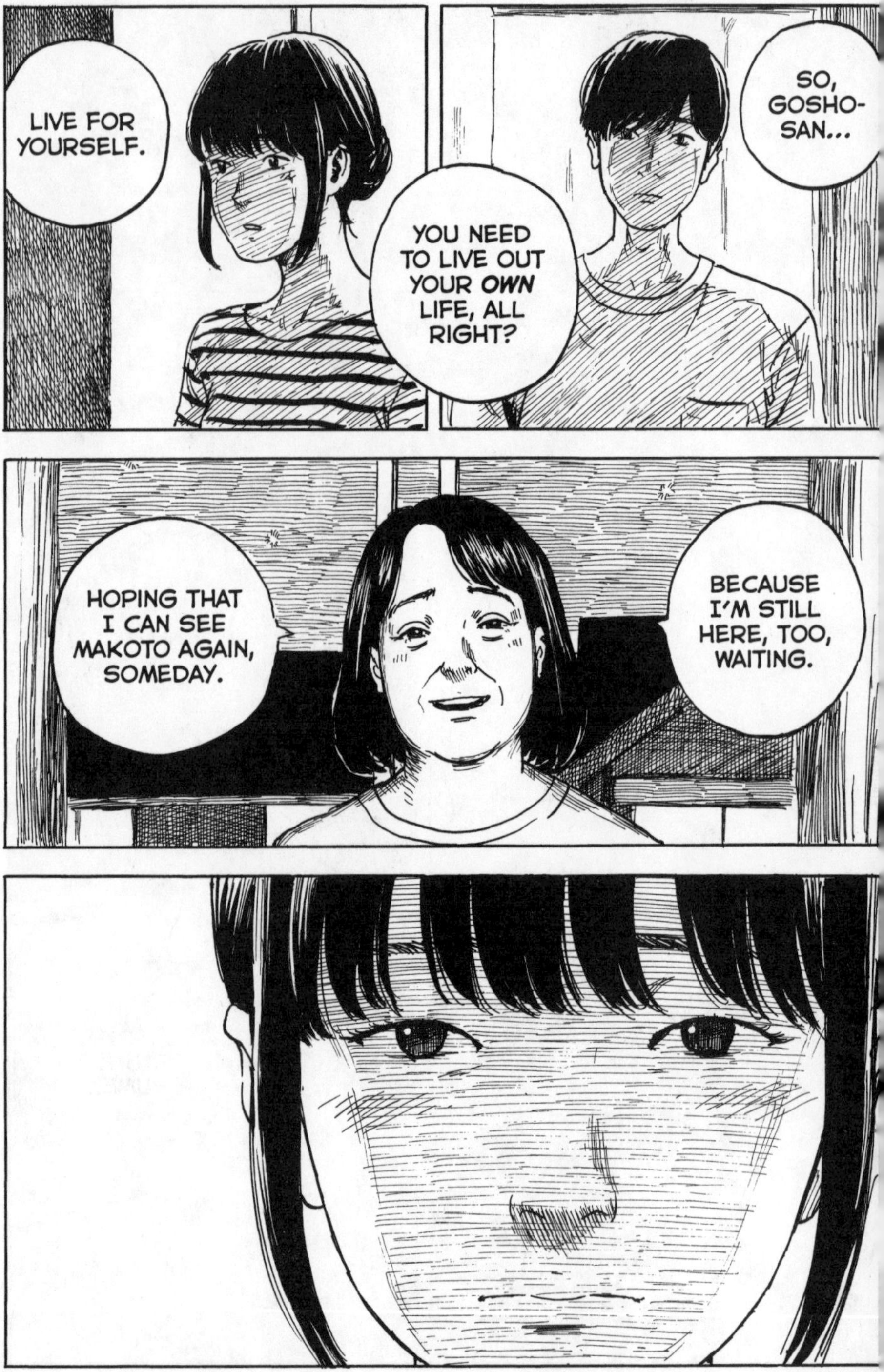
SO, GOSHO-SAN...
YOU NEED TO LIVE OUT YOUR *OWN* LIFE, ALL RIGHT?
LIVE FOR YOURSELF.
BECAUSE I'M STILL HERE, TOO, WAITING.
HOPING THAT I CAN SEE MAKOTO AGAIN, SOMEDAY.

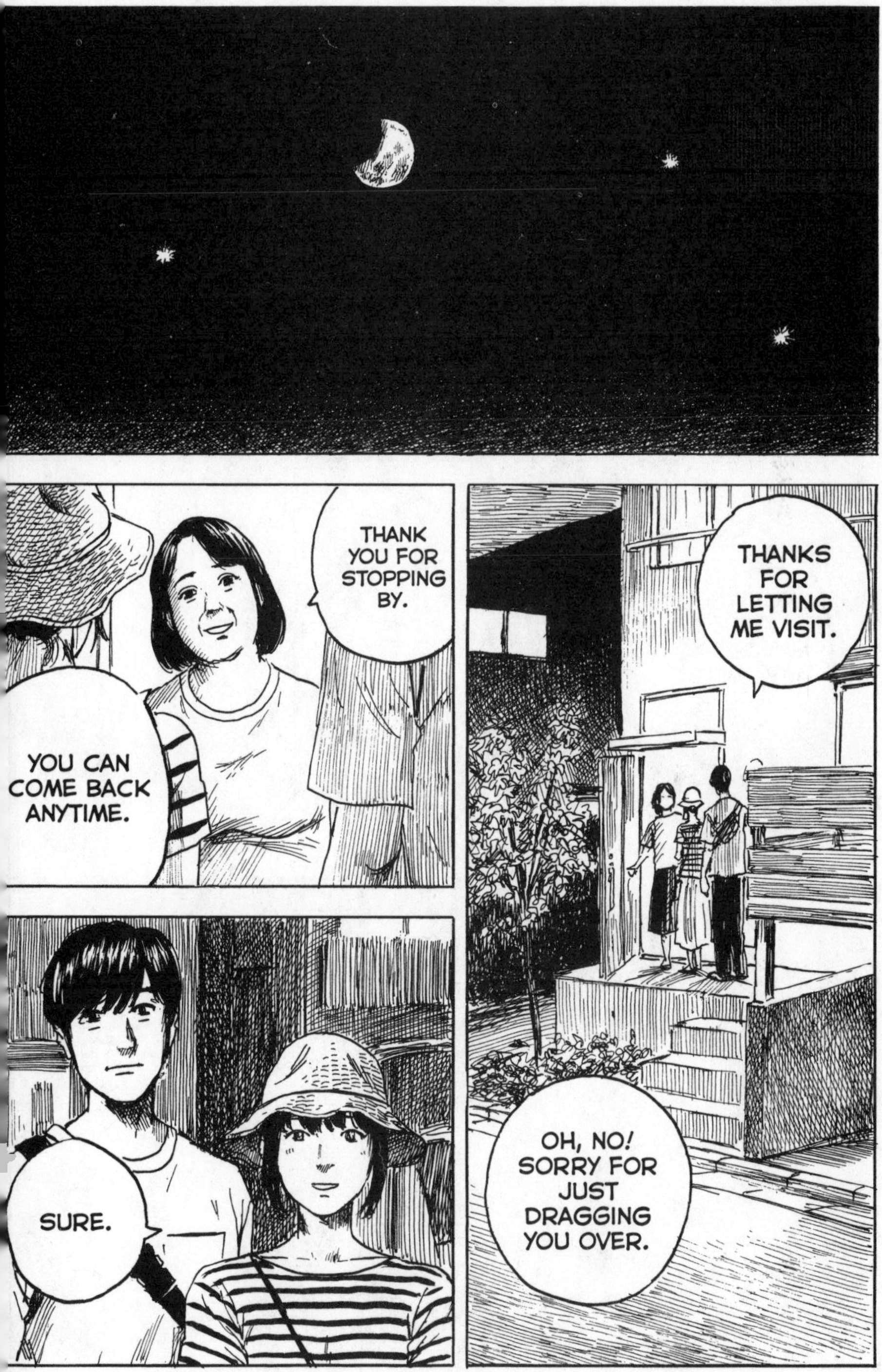
THANKS FOR LETTING ME VISIT.
OH, NO! SORRY FOR JUST DRAGGING YOU OVER.
THANK YOU FOR STOPPING BY.
YOU CAN COME BACK ANYTIME.
SURE.

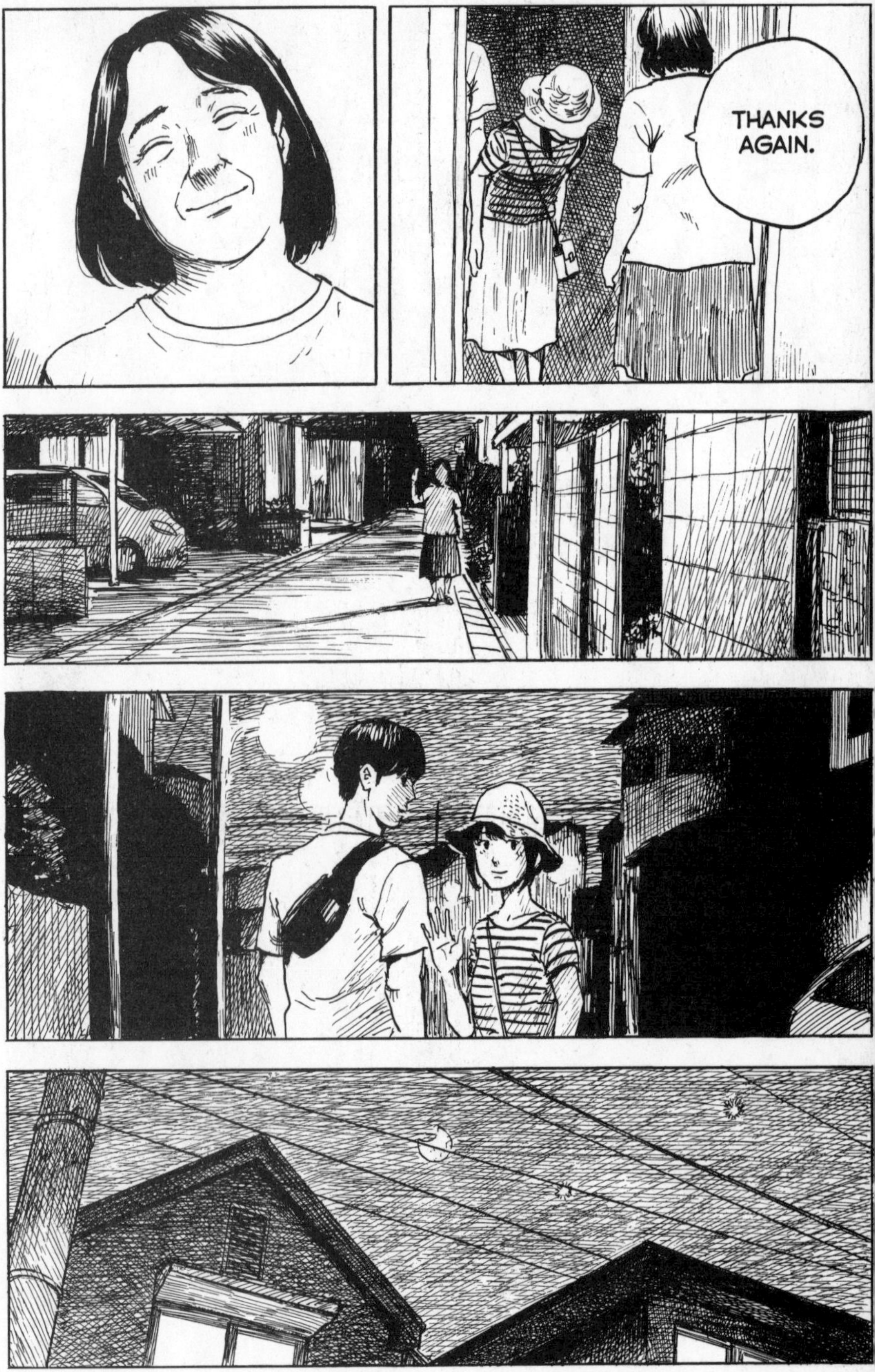
THANKS AGAIN.

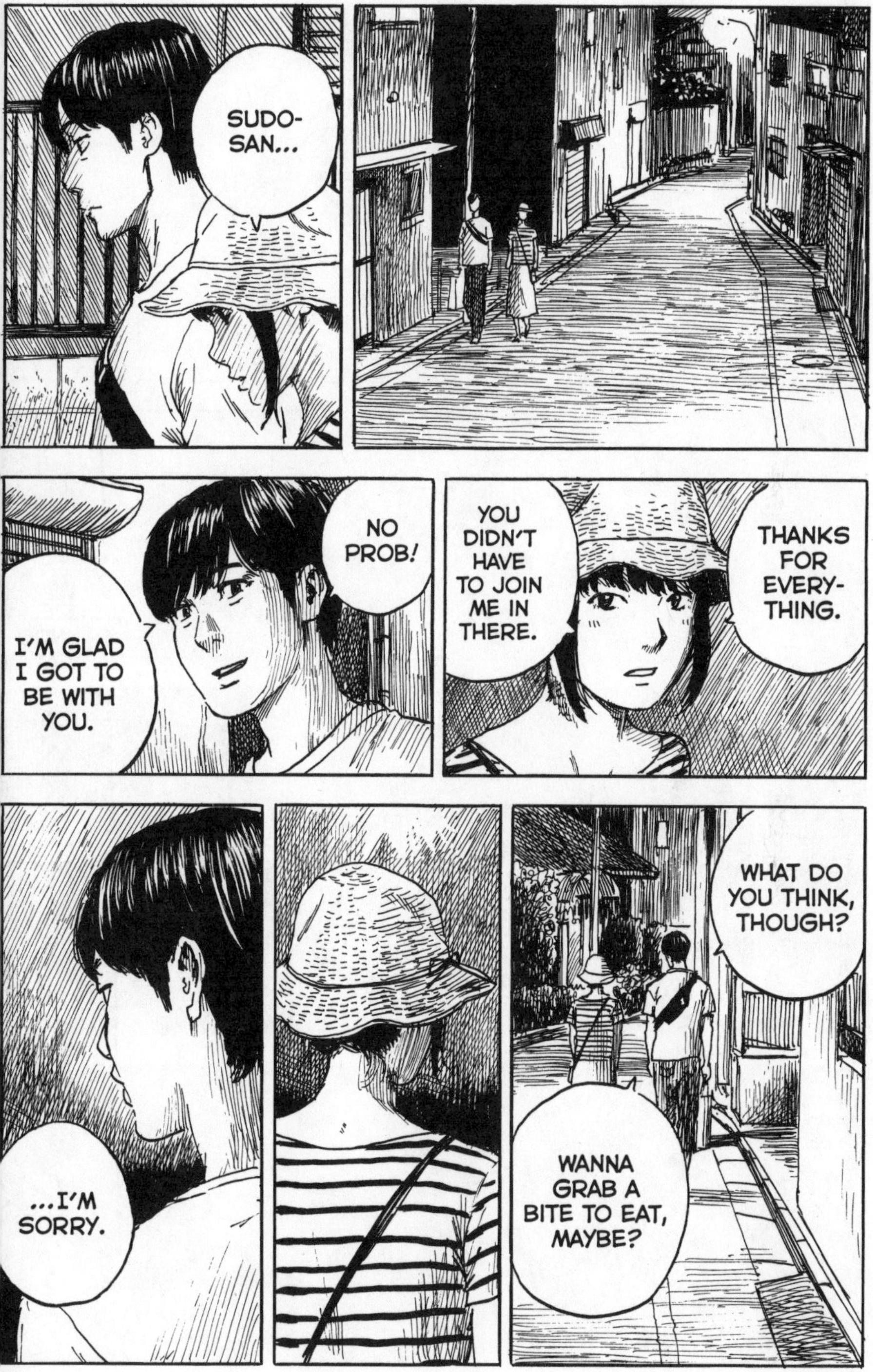
SUDO-SAN...
THANKS FOR EVERYTHING.
YOU DIDN'T HAVE TO JOIN ME IN THERE.
NO PROB!
I'M GLAD I GOT TO BE WITH YOU.
WHAT DO YOU THINK, THOUGH?
WANNA GRAB A BITE TO EAT, MAYBE?
...I'M SORRY.

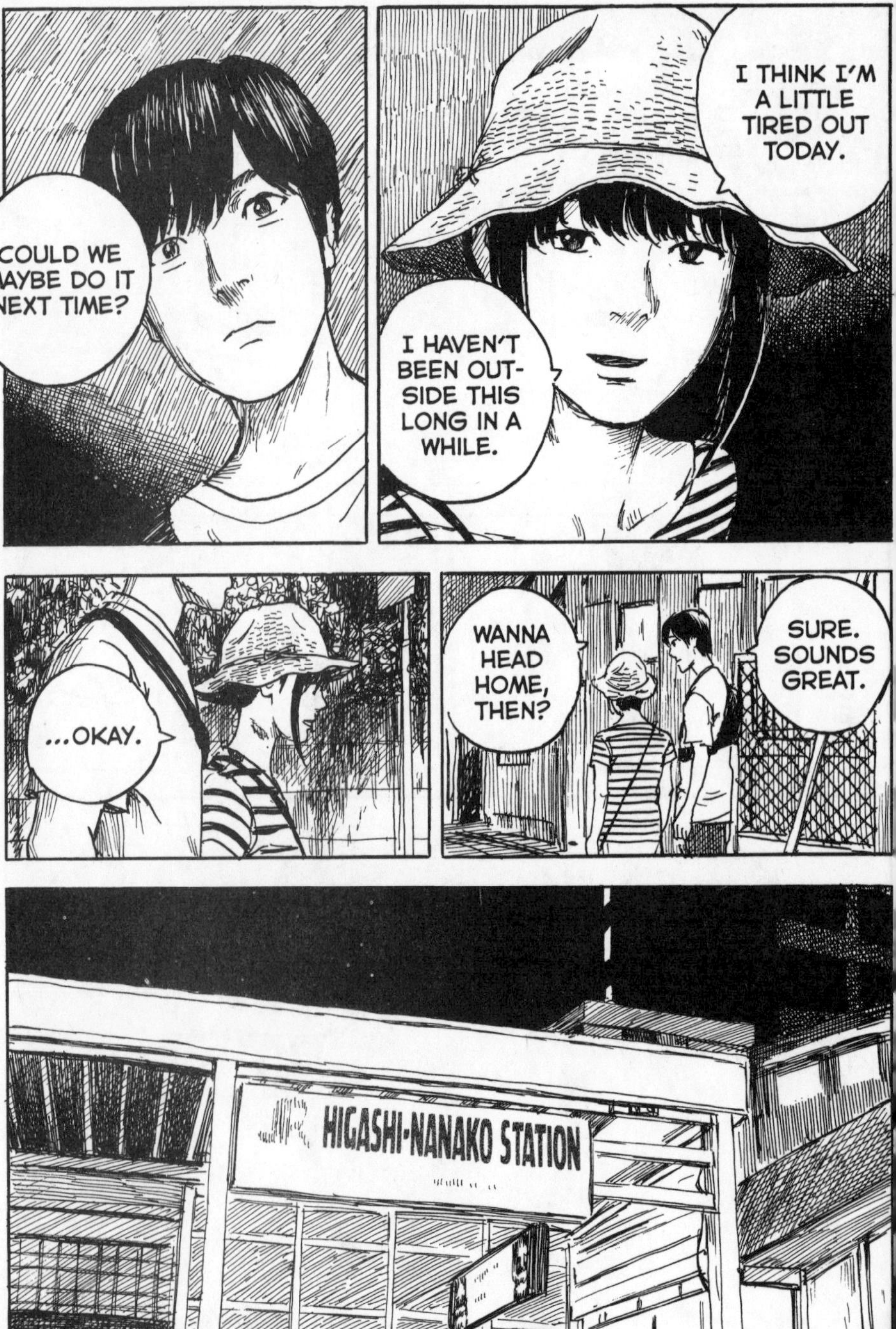
COULD WE MAYBE DO IT NEXT TIME?
I THINK I'M A LITTLE TIRED OUT TODAY.
I HAVEN'T BEEN OUT-SIDE THIS LONG IN A WHILE.
...OKAY.
WANNA HEAD HOME, THEN?
SURE. SOUNDS GREAT.
JR HIGASHI-NANAKO STATION

HERE'S GOOD?
YEAH.
UM...
SUDO-SAN?
TODAY WAS REALLY... REALLY FUN FOR ME.
AND THANKS, TOO...
...FOR THE HAT, I MEAN.

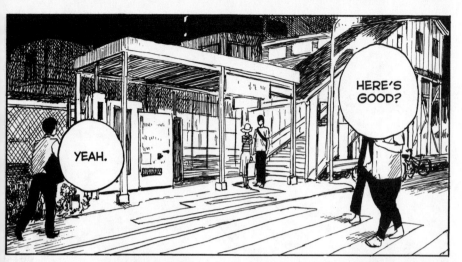

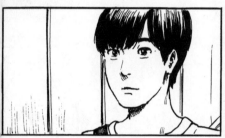

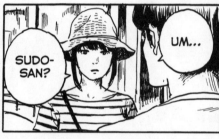

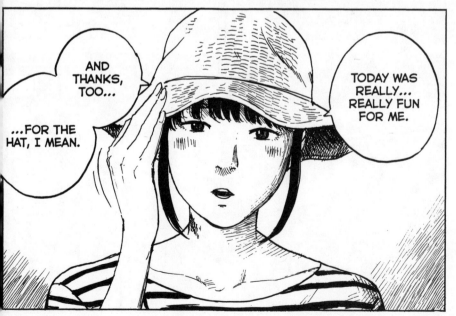

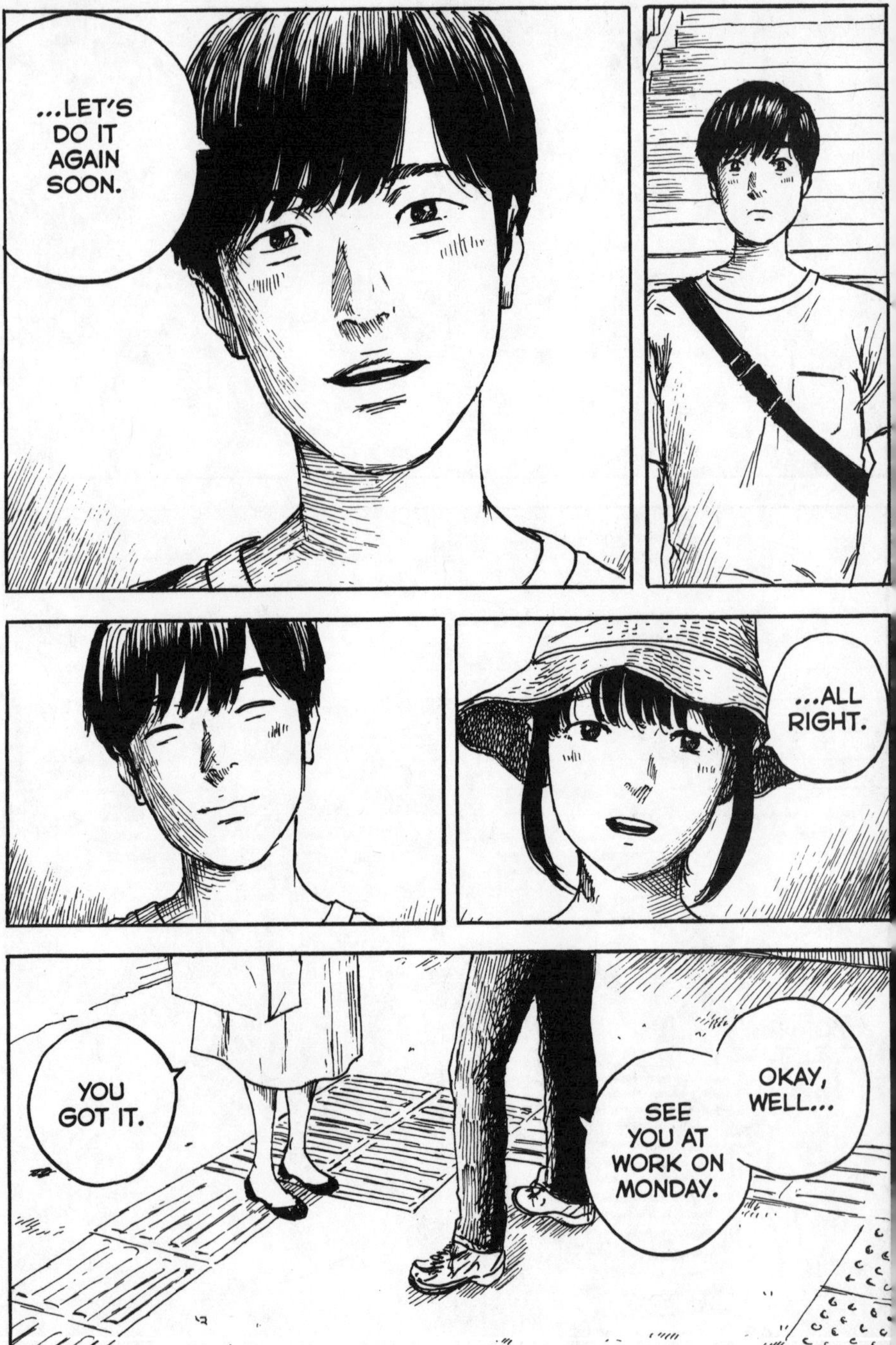
...LET'S DO IT AGAIN SOON.
...ALL RIGHT.
OKAY, WELL...
SEE YOU AT WORK ON MONDAY.
YOU GOT IT.

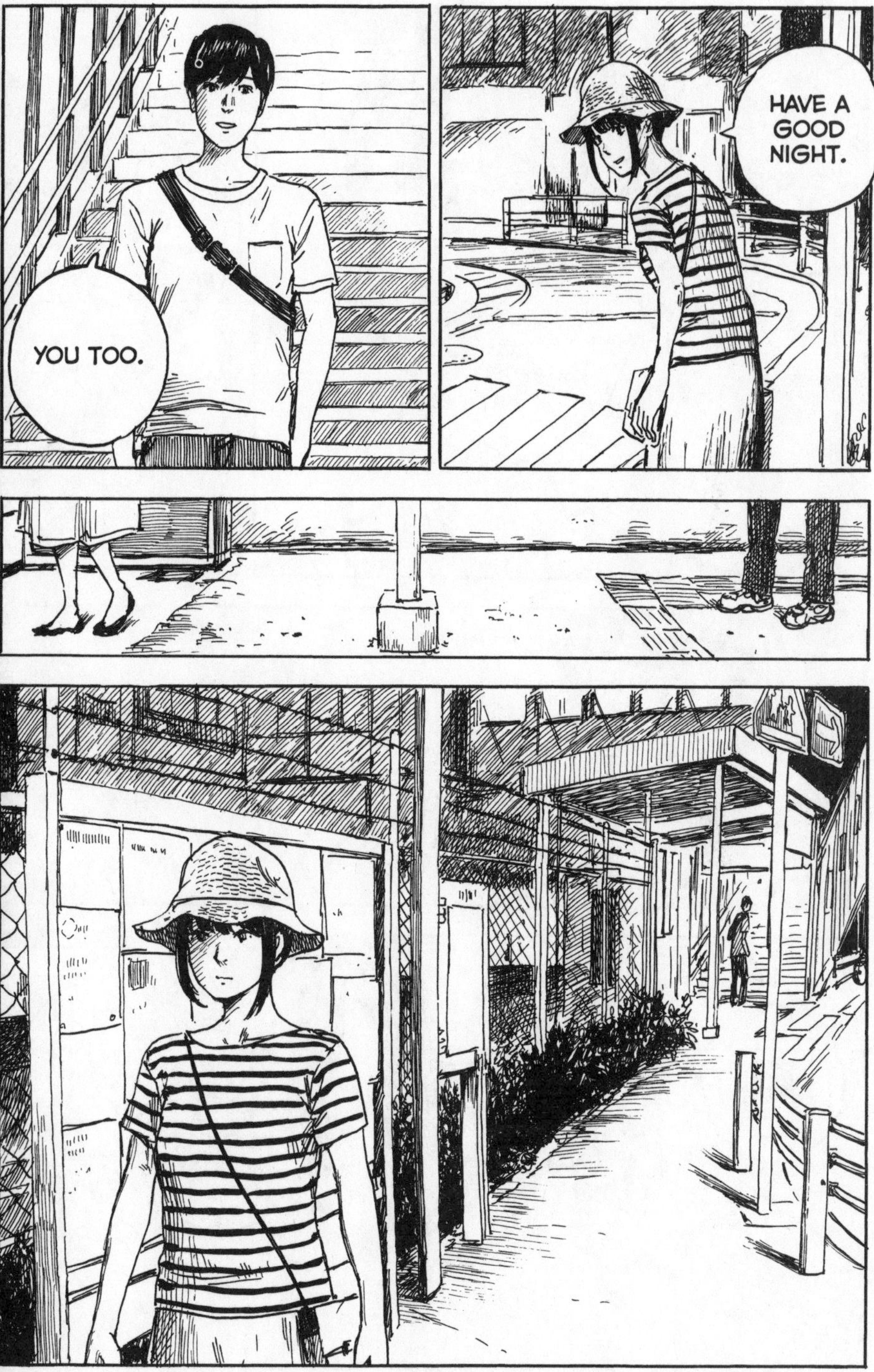
HAVE A GOOD NIGHT.
YOU TOO.

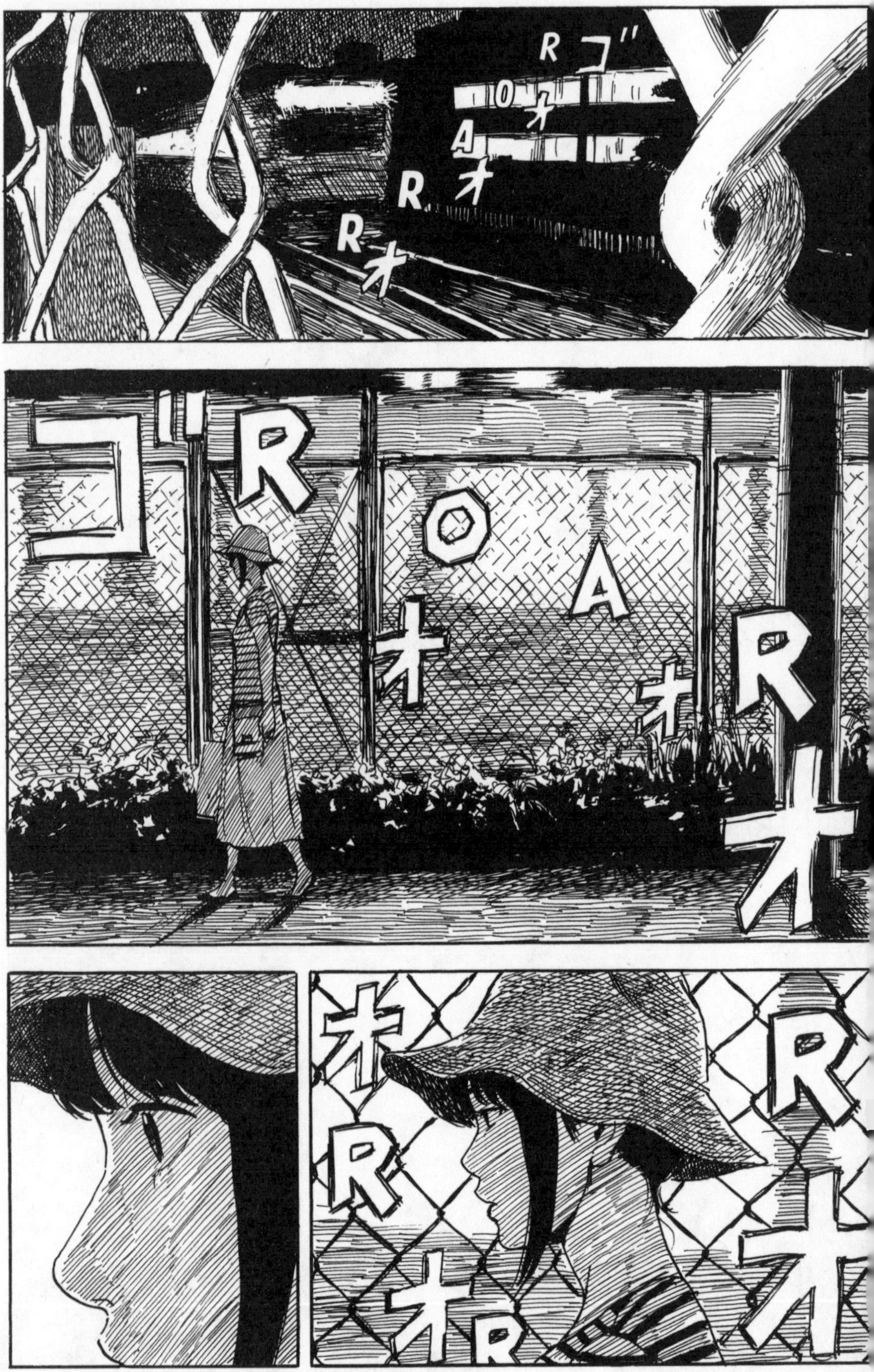
ゴオオオ
ROARR
ゴオオオ
ROAR
オオオ
RRR

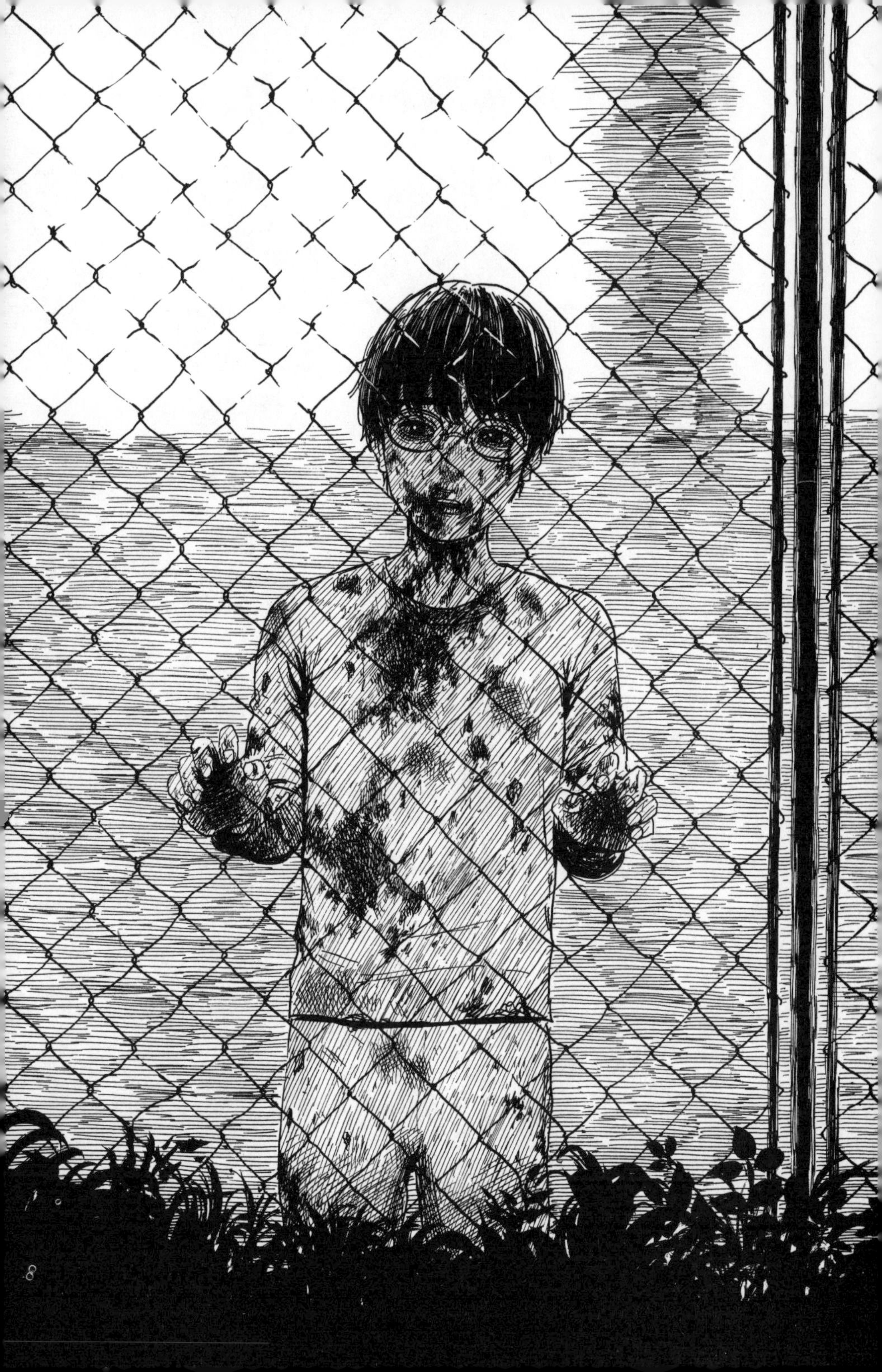

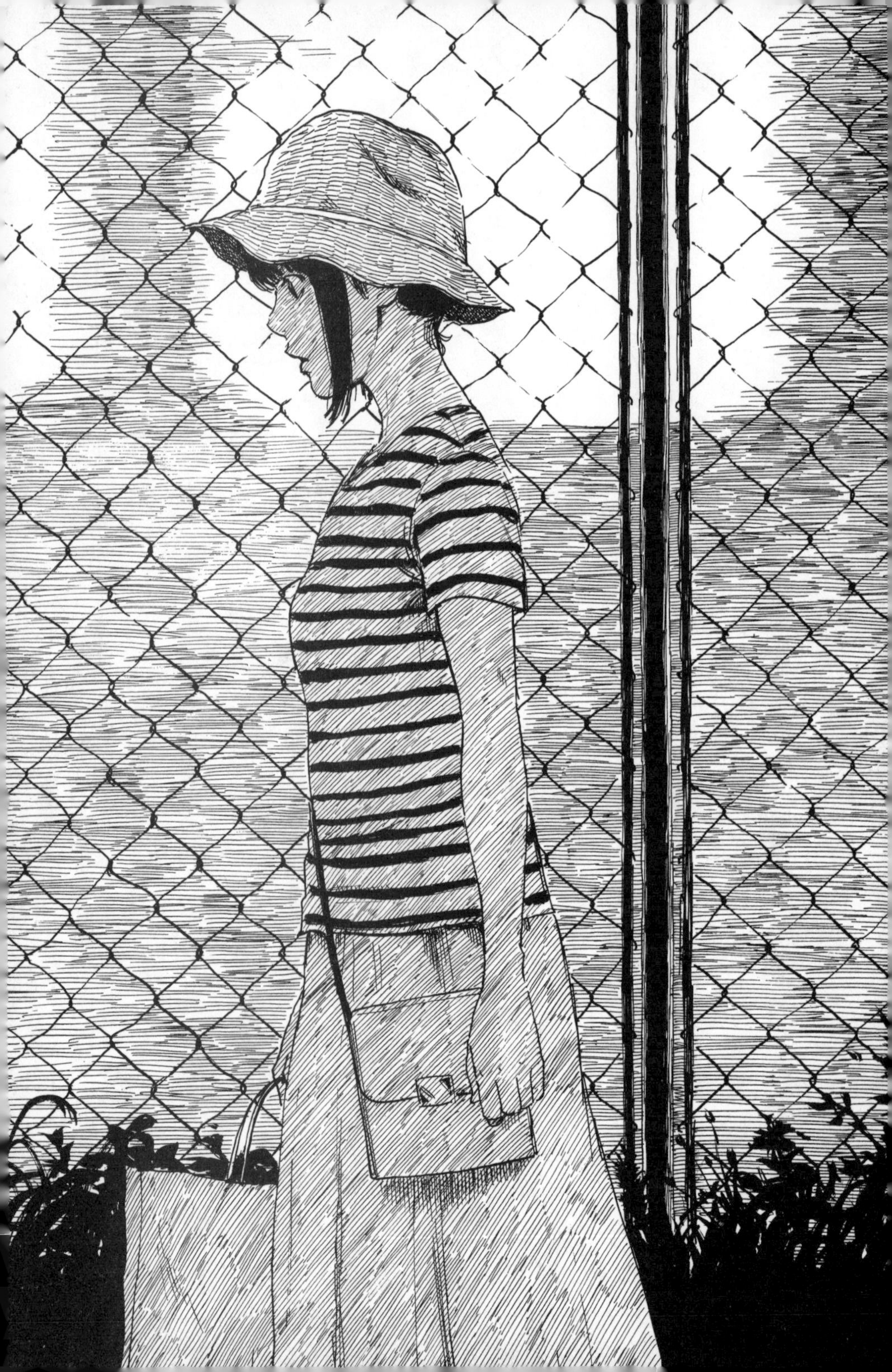

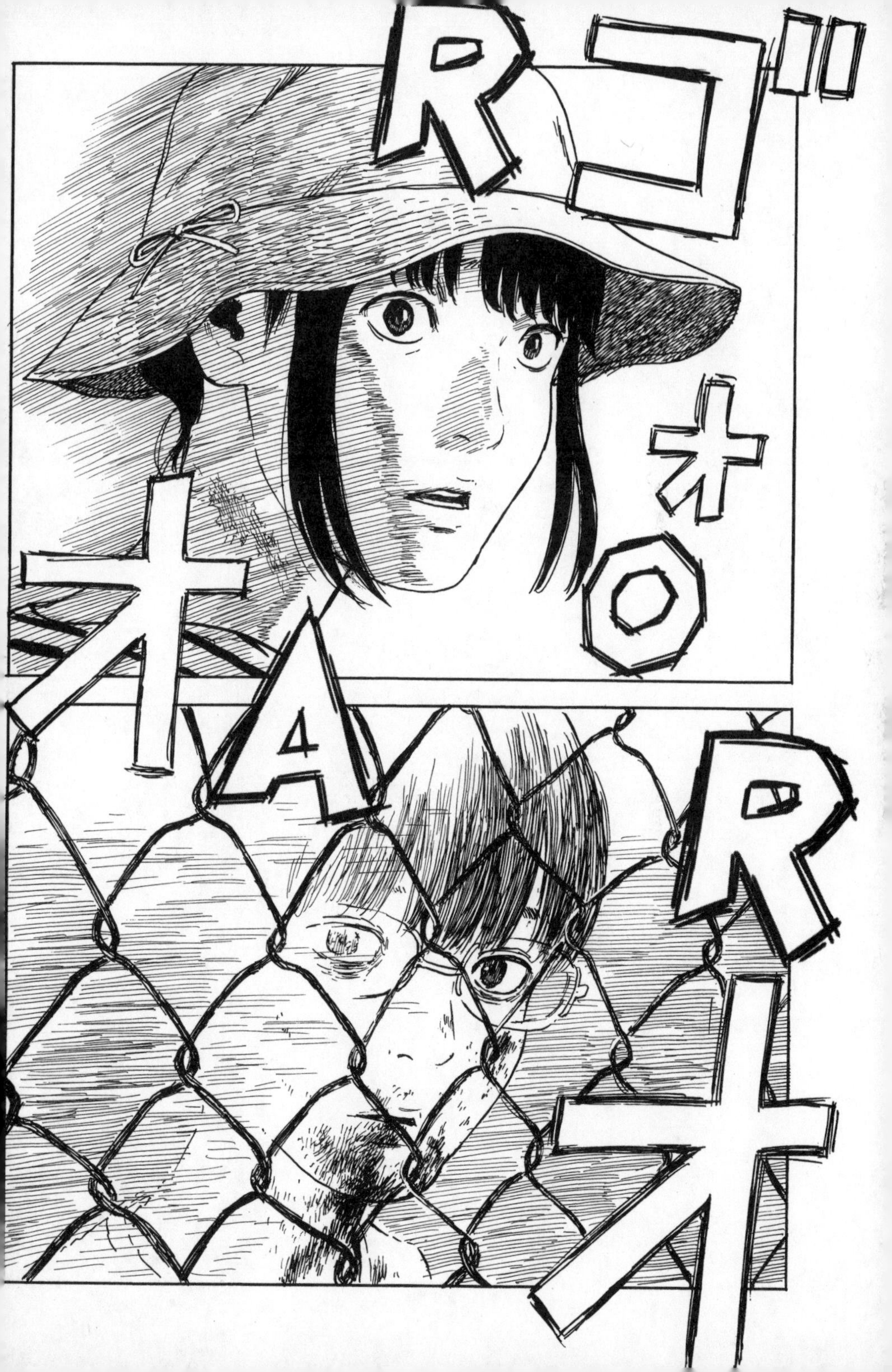

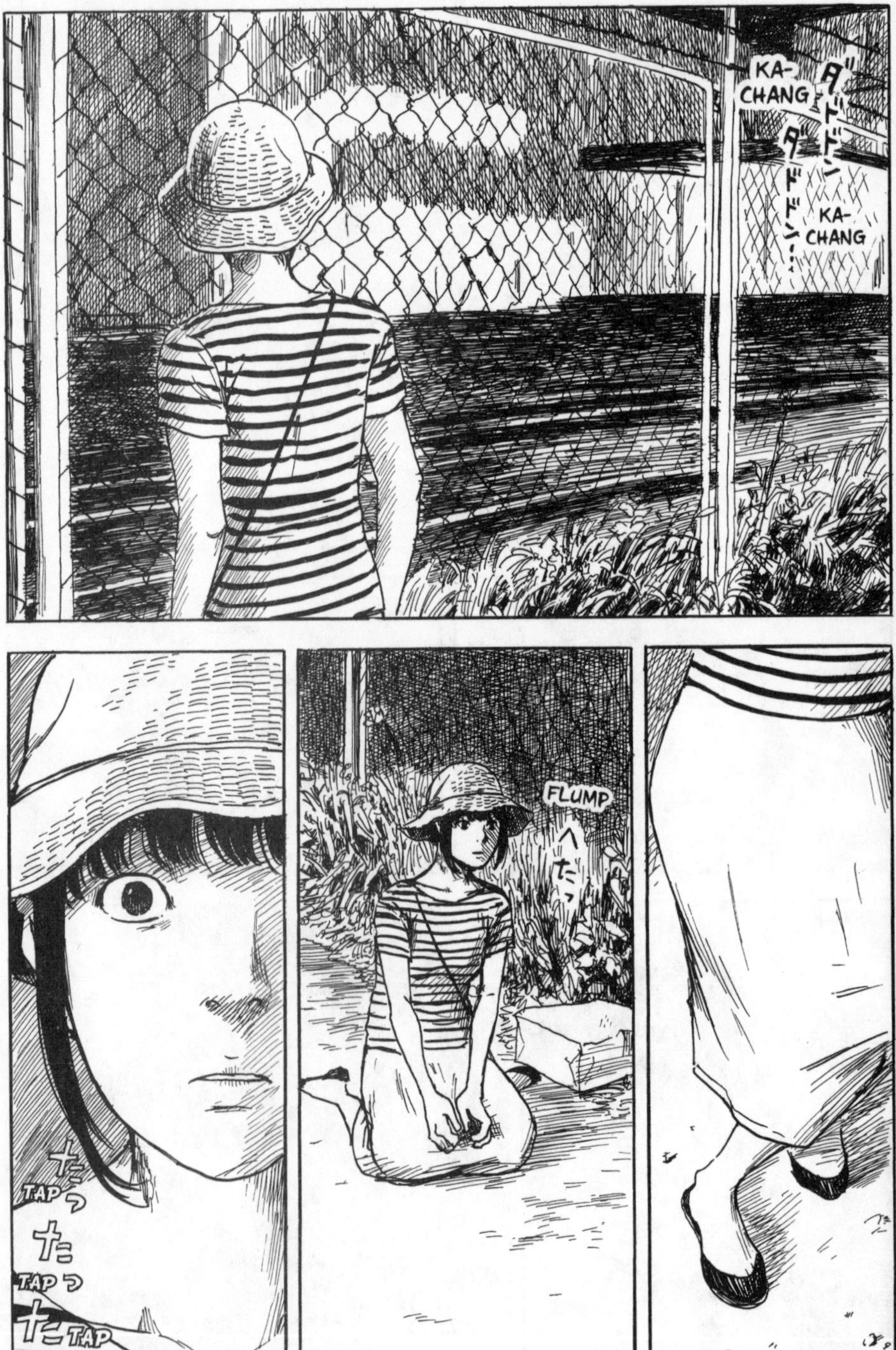
KA-CHANG
ダドドン
ダドドン…
KA-CHANG
FLUMP
へたっ
TAP
たっ
TAP
たっ
TAP
たっ

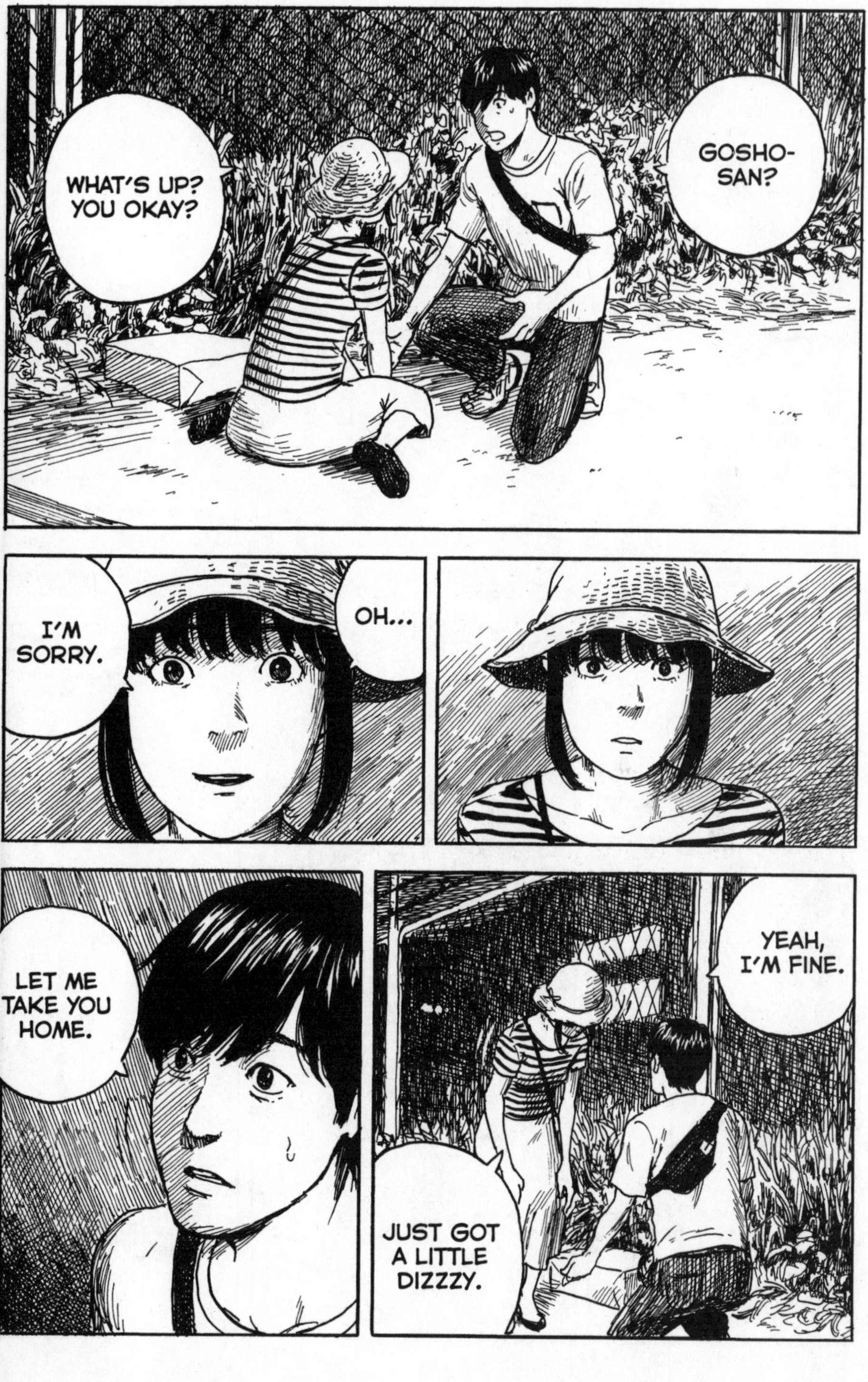
GOSHO-SAN?
WHAT'S UP? YOU OKAY?
OH...
I'M SORRY.
YEAH, I'M FINE.
JUST GOT A LITTLE DIZZZY.
LET ME TAKE YOU HOME.

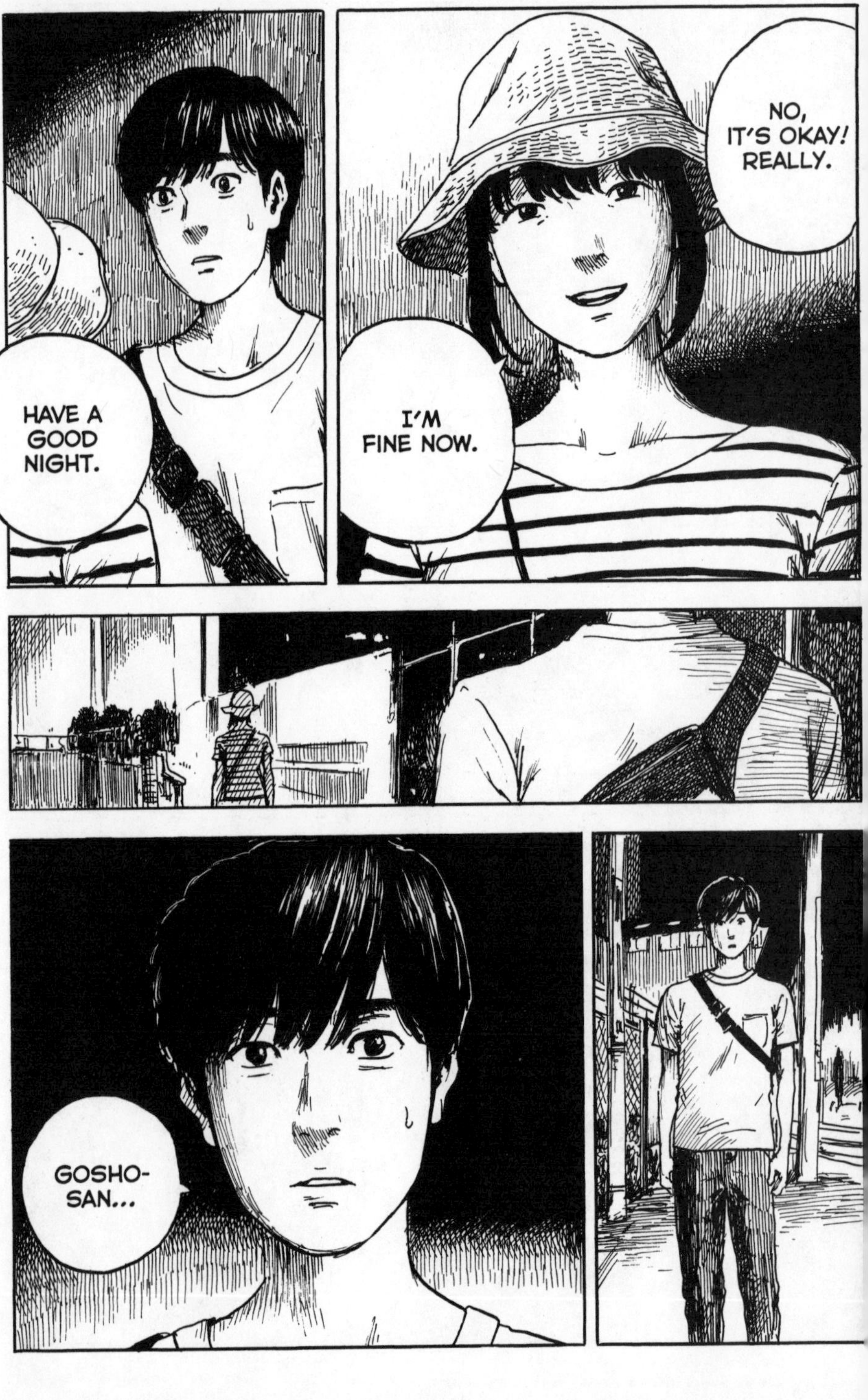
NO, IT'S OKAY! REALLY.
I'M FINE NOW.
HAVE A GOOD NIGHT.
GOSHO-SAN...

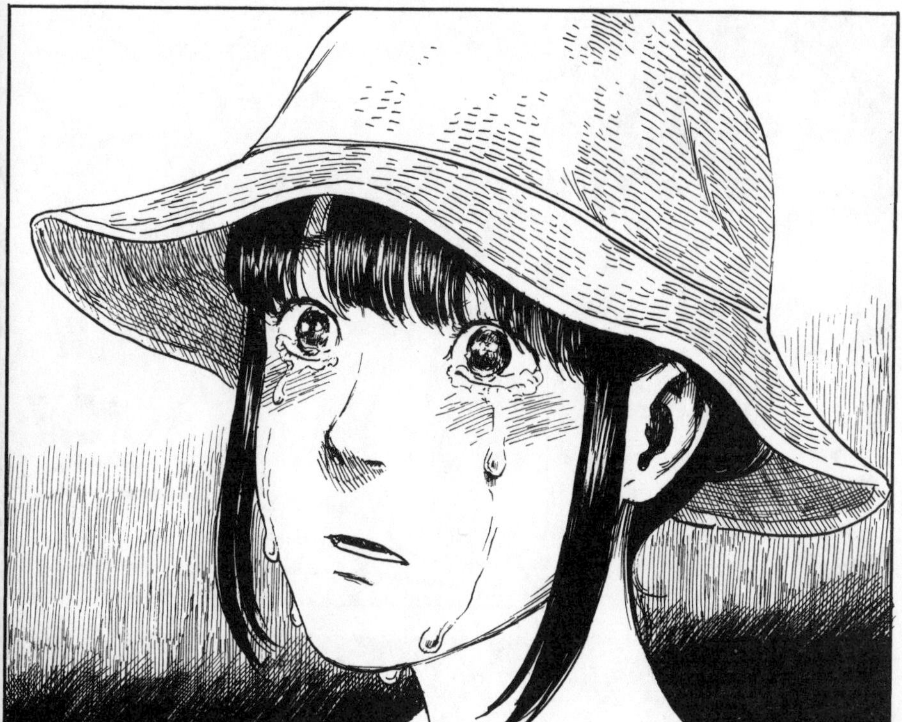

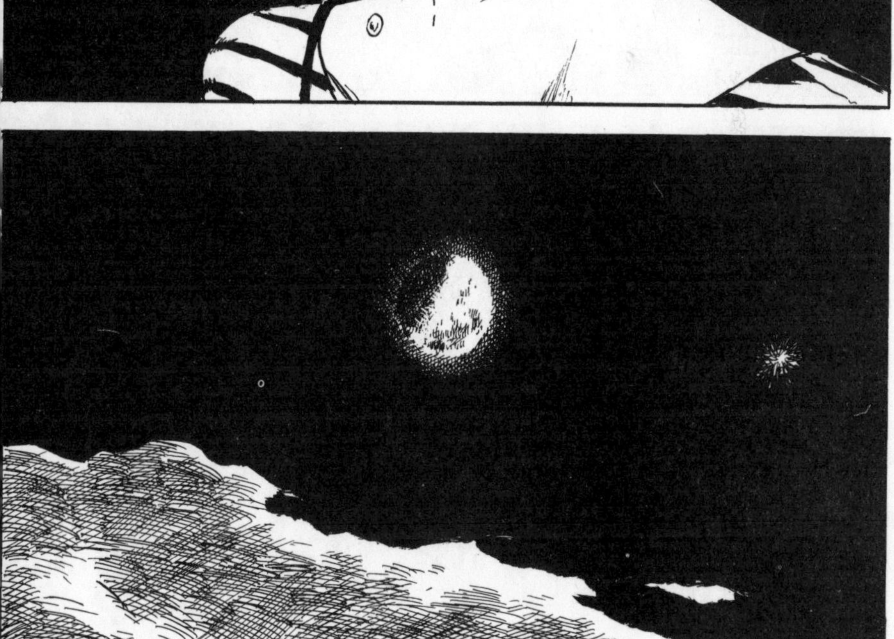

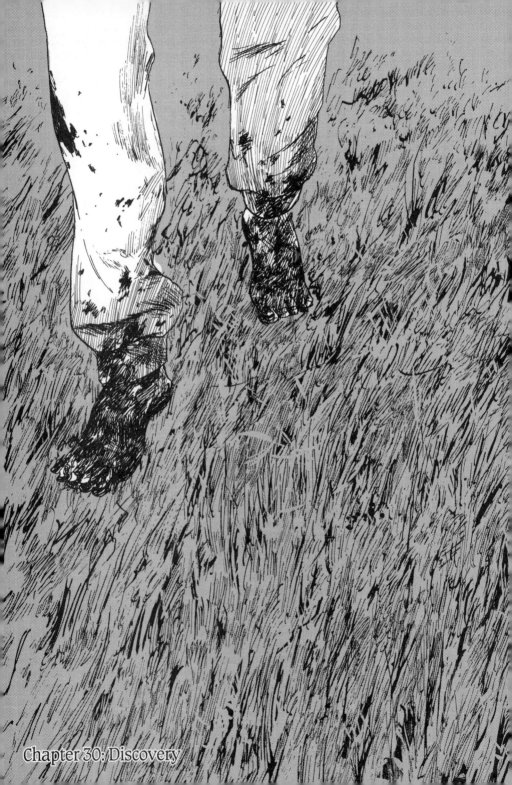

Chapter 30: Discovery

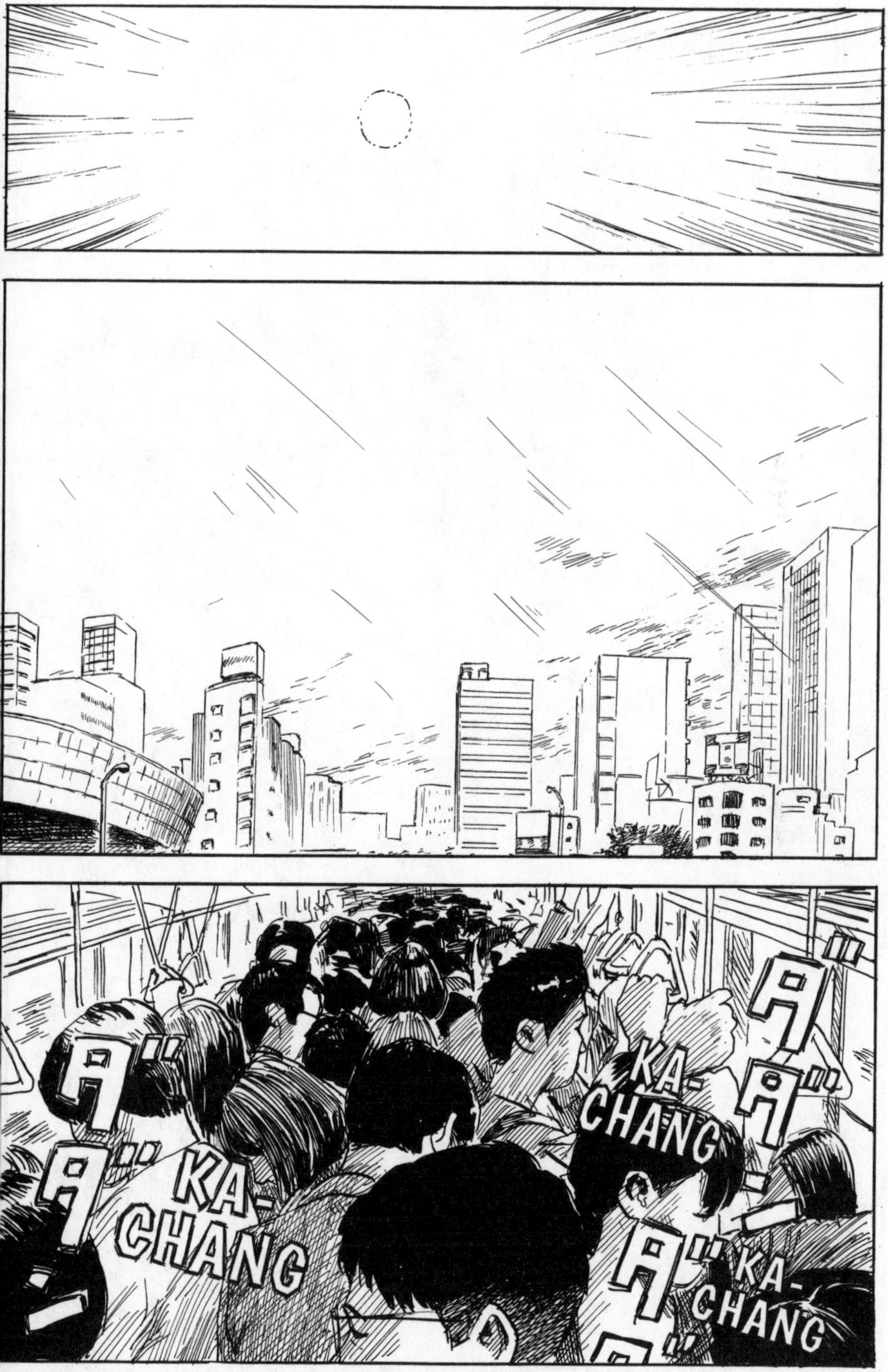
ダダ
KA-CHANG
ダダ
KA-CHANG
ダダ
KA-CHANG

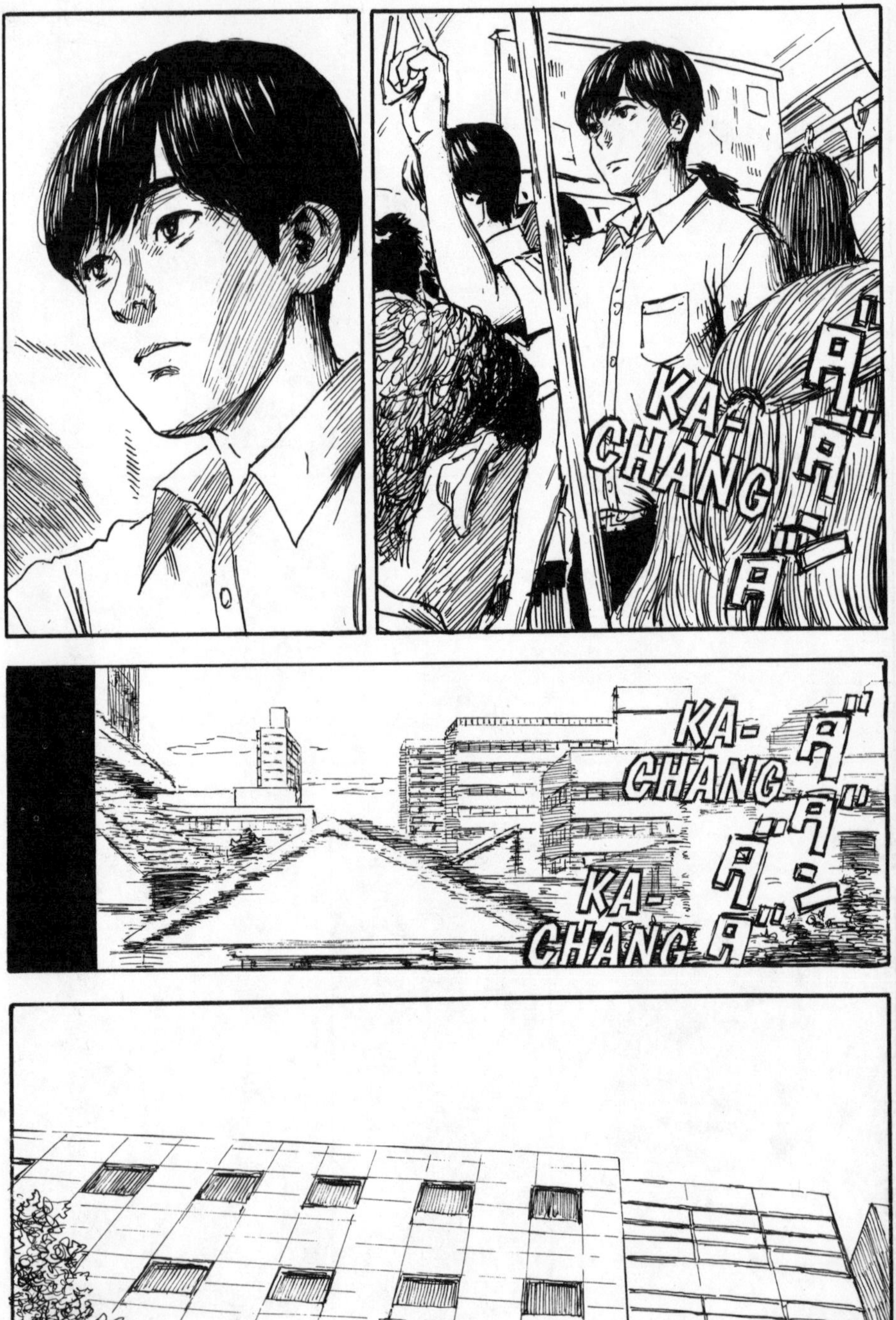
KA-
CHANG
KA-
CHANG
KA-
CHANG

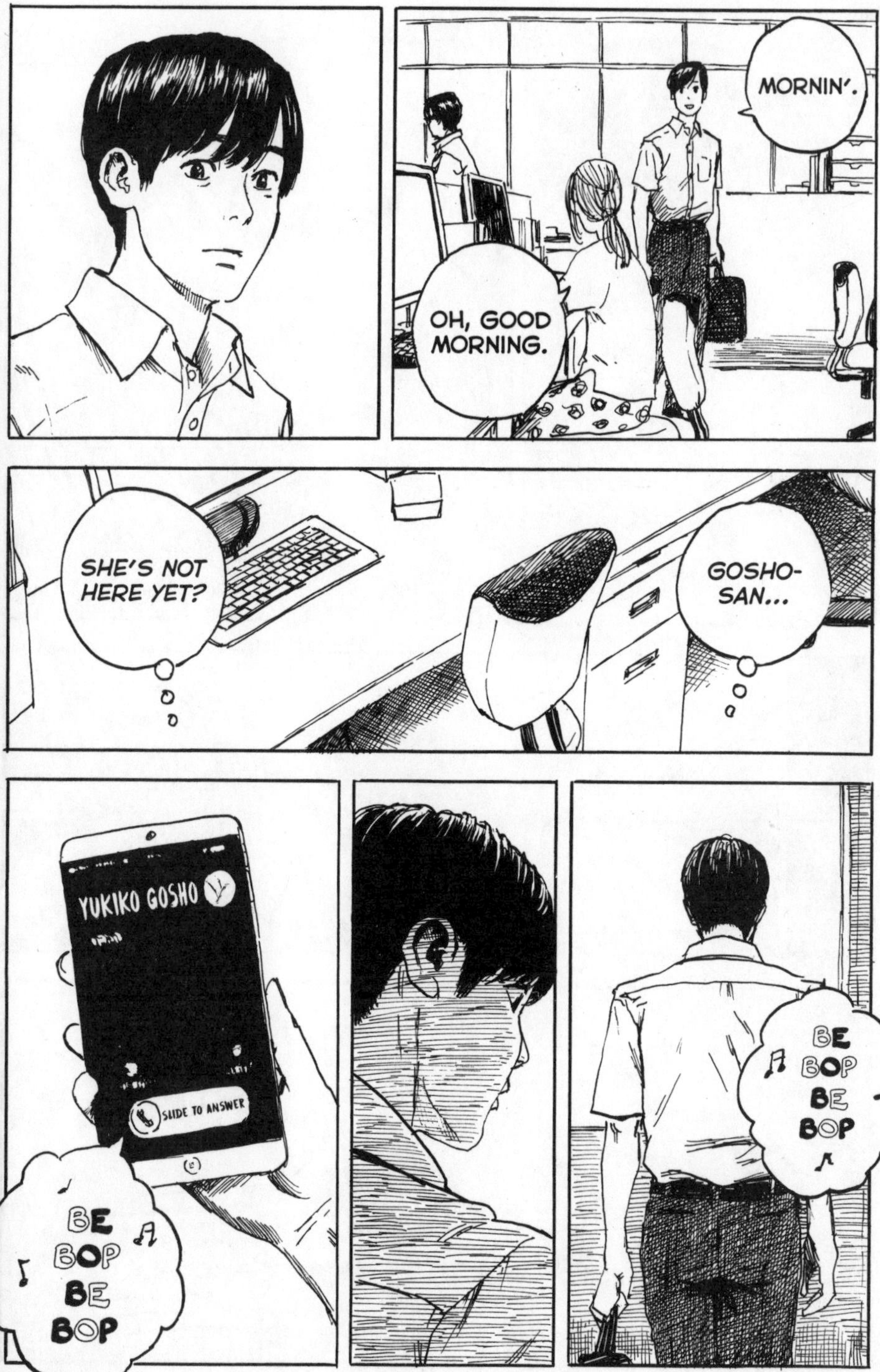
MORNIN'.
OH, GOOD MORNING.
GOSHO-SAN...
SHE'S NOT HERE YET?
BE BOP BE BOP
YUKIKO GOSHO
SLIDE TO ANSWER
BE BOP BE BOP

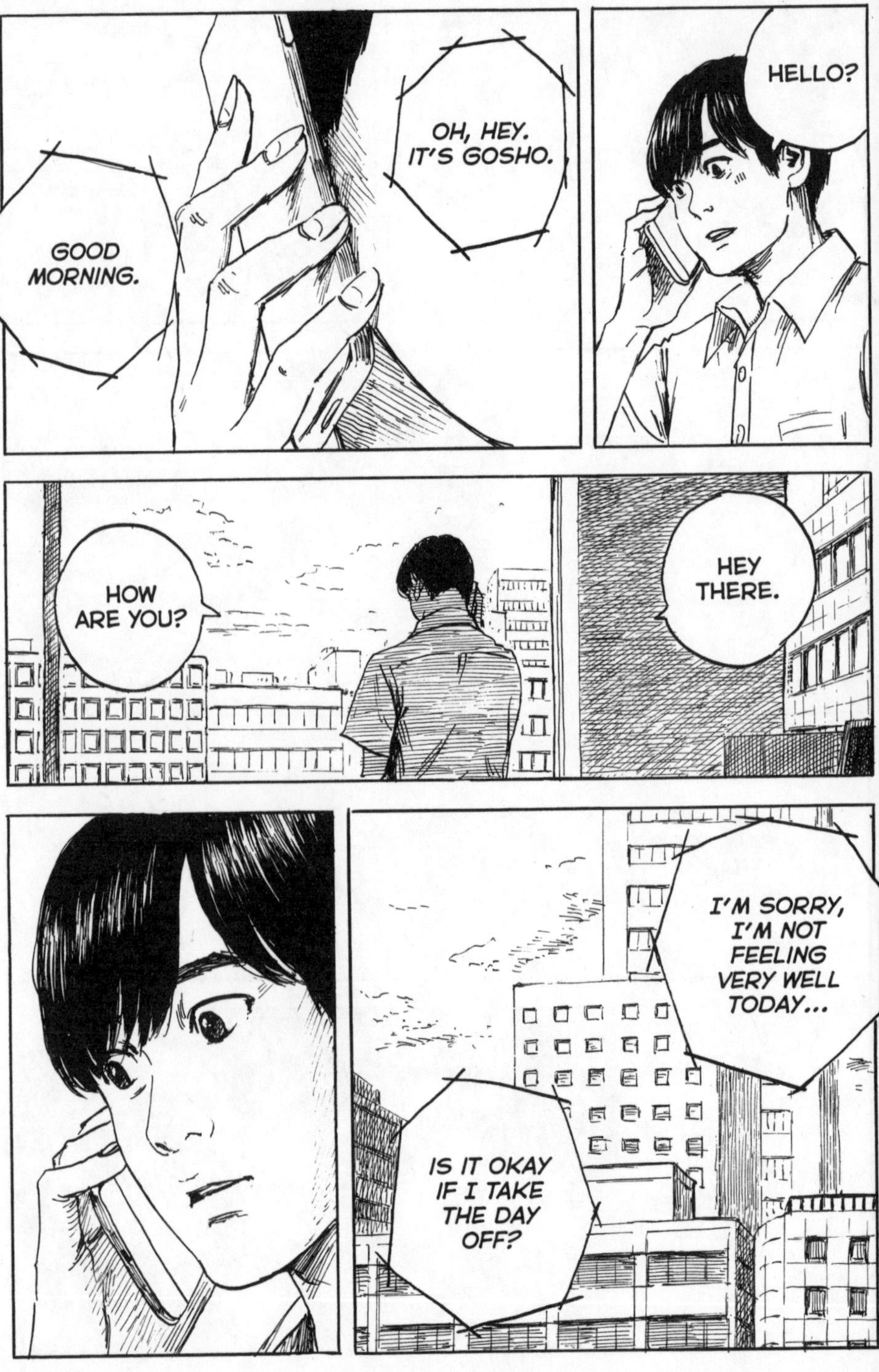
HELLO?
OH, HEY. IT'S GOSHO.
GOOD MORNING.
HEY THERE.
HOW ARE YOU?
I'M SORRY, I'M NOT FEELING VERY WELL TODAY...
IS IT OKAY IF I TAKE THE DAY OFF?

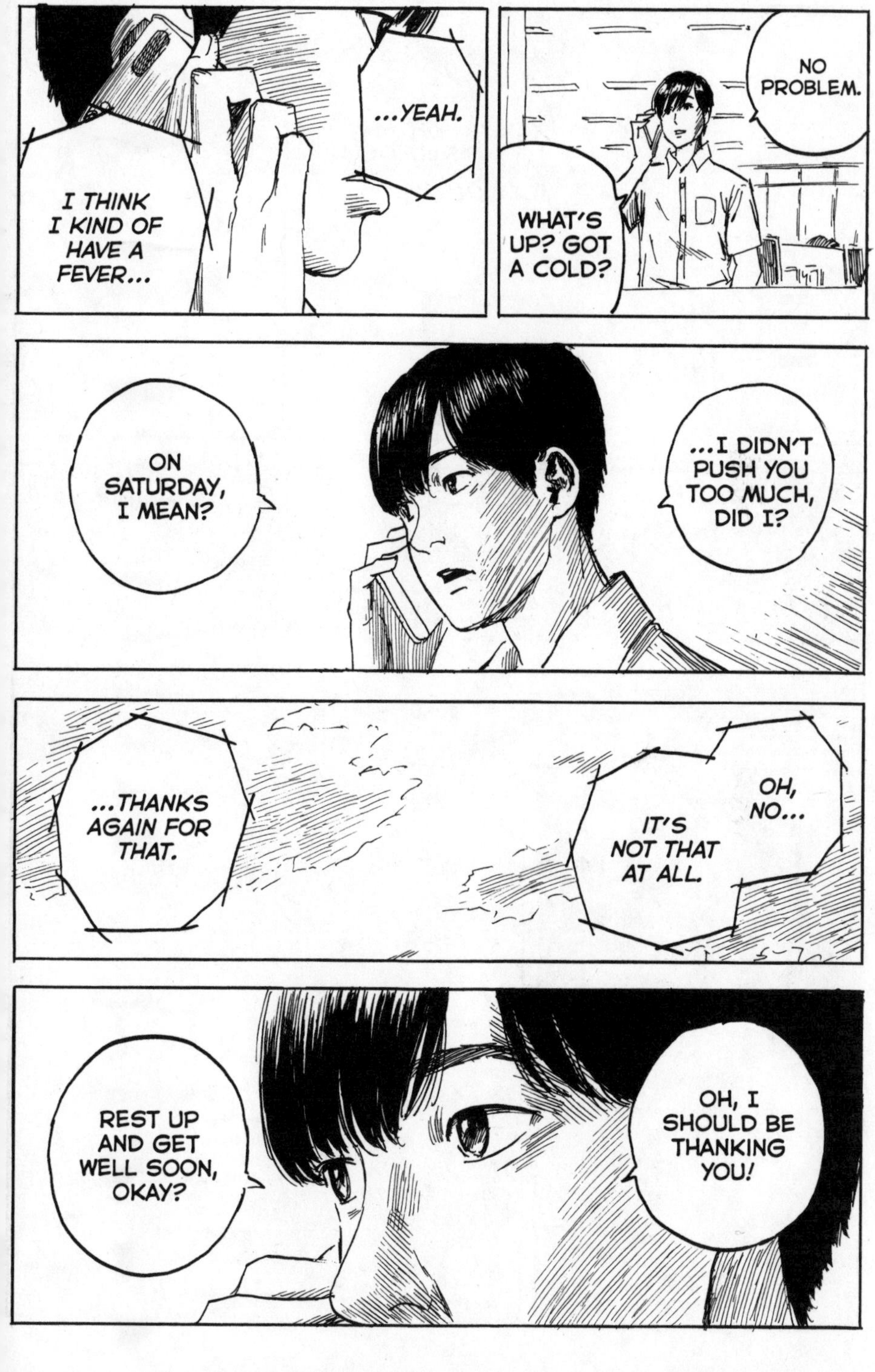
NO PROBLEM.
WHAT'S UP? GOT A COLD?
...YEAH.
I THINK I KIND OF HAVE A FEVER...
...I DIDN'T PUSH YOU TOO MUCH, DID I?
ON SATURDAY, I MEAN?
OH, NO...
IT'S NOT THAT AT ALL.
...THANKS AGAIN FOR THAT.
OH, I SHOULD BE THANKING YOU!
REST UP AND GET WELL SOON, OKAY?

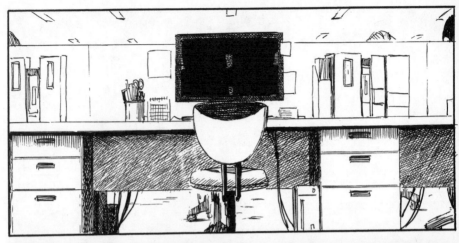

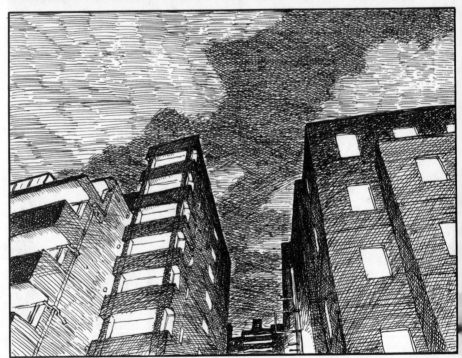

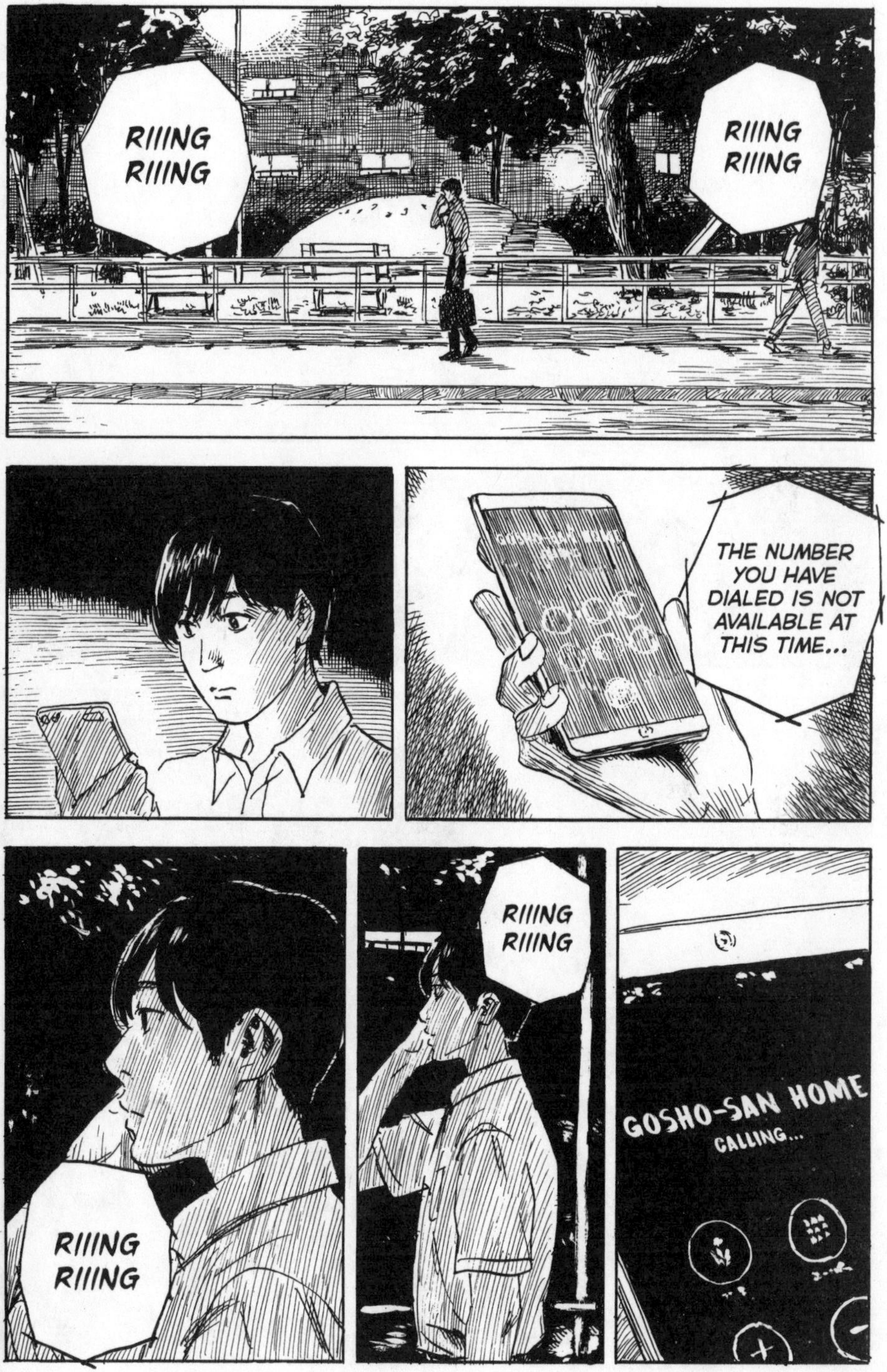
RIIING RIIING
RIIING RIIING
THE NUMBER YOU HAVE DIALED IS NOT AVAILABLE AT THIS TIME...
GOSHO-SAN HOME
CALLING...
RIIING RIIING
RIIING RIIING

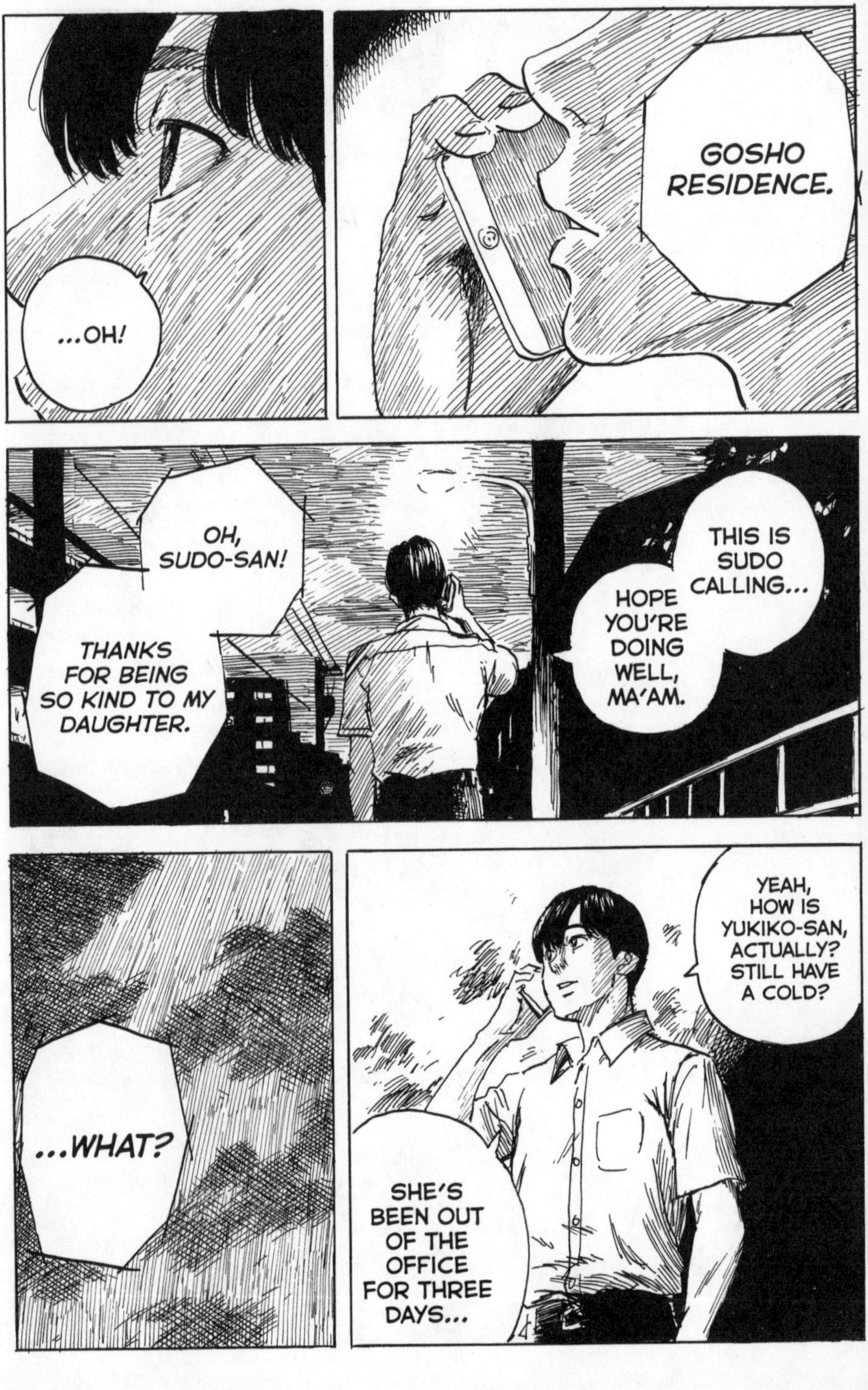
GOSHO RESIDENCE.
...OH!
THIS IS SUDO CALLING...
HOPE YOU'RE DOING WELL, MA'AM.
OH, SUDO-SAN!
THANKS FOR BEING SO KIND TO MY DAUGHTER.
YEAH, HOW IS YUKIKO-SAN, ACTUALLY? STILL HAVE A COLD?
SHE'S BEEN OUT OF THE OFFICE FOR THREE DAYS...
...WHAT?

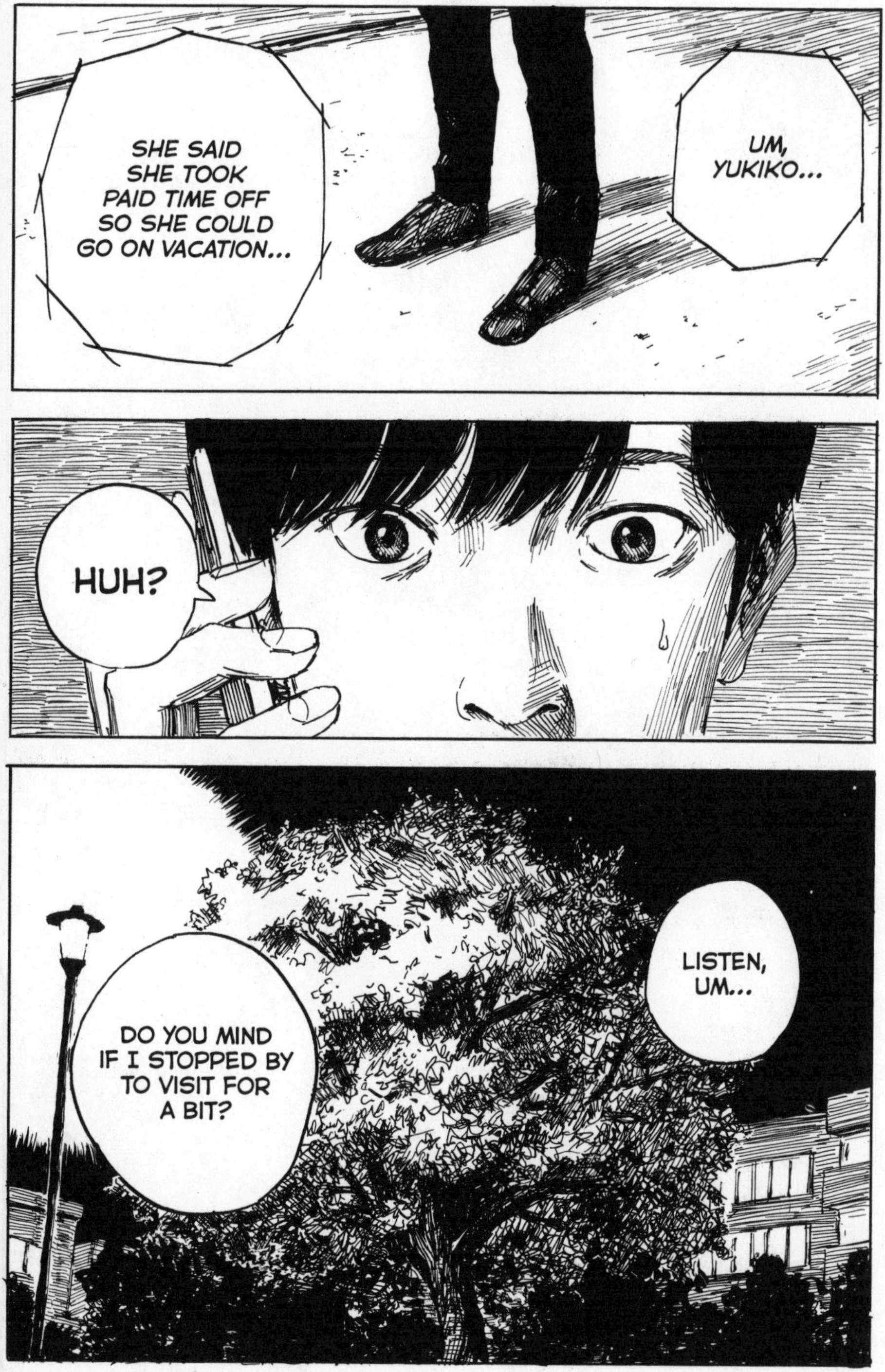
UM, YUKIKO...
SHE SAID SHE TOOK PAID TIME OFF SO SHE COULD GO ON VACATION...
HUH?
LISTEN, UM...
DO YOU MIND IF I STOPPED BY TO VISIT FOR A BIT?

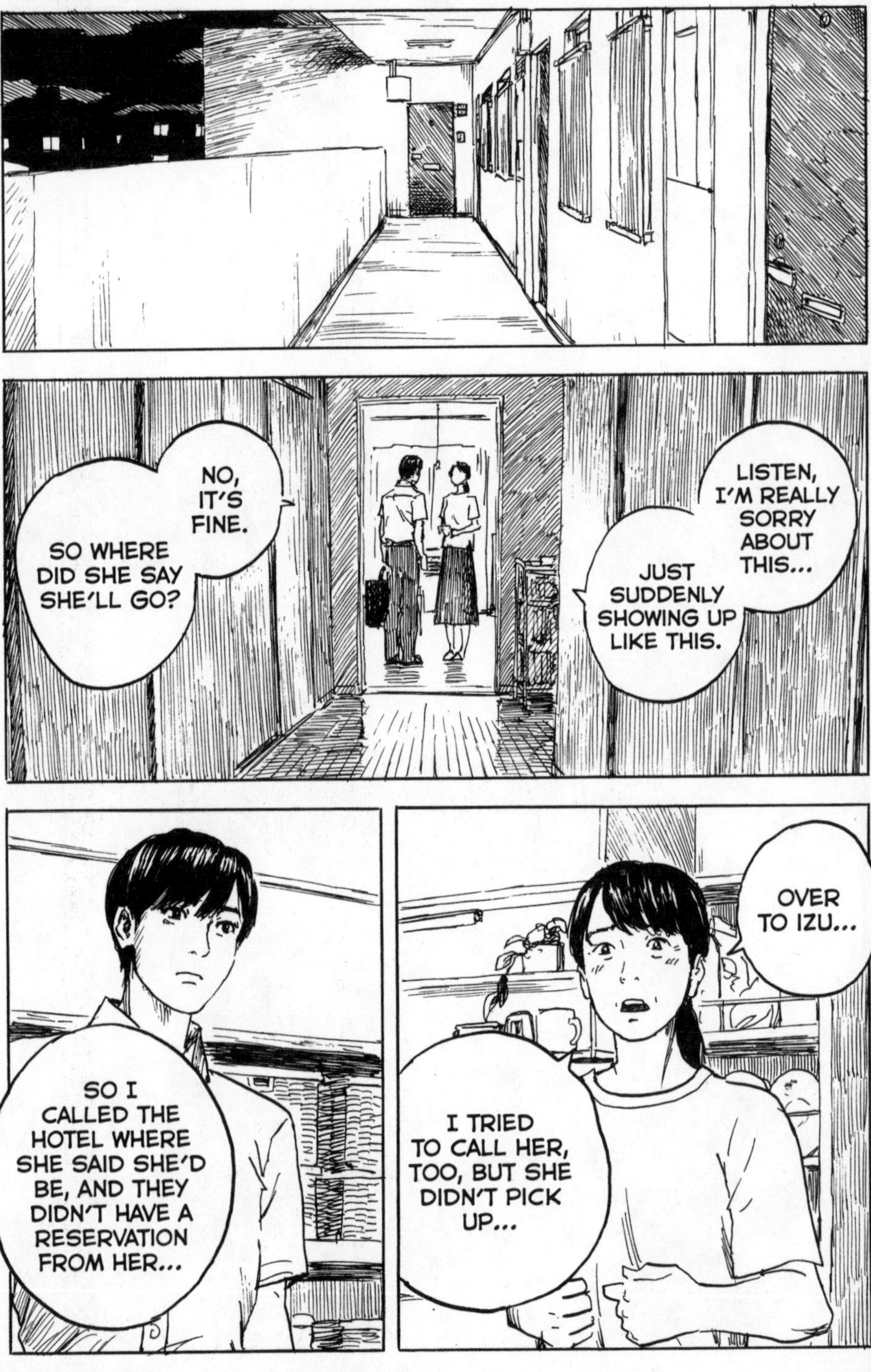
LISTEN, I'M REALLY SORRY ABOUT THIS...
JUST SUDDENLY SHOWING UP LIKE THIS.
NO, IT'S FINE.
SO WHERE DID SHE SAY SHE'LL GO?
OVER TO IZU...
I TRIED TO CALL HER, TOO, BUT SHE DIDN'T PICK UP...
SO I CALLED THE HOTEL WHERE SHE SAID SHE'D BE, AND THEY DIDN'T HAVE A RESERVATION FROM HER...

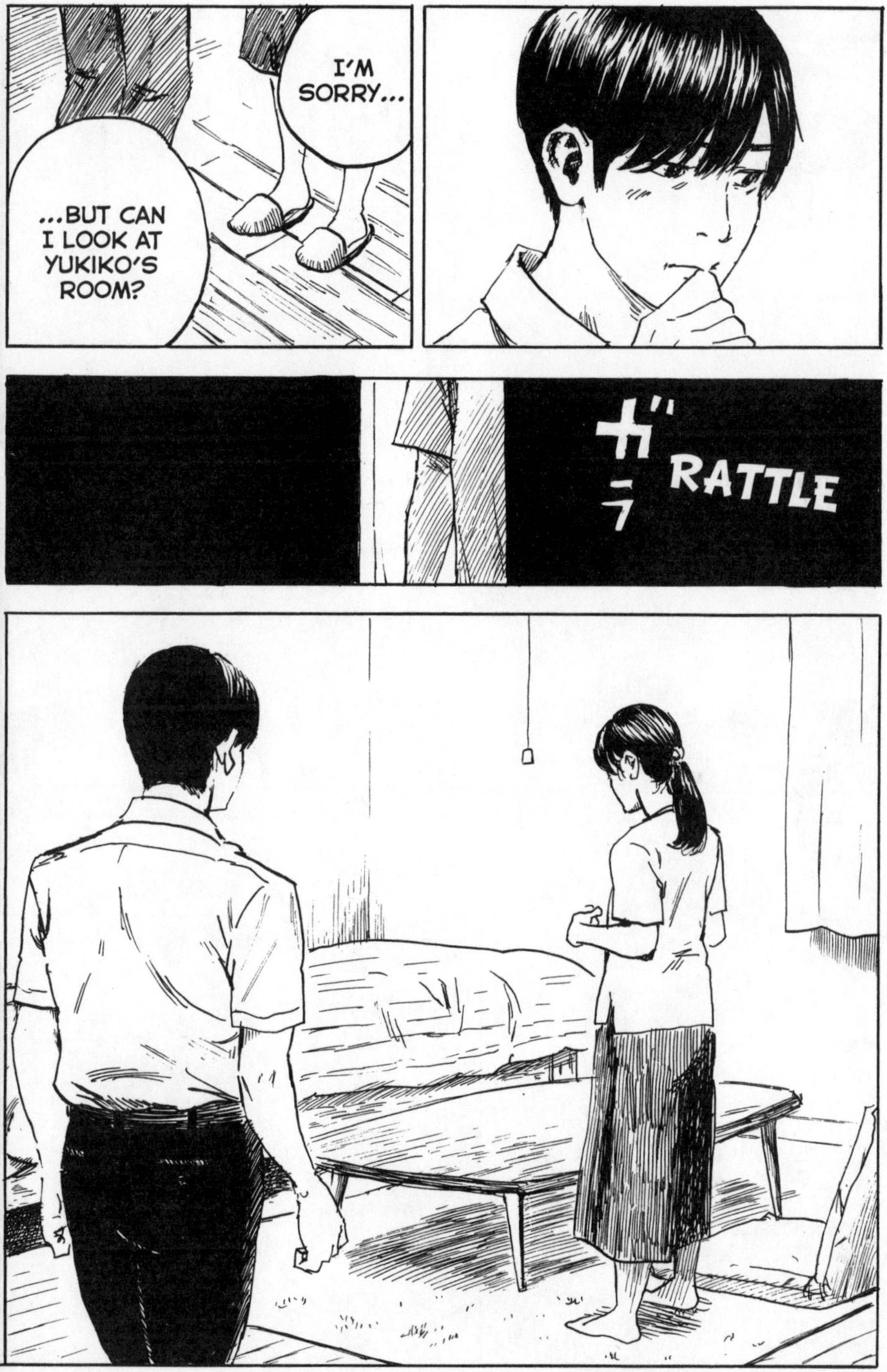
I'M SORRY...
...BUT CAN I LOOK AT YUKIKO'S ROOM?
ガラ
RATTLE

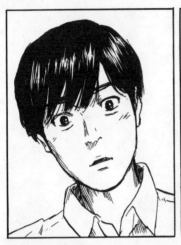
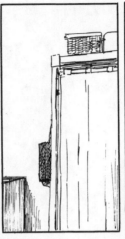
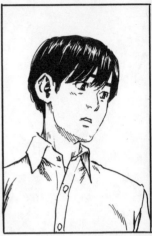
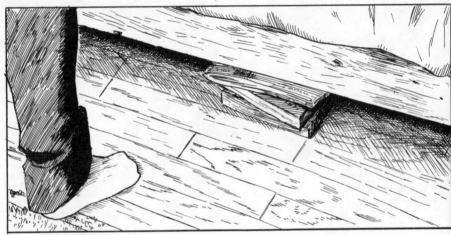
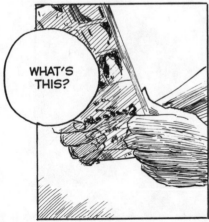

WHAT'S
THIS?

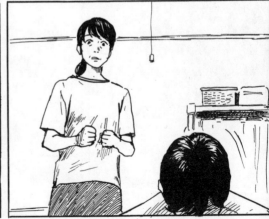

159

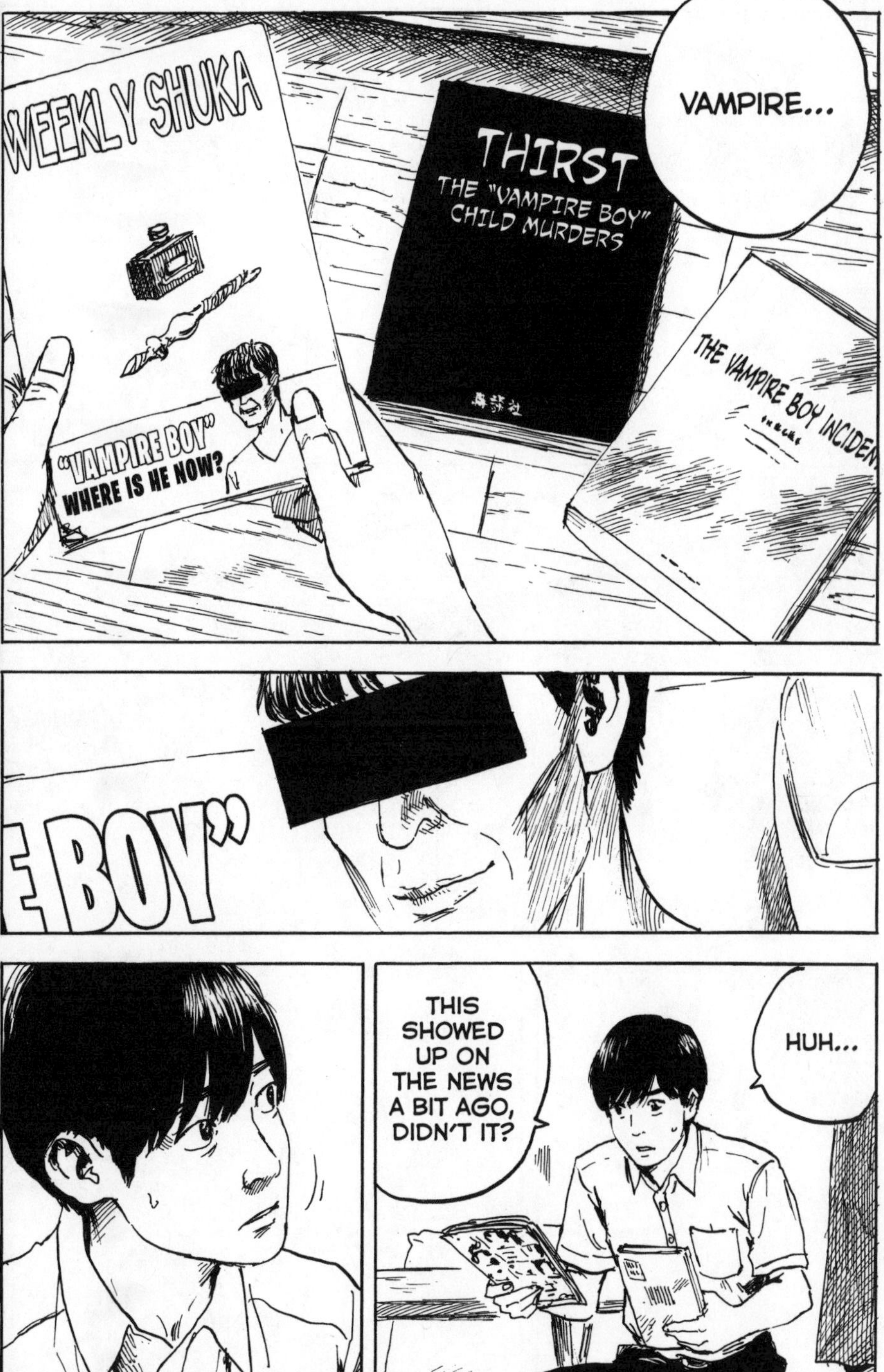
VAMPIRE...
THE VAMPIRE BOY INCIDEN
THIRST
THE "VAMPIRE BOY" CHILD MURDERS
WEEKLY SHUKA
"VAMPIRE BOY"
WHERE IS HE NOW?
E BOY"
HUH...
THIS SHOWED UP ON THE NEWS A BIT AGO, DIDN'T IT?

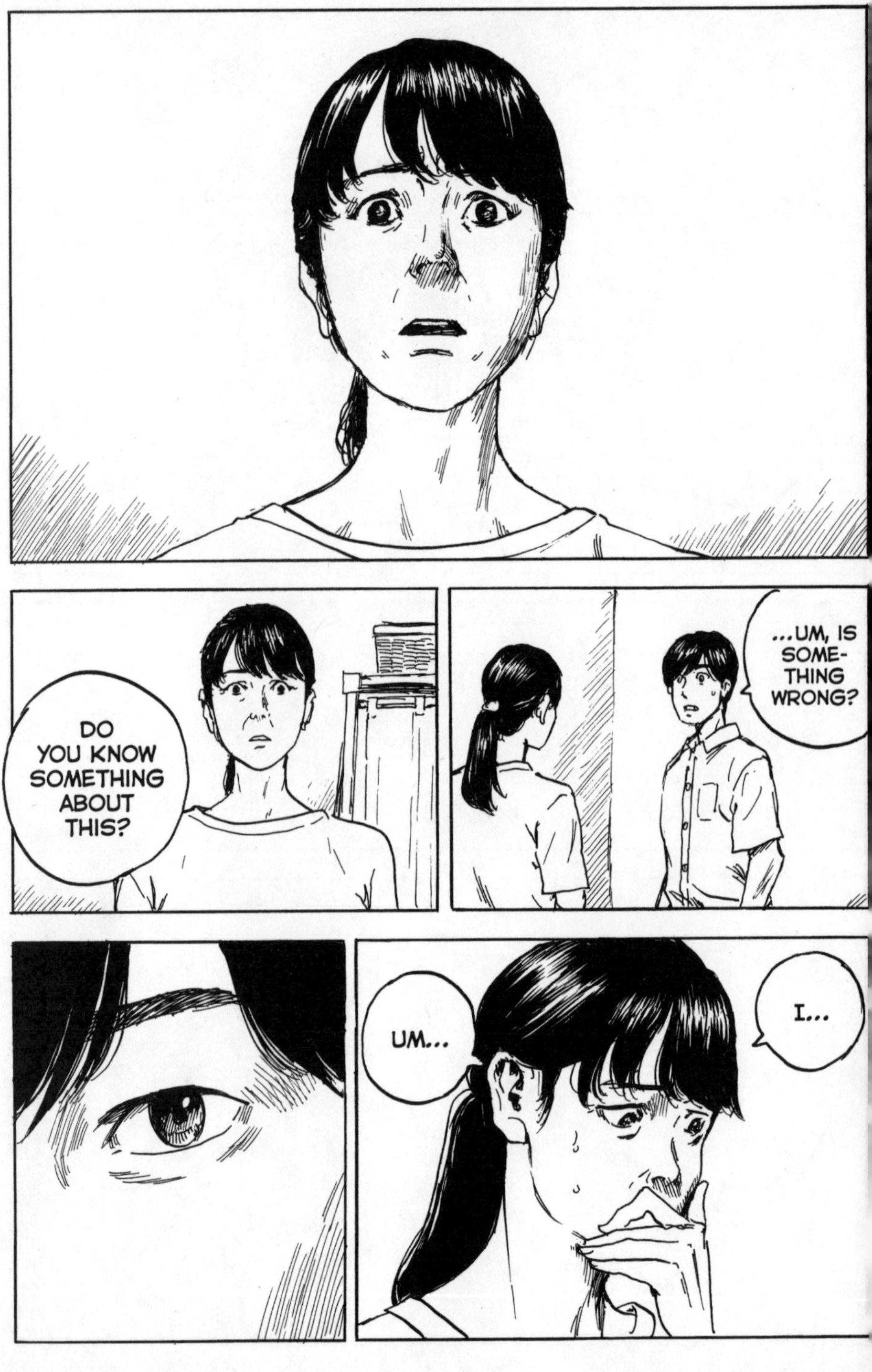
...UM, IS SOME-THING WRONG?
DO YOU KNOW SOMETHING ABOUT THIS?
I...
UM...

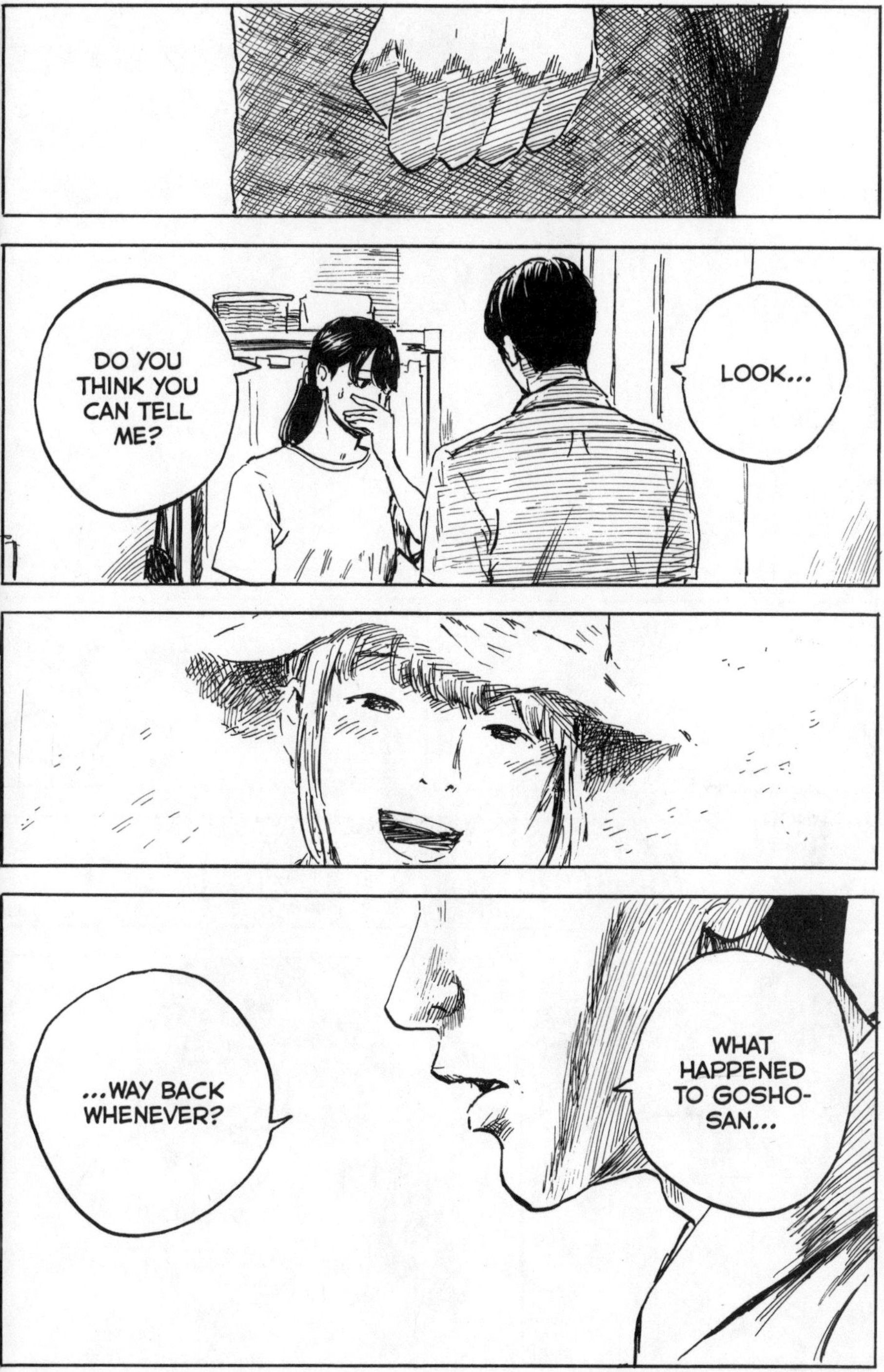
LOOK...
DO YOU THINK YOU CAN TELL ME?
WHAT HAPPENED TO GOSHO-SAN...
...WAY BACK WHENEVER?

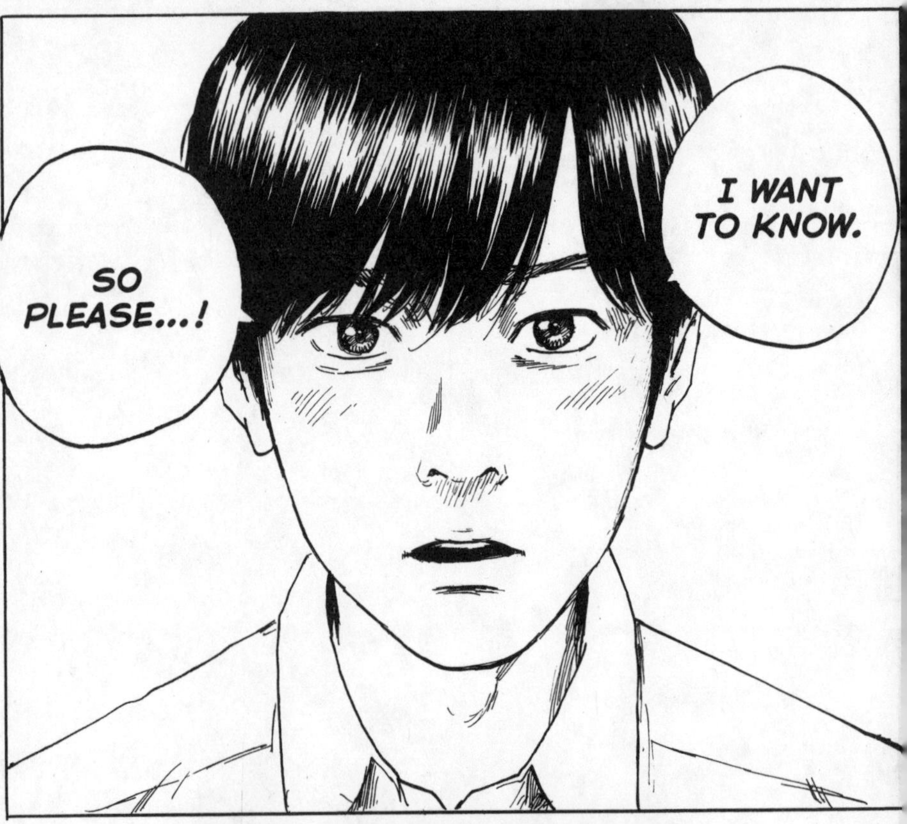
I WANT TO KNOW.
SO PLEASE...!

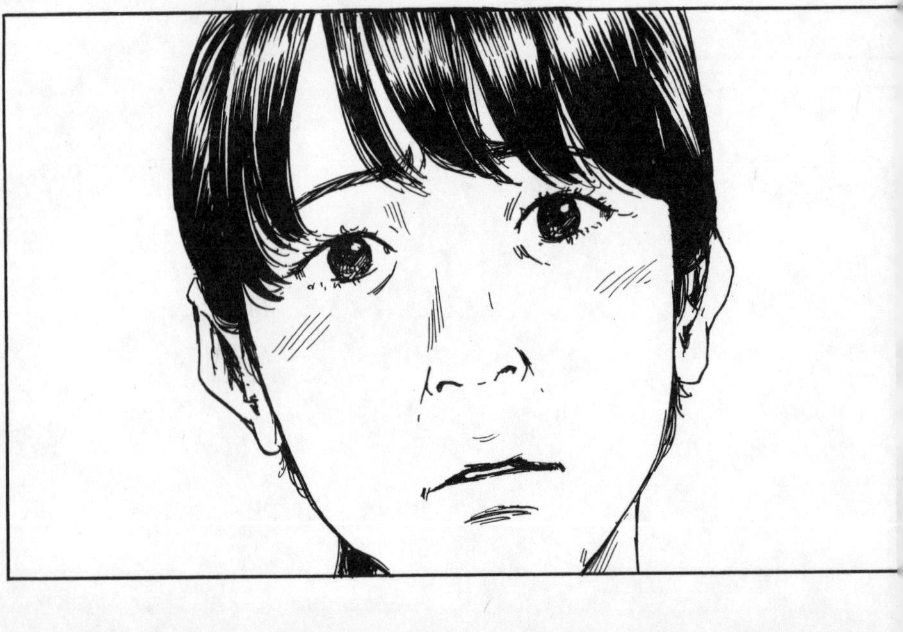

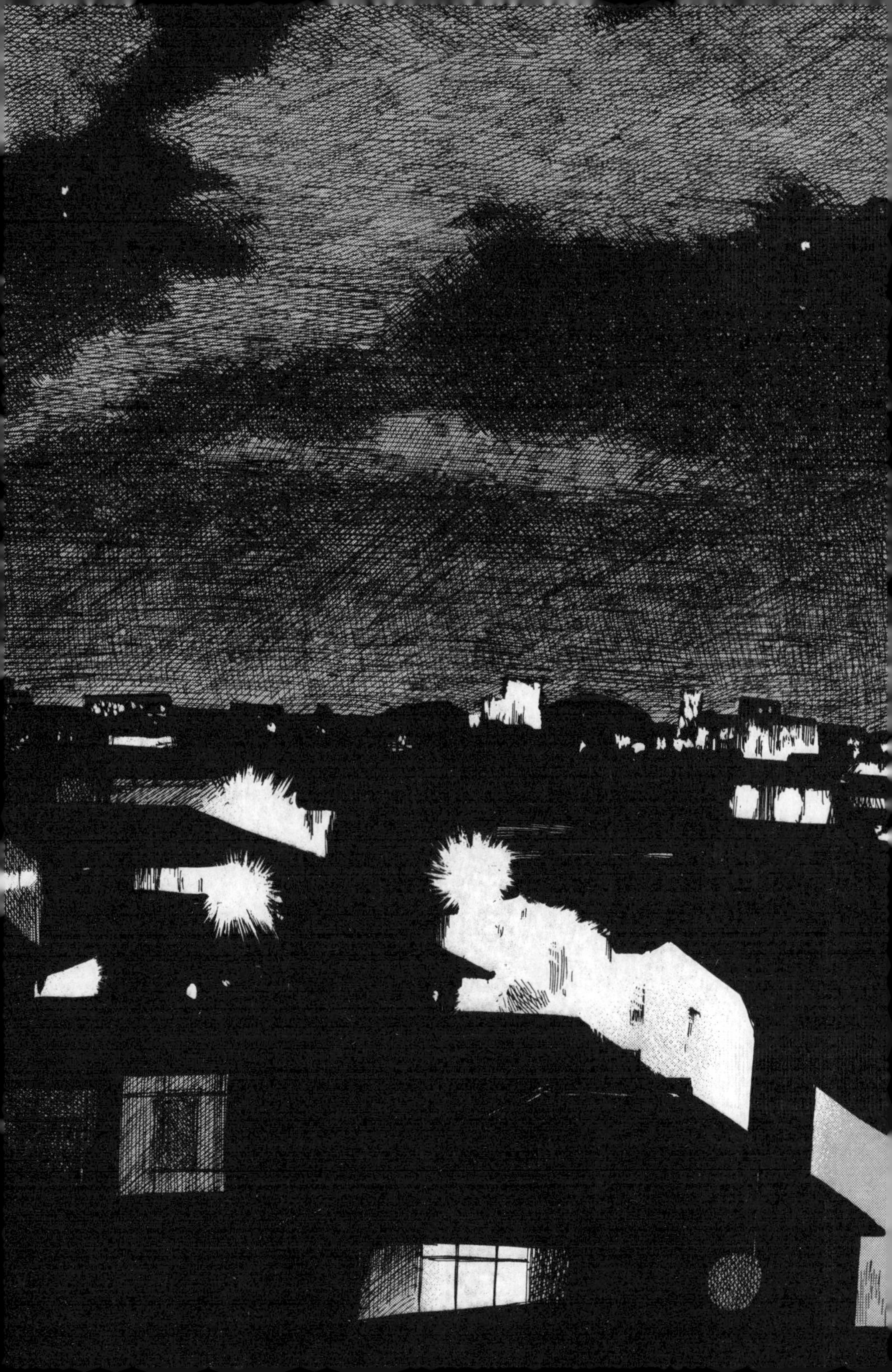

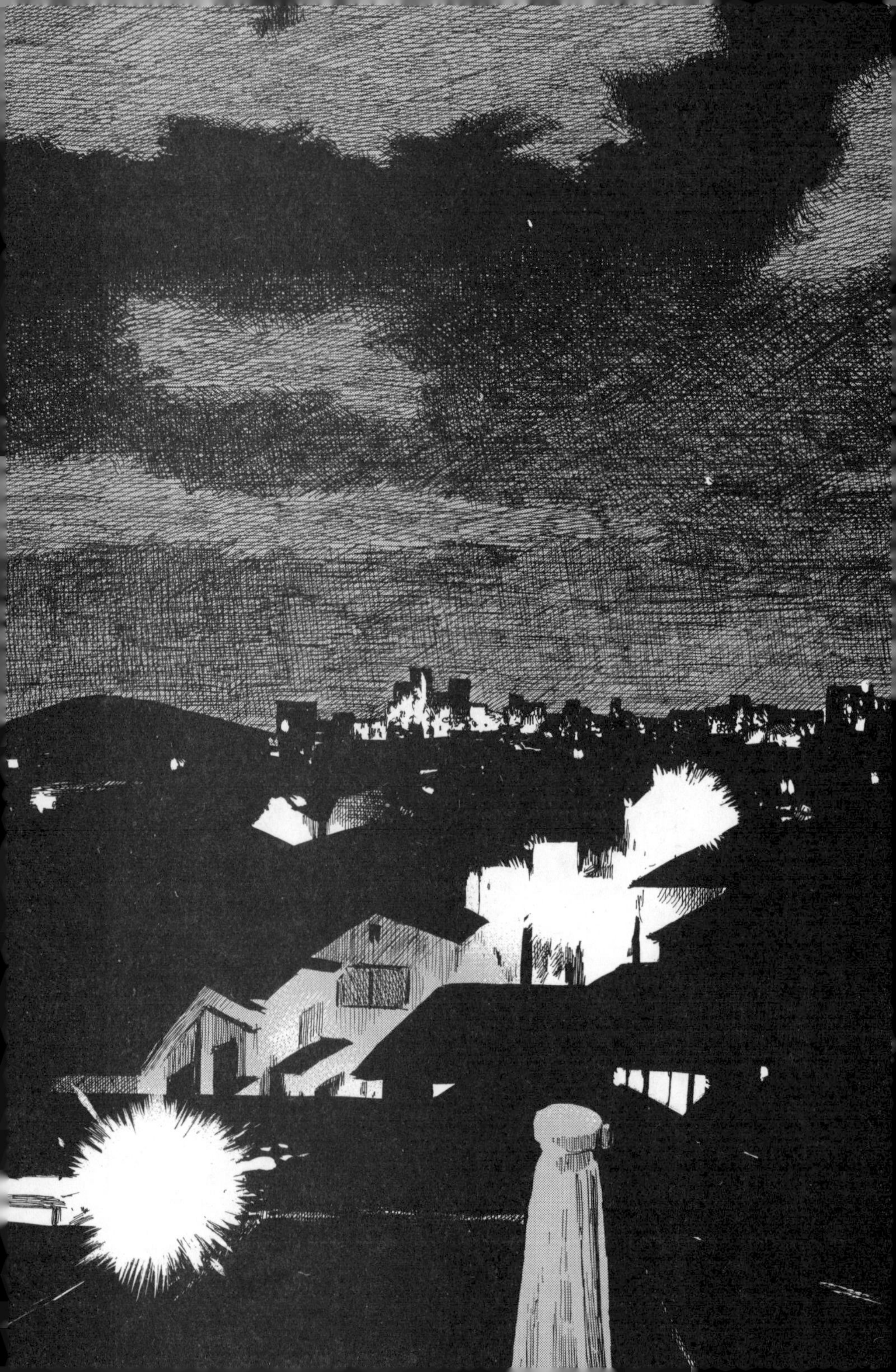

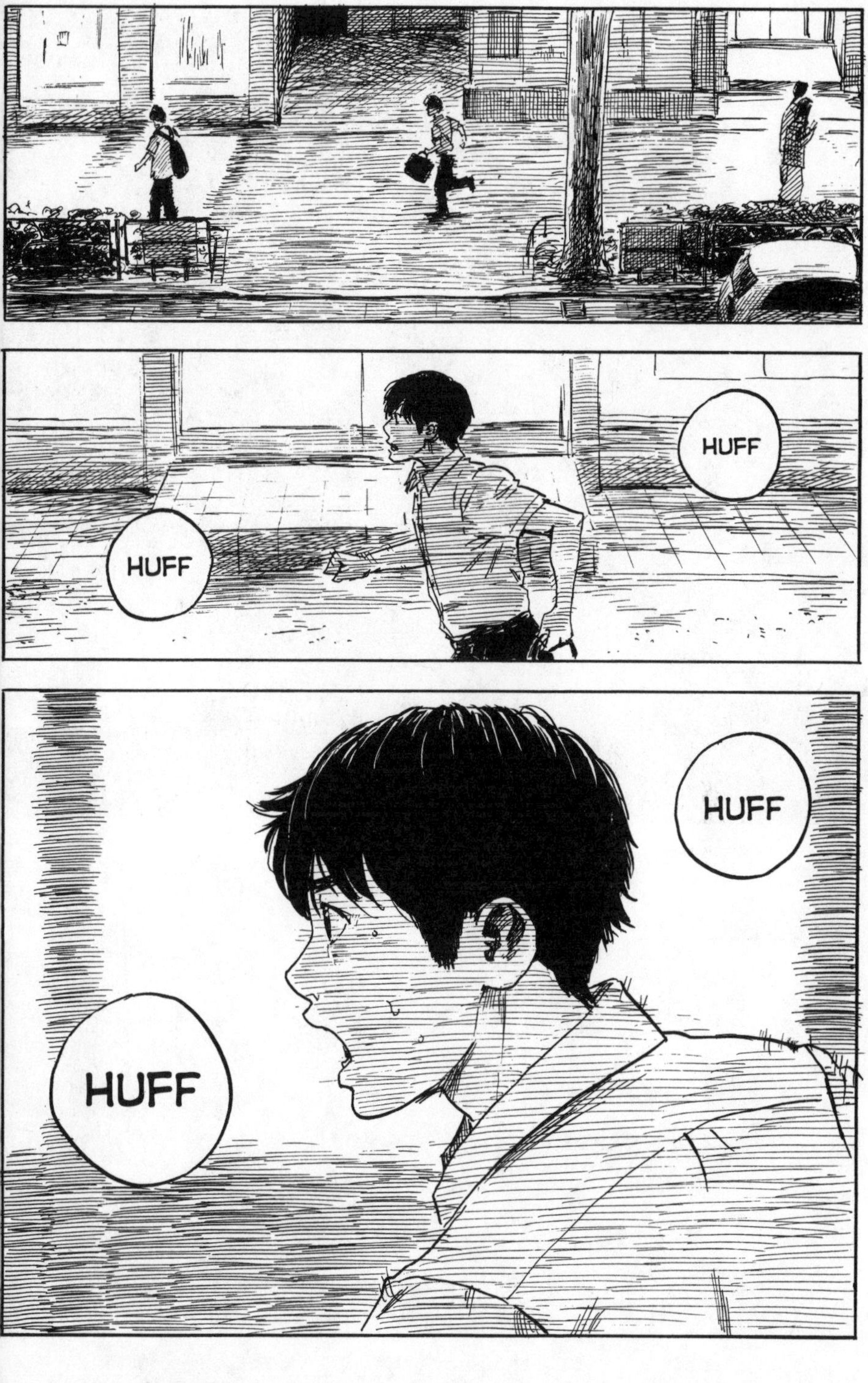
HUFF
HUFF
HUFF
HUFF

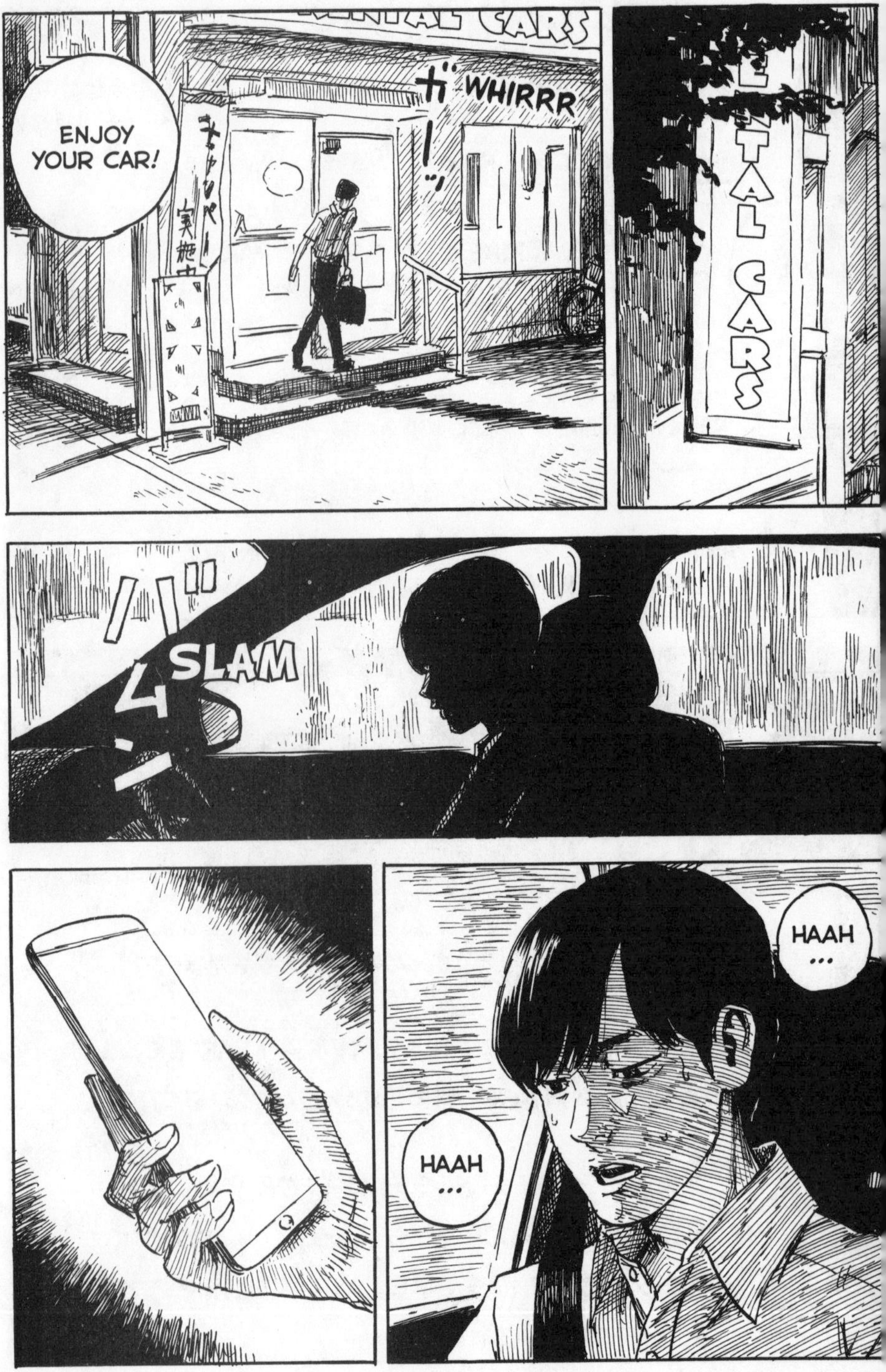
ENJOY YOUR CAR!
WHIRRR
SLAM
HAAH ...
HAAH ...

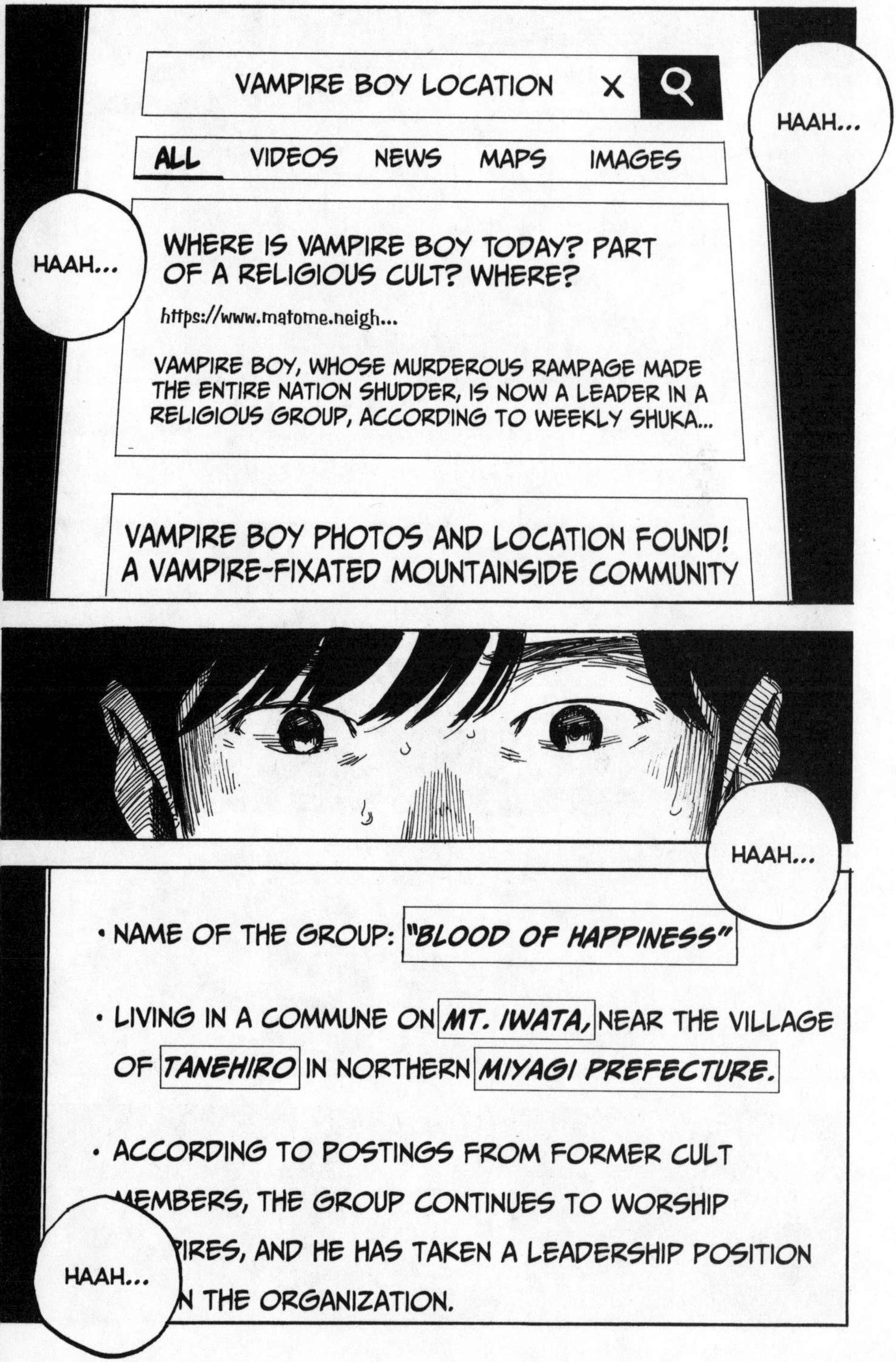
HAAH...
VAMPIRE BOY LOCATION X
ALL VIDEOS NEWS MAPS IMAGES
WHERE IS VAMPIRE BOY TODAY? PART OF A RELIGIOUS CULT? WHERE?
https://www.matome.neigh...
VAMPIRE BOY, WHOSE MURDEROUS RAMPAGE MADE THE ENTIRE NATION SHUDDER, IS NOW A LEADER IN A RELIGIOUS GROUP, ACCORDING TO WEEKLY SHUKA...
HAAH...
VAMPIRE BOY PHOTOS AND LOCATION FOUND! A VAMPIRE-FIXATED MOUNTAINSIDE COMMUNITY
HAAH...
• NAME OF THE GROUP: "BLOOD OF HAPPINESS"
• LIVING IN A COMMUNE ON MT. IWATA, NEAR THE VILLAGE OF TANEHIRO IN NORTHERN MIYAGI PREFECTURE.
• ACCORDING TO POSTINGS FROM FORMER CULT
EMBERS, THE GROUP CONTINUES TO WORSHIP
PIRES, AND HE HAS TAKEN A LEADERSHIP POSITION
N THE ORGANIZATION.
HAAH...

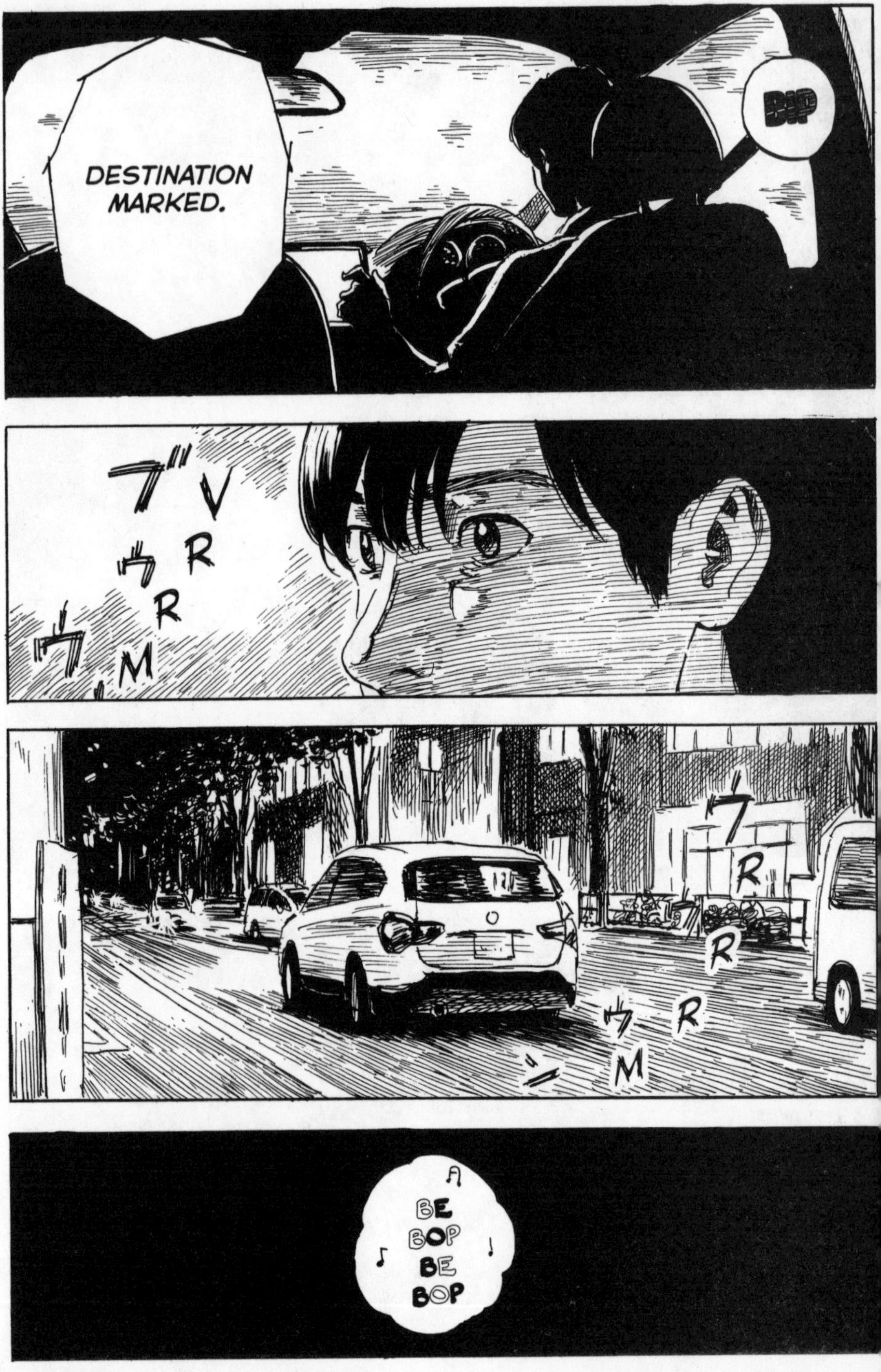
BIP
DESTINATION MARKED.
VRRM
RRRM
BE BOP BE BOP

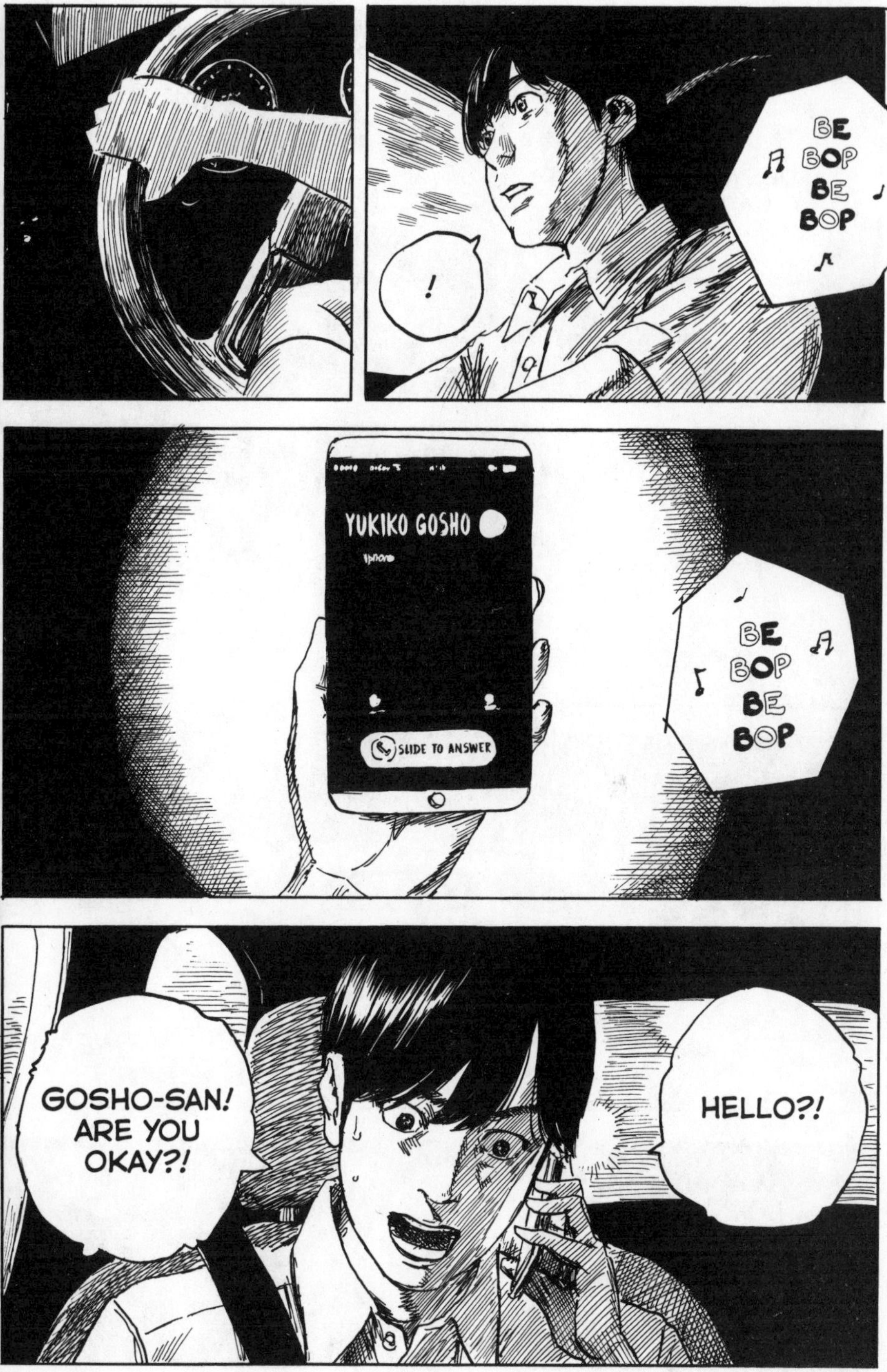

BE BOP BE BOP
!
YUKIKO GOSHO
SLIDE TO ANSWER
BE BOP BE BOP
HELLO?!
GOSHO-SAN! ARE YOU OKAY?!

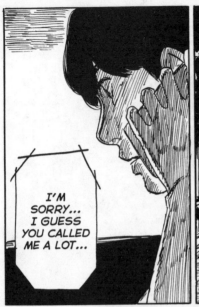
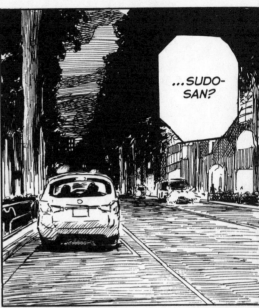

...SUDO-SAN?

I'M SORRY... I GUESS YOU CALLED ME A LOT...

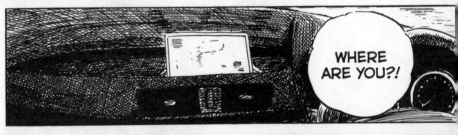

WHERE ARE YOU?!

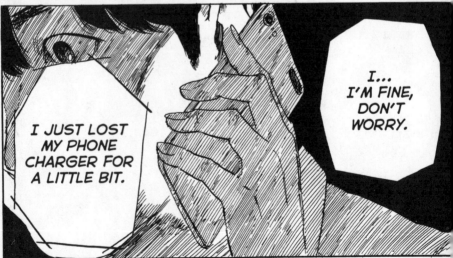

I... I'M FINE, DON'T WORRY.

I JUST LOST MY PHONE CHARGER FOR A LITTLE BIT.

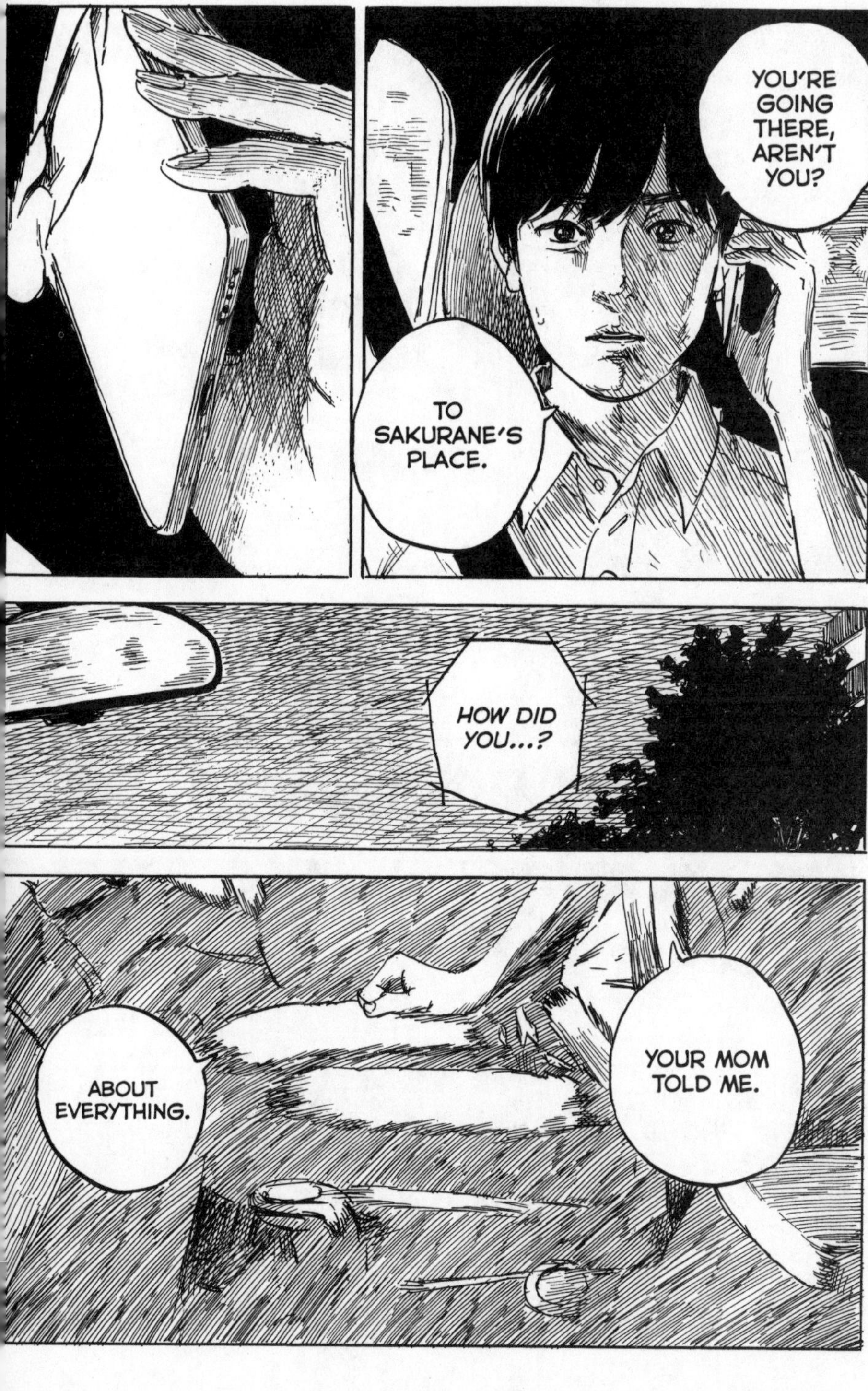
YOU'RE GOING THERE, AREN'T YOU?
TO SAKURANE'S PLACE.
HOW DID YOU...?
YOUR MOM TOLD ME.
ABOUT EVERYTHING.

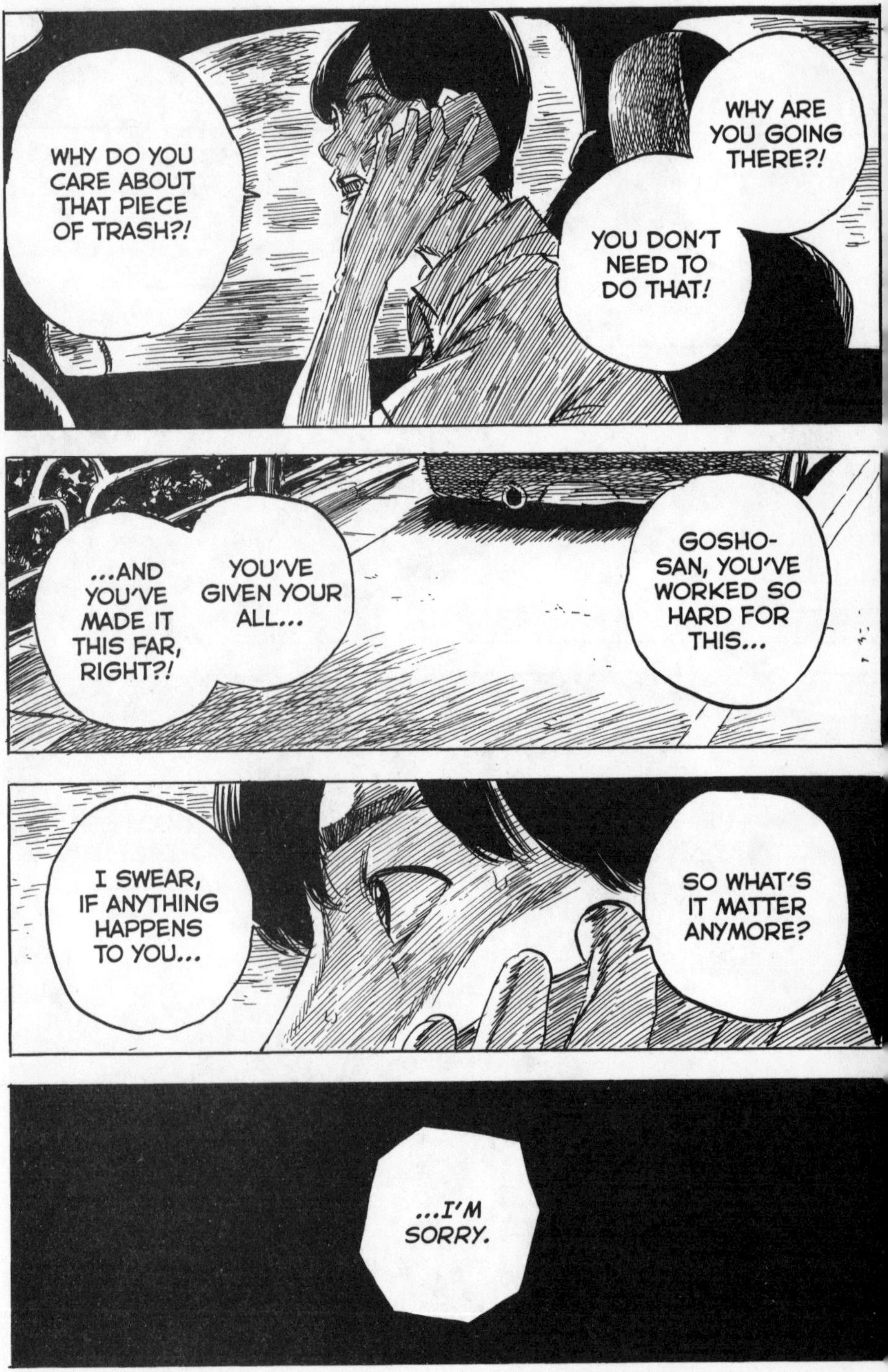
WHY ARE YOU GOING THERE?!
YOU DON'T NEED TO DO THAT!
WHY DO YOU CARE ABOUT THAT PIECE OF TRASH?!
GOSHO-SAN, YOU'VE WORKED SO HARD FOR THIS...
YOU'VE GIVEN YOUR ALL...
...AND YOU'VE MADE IT THIS FAR, RIGHT?!
SO WHAT'S IT MATTER ANYMORE?
I SWEAR, IF ANYTHING HAPPENS TO YOU...
...I'M SORRY.

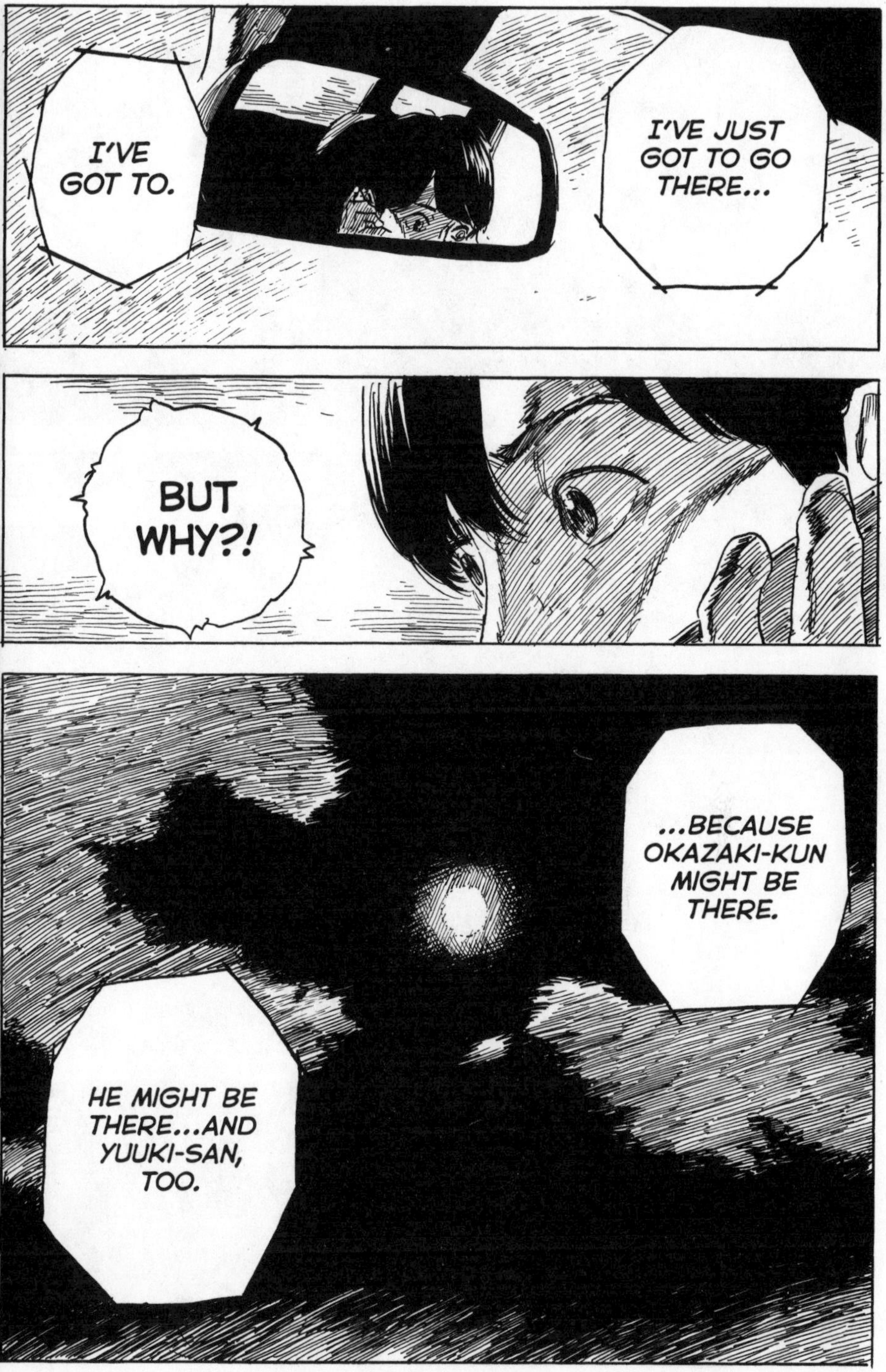
I'VE JUST GOT TO GO THERE...
I'VE GOT TO.
BUT WHY?!
...BECAUSE OKAZAKI-KUN MIGHT BE THERE.
HE MIGHT BE THERE...AND YUUKI-SAN, TOO.

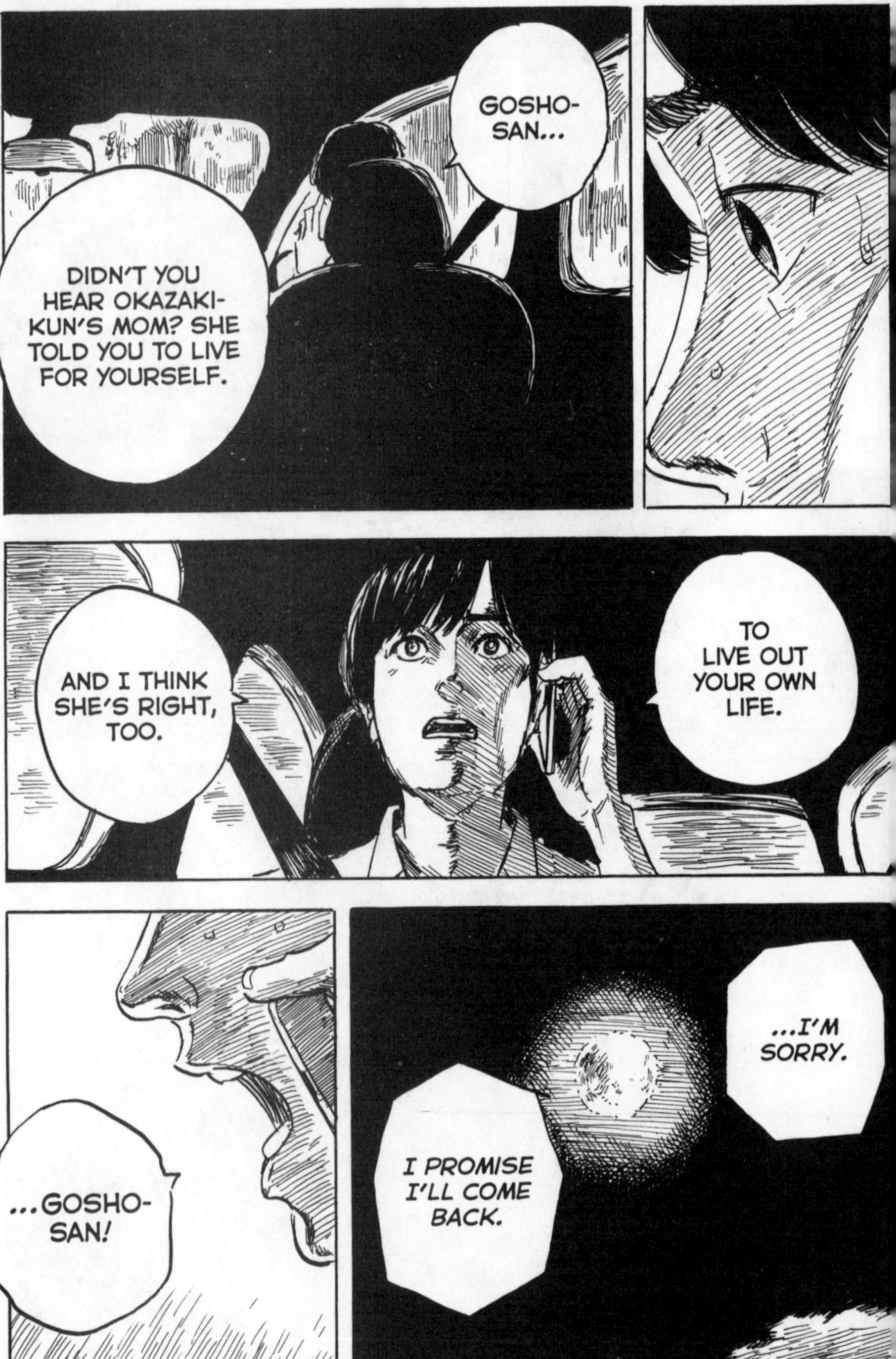
GOSHO-SAN...
DIDN'T YOU HEAR OKAZAKI-KUN'S MOM? SHE TOLD YOU TO LIVE FOR YOURSELF.
TO LIVE OUT YOUR OWN LIFE.
AND I THINK SHE'S RIGHT, TOO.
...I'M SORRY.
I PROMISE I'LL COME BACK.
...GOSHO-SAN!

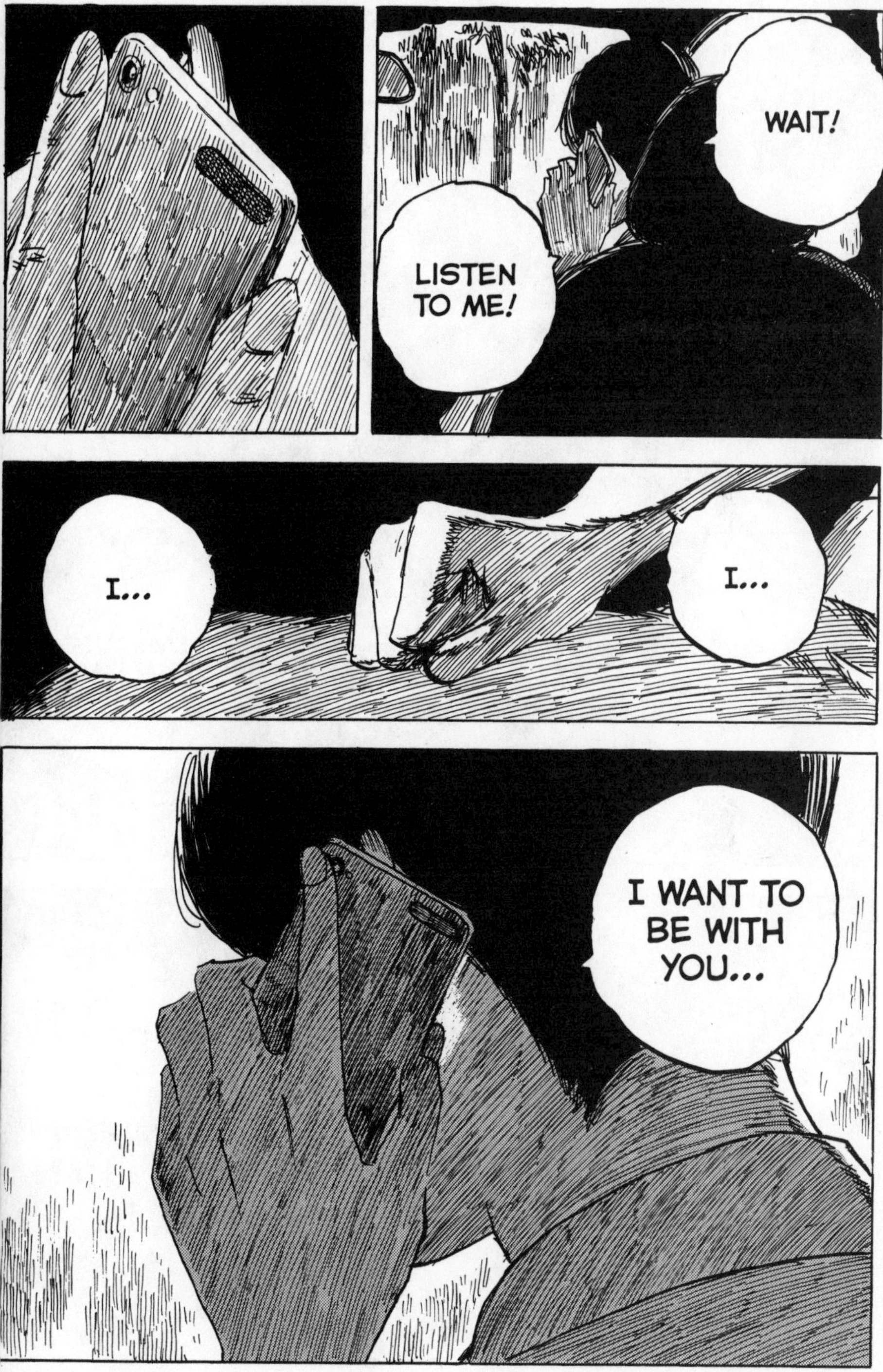
WAIT!
LISTEN TO ME!
I...
I...
I WANT TO BE WITH YOU...

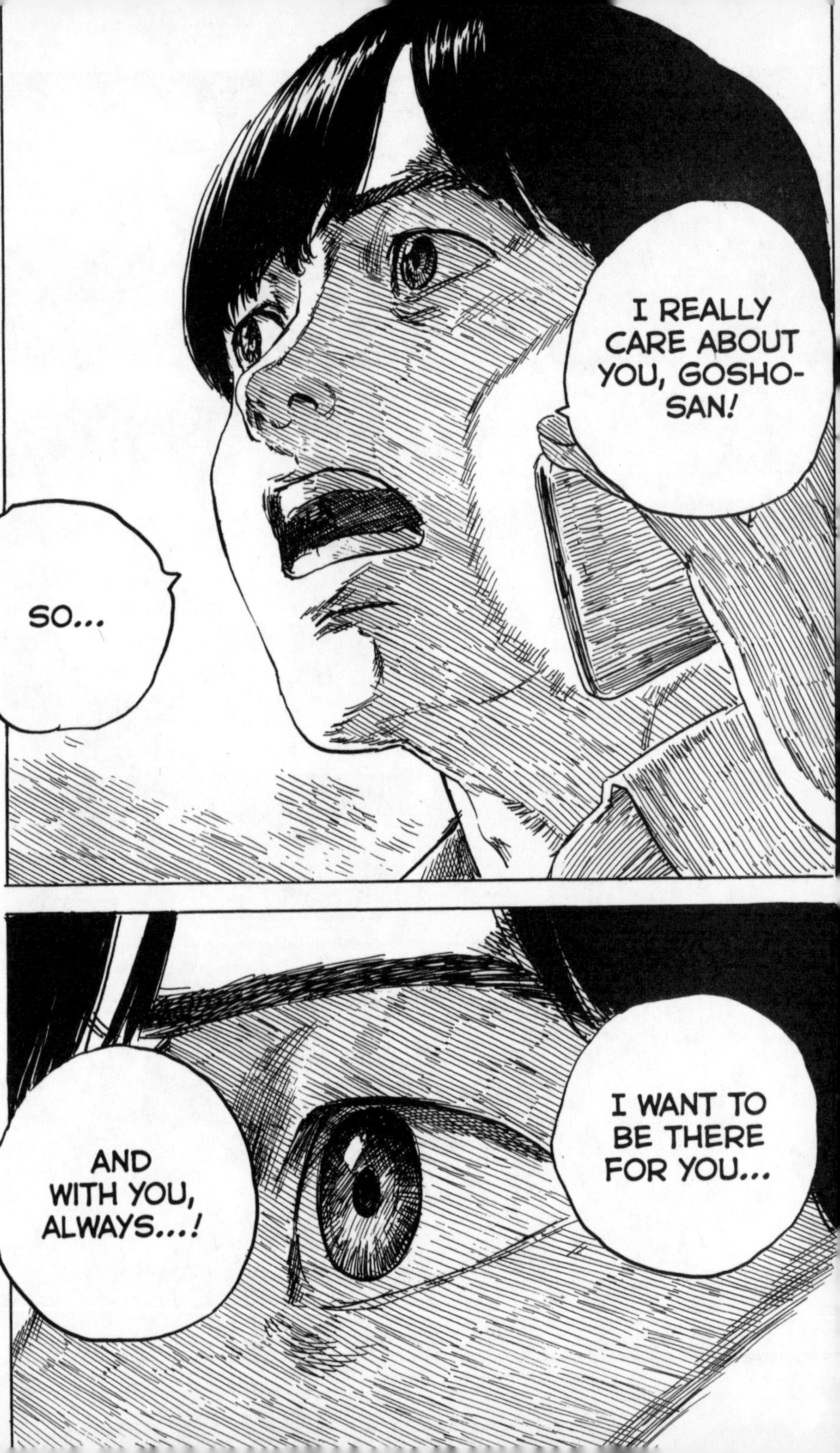
I REALLY CARE ABOUT YOU, GOSHO-SAN!
SO...
I WANT TO BE THERE FOR YOU...
AND WITH YOU, ALWAYS...!

VRRM
ゴオオオ
...WELL, THANK YOU.
JUST HEARING THAT FROM YOU... IT MAKES ME HAPPY.
CLICK
BEEP
BEEP

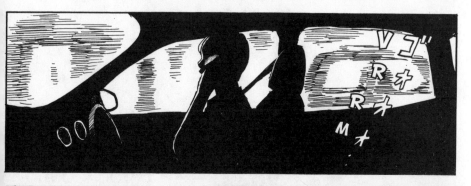

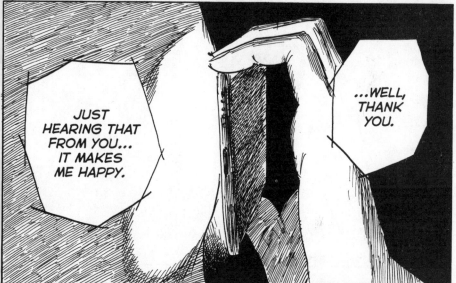

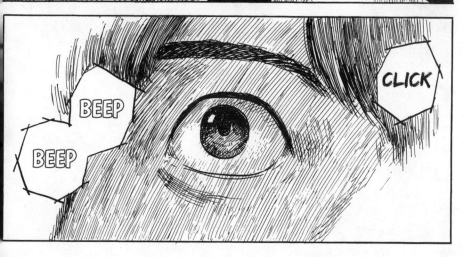

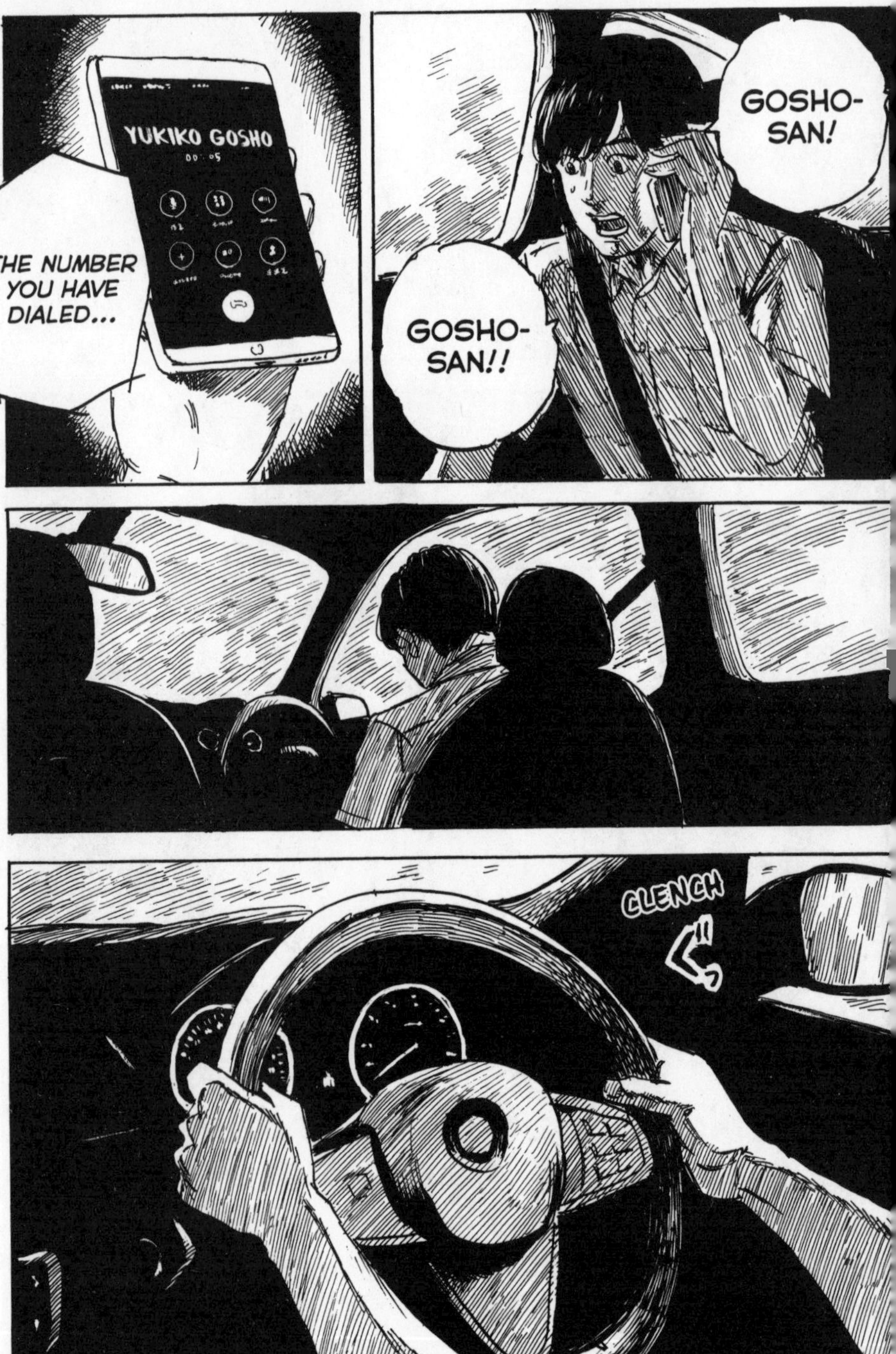
GOSHO-SAN!
GOSHO-SAN!!
YUKIKO GOSHO
00:05
THE NUMBER YOU HAVE DIALED...
CLENCH

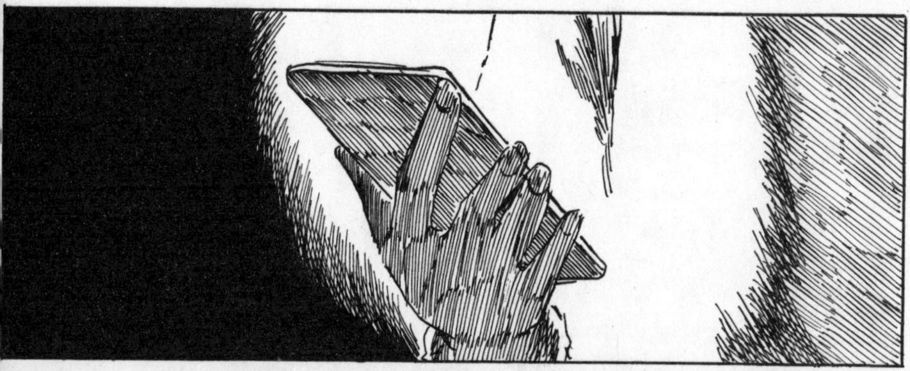
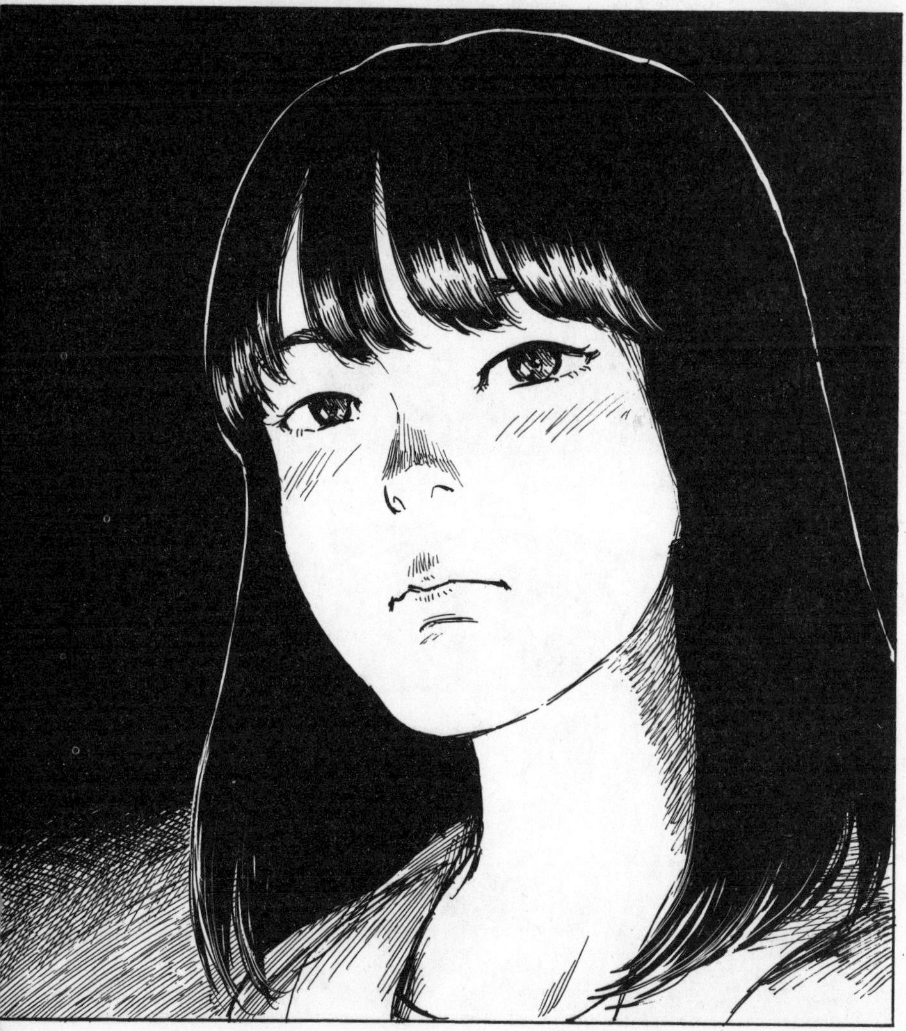

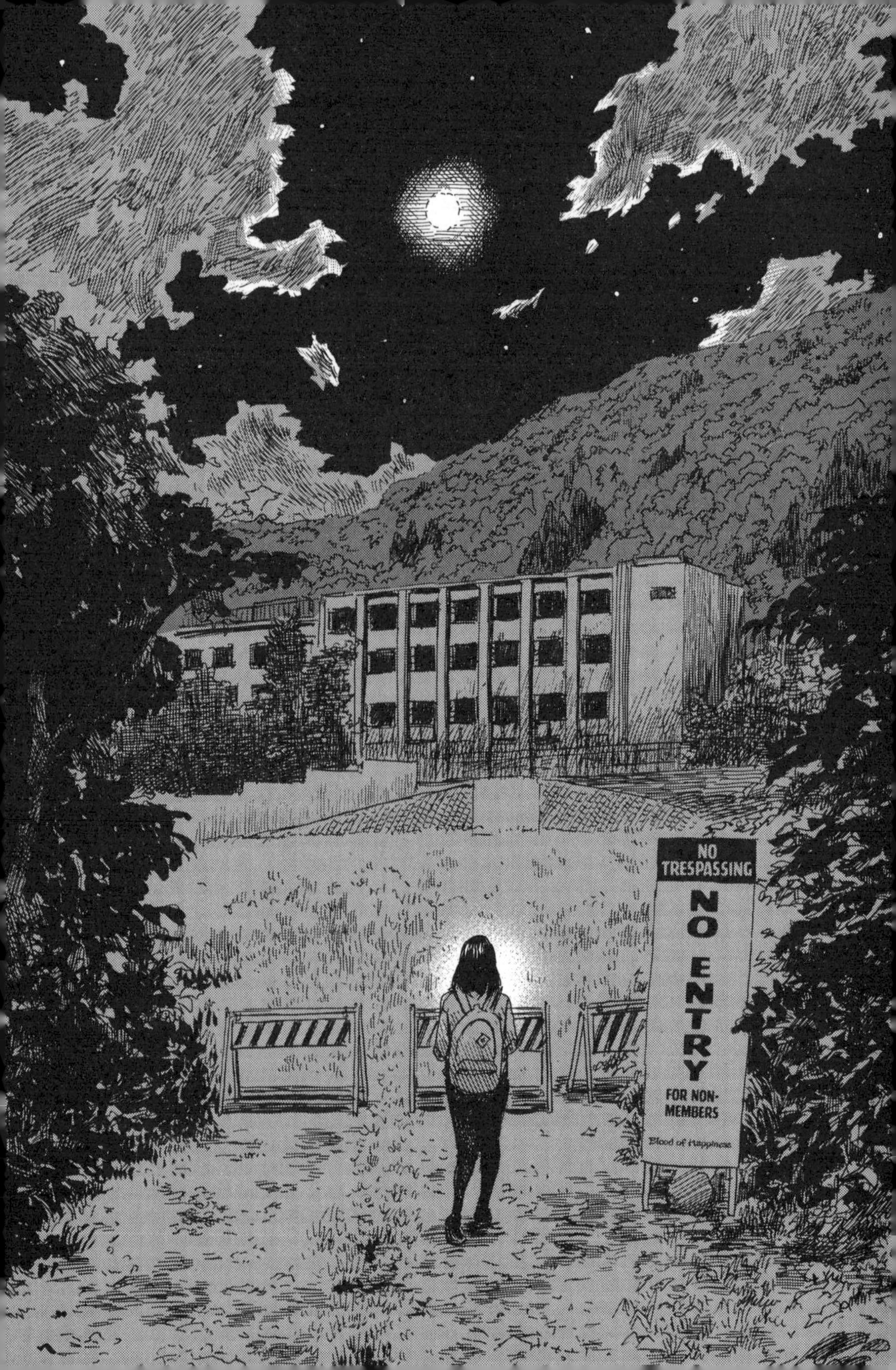
NO TRESPASSING
NO ENTRY
FOR NON-MEMBERS
Blood of Happiness

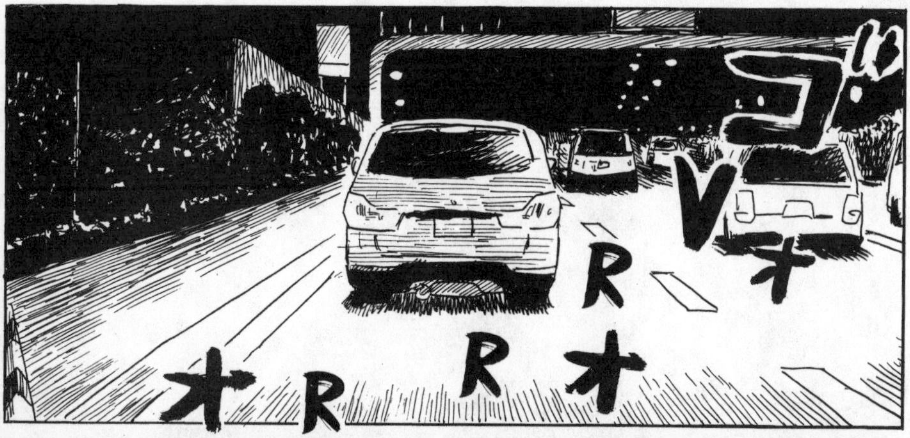

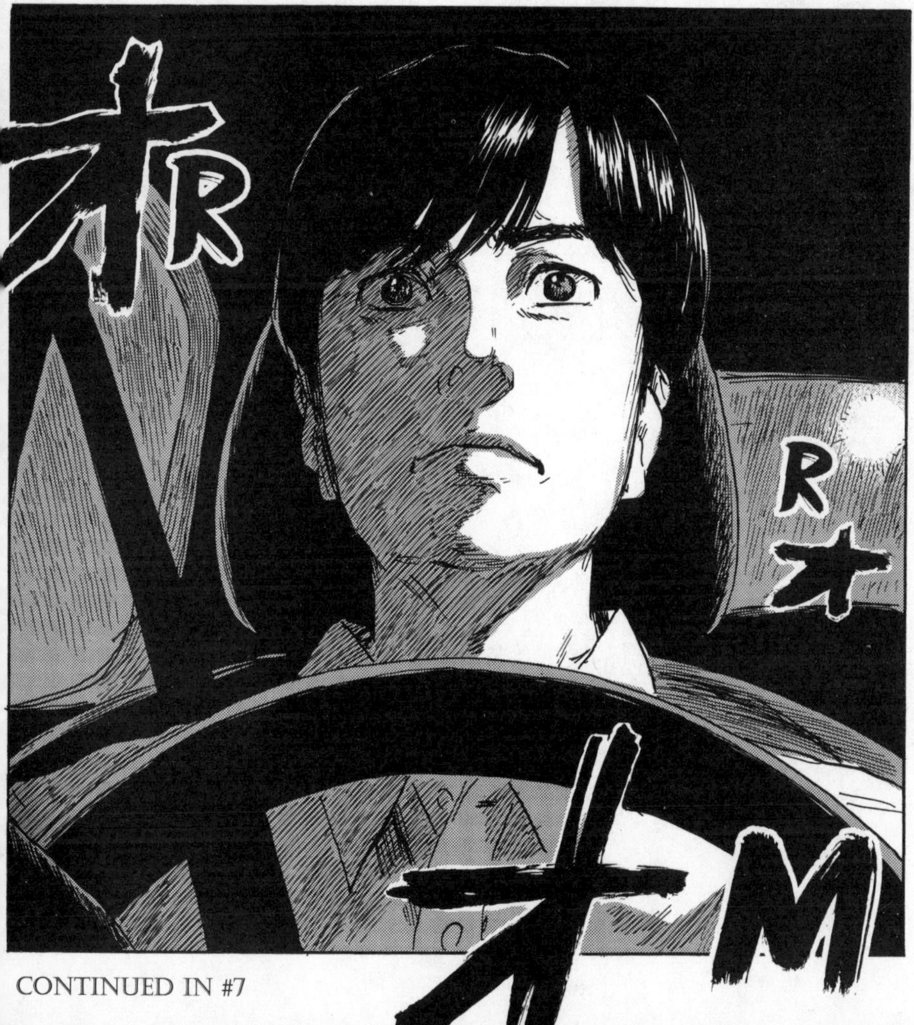

CONTINUED IN #7

HAPPINESS

HAPPINESS

NEXT VOLUME

A RISKY INFLITRATION ON A DARK NIGHT...
AND AN ENCOUNTER WITH SAKURANE,
THE MURDEROUS CRAVER OF BLOOD!

A VAMPIRE

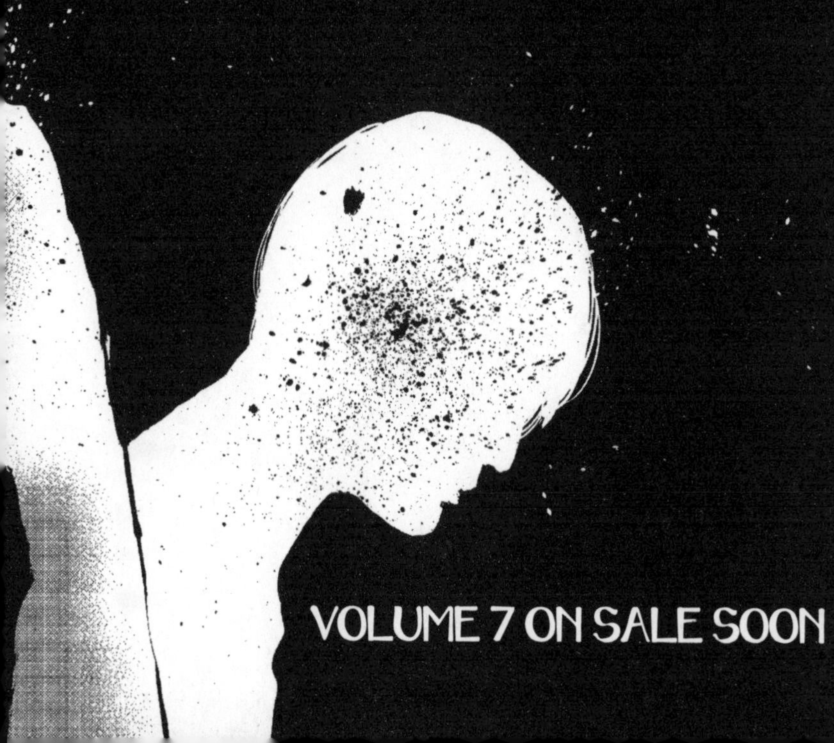

VOLUME 7 ON SALE SOON

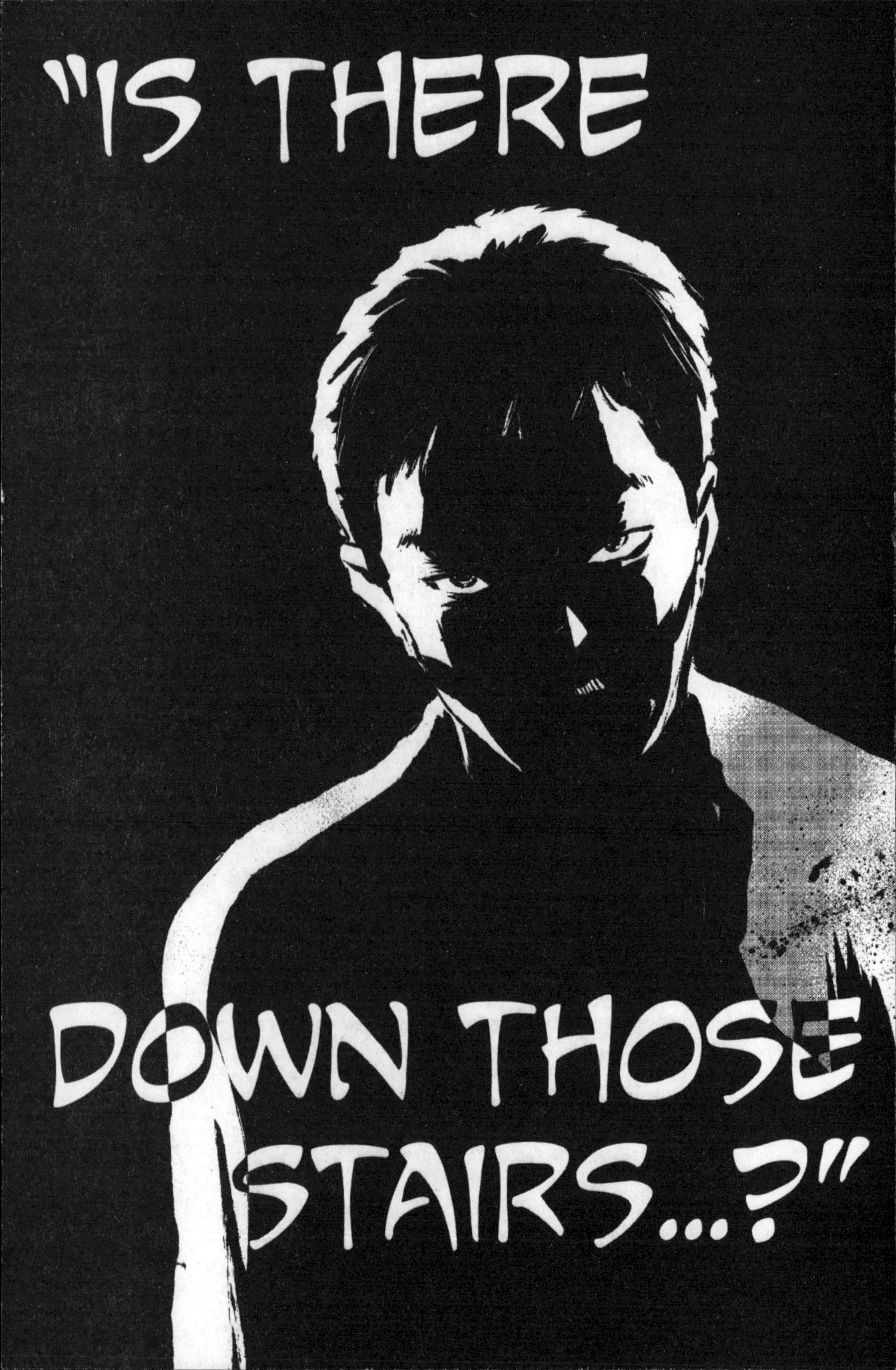
"IS THERE
DOWN THOSE
STAIRS...?"

AAH...

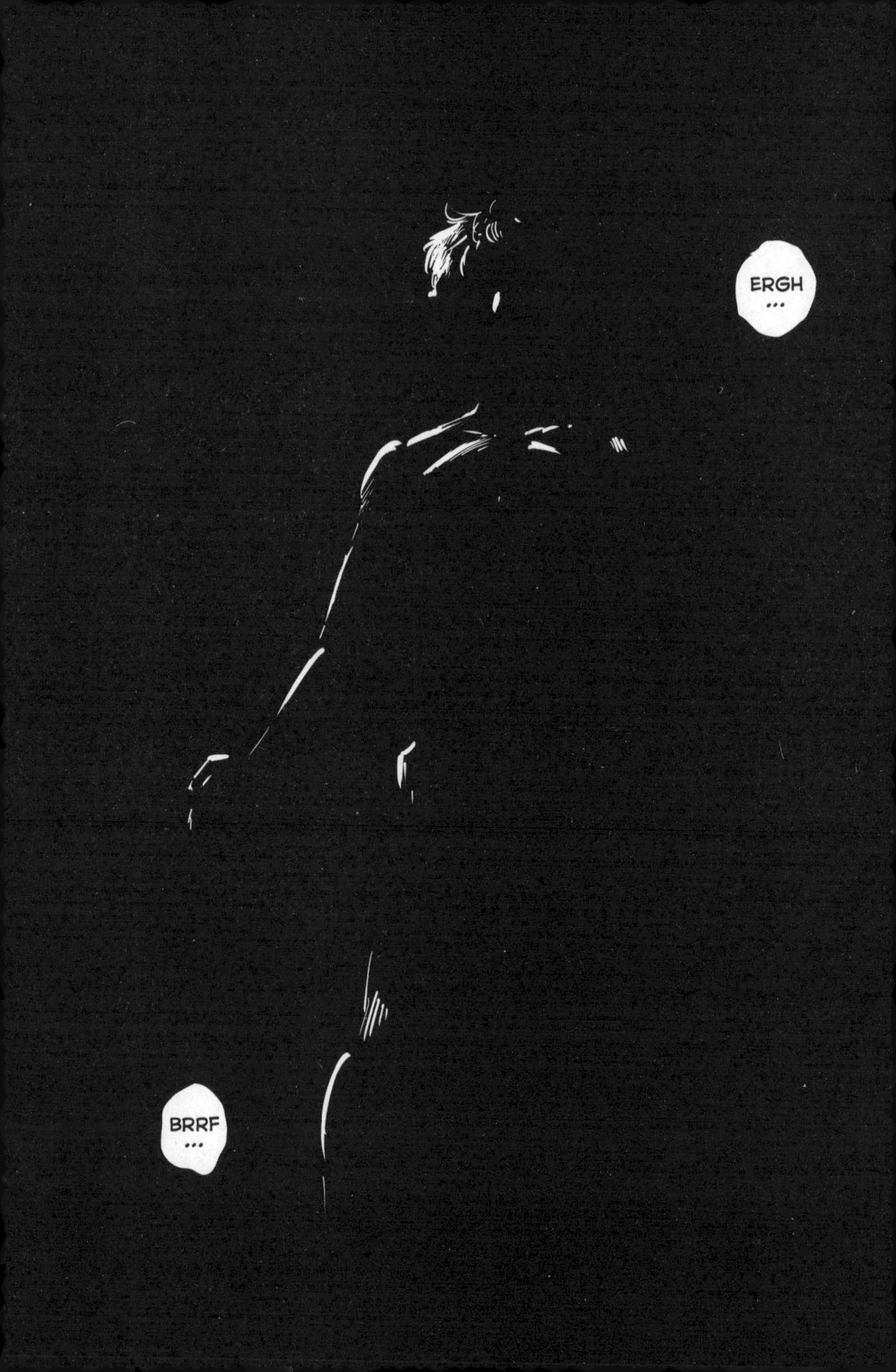
ERGH ...
BRRF ...

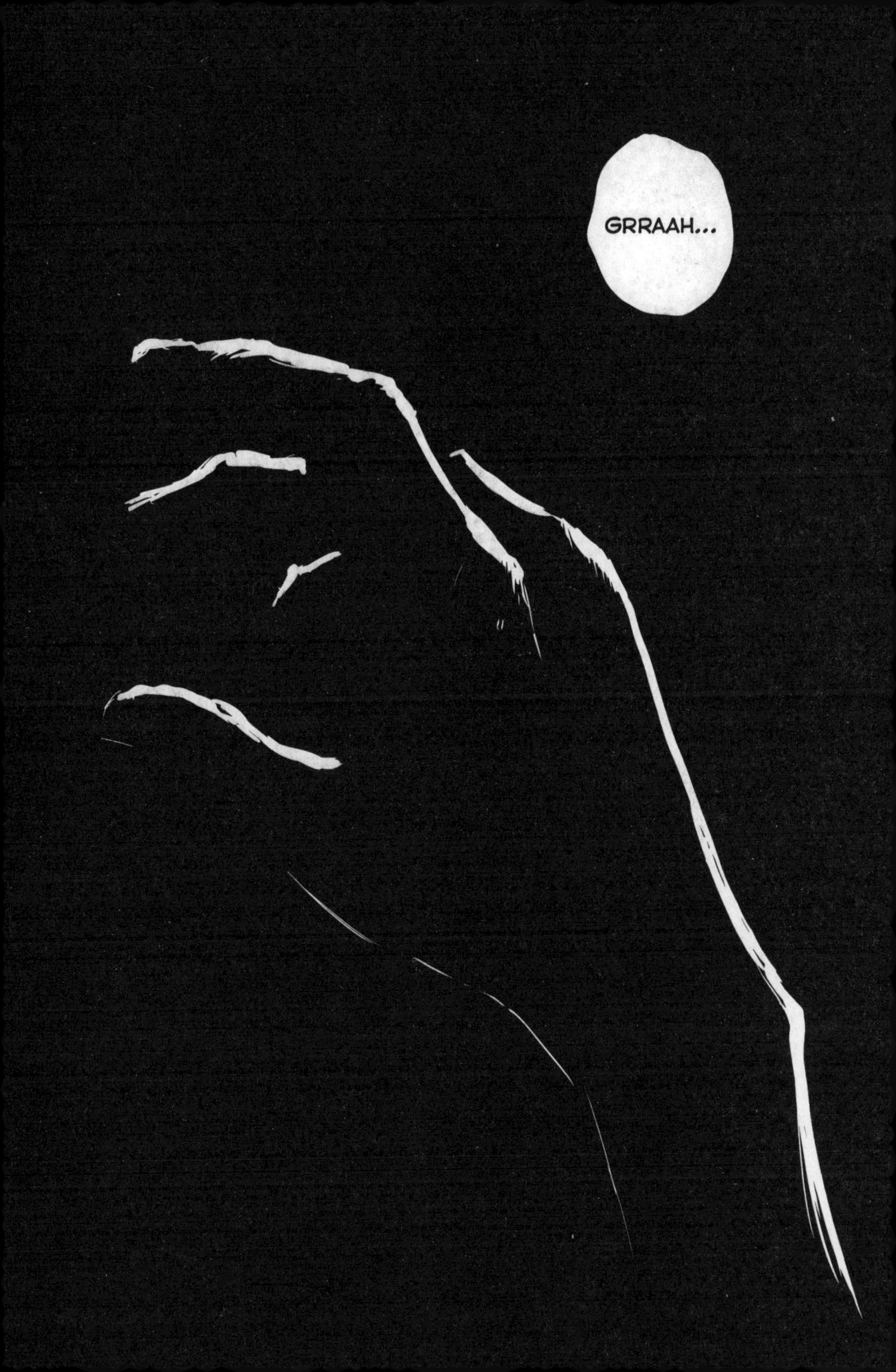
GRRAAH...

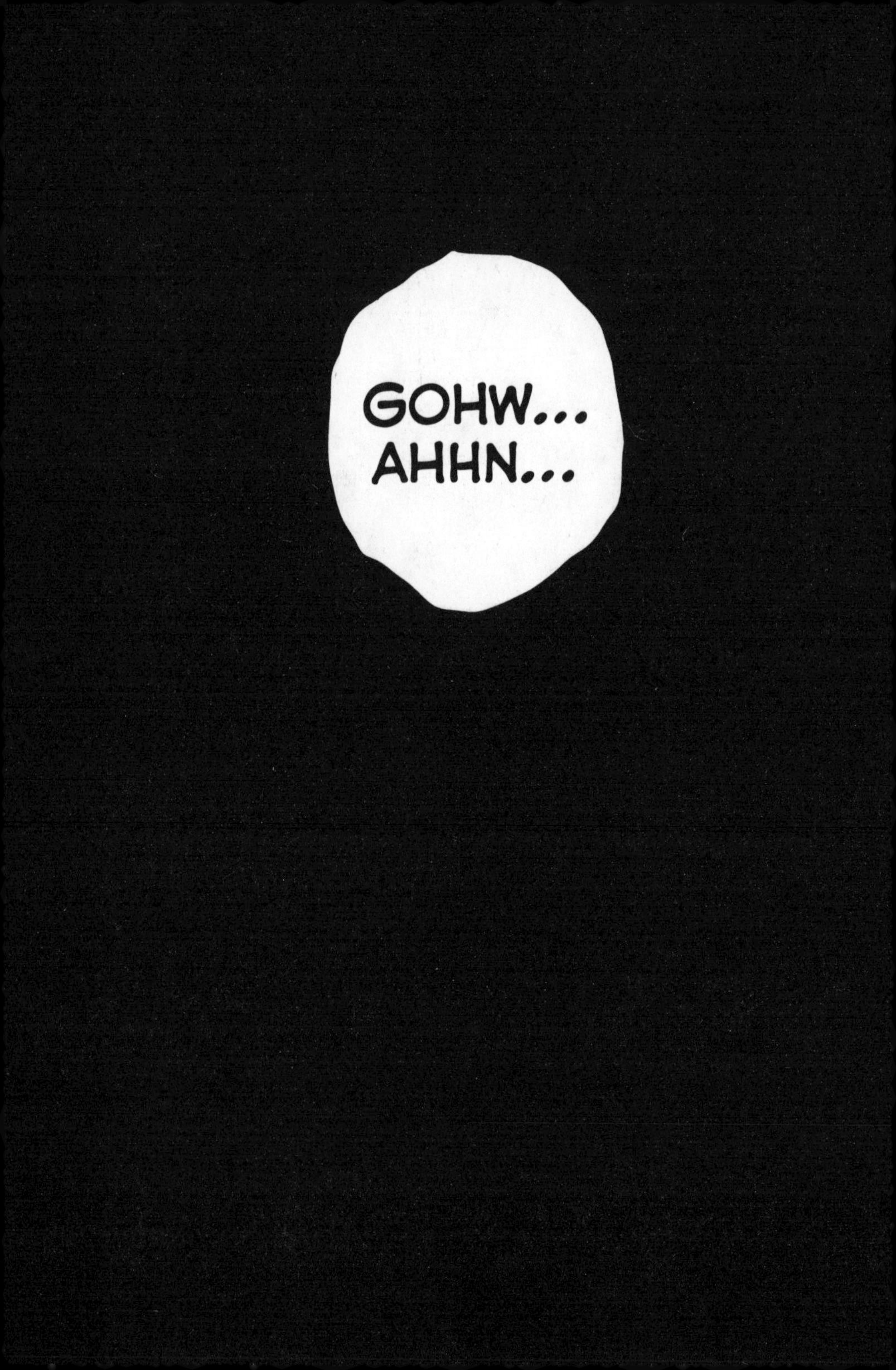
GOHW... AHHN...

New action series from Hiroyuki Takei, creator of the classic shonen franchise Shaman King!

In medieval Japan, a bell hanging on the collar is a sign that a cat has a master. Norachiyo's bell hangs from his katana sheath, but he is nonetheless a stray — a ronin. This one-eyed cat samurai travels across a dishonest world, cutting through pretense and deception with his blade.

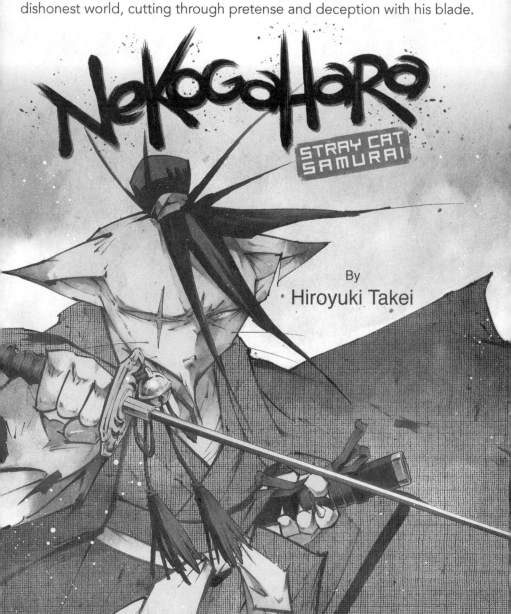

By
Hiroyuki Takei

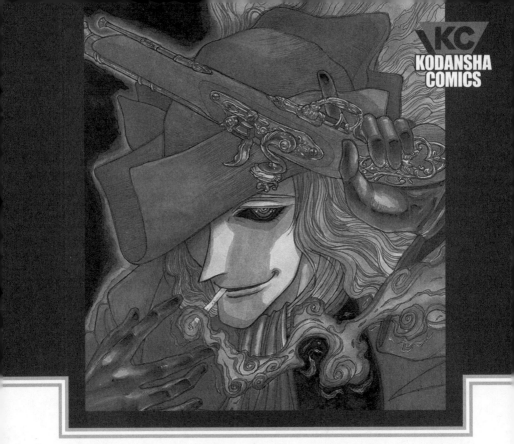

The Black Museum The Ghost and the Lady

By Kazuhiro Fujita

Deep in Scotland Yard in London sits an evidence room dedicated to the greatest mysteries of British history. In this "Black Museum" sits a misshapen hunk of lead—two bullets fused together—the key to a wartime encounter between Florence Nightingale, the mother of modern nursing, and a supernatural Man in Grey. This story is unknown to most scholars of history, but a special guest of the museum will tell the tale of The Ghost and the Lady...

Praise for Kazuhiro Fujita's *Ushio and Tora*

"A charming revival that combines a classic look with modern depth and pacing... **Essential viewing both for curmudgeons and new fans alike.**" — Anime News Network

"**GREAT!** The first episode of Ushio and Tora captures the essence of '90s anime." — IGN

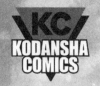

KC
KODANSHA
COMICS

Japan's most powerful spirit medium delves into the ghost world's greatest mysteries!

Story by Kyo Shirodaira, famed author of mystery fiction and creator of *Spiral*, *Blast of Tempest*, and *The Record of a Fallen Vampire*.

Both touched by spirits called yôkai, Kotoko and Kurô have gained unique superhuman powers. But to gain her powers Kotoko has given up an eye and a leg, and Kurô's personal life is in shambles. So when Kotoko suggests they team up to deal with renegades from the spirit world, Kurô doesn't have many other choices, but Kotoko might just have a few ulterior motives...

IN/SPECTRE

STORY BY KYO SHIRODAIRA
ART BY CHASHIBA KATASE

Having lost his wife, high school teacher Kōhei Inuzuka is doing his best to raise his young daughter Tsumugi as a single father. He's pretty bad at cooking and doesn't have a huge appetite to begin with, but chance brings his little family together with one of his students, the lonely Kotori. The three of them are anything but comfortable in the kitchen, but the healing power of home cooking might just work on their grieving hearts.

"This season's number-one feel-good anime!" —Anime News Network

"A beautifully-drawn story about comfort food and family and grief. Recommended." —Otaku USA Magazine

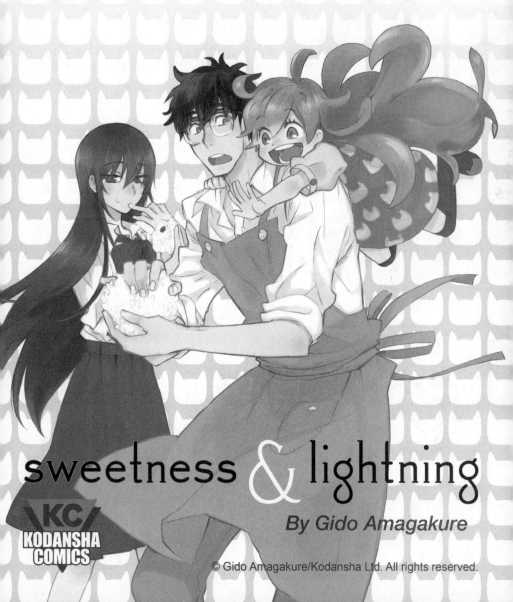

sweetness & lightning

By Gido Amagakure

KC KODANSHA COMICS

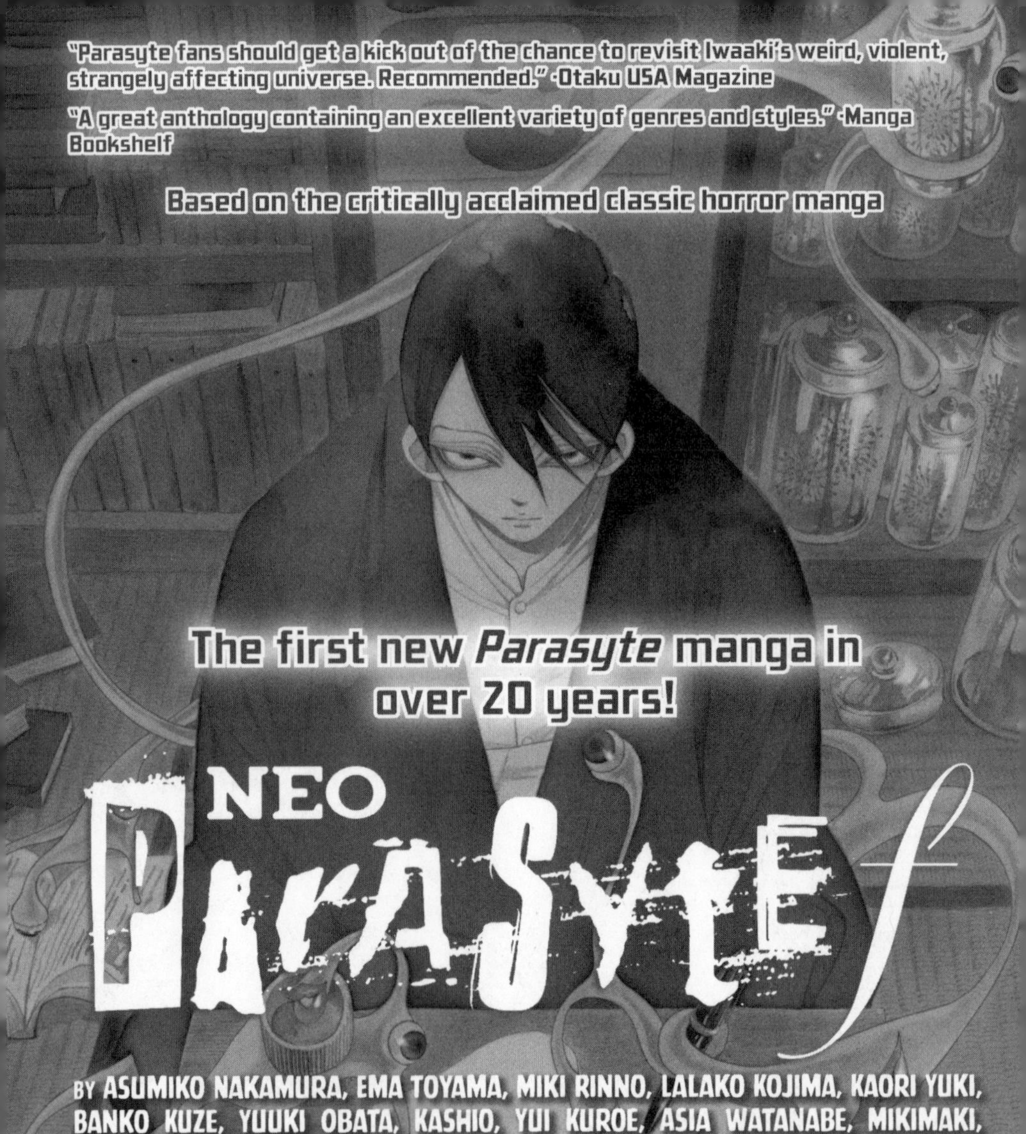
"Parasyte fans should get a kick out of the chance to revisit Iwaaki's weird, violent, strangely affecting universe. Recommended." -Otaku USA Magazine
"A great anthology containing an excellent variety of genres and styles." -Manga Bookshelf
Based on the critically acclaimed classic horror manga
The first new *Parasyte* manga in over 20 years!
NEO Parasyte f
BY ASUMIKO NAKAMURA, EMA TOYAMA, MIKI RINNO, LALAKO KOJIMA, KAORI YUKI, BANKO KUZE, YUUKI OBATA, KASHIO, YUI KUROE, ASIA WATANABE, MIKIMAKI, HIKARU SURUGA, HAJIME SHINJO, RENJURO KINDAICHI, AND YURI NARUSHIMA

A collection of chilling new *Parasyte* stories from Japan's top shojo artists!

Parasites: shape-shifting aliens whose only purpose is to assimilate with and consume the human race... but do these monsters have a different side? A parasite becomes a prince to save his romance-obsessed female host from a dangerous stalker. Another hosts a cooking show, in which the real monsters are revealed. These and 13 more stories, from some of the greatest shojo manga artists alive today, together make up a chilling, funny, and entertaining tribute to one of manga's horror classics!

KC KODANSHA COMICS

Happiness volume 6 is a work of fiction. Names, characters, places, and incidents are the products of the author's imagination or are used fictitiously. Any resemblance to actual events, locales, or persons, living or dead, is entirely coincidental.

A Kodansha Comics Trade Paperback Original.

Published in the United States by Kodansha Comics, an imprint of Kodansha USA Publishing, LLC, New York.

Publication rights for this English edition arranged through Kodansha Ltd., Tokyo.

First published in Japan in 2017 by Kodansha Ltd., Tokyo, as *Hapinesu* volume 6.

ISBN 978-1-63236-483-8

Printed in the United States of America.

www.kodanshacomics.com

9 8 7 6 5 4 3

Translator: Kevin Gifford
Lettering: David Yoo
Editing: Paul Starr
Kodansha Comics edition cover design by Phil Balsman